A MACHINE GUNNER'S WAR

From Normandy to Victory with the 1st Infantry Division
in World War II

ERNEST ALBERT "ANDY" ANDREWS, JR.

with the assistance of

DAVID B. HURT

CASEMATE

Philadelphia & Oxford

Published in the United States of America and Great Britain in 2022 by
CASEMATE PUBLISHERS
1950 Lawrence Road, Havertown, PA 19083, USA
and
The Old Music Hall, 106–108 Cowley Road, Oxford OX4 1JE, UK

Hardback Edition: ISBN 978-1-63624-104-3
Digital Edition: ISBN 978-1-63624-105-0

A CIP record for this book is available from the British Library

Printed and bound in the United Kingdom by TJ Books Ltd.
Typeset in India by Lapiz Digital Services, Chennai.

For a complete list of Casemate titles, please contact:

CASEMATE PUBLISHERS (US)
Telephone (610) 853-9131
Fax (610) 853-9146
Email: casemate@casematepublishers.com
www.casematepublishers.com

CASEMATE PUBLISHERS (UK)
Telephone (01865) 241249
Email: casemate-uk@casematepublishers.co.uk
www.casematepublishers.co.uk

Contents

Preface

When I look back on the more than one hundred public talks I have given about my experience as a machine gunner in World War II, it is children who have provided my most appreciative audiences.

After speaking to a class of elementary school students, I received a number of thank-you letters from the kids.

"Dear Mr. Andrews, Thank you for coming to our fourth grade class today. If you had not come, I very probably would have made an 'F' on my history test," one wrote.

A young girl expressed a more profound sentiment.

"Dear Mr. Andrews, Your talk was so cool. I am so glad you are alive. My daddy said that most veterans your age are already dead."

Naturally, I drew great encouragement from her kind words.

Whether speaking to children, university students, civic clubs, or senior citizens, I never cease to be amazed at the heartfelt reaction. It is a response that reflects the abiding gratitude and deep respect that Americans continue to feel for all those who served in World War II, especially toward those who sacrificed their lives. With so many veterans of that conflict now passing away, my friends of historical bent have convinced me to put my account of the war in writing so that it would not be lost to future generations.

My story is that of a Signal Mountain, Tennessee boy. Upon finishing my senior year at Central High School in Chattanooga in the summer of 1943, I practically stepped off the graduation platform and into the back of an Army truck. The small convoy of trucks delivered 250 of my fellow high school graduates and me to the induction center at nearby Fort Oglethorpe, Georgia, where we raised our right hand and were sworn into the U.S. Army.

Following the completion of our training at Fort McClellan, Alabama, and Bridport, England, my war began on D-Day, June 6, 1944, when I landed on Omaha Beach in German-occupied France as part of the Allied invasion. Serving in the second machine-gun squad, second section, second platoon, H Company, 2nd Battalion, 16th Infantry Regiment, 1st Infantry Division, I was engaged in the terrible fighting that stretched from the invasion of France until the end of the war in Czechoslovakia in early May 1945.

The resulting memoir does not present a broad chronicle of the war, but rather my own small window on the events of that time. Indeed, a battle that merits only a passing sentence in a history of the 1st Infantry Division may fill an entire chapter in this book. My account of the war will have much in common with the millions of other GIs ("Government Issues," slang for American soldiers) who went off to fight, except that it tells my own unique story.

The reader will find no reports of spectacular feats or heroic actions on my part, just an effort to describe the war as I personally witnessed and experienced it. Even after the passage of seven decades, my days as a soldier are almost as fresh to me as if they had taken place last week. Indeed, those intense moments in combat remain as vivid and terrifying for me now as they were at the time.

While part of me seeks to stay as far away from the horrors of the battlefield as possible, the war forces itself back into my consciousness again and again. Memories from the war do not haunt me, but they do often fill my thoughts and flash uninvited through my mind.

Grinding physical exhaustion. Dust, mud, rain, ice, snow, and cold. Constant orders to attack no matter the weather. Slogging forward with the heavy machine-gun tripod slung over my aching shoulders. Sinking into freezing mud as I "catnapped" in a foxhole. Forever trying to wipe mud from my eyeglasses. Pitying the war's destitute and homeless refugees and the sick and starving little children with beautiful sunken eyes in pain-racked faces.

Sudden firefights. Muzzle flashes from enemy rifles aimed at my machine-gun position, knowing my devastating weapon makes me their target. Bullets buzzing by my head and snapping off the twigs and small branches around me. Shooting my .45 pistol at German soldiers from pointblank range.

The dreadful metallic creaking of an approaching enemy panzer. The swoosh of an incoming German mortar round. A deafening explosion yards from my position. The shrill whine of incoming artillery shells. Their earth-shaking and air-convulsing detonations that fling lethal shrapnel and mud in every direction. The gut-wrenching cries of the wounded in the midst of night combat.

When remembering battles where so many soldiers crouching or running along beside me at one moment were killed by bullets or shrapnel in the next, I remain amazed at the countless times God spared my life. In reliving the brutal fighting in the Hürtgen and Battle of the Bulge, where I survived with only wounds while thousands of other men were slaughtered, I recall my constant prayers, pleading over and over to God to give me the physical strength to endure, to keep me in His protection, and to let His will be done with my life.

At the end of firefights so fierce that my entire concentration had been on killing the enemy, I always took time to thank God for my survival. With my eyes blurred by tears, I also prayed for the mothers, dads, wives, and sweethearts of those men who had just fallen before my machine gun.

My war story is first and foremost a testimony of how God in His grace held me close to Him from my war's beginning in Normandy on D-Day to its longed-for end in Czechoslovakia on VE-Day. Other guys claimed to possess some lucky token, but my "lucky piece" was the Lord, and I trusted Him to protect me. He blessed me with a long, full life that so many other boys from that time never got the chance to know.

This memoir is dedicated to the memory of my friends and my buddies as well as all those Americans who made the ultimate sacrifice during the war and cannot tell their stories. By sharing my own account, I hope to bring a little greater understanding of that war in which they gave their lives and thus honor their memory.

On a more personal level, I wish to dedicate this book to the memory of my late wife, and love of my life, Hellon Andrews. My more than 50 years with her were a celebration of the peace and freedom for which we fought and so many fell.

In a larger sense, I leave this memoir as my testament to the younger generation and all the future generations of Americans yet unborn. In sharing my combat experiences, it is my fervent prayer that they may never know war firsthand.

Ernest Albert "Andy" Andrews, Jr.
Black Mountain, North Carolina
Fall, 2015

Foreword

My sister, Sarah, and I were born seven and nine years after our father returned home from the war, having survived from D-Day through the remainder of the conflict in Europe. Its horrors and ravages were ever present in his heart and soul, but in our early life, we never knew of them. Instead, both he and my mother were committed to offering the opposite of what he had experienced—a home of peace and tranquility. And that was exactly what they provided—a place of creativity, humor, friendships, and love.

Looking back, I don't know how he did it. Somehow, he was able to push down the memories—the images, the violence, and the blood. And if he didn't suppress them, he hid them from our view. As we grew a little older, a few stories began to emerge, but they'd been sanitized for children—more like a war story in a Disney cartoon, cleaned up with a good ending.

It all changed when he signed me up to accompany him on a trip to Europe commemorating the 50th anniversary of D-Day. Fifteen veterans and their sons traveled together from one memorial to another, the old men basking in the hearty welcomes and celebrations in village after village. For all of them, memories came flooding back as they passed by familiar landscapes and towns. Quiet tears slowly seeped from their eyes and frequent times of silence fell over the group. And then, they began to tell stories.

When we walked on Omaha Beach together, followed by weaving our way through the white marble graves at the Allied cemetery at Normandy, Dad was quiet and thoughtful, kneeling at the graves of fallen comrades he remembered.

Our next visit on the tour was the nearby German cemetery where their men and boys were buried. As the bus arrived at the cemetery, many of the old soldiers didn't want to leave their seats. The understandable pain and anger inside were just too much for them. But Dad was at the front of the bus before it came to a complete stop and, when the doors opened, he got out and walked quickly to the nearest grave, one of the many black granite crosses, each representing five German men who had died on D-Day.

He bowed down, wrapping his arms around the cross as if it were an old friend, and began to sob. Through his tears, he said, "I'm so sorry I killed you. I took you from your mom and dad, your brothers and sisters, your wife, your children.

I'm so sorry. Please forgive me." Somehow in that moment, he felt their grace. It was as if one of his former enemies said, "You are forgiven. I understand. We all did what we had to do." From that day on, that which had been suppressed began to be released and, over time, we began to get the rest of the story—the nightmares, the reason he never finished college (PTSD), witnessing his buddies die, remembering the men he had killed, and the innumerable horrors of war. Stories upon stories. "I've thought about the war every day since I got off the boat at the war's end," he said. "I still think about it."

Since then, he was interviewed often, spoke at countless schools and events, and was a regular on the small-town parade circuit. A former German soldier who lived nearby became a dear friend. He found healing in the stories and wanted them to have a purpose. Through years of interviewing, writing, and re-writing, David Hurt has honored my father with this rich collection of stories and we, his family, are grateful.

Andy Andrews was a man of peace, and it was his mission to promote peace until his dying day. And just like the good soldier he accomplished his mission, and now his story lives on.

Al Andrews

Son of Private First Class Ernest A. Andrews Jr.

Summer, 2021

Introduction

War is a great paradox. In one respect, it violates society's fundamental moral prohibition against taking the lives of our fellow human beings. In another, it asks the soldier to lay down his or her own life for comrades and country, embodying one of mankind's highest virtues. War might thus be said to epitomize both inhumanity and humanity.

This profound ethical tension is perhaps best understood through a soldier's individual encounter with war. A military history can describe the overall course of a war or a particular unit's record, but only a firsthand account can begin to capture the deeply searing and utterly terrifying experience each human being endures in combat.

My first opportunity to speak at length with Andy Andrews about his service as a machine gunner during World War II came when I joined a group from Asheville, North Carolina, on a trip to the National WWII Museum—formerly the National D-Day Museum—in New Orleans in early 2003. Despite the passage of decades, Andy described his combat experiences in vivid detail, bringing those events to life as if he had just returned home from the war in 1945.

Though it was immediately apparent to me that his war story would make an enthralling book, I had to wait to approach Andy about such a project. At that time, I was assisting Andy's good friend William Lubbeck in writing about his experiences as a soldier in Germany's *Wehrmacht* (Armed Forces) during World War II. However, shortly after the 2006 publication of Lubbeck's memoir, *At Leningrad's Gates: The Story of a Soldier with Army Group North*, Andy and I began work on his book. Over the next nine years, we collaborated to develop a full account of his experiences in World War II.

Sadly, Andy passed away on April 22, 2016, at the age of 92. Although his memoir was not yet finished when he died, Andy had helped me develop a rough draft of all 22 chapters of the manuscript that allowed me to complete the writing and editing over the ensuing five years. While Andy did not live to see the publication of his account, I cannot think of any better tribute to his life and his military service than to see his compelling story come out in print.

No words are adequate to fully communicate the intense terror and unrelenting horror of combat, but Andy forcefully conveys the physical and psychological reality of the battlefield at the personal level. He also eloquently recounts his struggle to retain both his basic human decency and his deep commitment to his Christian faith amid the war's brutality and carnage.

Although war memoirs tend to concentrate almost exclusively on the events that occurred during the conflict, Andy and I felt it was essential to include a little about his background growing up in Tennessee before the war. Not only does his account provide a window into how one American family witnessed the rise of Hitler and Nazi Germany, it also offers a firsthand look at wartime America after Pearl Harbor. Likewise, this memoir also briefly covers the decades after the war in an effort to describe the ways in which the conflict shaped Andy's postwar life.

In preparing the narrative, we have made every effort to produce a faithful chronicle of Andy's personal experience. Though the "truth" of any such testimony is always subject to the limits of individual perception and the frailties of human memory, Andy's retelling of his story in dozens of public talks since the war has been extremely helpful in preserving his recollections.

While acknowledging that memory is imperfect, we have nonetheless decided to include Andy's recollection of various wartime conversations in the book. Certainly, it is not possible to produce anything even close to a verbatim record at this distance in time, but we deemed it useful to retain his account of these verbal exchanges in the belief they reflect the basic content of what was said. On a more practical level, it is far more engaging to read dialogue than simply a summary of these conversations.

Beyond relying on his own memories of the war, we have also referenced Andy's discharge papers and other U.S. Army records for historical details. Particularly useful were two official daily reports on the wartime movements and actions of Andy's company: *History of Company "H," 16th Infantry Regiment*, covering the period before June 6, 1944, and *Organization History of Company H, 16th Infantry: The Invasion of the Continent*, covering the period after June 6.

Though U.S. Army documents provided us with the detailed historical context for Andy's war memoir, the books *Danger Forward: The Story of the First Division in World War II* by H. R. Knickerbocker et al. (1947), *The 16th Infantry, 1798–1946* by Lt. John Baumgartner et al. (1946), and *Blood and Sacrifice: The History of the 16th Infantry Regiment from the Civil War through the Gulf War* by Steven E. Clay (2001) were also beneficial in helping us gain a broader overview of the larger operations in which Andy's company was involved.

In sum, we have worked diligently to ensure the memoir is as historically accurate as possible but acknowledge that inaccuracies and other inadvertent mistakes may yet exist. For any such errors, we apologize in advance.

Andy Andrews was a member of what the journalist Tom Brokaw has aptly called America's "Greatest Generation." Growing up amid the hardships of the Great Depression, these men and women labored, fought, and sacrificed to achieve victory in World War II and secure the postwar peace. Like Andy, that generation is passing from the scene, but their extraordinary legacy will be lasting.

In telling one small part of that epic story, Andy's memoir sheds a little more illumination on the war and that time. I hope the reader will find his tale as gripping and as moving to follow in print as it was to hear in person. It has been my great privilege to assist Andy in writing this account and helping to see it to publication after his passing.

David B. Hurt
Knoxville, Tennessee
Spring 2022

Prelude to Invasion:
Dawn, June 1–8:30am, June 6, 1944

Camp D-8, a pre-invasion marshalling area at Down Wood, just north of Bincombe in Dorset, England: Dawn–8am, Thursday, June 1

The shrill blast of Sergeant Gentry's whistle abruptly jarred me out of my slumber, leaving me just alert enough to comprehend his ensuing orders.

"Get your ass out of the sack and fall out for roll call and calisthenics. You got 10 minutes!" he bellowed, commencing our morning routine.

Now wide awake, I hurriedly threw on my green pants, tee shirt, and green jacket. Jamming on my boots that were still damp from the previous day's hike through the rain, I darted out the door to claim my assigned spot in H Company's second machine-gun platoon.

Dawn colored the overcast English skies as everyone came to attention in neat rows outside our wooden huts. Following roll call and half an hour of strenuous calisthenics under a light drizzle, we trekked to the mess hall for breakfast. Between cramming in mouthfuls of eggs, bacon, and toast washed down with big swigs of coffee, all of us speculated excitedly about the coming Allied invasion of German-occupied France.

"You got 15 minutes to shit, shower, and shave! And then we're gonna go to bayonet practice," Sergeant Gentry boomed 30 minutes later, just as we were swallowing the last bites of that morning's chow.

After washing up, I grabbed my M1 Garand rifle and formed up with the rest of our platoon outside. When everyone had fallen in, we marched out to the drill field a half mile away for bayonet practice. Here, in the peaceful English countryside a few miles south of Dorchester in the county of Dorset, our training for war continued.

Charging forward six at a time, we assaulted the "enemy" with our rifle bayonets, repeatedly jabbing one of the six straw-stuffed dummies that hung down on ropes attached to a wooden scaffold. Once the dummy was satisfactorily subdued, each of us thrusted his bayonet out and froze, maintaining that awkward stance until the sergeant gave permission to relax.

Just after the drill got underway, another GI was bayoneting one of the straw dummies when guts suddenly began flying out of it.

"Holy mackerel!" the man cried, stunned at what he had done. The rest of us stood there gawking in open-mouthed surprise at the gory sight.

"That's what it's gonna look like, soldier ... get used to it!" the sergeant hollered. It turned out the sergeant had requisitioned a bunch of chicken innards from the mess hall the previous night. Concealing them inside one of the dummies, he gave it lifelike guts in an effort to prepare us for the real thing.

When my turn came, I followed the prescribed drill, stabbing my dummy over and over. After thoroughly brutalizing the poor fellow, I took a few steps backward and lunged at empty air with my bayonet.

At the moment my rifle was fully extended, I froze in position. With the heavy rifle jutting out in front of me, I held myself stiff as a statue, waiting for the sergeant to affirm I had adopted the proper form for a bayonet thrust.

"Keep holding that rifle out, out, out!" he barked, determined to keep us from slacking in the meantime.

Before long, excruciating pain began spreading through my body. The nine-and-a-half pound Garand rifle was growing heavier by the second. Every muscle in my body throbbed in angry protest. My back ached. My leg muscles cramped. My arms felt as if they were about to snap off my shoulders.

Finally, at the end of several long minutes, the sergeant came over to inspect me. Upon determining that my rifle was acceptably straight, he ordered me to the end of the line to relax for a few minutes before I repeated the drill.

As the rest of us watched the others who had not yet been released, the strain became too great for one of the men. Fainting from exhaustion, the soldier simply toppled forward onto his rifle, causing the sergeant to explode in laughter. The incident momentarily broke the tension, but discipline was swiftly restored, and the exercise resumed.

No aspect of our infantry training was more physically grueling, nor more widely despised, than these two hours of bayonet drill, the tempo of which had been increasing. If there was some limited benefit in practicing a bayonet assault on dummies, all of us thought holding the rifles out for several minutes was a complete waste of time. This part of our bayonet drill did nothing to enhance our combat skills, especially since our company was made up of machine-gun and mortar squads. Of course, any complaints about an Army drill, no matter how reasonable, fell on deaf ears.

Worthwhile or not, such training exercises made up our company's daily routine in England. But neither bayonet drill, a steady drizzle, nor fatigue could dampen the electric mood in our company.

Less than a year earlier in July 1943, I had left my family's home on Signal Mountain, Tennessee, for 17 weeks of basic training at Fort McClellan in Alabama.

In January 1944, I had shipped across the Atlantic to Scotland and ridden a train down to the town of Bridport, Dorset, in southern England.

Stationed in Bridport, I began advanced combat training with H Company, 2nd Battalion, 16th Infantry Regiment, 1st Infantry Division, the division famously known as "The Big Red One." As the heavy weapons company that would support the 2nd Battalion's E, F, and G infantry companies, H Company contained two machine-gun platoons and a mortar platoon. Each of the 36-man machine-gun platoons was divided into two 15-man sections, with each section containing two seven-man squads. Assigned to the second machine-gun platoon, I was a member of the second squad, second section.

Just one outfit among the innumerable Allied units based in southern England, our 2nd Battalion had undergone months of intensive drilling that spring in preparation for the landings in German-occupied France. On May 17, H Company and the rest of the battalion transferred to a marshalling area in Dorset, which placed us closer to the twin ports of Weymouth and Portland on the English Channel. Based at Camp D-8 at Down Wood, we were now about 15 miles east of Bridport and roughly four miles north of the port of Weymouth.

On May 25, the D-Camps had been sealed for security. The next day, our officers presented a detailed briefing on our outfit's invasion plans, revealing the Normandy region of France was to be the Allied target. On D-Day, British and Canadian forces would attack Gold, Juno, and Sword Beaches on the coast of Normandy, while American troops would assault two neighboring beaches codenamed Omaha and Utah.

Though receiving little information on the big picture, we learned our 16th Infantry Regiment of the 1st Infantry Division would spearhead the American assault on Omaha Beach in the Colleville-sur-Mer area of Normandy. Assigned to the Easy Red sector of Omaha Beach, the 2nd Battalion would be landing during the first hours of D-Day, with H Company arriving in the third wave of the battalion's assault team. The exact date of the long-anticipated cross-channel invasion remained unspecified, but we knew our departure from Camp D-8 to a nearby English port was now imminent.

The struggle to secure a beachhead in France was certain to be bloody, but our training had given us a deep sense of confidence and we felt ready. If combat itself was something we could not yet truly comprehend, heading off to battle seemed a thrilling climax to all our preparation.

We knew we were tough. Indeed, in our youth, we felt indestructible and acted the part. A couple of months short of my 21st birthday, I felt primed for action physically and psychologically. Like every other GI, I just wanted to get on with the operation.

Around eight o'clock on that morning of Thursday, June 1, an hour or so into our bayonet drill, a jeep led a column of Army trucks onto our training field. Standing in the jeep's passenger seat, our company commander Captain Robert Irvine called us to attention with a bullhorn. The tension in the air was palpable.

"Men, the invasion of Normandy, France, is on! Let's go!" he announced.

Our reaction to the long-awaited news was instantaneous and overwhelming. All of us spontaneously burst into wild yelling and cheering, clapping our hands and thrusting our fists into the air, celebrating his announcement as if the war was already won. Our burst of enthusiasm was an emotional release, a display of our relief at finally going into action.

The months of damnable training were over. Now, we were at last joining the battle against Hitler's Nazi empire!

Moving out: 8am–7pm, June 1

"Get aboard the trucks and get your combat gear! We're going to get on the troopships to take us to France," Captain Irvine ordered, once the din subsided.

After his jeep sped off, other officers and noncoms (noncommissioned officers or NCOs; sergeants and corporals) took charge. In moments, we loaded up on the trucks, which took us to the D-Camp's quartermaster building. Very little gear had been issued to us up until this time, but that was about to change.

Our company's quartermaster was housed in a 100-foot by 50-foot Nissen hut, a prefabricated shed topped with a semicircular corrugated metal roof that gave it the appearance of a giant aluminum pipe cut in half. Its shelves were piled high with every imaginable item of military equipment an infantryman would need.

As soon as we entered the Nissen hut, all of us immediately began gagging, struck by an overpowering rancid odor that emanated from every piece of clothing inside. The stinking, stiff fabric resulted from the clothing's impregnation with a special chemical designed to shield the skin from exposure to mustard gas in case the Germans deployed that weapon against us. None of us knew whether the chemical treatment would really provide effective protection from mustard gas, but we all agreed the Germans were sure to smell us coming.

Passing in front of a series of quartermaster clerks, each man received a field pack; one full set of chemically treated uniforms; a battle jacket with large pockets; a raincoat; a new pair of boots; an extra pair of gas-protected socks; a short-handled entrenching tool; a canteen filled with water; water purification tablets; anti-seasickness pills; a mess kit; a couple of small boxes containing two days of "C" food rations; ration heating units with a fuel tablet; two extra candy bars; extra chewing gum; extra cigarette packs; an extra razor blade for shaving; insecticide powder; and a waterproof first-aid kit with morphine, sulfanilamide powder, and a small bandage. The clerks also issued us a smaller six-pound backpack containing various general-purpose items. The provision of this supplemental pack reflected the Army's expectation that a great deal of equipment would be lost during the invasion.

To replace the lightweight gas masks which we used during our training, the first sergeant in charge issued us "assault" gas masks. As he did so, he tried to make sure we adjusted the straps so the new masks would fit snuggly on our heads and around our faces.

Each member of our heavy weapons company also received a .45-caliber pistol, an M1 carbine, and two ammunition bandoliers, which included fully loaded ammo clips for each weapon. The carbine was smaller and lighter than the standard Garand rifle carried by the regular infantry, but still packed a wallop. Grenades were distributed later out of concern that some jackass might accidentally detonate one aboard ship, killing himself and everyone around him.

If for some reason we lost any of our weapons prior to reaching the beach at Normandy, Captain Irvine promised us replacement weapons would be available from among the troops killed in the two waves of troops landing ahead of us, an assurance that was not especially reassuring.

With our gear in hand, we proceeded to a large open area within the Nissen hut to change into our new clothes and boots, strap the gas masks to our legs, cram everything we could into our soon-bulging backpacks, and stuff the rest into our pockets. Though heavily burdened with roughly 70 pounds of equipment, all of this newly issued gear further boosted our confidence.

Leaving the quartermaster, we headed to our barracks to retrieve our personal items, underwear, extra socks, shaving articles, and soap and then ate a hurried lunch. The rest of the afternoon was spent cleaning and packing up equipment as we awaited the arrival of our transportation.

About six o'clock that evening, everyone in H Company assembled at the main gate of the D-Camp, where we boarded trucks for the trip down to our embarkation port. Our destination was the loading docks in the town of Portland, located on the south side of Portland Harbour from Weymouth.

As our convoy weaved its way slowly through a small town along the route to the port, both sides of the cobblestoned street were lined with the local ladies who had come to see us off. Presenting a jumble of emotions, they waved, blew us kisses, and wept.

When the truck in which I was riding momentarily halted for traffic, I overheard a distraught English woman standing nearby.

"Something dreadful is happening! Something dreadful is happening! The jeeps and lorries, they're all going. Dear Jesus! Dear Jesus!" she exclaimed before raising her handkerchief to wipe the tears from her eyes. The English had always known this day would eventually arrive, but that foreknowledge did not make our abrupt departure any less dramatic when it came.

With our snaking caravan of vehicles motoring southward at little more than walking speed, we had plenty of time to eat the peanut butter and jelly sandwiches prepared by H Company's mess and revel in the grand parade.

Everything seemed to be on wheels. Hundreds of infantry-filled trucks, jeeps, half-tracks, and Red Cross ambulances had to share the narrow, tree-lined country lanes with huge trucks hauling tanks and artillery pieces. All the jam-packed traffic was flowing in just one direction, as if some giant had tilted the land sideways, sending everything spilling toward the coast.

Equipment not on the road was stashed in the countryside along the route. Stretching as far as the eye could see, there were neat, densely packed rows of parked tanks, half-tracks, jeeps, ambulances, artillery pieces, and airplane parts. Countless Nissen huts warehoused other supplies. Everything was carefully camouflaged to conceal it from aerial surveillance.

While the amount of equipment around us was truly staggering, it represented only a minute fraction of the total provisions stockpiled for the Allied invasion of Europe. Such was the quantity of men and material that I found it amazing Britain itself did not sink into the sea under the weight of it all. Indeed, it seemed to me the island would surely rise a few inches, if not a few feet, once freed from this colossal burden.

Contemplating the mammoth logistical effort behind the coming campaign, it was evident why it would take a dozen people working behind the front line to support a single American soldier in combat. If it was hard to comprehend the number of individuals involved in the operation, it was even more astonishing that much of the responsibility fell upon people my age. Thrilled to be a part of this historic endeavor, I felt an overwhelming sense of awe at the scale and complexity of it all.

With preparations for the invasion of France completed, the combined force from America, Britain, Canada, and the other allies was finally ready to open the "second front" in the west, an offensive long demanded by the Soviet Union. Fully recovered from its defeats in 1941–1942, the Soviet Red Army was now grinding toward Germany from the east. If our invasion of the continent proved successful, the Nazi regime would be caught in a vice between two vast Allied armies. Already, there was talk the war could be over by Christmas.

However, the gigantic amassing of troops, vehicles, and ships by the Allied armies in Britain had been matched by an enormous construction program and military buildup of the *Wehrmacht* in France.

Under the command of the famous German General Erwin Rommel, hundreds of thousands of tons of steel and concrete had gone into constructing Hitler's Atlantic Wall along the neighboring French coast. The dense network of enemy bunkers was augmented by extensive beach obstacles, miles and miles of barbed wire, and hundreds of thousands of anti-tank and anti-personnel mines. Designed to defeat any Allied assault at the water's edge, these Atlantic Wall fortifications were now manned by tens of thousands of German troops.

The collision of these two immense armies in Normandy was certain to produce incalculable anguish, suffering, devastation, and death. It was up to us to ensure our side claimed victory in the titanic battle.

Portland Harbour: 7pm, June 1–5:30pm, June 5

Around seven that evening, H Company's small convoy motored into the port of Weymouth, about four miles south of our D-Camp. To reach the ships loading at Portland on the south side of the harbor, our column of trucks now had to travel a further four or five miles along a semicircular route that passed southwest through Weymouth, south-southeast down a narrow causeway, and then east-northeast through Portland to the docks.

Trapped in even heavier traffic, we crept along at a snail's pace through Weymouth and down the causeway, only reaching Portland's harbor area around 10 o'clock, just as the last light was fading from the sky at the end of the long summer day. After inching forward for another hour, our company's trucks finally pulled to a halt within a dozen yards of a long wooden gangplank that led up to the deck of a massive vessel.

"Our ship!" a buddy in my truck yelled as he pointed up at the USS *Henrico*, the attack transport assigned to carry our 2nd Battalion across the Channel.

As we dismounted from the truck in the misty twilight, I finally got a good look at what was going on around us. Thousands of troops and vehicles swarmed over Portland's docks. Providing direction to this blur of constant motion, the ships of every size that crowded the harbor's berths appeared to be giant magnets, irresistibly drawing everything on the dock toward them.

Traffic controllers wearing special armbands were everywhere, waving men and vehicles into their proper queues on the docks. While thousands of GIs were lined up to ascend one of the numerous gangplanks leading up to the troopships, hundreds of tanks, trucks, jeeps, ambulances, half-tracks, and other vehicles were waiting to load aboard specialized ships. Driving up steel ramps, the vehicles passed through huge rear doors built into the hulls and entered the vast "parking areas" in the interior bays of the ships. Here, they were backed in so they would be facing the beach when they debarked in France.

With the descent of darkness, the drivers had switched on miniature blackout drive lights in place of their headlights. Shielded from above by small hoods, these fingertip-sized lights provided just enough illumination for the vehicles to maneuver, while concealing the process from any enemy surveillance aircraft that might be lurking along the English coast. If any low-flying German planes did attempt to approach the airspace near the ports, they would have to dodge the hundreds of cables that hung from the dozens of oblong barrage balloons floating in the sky overhead.

The loud noise of creaking treads and rumbling engines filled the air, but the thousands of men waiting to board the ships seemed strangely quiet. The only audible words came from the traffic controllers, who were zealously cussing out drivers and the infantry as they worked to keep everyone in their proper lines. To accomplish their mission, these traffic controllers employed a limitless array of expletives that could fill a dictionary on the art of swearing. Listening to them, I found it interesting to imagine the training program for this assignment.

As soon as we had dismounted from our truck, we witnessed a display of a traffic controller's authority when the sergeant in charge of troop movement in our sector of the harbor was confronted by an officer from one of the outfits loading nearby. Having ordered his squad car to pull out of the queue and drive over to the sergeant, the big heavyset officer climbed out and demanded to know where his men needed to be. Unintimidated by the man's rank, the sergeant was not about to let any vehicle get out of line in his area.

"Hey, sir, who the hell told you that *you* could drive over here?" he roared, warning the officer to return his vehicle to its spot in the queue.

As the officer started to object, the sergeant instantly quashed his protest.

"Don't argue with me, you sonovabitch. You get your big fat ass back in that squad car. I'm in charge here and, if you don't like it, you can call General Bradley! General Bradley assigned me to this loading area and told me not to take any shit from anybody!" the sergeant thundered.

Unable to dispute orders from the top brass, the officer drove off in a huff, directing his vehicle back to its original place in line. But though tempers often flared, the episode was just typical Army all the way. Any tensions that might arise from the inevitable snafus were always diffused with plenty of humor.

"H Company, go to gangplank number two!" one of the traffic controllers shouted a moment after this incident.

Heading to a gangplank sign marked with a great big number two, we formed up in line to board the *Henrico*. While waiting, I chatted a little with my buddies Wayne Newsome, Lincoln Welser, and Hector Gonzalez, fellow members of my machine-gun squad. After months of training, we were all excited to be on our way at last.

When my turn came to ascend the gangplank, I climbed most of the way up before briefly turning my head to take in the whole, incredible scene unfolding on the docks below me. Only a meticulously choreographed loading schedule could have maintained clockwork order in what would otherwise have fallen into total chaos. Even before the battle in Normandy had been fought, a crucial logistical triumph was already being won in England.

At the top of the gangplank, a soldier holding a clipboard stood waiting to greet us. Using a miniature flashlight, he was checking for each man's name on H Company's roster.

"Ernest Andrews?" the soldier inquired with perfect timing as my boot landed on deck.

"Yeah, that's me," I affirmed.

"Okay, get on the ship," he said, checking off my name with his pencil.

By the time I had acknowledged my name and was moving past the soldier, he was already calling the next name. With this truly amazing display of efficiency that belied its well-deserved reputation for screw-ups, the U.S. Army was demonstrating it knew the exact location of every one of its GIs.

Once aboard the *Henrico*, we never stopped moving. A sailor promptly directed us to proceed below deck to our assigned quarters. As we awkwardly descended several steep, narrow flights of metal stairs encumbered by all our gear, there was just adequate light for us to see. With everything inside the ship uniformly painted a depressing medium gray monotone, the walls, ceiling, steps, and floor seemed almost to merge together and close in around me.

On reaching our accommodations down in the claustrophobic bowels of the ship, my eyes had to adjust to the even dimmer lighting coming from miniature bulbs recessed into the hull. Located about three feet above the deck and spaced every 10 feet, the tiny bulbs barely illuminated our surroundings.

Despite the removal of the ship's sleeping bunks to make room for the roughly 1,500 men assigned to the *Henrico*, much of the available space was already occupied by the troops who had loaded ahead of us. Once we did find seats on the hard steel deck, everyone was crammed shoulder-to-shoulder like sardines. Most of the GIs near me belonged to H Company, but a few guys from the 2nd Battalion's three regular infantry companies were scattered among us.

When we boarded the *Henrico* about 11pm on Thursday, June 1, our expectation was the ship would set sail within a few hours, but this did not happen. As the hours of waiting stretched into days, our discomfort mounted.

From the moment I sat down, my overstuffed backpack, carbine, and other equipment began shifting position on me. Despite my efforts to reallocate my gear, I never really managed to stabilize it effectively. Inevitably, I was repeatedly bumping into the rifles, canteens, or sheathed bayonets of the soldiers seated around me, which made any real sleep impossible.

Our chow aboard ship consisted mostly of sandwiches, fruit, cookies, and cups of pudding handed out by members of the *Henrico*'s crew. When we needed to relieve ourselves, we had to wind our way among the bodies to reach the nearest head, trying not to step on anyone else in the process.

Shortly after our arrival on board, one heavily utilized commode overflowed, which sent raw sewage oozing down the narrow corridor just outside the door to our compartment. The ship's crew were quick to repair the toilet and mop up the mess, but the foul stench lingered in the stagnant air. Comingling with the smell of sweating bodies and the horrible odor emanating from our chemically impregnated uniforms, it spawned a sort of toxic fog. Without any portholes to allow fresh air to enter from outside, our cramped and crowded quarters grew increasingly stuffy and smelly.

Down in the dark bowels of the ship, we had only a vague sense of time as Friday and Saturday passed with no word on our departure date. Sunday, June 4, brought a scripture reading, hymns, and prayer over the *Henrico*'s loudspeakers. Early that same morning, the Allied high command postponed the invasion by 24 hours, but we knew nothing of their decision, leaving only rumors to circulate among us. With a storm roiling the waters of the harbor outside, it was hard to believe the invasion could get underway anytime soon.

Sailing for Normandy: 5:30pm, Monday, June 5/1:15am, Tuesday, June 6

Late on the afternoon of Monday, June 5, just under four days after we had boarded the *Henrico*, the ship's great turbines finally rumbled to life, shaking the deck beneath us. About 5:30pm, our troopship departed the calm waters of Portland Harbour and entered the English Channel, where we joined other ships assembling in one of the mammoth invasion convoys sailing for France.

Except for the *Henrico*'s engine and the waves splashing against the ship's hull, almost the sole distinguishable sound in our crowded compartment was the steady breathing of the hundreds of men around me.

By now, the mood of excited anticipation that had predominated back in our D-Camp, and upon boarding the *Henrico* four days earlier, had faded. All the shouting, joking, and laughter had ceased. No one played cards or dice. The quiet was only occasionally disturbed by brief whispered conversations.

In the darkness, fear of the unknown gripped and silenced us. Each of us knew the ship's embarkation meant we were headed to war. Perhaps oddly, it was only now that the reality of going into battle finally hit home to me.

Over the preceding months, most of us had treated our training as a program of physical exercise, almost as if we were practicing for some kind of military sporting event, rather than drilling for combat. The admonitions of our officers to take our training seriously were dismissed as some great joke.

We simply had not been able to come to terms with the idea that we were about to go into battle against the enemy. Despite all of the evidence to the contrary, the imminent reality of combat had somehow remained remote to us, though maybe such self-delusion or detachment is psychologically healthier than dwelling on the savage brutality of fighting, killing, and dying.

But now it all seemed very close. The short crossing of the English Channel would mark a momentous event in our lives—if we survived the war.

For our chow that night, we received a paper bag with small containers of Spam, bread, applesauce, jelly, and a small can of prune juice. With anxiety churning our stomachs, many of the guys could not eat much.

Right after supper, the captain came over the ship's intercom system.

"Soldiers, we're glad to have you aboard our ship. We're going to be crossing a hundred miles of open water. There may or may not be German subs, but we don't think so because we've got submarine hunters out there. When you hear the ship's turbines stop, you will be 12 miles from France, 12 miles from battle. You'll sit where you are sitting until it's time to go up on deck. Good luck."

After this welcome, we heard a message from General Dwight D. "Ike" Eisenhower, Supreme Commander of the Allied Expeditionary Force.

> Soldiers, Sailors and Airmen of the Allied Expeditionary Forces: You are about to embark upon the Great Crusade, toward which we have striven these many months. The eyes of the world are upon you. The hopes and prayers of liberty-loving people everywhere march with you. In company with our brave Allies and brothers-in-arms on other Fronts you will bring about the destruction of the German war machine, the elimination of Nazi tyranny over the oppressed peoples of Europe, and security for ourselves in a free world.
>
> Your task will not be an easy one. Your enemy is well trained, well equipped and battle-hardened. He will fight savagely.
>
> But this is the year 1944! Much has happened since the Nazi triumphs of 1940–41. The United Nations have inflicted upon the Germans great defeats, in open battle, man-to-man. Our air offensive has seriously reduced their strength in the air and their capacity to wage war on the ground. Our Home Fronts have given us an overwhelming superiority in weapons and munitions of war, and placed at our disposal great reserves of trained fighting men. The tide has turned! The free men of the world are marching together to Victory!
>
> I have full confidence in your courage, devotion to duty and skill in battle. We will accept nothing less than full victory!
>
> Good Luck! And let us all beseech the blessing of Almighty God upon this great and noble undertaking.

When the ship's commander signed off for the night, our quarters again fell quiet, but Ike's encouraging words seemed to settle everyone down. Reassured of the justice and importance of our mission, each of us tried to ready ourselves for the fight that lay ahead. Most of the guys around me used the time to try to grab some sleep, but I was too keyed up and cramped to manage more than quick catnaps. Many questions passed through my mind.

How long would it take the ship to reach our assigned spot 12 miles from the beach? What would it be like when we hit the beach? Would we come under enemy fire? Will I be afraid? Heck, I'm already afraid!

Although a two-month temporary assignment back in England had caused me to miss out on most of H Company's training with Higgins boats (or LCVPs for Landing Craft, Vehicle, Personnel), I had heard plenty of stories about the difficulties involved in downloading from the ship to the landing craft.

Is it going to be difficult to climb down the rope "scramble nets" to the landing craft with all this gear? Could I slip and fall into the ocean? What's a Higgins boat really like?

My focus gradually drifted from what lay ahead to what I had left behind back home, engulfing me in a flood of memories of my mother, my father, my four brothers, my sister, and even my dog. I recalled fun times with my friends at church and school, hot summers mowing grass, days spent fishing, hunting, and camping, and laughter over home-cooked meals.

Will I return to that happy life again?

My mind turned to two of my brothers who were also a part of this historic undertaking. They were out there somewhere amid the vast multitude of troops heading toward Nazi-occupied France.

Will I see them again? Will I make it through? Will my landing craft even make it to the beach? Will God protect me? Please, God, help me!

As I sat lost in my own thoughts, nearly all the soldiers closest to the tiny bulbs in the hull were using their faint illumination to read. Many sought solace in their pocket-sized copies of the Bible's New Testament and the Psalms which had been passed out by Army chaplains a few days earlier.

Most prayed silently, though an audible prayer was occasionally uttered by men whose apprehension about the coming day had brought their total dependence upon God to the forefront. About halfway through the night, one GI sitting a few feet away from me began softly reciting the Lord's Prayer aloud.

> Our Father, who art in heaven, Hallowed be thy name. Thy kingdom come, Thy will be done on earth as it is in heaven. Give us this day our daily bread. And forgive us our trespasses, as we forgive those who trespass against us. And lead us not into temptation, but deliver us from evil. For thine is the kingdom, and the power, and the glory forever. Amen.

With his hands clasped tightly in front of him, the soldier repeated the words over and over and over, like it was the only prayer he knew. Sharing his fears, I found the familiar scripture tremendously comforting.

The spectacle of war: 1:15am–8:30am, June 6

Reveille for H Company and the rest of the 2nd Battalion came at 1:15am on June 6. D-Day had arrived.

Following our breakfast of bologna sandwiches and coffee, we expected that all the troops on board the *Henrico* would immediately start heading up to the ship's top deck in preparation for downloading onto the landing craft.

Instead, an agonizing delay ensued after breakfast as we waited for information, orders, or some direction. The hushed stillness of the previous few hours persisted. Little talking or joking could be heard. There was almost no movement around me.

The silence in our dimly lit compartment seemed to grow deafening. In the midst of hundreds of men, I felt completely isolated and alone.

At last, the *Henrico*'s loudspeakers began calling units of the 2nd Battalion topside, company by company. Shortly afterward, we heard the anchor unwinding. Roughly 10 hours and 100 miles from Portland, our ship had reached its assigned station 12 miles off the coast of Normandy.

With the ship anchored, boat teams from the 2nd Battalion's E, F, and G Companies started loading aboard their assigned Higgins boats for the long trip to shore. Assigned to the first waves of the assault, these three rifle companies would form part of the spearhead of the 175,000 men in the Allied invasion force. Our H Company would go in right behind them.

"H Company, H Company on top! Let's go!" a voice finally announced over the intercom. Only at this point did conversation resume among the men around me, ending my sense of isolation.

"Boys, we're going in on Easy Red!" Captain Irvine called out in encouragement, using the codename for our company's sector of Omaha Beach.

Struggling to our feet, we ascended the several flights of stairs with our gear, a climb which proved to be even more challenging than our descent a few days earlier. When we emerged out onto the *Henrico*'s top deck, a brisk wind and light drizzle made it feel cooler than the 60-degree temperature, but my senses were so overwhelmed that I hardly noticed the weather.

Even in the still faint predawn light, the panorama of the invasion was utterly awe-inspiring. For as far as the eye could see an innumerable armada of ships and boats of every size and description filled the horizon. Overhead, small dirigibles tethered to ships floated in the sky to hamper enemy planes from conducting strafing runs on the assembled fleet.

Glancing to my right, I was astounded to observe what appeared to be a gray wall looming up from the sea. *What in the world is this thing?*

A dozen yards above me, the muzzles of massive deck guns protruded over the top of what I now realized was a ship's steel hull. Larger than anything in my wildest imagination, the enormous vessel was a battleship, the USS *Texas*.

Moments later, there was a brilliant flash and deafening boom as its 14-inch guns blasted giant shells toward enemy targets ashore. Each time the battleship fired off another salvo, the wind blew a thick cloud of smoke from its guns toward the deck of the *Henrico*, saturating the air around us with the pungent, nauseating smell of cordite. It was the smell of battle.

The *Texas* was at one end of a row of three battleships the deckmaster told us included the *Nevada* and the *Arkansas*. Stationed bow-to-stern, they were delivering a tremendous pounding of the German positions ashore. Yet the immense firepower of these battleships was just a small fraction of the total bombardment targeting the enemy's coastal fortifications and objectives further inland. In scale and intensity, the military might of the Allied naval and air forces was beyond words, power that was as reassuring as it was fearsome.

In the sea nearby, there were about 50 Higgins boats, split up into groups of a dozen circling craft each. Churning up white foam wakes as they made repeated circuits in the water, each 36-foot long, 11-foot wide Higgins boat awaited its turn to break away from the circle and download men from the troopships.

Man alive, what a show! I wouldn't miss this for anything in the world! Gaping at the spectacle around me, I felt part of an unbeatable team. Victory seemed certain. Failure seemed unimaginable.

By the time H Company arrived up on the *Henrico*'s deck, the boat teams from E, F, and G Companies had just about finished downloading onto the Higgins boats. With each landing craft carrying three dozen troops, they formed up into convoys of a dozen boats. Heading off through choppy seas like a one-way parade of oversized water spiders, they started the trip to shore.

As part of the first and second waves, the 2nd Battalion's infantry companies were designated to begin landing at 6:30am (H-Hour) on Easy Red Beach, a nearly mile-long sector of Omaha Beach. Scheduled to follow them onto the beach in the third wave at 7:10am (H-Hour plus 40), H Company began moving to the *Henrico*'s rails about 4am to download onto the Higgins boats.

Just at this moment, a large portion of our second machine-gun platoon received word that we would not be able to download with the rest of H Company. The officer serving as the deckmaster informed us the Higgins boat assigned to our boat team was unavailable, though it was unclear whether this was due to a mechanical problem or some other issue. As a result, our boat team would have to wait for a landing craft to return from shore before we could make the trip to the beach.

Stunned and frustrated by this last-minute delay, there was nothing we could do about it. Even if those of us who had to remain behind knew we would be hitting the beach only a few hours after the rest of our company, it still felt strange to stand by as we watched the other men downloading onto the Higgins boats in the pre-dawn light.

Sometime around 5am, the convoy of boats carrying the bulk of H Company set out for shore. They were scheduled to land on Easy Red Beach at 7:10am, but we later learned our company did not reach the beach until a little before 7:30am because of a delay in contacting their Navy control boat.

Back on the deck of the *Henrico*, time seemed to pass slowly as my boat team and I waited impatiently for a returning landing craft to become available.

Looking southward, there was just enough daylight to make out the French coastline, but a thick cloud of white smoke caused by our naval and aerial bombardment largely shrouded the shoreline from view. German artillery batteries ensconced in concrete bunkers retaliated against our invasion armada with long-range fire of their own. The deckmaster us told us that our ship's position placed us just beyond the range of their guns, but we observed what appeared to be several enemy rounds exploding in the sea nearby.

About 7:30am, an hour after the first landings on Easy Red, the deckmaster alerted our boat team and the other boat teams on deck to move to the ship's rails. We would start downloading as soon as the returning Higgins boats arrived.

While our boat team began queuing up, radio messages started to arrive from the beachmaster, an officer who directed the movement of forces on the beach. Broadcast over the *Henrico*'s loudspeakers, these radio transmissions from shore were clearly audible to all of us on deck.

As we listened intently over the next hour, it increasingly began to sound like a crisis was developing on Omaha Beach. In the meantime, the anticipated order to download onto returning Higgins boats did not come.

About 8:30am, the beachmaster radioed back an urgent message.

"Don't send the troops yet. There are too many dead men ... too much destruction on the beach. Tanks are blown up and jeeps are all to pieces. There's no place to land. Hold up till further notice."

CHAPTER I

Easy Red Beach:
8:30am, June 6–Night, June 6/7

Waiting to join the battle: 8:30am–2:30pm, June 6

Shaken by this ominous news, all of us mutely pondered what it meant, concerned for the fate of our buddies fighting on the beach 12 miles away.

Would the troops ashore be forced back off the beaches? Could they possibly reload onto the Higgins boats to return to the troopships?

Standing on the deck of the *Henrico* amid the ceaseless firing of the naval guns, it seemed impossible this colossal invasion force could be defeated.

We had to be successful in our landings and push inland. But what awaited us when the landings resumed?

Following the postponement of further landings, the deckmaster ceased playing radio traffic from shore. His action was undoubtedly taken out of concern for our morale, but it left us completely in the dark as to what was happening on the beach over the next few hours.

Around 9:30am, we ate an early lunch of peanut butter and jelly sandwiches and an apple. After downing our chow, some of the GIs around me tried to nap where they sat on deck, but no one got much rest amid the ongoing noise of battle and apprehension about what lay ahead.

Sometime before 2pm, more than five hours after the landings had been suspended, the radio message we had been waiting for finally crackled over the ship's loudspeakers, which had just resumed broadcasting the beachmaster's transmissions from shore.

"It's not all clear, but it's clear enough to land," he announced.

"Okay, guys, let's go!" the deckmaster ordered.

After roughly 10 hours of waiting up on the *Henrico*'s deck, the command to download onto the Higgins boats came as a relief to us. More importantly, the order to proceed with the landing meant our guys were successfully fighting their way off the beach.

All of our training was a prelude to this moment. The long days of drilling were over. We were finally heading into the battle for Normandy.

Made up of GIs from H Company's second machine-gun platoon as well as men from other outfits, our 36-man boat team was assigned to the second Higgins boat to load. This meant another half-hour of waiting as the boat team ahead of us downloaded.

When the deck master at last signaled our boat team to download, we formed a queue along the rails of the *Henrico*. Located a dozen or so men back from the front of the line, I watched as three men at a time went over the rail.

In order to reach the Higgins boat two or three stories below the deck of the *Henrico*, we would have to descend a wide scramble net hanging down the side of the ship. At each step down the latticed squares of the net's thick hemp ropes, a heavily laden GI had to avoid entangling his arms and boots, all the while tightly maintaining his handholds and footing.

A soldier burdened with up to 70 pounds of equipment would face a difficult descent even in good conditions, but the rough seas off Normandy made the climb truly perilous. The struggle to maintain one's balance and hold on to ropes made slippery with sea spray was made infinitely more challenging by the rocking of the *Henrico* that caused the scramble net to swing away from the ship and then slam back into the hull.

The severe sea swells created even bigger problems for the Higgins boat positioned beneath the *Henrico*. Like some over-sized cork, the landing craft bobbed up four or five feet as it crested each wave and then plunged back down into the ensuing trough. As the boat rose and fell, the waves were also pitching the craft several feet away from the ship and then driving it back, causing it to bump up hard against the hull.

On reaching the bottom of the net, each man had to carefully time his final backward drop in order to land inside the boat, which only stayed in position at the crest of a wave close to the ship for a few seconds.

Downloading to the Higgins boat: about 2:30pm–3:30pm, June 6

Descending the scramble net three men at a time, the first several members of our boat team successfully made their way down to the landing craft over the next 10 minutes. As I was moving to the *Henrico*'s rails to start my own descent, a lieutenant overseeing our loading reached into a big box and handed me a small, neatly folded sheet of white cotton.

"What is this?" I asked.

"That's a mattress cover for your dead body, soldier. Stick it in your jacket. In case you get killed, all they gotta do is reach into your shirt, pull out the mattress cover, stick you in it, and stack you up like cordwood. You may need it. You probably will," he quipped with a smile. That was a real encouragement.

Yet despite his morbid humor, I never expected I would be killed. As I stuffed the mattress cover into my field jacket, I was thinking that it might be needed for someone else or for some other purpose.

After issuing the mattress cover, the officer next handed me a condom.

"Put this on your rifle," he directed. Rolled down over the barrel of my carbine, the prophylactic would shield the weapon from seawater. Not having time to do it at that moment, I decided to wait until I was down on the boat.

"Throw your leg over the side and take hold of the rope!" the lieutenant shouted. Standing at the *Henrico*'s rail, I leaned out so that I could observe the GIs already descending the scramble net below me.

At that same moment, one of the soldiers who had reached the bottom rung of the net dropped backward toward the Higgins boat just as a swell pitched the craft away from the ship. In what seemed like slow motion, the man plummeted into the gap that had opened between the ship and the boat.

Plunging into the sea, the GI was instantly dragged under the surface by the weight of his gear, almost certainly making any rescue impossible. Though I was not well acquainted with this soldier, the pity I felt for him was magnified by the knowledge that I risked meeting the same fate. Indeed, his disappearance beneath the waves was as unnerving as it was gut-wrenching.

"Get moving, soldier!" the officer impatiently yelled from behind me, bringing me back to the moment.

How am I going to make it down to that boat? I wondered. Though strong and honed at 185 pounds, my shorter five-foot-six-inch height would make the already risky descent down the scramble net that much more physically demanding for me. The challenge it posed deepened my regret at having missed out on the main portion of our boat loading drills in England during a two-month temporary assignment away from H Company.

Hampered by my carbine and pack, I swung my left leg over the side until my boot was secured on a horizontal rope rung. After tightly grabbing hold of the ropes with both my hands, I then pulled my right leg over, awkwardly maneuvering my entire body onto the net. Despite being a bit slick with sea spray, the ropes were as thick as my wrists, giving them a sturdy, reassuring feel.

More powerful encouragement came from the big guns of the USS *Texas* which continued blasting away at enemy targets ashore. The acrid smell of cordite in the drifting smoke intensified the reality of battle for me. Caught up in the moment, I felt adrenaline flooding through my body and sharpening my senses, giving me a hyperawareness about everything that was happening.

With my fingers clenched around the rope, I tried to take my first step down the net toward the Higgins boat bobbing on the waves below me. From my position, it was impossible for me to look directly down to the next rope rung, so I had to blindly fumble downward with my left boot while clinging tightly to the net with my hands and struggling to retain a footing with my right boot.

Even stretching the toe as far as I could, my boot simply flailed in the air, unable to locate the next rung a couple of feet down. A paralyzing terror swept through me as I realized the climb would be even harder than I had anticipated.

But at this moment of crisis, an idea flashed through my mind. By using the edge of my left boot along the vertical strand of the rope, I could guide my foot down to the next horizontal rung on the net. With this method, I was finally able to find my footing on the rung below and shift my weight down to it.

As adrenaline continued to pump through my body, I repeated the process again and again, but each step down the net was a precarious balancing act that tested me physically. Any misstep would almost certainly be fatal.

Despite stern warnings to keep our attention focused on our own descent and avoid looking down, my curiosity got the better of me. Just as I glanced to my right to check on the progress of the other guys a little further down the net, a soldier below me lost his grip on the rope.

Momentarily thrashing in the air without making the slightest sound, he splashed into the water right beside the Higgins boat.

The nightmarish sight of this second soldier falling from the scramble net sent a shockwave through my whole system. Almost overwhelmed by fear, I placed my life in God's hands. There had already been a good bit of praying on my part even before I began my descent, but the desperation of my situation now intensified the urgency of my plea.

God, please help me make it down the net to the Higgins boat.

At that same instant, I heard orders being issued to the men already aboard the landing craft to pull the bottom of the net into the boat and hold it there until everyone had safely downloaded. After observing a second soldier fall into the water, the commander of our boat team had devised this simple solution to ensure the rest of us would land in the boat when we released our grip on the net. His action might well have saved my life.

On my next glance down the net, I saw that the guys aboard the Higgins boat had succeeded in rescuing the GI who had just fallen into the sea. As the others applauded, one of them started CPR on the man, who appeared to revive.

By the time I reached the bottom of the net, I was almost overcome with exhaustion. The climb down had seemed to last an hour, though only 10 grueling minutes had passed since I had swung over the side of the *Henrico*. But even with the net now pulled into the boat, it would still be pretty easy for me to break my neck when I let go and dropped backwards into it.

"Okay, let loose!" shouted one of the GIs already aboard.

Surrendering my grip on the rope, I tumbled backwards three or four feet into the Higgins boat.

Landing hard on my backpack, I careened several feet across the deck of the boat which was greased slick as ice with a couple of inches of vomit. My slide ended with me slamming against the boat's hull as I came to a stop in a shallow pool of puke. Coating my hands and arms, its stinking, pungent odor immediately left me gagging.

Violently seasick, almost everyone already on board had been throwing up. Packed tightly together, many men had been unable to reach the side of the boat to vomit into the sea. Though disgusted by the conditions aboard and bruised by my fall, I knew I was just lucky not to have broken any bones.

A moment later, several guys helped pull me to my feet in order to make space for the next GIs coming down the net. Because I had missed out on most of the training with landing craft back in England, it was only now that I had my first opportunity to inspect a Higgins boat up close. I was utterly shocked to discover the 36-foot-long craft was constructed almost entirely of plywood. Indeed, the boat's only armor was its steel ramp up front.

"Wait a minute! Wait a minute! We're going into all that machine-gun fire with a plywood boat!" I protested to no one in particular.

"Yeah, c'mon, Andy. You know what a canoe is, don't ya? This is just a big canoe," the captain in command of our boat team joked. Though the officer knew my name, I had never seen him prior to our arrival on the deck of the *Henrico* earlier that day. A tough-looking son of a gun, he seemed like a capable leader.

With the relentless rolling of the boat and the slippery deck underfoot, it required a constant effort just to remain upright while the rest of our boat team finished loading. Meanwhile, three soldiers were probing the water around our boat with long poles in an attempt to locate the first GI who I had seen fall into the sea. Since they failed to retrieve him, I can only assume the man drowned.

Roughly half an hour after the loading process had begun, the last members of our boat team made it down to the landing craft without further incident. Pulling away from the *Henrico*, our boat joined several others circling in the water nearby to await the rest of the landing craft in our convoy.

As we motored through the water, four to six-foot white-capped waves continued to toss our Higgins boat up and down and side to side, while diesel fumes from the boats circling ahead wafted back over us. On top of that, the foul odor emanating from our uniforms treated with the anti-gas chemicals had become even more pungent now that the fabric was wet.

Between the jostling and bouncing around and inhaling noxious diesel fumes comingled with the awful stench of our uniforms, most of the guys who had fought off seasickness up until this point soon lost the battle. While the men at the edge of the boat were generally throwing up into their helmets and dumping the contents overboard, the conditions for those of us in the boat's cramped interior were even worse. My own nausea did not grow bad enough to make me sick, but the fellow right behind me was not so lucky.

Unable to keep down his last meal, he let out a loud belch and vomited. Striking my right shoulder and neck, the stream of hot puke oozed under the collar of my uniform and then seeped down my back under my shirt. The revolting stench left me dry heaving, but I just managed to avoid becoming sick.

Ordered to take seats on the deck of the boat, we sat down where we were standing. The discomfort of being crammed together shoulder-to-shoulder was minor compared to the gross indignity of sitting in three inches of accumulated vomit. However, my main thought at that moment was how the seasickness might affect our ability to fight once we were ashore.

Into the fight: about 3:30pm–6pm, June 6

A violet-colored flare bursting up in the sky signaled our small flotilla of Higgins boats to head for the landing beach. After a half-hour breathing diesel fumes from the boats circling ahead of us, all of us were ready to get under way.

Turning the boats toward shore, the coxswains started the 12-mile run toward the Easy Red sector of Omaha Beach. Popping my head up a moment later, I saw we were racing along just an arms-length away from another boat. Packed so closely together, it was incredible there were no deadly collisions.

My position three-quarters of the way back in the boat placed me a half-dozen feet from the coxswain piloting our craft at his post close to the stern. As the only man aboard whose head peaked out above the side of the boat, the coxswain struck me as a battle hero. His assignment was to bring our Higgins boat close to shore before dropping the steel ramp at the front. Disembarking in shallow water, we would wade the rest of the way to the beach.

All sense of time was soon lost as the powerful motor of the boat propelled us toward shore at what seemed amazing speed. Unfortunately, the steady shower of sea spray drenched and chilled us, while also adding several inches of cold water to the puke sloshing around on the deck where we sat.

Though a large number of the guys on board were from H Company's second machine-gun platoon, I only knew a few of them well. None of my buddies from my gun squad were sitting near enough for me to speak with them. Even if they had been closer, the loud hum of the boat's engine would have made any conversation difficult, which was okay since no one really felt much like talking anyway.

Every so often, there was a boom from behind us as the battleships fired another salvo. A moment later, we could see three huge shells at a time rocketing through the air toward shore with a noise resembling a speeding freight train.

As we drew closer to the beach, our ears began focusing on the whistle of incoming German artillery rounds. Coming down at a rate that increased in direct proportion to our diminishing distance from the beach, the enemy shells splashed into the sea around us, casting up geysers where they exploded.

By now, my adrenaline was really pumping, but the earlier enthusiasm I had felt at being a part of the invasion's epic drama had faded. The stark reality of what loomed ahead generated a torrent of conflicting emotions. While still feeling a sense of anticipation and pride about our mission, I now also experienced real fear as I pondered what awaited us ashore.

What did the earlier waves of troops go through on the beaches? What are we going into? What are we going to see? Will the beach obstacles still be there?

If given a choice at that moment, I would rather have been somewhere else—almost anywhere else. That was probably true of every man around me, but we were here and determined to do our duty as soldiers. None of us wanted to let down our buddies.

Lord, we just gotta get to the beach. Please help us get to the beach, I began silently pleading to God, repeating my prayer over and over.

Roughly two hours after our small convoy of landing craft had set out for shore, a loud scraping noise resonated up through the hull. At the same instant, all of us lurched forward as our boat came to a juddering halt.

We had run aground but were still at least 300 yards away from the beach. Coming in on the evening's low tide, our boat had struck an outlying sandbar pushed up by wave action. The loud sound of the sea washing around us made it clear our landing craft was still surrounded by deep water.

Over on our left, a two-story tall landing craft for vehicles, an LST (Landing Ship, Tank), had also halted, apparently having run aground on the same sandbar. As we watched, three amphibious Sherman tanks began driving off the LST's ramp into the water one by one. Specially modified, they had big rubber aprons wrapped around their hulls to keep them afloat as they motored through the surf to the beach, where they would go directly into action.

But instead of "swimming" as designed, the tanks immediately sank like stones, their protective rubber skirts completely failing as they were hit by the big waves thrust up by the heavy surf. In one case, a particularly strong gust of wind appeared to rip off a tank's apron just before it entered the water. As this tank sank, we saw at least a couple of crew members bail out, but some of the crews appeared unable to escape as seawater flooded into their vehicles.

Taller than a man, only the topmost part of the tank turrets remained visible above the waves. With the sunken tanks confirming the true depth of the water, there could now be no doubt in anyone's mind that we would all drown if we exited our boat this far out from shore. When we charged off the ramp with all our gear, we would be plunging to certain death.

However, within 30 seconds of grounding on the sandbar, our coxswain had apparently concluded this was as far as our Higgins boat could proceed. Unable to motor any further toward the beach, he followed the next step in the landing procedure drilled into him during his training.

"Ramp down! Ramp down!" he shouted, seemingly oblivious to the danger of sending us off the boat this far out.

In the split second before the ramp was dropped, the captain in charge of our boat team whipped his .45 pistol out of its holster. As I watched from six feet away, he jammed the muzzle right up against the coxwain's temple.

"I'll be damned if we're gonna stop right now!" he roared, speaking in a tone that brooked no argument. "You back this damn thing up. You're gonna hit that sandbar wide open and go further toward the beach or I'll blow your damn head off and drive this thing to the beach myself."

"Yes, sir, whatever you say, sir!" the coxswain responded with a look of sheer terror on his face. Reversing our Higgins boat 50 feet, he gunned the engine, getting it up to full speed before we rammed the sandbar.

The impact was again jarring, but this time the boat's hull slid across the sandbar with a loud grinding noise to reach the water beyond. No one said a word, but our collective sense of relief was palpable.

As we came closer to shore, the bodies of our troops who had been killed in the fighting earlier that day began to appear in the water alongside our boat. The gut-wrenching sight of these dead Americans tore my heart out and brought tears to my eyes. It was as if the war was stretching out into the sea to meet us, delivering an ominous warning of what lay ahead.

Meanwhile, German artillery rounds were exploding in the water around us with ever increasing frequency, though none fell close enough to cause any damage to our boat. But on top of the danger posed by incoming shells, we also knew the enemy had planted mined underwater obstacles in the shallow water nearer to shore.

During our pre-invasion briefings, an officer had explained that the *Wehrmacht* expected the initial Allied assault would come at high tide to shorten the width of beach troops would need to cross. In preparation, the Germans had deployed thousands of the tetrahedral obstacles constructed from crossed steel beams welded together. Driven into the sand at low tide, many of these obstacles had explosive charges mounted atop them. These charges were designed to detonate when they came into contact with the hulls of the landing craft arriving at high tide. Fortunately, we were coming in at the evening's low tide, which minimized our risk of hitting any mined underwater obstacles.

Moments after crossing over the sandbar, our landing craft again ground to a halt in the sand much closer to shore. Though still roughly a hundred yards away from the beach, it was clear the boat had gone as far as it could. More importantly, the water was now shallow enough that we would not drown.

"Ramp down! Ramp down!" the coxswain hollered, after making certain that he had the captain's approval.

But any reprieve we felt at having avoided drowning further out instantly evaporated. At the same moment our boat's front ramp dropped, another Higgins boat 30 yards to our left suddenly blew apart in a tremendous explosion. As we looked on in horror, the bodies of the soldiers aboard and pieces of the landing craft were hurled into the air in a huge cascade of water.

Within seconds, almost every trace of the boat and its three dozen GIs had vanished. The powerful blast had obliterated the craft, suggesting it had suffered a direct hit from an artillery shell. While the explosion could have been caused by the boat striking an underwater mine, it seemed to me a mine would likely have destroyed only the vessel's front end.

There was no time to mentally process this terrible scene, but the destruction of one of the landing craft in our flotilla sparked us into action. No one wanted to linger on our own boat after what we had just witnessed.

Without further delay, we began our disembarkation. Raising my carbine over my head, I followed the two dozen men rushing forward ahead of me.

As we stepped off the boat's steel ramp into the water, we had feared German machine gunners would be zeroed in on our landing craft, just waiting to scythe through us. Even when our boat had been grounded further out on the sandbar, a few bullets had pinged off our boat's steel ramp. But now, to our great surprise and relief, the anticipated enemy machine-gun and small arms fire from shore was nonexistent, a situation we could only hope would last.

Despite immediately sinking up to my armpits in the frigid, five-foot-deep water, I hardly noticed the cold, drenched and chilled as I already was from the sea spray. In fact, the depth of the water greatly aided my efforts to wash off the puke that still clung to my body and clothing. But though glad to have escaped the rolling, crowded, and vomit-filled confines of the landing craft and plant my boots on the sand, I mainly felt relieved to have made it this far.

Thank you God! I prayed as we started the slow trudge through the surf toward the beach. Like everyone else, I wondered about my odds of survival.

Lord, please help me to get to the beach, I began to repeat silently.

Around me, some of the other GIs were joking with one another in an effort to cope with the danger.

"Hey, guys, we'll be in France in just a few minutes," they exclaimed, making it sound like we were arriving in Normandy for a holiday.

In truth, every one of us felt scared to some degree. The only way to overcome fear and its paralyzing effects was simply to find raw courage inside ourselves and rely on our training. Whatever we might face, we all had to do our best to carry out the mission for which we had trained—and pray hard.

As we waded closer to shore through a forest of steel tetrahedral and log obstacles, German artillery rounds continued to drop into the water around us. However, it was the tragic consequences of the earlier fighting that gripped my attention. Nearby, the bodies of eight or ten GIs floated amid the debris of battle in water tinged red with blood in places. As waves carried some of the dead toward the shore, other bodies were dragged out to sea.

Lord, please get me to the beach. Lord, get me to the beach.

Easy Red Beach: about 6pm–7pm, June 6

Around six that evening, we at last made it ashore following our slow slog through the waves. A biting wind whipped against my soaked clothing, but I was deeply grateful to God to have arrived safely on land. At the same time, it was still hard to come to grips with the reality of where I was.

This is France. What in the world am I doing here? I asked myself fleetingly. But all of the thousands of us landing here knew we had been given a mission to end the Nazi occupation of Europe. We had to overcome that wicked tyranny.

As I looked around the beach, it was clear the battle here was largely over, but the price of our victory had been high. Here and there, the corpses of more dead GIs were stacked like firewood, awaiting a Graves Registration detail. The human toll was echoed by the wreckage of knocked-out jeeps, half-tracks, and tanks that littered the sand. Some had been blown apart, while others had flipped onto their sides and were still smoldering. The unbelievable scale of the carnage and waste inscribed an indelible image in my mind.

Here is the true face of war, I reflected.

But even amid this terrible destruction, the beach was humming with activity. Up and down the shoreline, more tanks, half-tracks, trucks, jeeps, ambulances, and other vehicles were steadily rolling out of large landing craft like the LST we had just seen offloading the doomed tanks further out.

Often towing artillery or trailers, most of the vehicles had to motor a short distance through the shallow surf. Coming ashore, the drivers headed for beach exits that led up to the high ground from where they could proceed further inland. Already, long queues of vehicles were forming up on the sand.

In the absence of German small arms fire, the only incoming fire came from the enemy's artillery, which was lobbing a round toward the beach every couple of minutes. Even if the artillery fire was not well-aimed, the presence of so many American targets moving across the sand still gave it lethal effect. Meanwhile, more shells whistled loudly through the air overhead as German artillery continued to fire on the incoming landing craft further out in the water.

To my astonishment, a mobile crane perhaps three or four stories high was already hard at work clearing the beach. Puzzled how it had reached the beach so fast, I watched as the soldier operating the crane locked the machine's big jaws on the burned-out hulk of an American vehicle. Hoisting it up into the air, he swung the wreck over and dumped it on top of a large heap of wreckage. Alongside the crane, two oversized bulldozers were shoving more wreckage into another massive pile.

To clear the beach while the enemy was still shelling the area required brave souls. Perhaps as much as any other element of the invasion, the presence of the crane and dozers at such an early moment provided further evidence of the meticulous logistical planning that had gone into the operation.

A short distance away, an officer serving as the beachmaster in this sector was walking back and forth across the sand with a baton, orchestrating the movement of human and vehicular traffic like he was conducting a symphony.

"Go this way!" he barked through a bullhorn at one group of GIs, ordering them off in one direction. He next turned to greet our boat team.

"You guys, c'mon this way!" he shouted, directing our party of three dozen or so GIs toward a beach exit. Because our landing had occurred at low tide, we would have to cross a flat 200-yard expanse of sand in order to reach a path that led up to the high ground above the beach.

Without attempting to get organized into our units, everyone immediately moved out toward the beach exit at a plodding gait, unable to proceed any faster under the weight of 70 pounds of gear and our waterlogged clothing. Whatever courage drove us toward the battle ahead was reinforced by the absolute certainty there was no way to go back and no safety in remaining where we were. As we went forward, my appeal to God now underwent another revision.

Lord, I've got one more prayer. We're here at the beach, now I really need to get to the high ground. Please Lord, I just need you to help me get to the high ground. Help us to get to the high ground.

Other than the occasional German artillery round, our greatest concern was enemy mines. But thanks to the earlier work of mine-clearing teams, there were now safe routes through minefields and barbed wire, marked out by small black and white signs to our right and left that warned of unexploded mines. With our sluggish pace through the cleared passage presenting an inviting target for any remaining enemy artillery observers, our group spread out and hunched down in order to minimize our vulnerability.

Not knowing when a German artillery shell might come whistling down in our direction, we searched the sand in vain for the expected craters where we could dart for cover. Unfortunately, most of the Allied ordnance had targeted the enemy's positions further inland, rather than the beach. However, the lack of craters proved inconsequential due to the low intensity of incoming enemy artillery fire by this point in the day. Though a dozen or so rounds struck the beach as we crossed the sand, none landed closer than about 50 yards from us.

At the end of several long, tense minutes, our boat team reached the beach exit, which was located at the base of a well-worn trail. The path followed a natural ravine up to the high ground near the top of the roughly 150-foot ridge which rose above the beach.

To defend the beach exit, the Germans had constructed a concrete bunker for their machine gunners about six feet away from the start of the path. Captured by American troops earlier in the day, the bunker now housed a U.S. command post. As we passed it, a half-dozen GIs at its entrance were talking into field telephones with extra-long antennas to extend the range of their signal.

Still sopping wet and feeling the weight of our packs, we immediately began our ascent, cautiously advancing up the gently rising two-foot-wide path that cut through the green scrub blanketing the hillside. If the roar of our heavy equipment on the beach behind us was reassuring, the staccato noise of rifle and machine-gun fire and an occasional whiff of cordite in the air provided a strong reminder that fighting was underway nearby. I kept praying.

Now Lord, I've got one more request. I need a hole to get in. And thank you for protecting us as we come up the pathway.

About halfway up the trail, we came upon several dead German soldiers, who lay one on top of the other in a ditch just to the left of the path. While seeing dead American GIs in the water and on the beach had torn my heart out, the sight of these dead Germans did not really register with me.

Passing within three feet of the bodies, we all greedily eyed and remarked upon the shiny Luger pistol in the hip holster of the dead German whose body lay on top of the others. Each of us was sorely tempted to grab such a highly prized war souvenir, but we had been warned repeatedly that enemy bodies would likely be booby-trapped. No one wanted to risk his life for a pistol.

But a GI who came up the trail just behind me had no such apprehension. On reaching the bodies, he bent down, whipped the Luger out of the dead man's holster, and jammed the weapon under his own belt.

"That's the way we do it back home," he proudly proclaimed to anyone in earshot. Regretting my overabundance of caution, I vowed not to miss out on any future opportunities to claim an enemy pistol.

By this point in our climb, I was starting to believe we would make it up to the high ground without incident. Just at that moment, machine-gun fire and then rifle shots rang out from somewhere a little way ahead. Quickening my pace, I hustled forward as fast as I could manage under the weight of my gear. By the time I reached the scene 50 feet further up the trail, the action was all over, but everyone was recounting what had happened.

From a concealed position behind some brush to the left of the path, a German soldier had been watching the advance of our group. After the soldiers leading our column had passed him, the "Kraut" popped up and sprayed them from behind with his burp gun (an MP 40 or *Maschinenpistole* 40 submachine gun).

Almost instantly, another GI in our column drilled the German in his back with a shot from his rifle. Tumbling from the bushes, the enemy soldier's lifeless body had rolled out onto the trail where it now lay before us. He must have been one of the last few Germans still resisting in this sector of Omaha Beach.

Sadly, the burst of fire from the German's submachine gun had hit a couple of our guys. While one GI had suffered relatively minor arm wounds, the other had a string of bullet wounds stitched down his left arm. Several of these wounds appeared to be less serious, but one bullet had ripped into his shoulder, causing severe bleeding.

Looking down at the soldier's shredded arm, it was difficult to believe he would live. Although I barely knew this GI, the sight of his wounds and his suffering really shook me up. Like the other things I had witnessed over the past few hours, it was another part of my initiation to the harsh reality of war.

In response to our shouts, a couple of medics rushed up to the site from the beach, reaching us within 10 minutes.

"Hey, this guy's still alive!" exclaimed the medic who examined him. After gently placing the wounded man on a stretcher, the medics carried him back down to the beach. Several weeks later, we learned he had been evacuated to a hospital ship where Army surgeons were able to save him.

On the high ground: about 7pm, June 6/4:30am, June 7

After a slow trek up the roughly 300-yard-long trail, our column finally reached the top of the ridge about half an hour after setting out. Emerging onto the high ground, we practically stumbled into a network of a dozen abandoned German foxholes. Established 10 yards back from the edge of the ridge and extending for about 40 yards, these foxholes had afforded the enemy an excellent spot from which to fire down at our troops on the beach or coming up the trail. Surveying the site, all of us were in awe of the GIs who had earlier seized such a strong position from the Germans.

From this location, we had a spectacular vantage point to observe the progress of the invasion. Vessels of all types were arriving to unload their cargos on the beach. Hundreds of men and vehicles were moving inland, including a stream of jeeps. Every jeep towed a trailer loaded with ammo, grenades, artillery rounds, food ration boxes, and all the other essentials of war. With each passing hour, our beachhead in France was growing more secure.

But we did not have much time to enjoy the view. Though the Germans had retreated a short distance inland from the ridge, a counterattack seemed likely. Uncertain of the enemy's present location and with no other American troops visible atop the high ground, the captain in charge of our boat team immediately directed us to take up a defensive position in the abandoned foxholes and prepare to resist any possible German assault.

Dropping into one of these deep holes, I was grateful to finally be in a relatively defensible location if we encountered the enemy. Still wet with a salty mixture of seawater and sweat, I began to assess my equipment. While I had kept my carbine out of the water, my .45 pistol had been completely submerged when I had plunged off the ramp. Firing off a couple of test rounds, I was happy to discover my pistol worked just fine. I felt ready for whatever came next.

After maybe an hour, it became apparent a German attack against our position was not imminent. While remaining alert, we now relaxed somewhat. Recovered from our seasickness, all of us were famished and ready for chow. As I broke out the canned C-rations stowed in my pack, my appetite was higher than it had been at any time over the past few days. Hungrily, I dug into my meal of Spam, crackers, and cheese like it was a gourmet feast.

Feeling an overwhelming sense of relief to have made it to this point, gratitude to God filled my heart.

Thank you Lord, thank you for bringing me to the safety of this foxhole and for this good food. Thank you for giving me protection coming up the path and in the boat.

About 10pm, just after sunset on that long summer day, we stretched our legs before settling back into our foxholes for the night. Though our part of the second machine-gun platoon was separated from the rest of H Company, we were at least largely united at one location. If things went according to plan, we expected to link up with our company near the village of Colleville-sur-Mer early the next day.

Still lacking any heavy equipment, we were waiting for our assigned jeep and trailer, which hauled the machine guns and other gear for the two squads in our section of the platoon. While we knew the jeep and trailer would disembark on the beach, we remained uncertain as to how the driver would locate us.

But shortly after 10:30pm, as full darkness descended, our jeep and trailer arrived. Naturally, we were all curious how our driver had managed to find us amid the chaos on the beach and in near darkness.

"The beachmaster pointed in the direction our outfit was supposed to be and I just drove 'til I found you," he explained.

Excitedly, our two squads from the second section gathered around the jeep and trailer. Both were jam-packed with our equipment: two .30-caliber water-cooled Browning machine guns, tripods, metal boxes filled with ammo belts, several metal water containers, rubber hoses, wooden crates of grenades packed like cartons of eggs, food rations, and other supplies. As each of us collected his designated component of the machine gun and other provisions, almost everyone tossed his heavy gas mask in the trailer in order to lighten his load, having concluded the risk of the Germans using poison gas was low.

Immediately afterward, the officer in charge ordered our section to deploy the two machine guns to defend against a possible enemy counterattack still expected all along the line. Our squad's gun was set up in front of my foxhole, while the other squad's gun was posted 40 yards to my right, giving us a cross-cutting field of fire. No sentry duty was assigned as all of us were awake and ready for action. If the Germans did try to assault our position, we now had the firepower and grenades to hold them off.

While we kept watch under a cold drizzle, Allied warships continued to send huge shells arcing through the skies over our heads, maintaining their relentless hammering of German targets further inland. Explosions and gunfire resounded off in the distance. The enemy was out there somewhere, but the anticipated counterattack against our position did not come.

Even after my turn on gun duty ended, I remained too keyed up to get much real sleep. As I kept watch for any sign of enemy movement from my foxhole, a GI came crawling through our position.

"Does anybody speak German? Does anybody speak German?" he repeated in a voice just loud enough for us to hear. An officer was trying to interrogate captured enemy troops and needed someone who could translate. Unfortunately, neither I nor anyone else around me spoke German.

Missing out on this opportunity made me regret not studying German in school. I could have helped question the prisoners to find out the size and location of the enemy's units, their assigned missions, and other vital information. Such intelligence would allow us to determine the type of threats we faced and the best route to advance. At a deeper level, my German heritage on my father's side, as well as my outgoing nature, made me especially curious to get to know and understand these German soldiers as human beings.

How old were these soldiers and where were they from? Were they practicing Christians? What motivated them to fight? Did they believe that Germany had the right to control France and the other occupied countries? Did they support Hitler and the Nazis?

If we could just sit around a campfire and get to know each other, we would get along just fine, I mused.

Still, whatever my more positive disposition towards the Germans as individuals, I wholeheartedly believed in the justice of our fight against the brutal Nazi dictatorship that controlled much of Europe.

Before long, my thoughts returned to our immediate circumstances. Despite our force's success in seizing a shallow foothold at Omaha Beach, the position remained tenuous. Like every other Allied soldier in Normandy that night, I was anxious about what lay ahead.

God had brought me safely through D-Day, my first day in combat. Trusting in His will, I wondered whether I would live to the end of the war to see my home and family again.

CHAPTER 2

Heading towards War:
July 1923–July 12, 1943

Our family farm: 1923–1929

My dad believed his kids should grow up on a farm where they would have the smell of clover fields and freshly cut hay, a barn for horses and cows, a barnyard alive with chickens and ducks, and a muddy pen filled with noisy pigs. So, it was in just such an idyllic setting that I spent the earliest years of my childhood, surrounded by love and happiness.

Born in Ohio in 1878, my dad, Ernest Albert Andrews, was a man of strong Christian belief, high integrity, and clean speech. While our family resided on a farm, he earned a living as a printer. Admired by all who knew him, he was hard-working, dependable, forthright, and honest to a fault. As a father, he balanced his sober side with good-natured humor and a sense of adventure.

My mother, Margarette Rebecca Lockwood, was born in 1888 in Pennsylvania and raised in West Virginia and Virginia. Caring, industrious, and outgoing, it was her deep Christian faith that truly defined her and everything she did. An accomplished pianist and piano teacher, she was passionate about music. As a loving mother, she managed to find time for each of her children, keep our house running efficiently, and still cook up wonderful meals.

When my parents married in 1914, my 26-year-old mother was a little older than the typical bride of that day, while my 36-year-old father was a good 10 years older than the typical groom. By the time I was born into the family on July 27, 1923, my parents already had three other sons: Karl, Don, and Bennett. Christened Ernest Albert Andrews, Jr., I was proud to be named after my father. By 1927, my parents had added another son, Bill, and a daughter, Peggy.

Our family lived in a large two-story home on a 13-acre farm located in the rolling hills a little east of Chattanooga, Tennessee. Our barn housed an old tractor, a wagon, and stalls to shelter our several cows and our horse in the winter. Beside the barn was the corncrib, which was built up off the ground to discourage incursions from varmints. Following the harvest of the corn crop, this crib held tons of golden ears of corn shucked from their husks.

Naturally, the barn held high fascination for us kids. Its hayloft was home to a multitude of mostly mid-sized rats that made regular forays across the iron pipe above the tractor in order to plunder the chicken feed in the granary. My older brothers and I made it our mission to curtail these rodent raids. Hiding behind barrels in the barn with an arsenal of sticks, we targeted the rats as they scurried along the pipe. When knocked off the pipe, the rats fell into the paws of the cats prowling below. Some days our count would go as high as 20 rats.

A big mulberry tree on our farm provided another source of entertainment. After its berries ripened in late summer, my brothers and I would climb up the trunk and shake the branches, causing mulberries by the thousands to rain down onto sheets under the tree. My mother would transform the collected berries into countless jars of jellies and mouthwatering pies.

Beyond her talents as a cook and a piano instructor, Mom was also a teacher about life. On warm summer nights, my brothers and I would lie down beside her on the lush green grass of our lawn. As we watched the sky for falling stars, she would point out the constellations to us. Reflecting on the heavens helped to open our young minds to the majesty of God's handiwork.

By the late 1920s, my father owned and operated a printing company with 52 employees. With business brisk and the future looking bright, he purchased a brand-new Ford Model-T truck. Unfortunately, this purchase came just before the Stock Market crash on October 29, 1929, an event that marked the start of the Great Depression.

As the Depression deepened over the ensuing months, Dad often expressed concern as more and more of his customers were unable to pay their printing bills. One night at supper, Dad told us he did not know how he was going to pay for the new truck. Not long after that, he sadly announced he would have to close his business and go to work for another printer. For the first time, he would not be his own boss.

Eventually, my dad was reduced to taking a job as a printer that paid only $25 a week, an income below what was needed to support our family. Listening to conversations between our parents about our continually worsening money problems, my brothers and I had little real understanding of what was happening but sensed the relentless financial pressure as they tried to figure out how our family would survive.

By early 1931, my parents' greatest worry was losing the farm, for which they still owed $1,500. Our family discussed how we might raise additional cash by selling off different assets such as our car, but each option had drawbacks and did not resolve the underlying shortfall in income. A few months later, we were forced to sell our beloved farm, a step that broke my dad's heart.

Signal Mountain, Tennessee: 1931–1939

Leaving our farm east of Chattanooga, we moved into a rental house in the town of Signal Mountain on the west side of Chattanooga, roughly 30 minutes from the city's downtown. Situated atop one of the low mountains surrounding the city, Signal Mountain was a friendly, close-knit community that provided us with a very different life from what we had known on the farm.

Despite our family's ongoing financial struggle, my mother still found a way to prepare something delicious for our meals, often buying eggs, produce, berries, and other items from local farmers who stopped by our house hoping to earn a little cash. When jobless men showed up at our door seeking food, she was always generous, offering them a small basket of food that came with the spoken assurance that God loved them.

Early on many Saturday mornings, Dad would wake me and several of my brothers to join him for a day of fishing at one of the region's many lakes. At nights, he sometimes took us frog-gigging. During these outings, my dad always found a way to teach us a moral lesson.

Of course, there were also school lessons. In the fall of 1931, when I was eight years old, I began second grade at Signal Mountain Grammar School. Most people rightly place great value on education, but I was more the active outdoor type and just never had much use for schooling.

By the spring of 1935, my lack of dedication to academic success caught up with me. Though I had developed a bit of a crush on my very attractive fifth grade teacher, I was pretty sure she had not come to sing my praises when she showed up at our home to see my mom toward the end of the school year.

Ushering my teacher into our living room, my mother invited her to take a seat on our couch where they could talk. Eavesdropping from the kitchen door, I heard every word of the conversation. My teacher got straight to the point.

"Mrs. Andrews, Ernest is a really nice boy, but he needs to take the fifth grade over," she bluntly stated. Unfortunately, being held back a year did little to bolster my already poor effort at scholastic achievement. Indeed, playing marbles and milk-bottle tops at recess were the highlight of my school days.

When summer arrived, my friends and I mowed lawns together. The money we earned was enough to finance the purchase of our annual fishing and hunting licenses. There was even a bit left over to buy a moon pie and RC cola for lunch and a five-cent Baby Ruth bar for a snack.

At night, my friends and I would often head over to "the brow" atop Signal Mountain, a bluff that provided an unobstructed vista of the surrounding area. Gathering there in the mid-1930s, we watched huge tractors and bulldozers begin construction of the Chickamauga Dam. At that distance, the huge earthmoving machines appeared to be tiny bugs crawling around in the dirt as they worked through the night under the illumination of brilliant floodlights.

From the age of 12, I was an active member of a Boy Scout troop on Signal Mountain. Our favorite night game was "Capture the Flag," played out on the fairway of the local golf course. Sneaking up on the keeper of the "enemy" flag was always the most nerve-racking moment since you could be spotted or heard at any moment. Learning to detect the slightest sound of movement helped me develop a critical skill that would one day aid me in real nighttime combat.

After turning 14, I began serving as a senior patrol leader in the Scouts, learning more invaluable skills that would benefit me throughout my life. Both inside and outside of Scouting, my free time was filled with fishing, hunting, hiking, canoeing, and camping. Fishing was my favorite pastime, but squirrel hunting ran a close second.

As teenagers, my brothers and I often went on day-long hunting expeditions on Signal Mountain. Mom told us we could bring home all the fish, fowl, and wild game that we wanted as long as these were scaled, skinned, gutted, cleaned, and re-cleaned before they entered her kitchen.

My mother spent much of her day teaching piano and at times had as many as 30 pupils, which supplemented my dad's income as a printer. Beyond helping to meet our family's rent and other regular expenses, her earnings also allowed us to set aside money toward building a new house of our own.

Naturally, Mom did everything she could to encourage my siblings and me to develop an interest in music, hoping we would be inspired to learn to play the piano or some other instrument. Despite never acquiring the ability to read music, I gradually learned to play a few songs on the piano by ear, eventually becoming an almost decent pianist. As my mom prophesied, even my limited skill on the instrument proved useful on numerous occasions.

Nearly every Sunday, our family worshipped at Signal Mountain Presbyterian Church. If my siblings or I missed the service, it was only on account of sickness, which was much worse than sitting through sermons. Missing church meant swallowing three doses of castor oil and staying in bed all day while the other kids went out to fly kites or ride their bikes after church.

The eight of us in my family pretty well filled up a pew. I loved sitting close to Dad so I could listen to his fantastic baritone as he sung the hymns. Sitting next to my father had another practical advantage, since I was far less likely to develop a case of the giggles in his immediate presence than if I was seated between a couple of my siblings. Anything funny raced up and down our pew like shockwaves, with laughter all the more difficult to suppress precisely because of the solemnity of the worship service.

Even if it was right in the middle of the sermon, any misbehavior was immediately punished. Dad would stand up in the center aisle of the church and aim his long finger at the guilty party, motioning the culprit to join him in a long walk of shame to the back exit under the scornful gaze of the congregation. Following this public humiliation, he would scold the perpetrator, "You've ruined the whole service for a lot of people." Dad would then lead the offender back to our pew, where we would all sit meekly for the rest of that day's service.

Our Sunday school classes provided Christian education, teaching us stories about Jesus, his disciples, his parables, his deeds, and the importance of knowing him as Lord and Savior. But it was a Thanksgiving Day trip with the class outside of church that taught me the true meaning of sharing and giving.

After collecting canned food and fresh vegetables from our homes, we loaded up in two big cars and drove out to an isolated rural area. A bumpy dirt road led up to a home, which was a large teepee-like tent with a side room added. The mother, the father, and their five children all lived in this tent. The kids were extremely short and emaciated. Trash was piled in one part of the yard as if put there for a garbage truck that never arrived. All the hardship of the Great Depression seemed to be epitomized in this single family.

Such encounters nourished the growth of my own Christian faith. I learned what it meant to love, believe, share, and live for Jesus Christ, God's son who was sent to redeem the world from sin. When I was 16 years old, I made the public profession of my faith, accepting Christ as my personal savior. This decision marked the major turning point in my life. It was a commitment from which I never backed away.

My acceptance of Christ instilled in me the belief God would be with me ever after and would never send me into any trials without giving me the grace to sustain me. Little did I realize that, within a few short years, my faith would be severely tested on faraway battlefields.

The growing threat from Nazi Germany: 1933–1939

A small, round-topped radio in our family's living room was our window to the wider world. Gathered around it, we listened to the important news of the day and public addresses given by President Franklin Delano Roosevelt, who had first been elected in 1933. FDR's folksy Fireside Chats helped lift our spirits during the difficult years of the Great Depression.

Radio networks also covered major sporting events such as the 1936 Summer Olympics in Berlin, Germany. We listened with excitement as Jesse Owens won four gold medals for the United States in track and field. Those Olympics gave me and many other Americans our first introduction to the Nazi regime that had taken power in Germany at the start of 1933.

Boxing was also broadcast over the radio. Dad was crazy about the American boxer Joe Louis and always rooted hard for him. After he got knocked out in a 1936 fight against the German, Max Schmeling, Joe was looking for redemption.

On the evening of June 22, 1938, an unforgettable second bout was to be held in New York City's Yankee Stadium, a grudge match of the first magnitude.

To accompany the event, Mom had fixed a huge platter of sandwiches and a couple pitchers of delicious fruit juice punch. While we sat hunched around our little radio, the announcer reviewed each heavyweight boxer's weight, height, arm reach, and past victories, indicating that the bout was soon to begin.

As if trying to get a better vantage point on the match, Dad moved closer to the radio when the bell rang. The announcer began spouting a rapid-fire, blow-by-blow description. All of a sudden, he yelled, "Max is down!" The crowd's shouting practically made the radio dance on its perch. In two minutes, Joe had won a technical knockout. Everybody in the stadium was stunned.

Our family was just as astonished. For the next 45 minutes, we rehashed the fight over our food and punch, wondering how poor Max could report back to Germany's Nazi *Führer* (Leader), Adolf Hitler. As it happened, Schmeling did not see him as the dictator could not bear talking to a loser.

Over the course of the 1930s, we gradually gained a clearer picture of Hitler and the Nazis. At the movie theater, newsreels that ran before the feature film showed the Nazi repression of Germany's Jews and political prisoners. Back at home, my dad, my brothers, and I occasionally tuned into radio broadcasts which included bits of Hitler's speeches to the German people. Though none of us understood German, it was evident the Nazi dictator was a fiery orator. Growing more and more impassioned as he spoke, Hitler would work his German audience into a wild emotional frenzy of cheering and shouting.

The first time we heard him, my dad shook his head sadly and warned, "That's the guy you fellas are going to have to go fight."

Coming only two decades after America had joined the British and French to help defeat Germany in World War I, the idea of another war against Germany was utterly unimaginable to my brothers and me. As Christians, none of us wanted to go fight and kill anyone. But our concern was also shaped by the fact we were of German ancestry on my dad's side of the family.

We all knew his family story well. My dad's parents, Hermann Faerber (born in 1841) and Luise Alfele (born in 1838) were both natives of Friesenheim, a municipality in what was then the Grand Duchy of Baden. Located on the border with France, Baden was a small independent German state allied to the Austrian Empire in Austria's mid-century rivalry with Prussia for political dominance in Germany.

Sometime in the 1860s, Hermann Faerber joined Baden's army as a medic. Following Prussia's defeat of Austria in the Austro-Prussian War during the summer of 1866, Baden accepted a military alliance with Prussia, which would go on to found the German Empire under the Prussian *Kaiser* (Emperor) in 1871.

After completing his military service, Hermann married Luise in Friesenheim in 1867. In 1872, the couple and their three very young children emigrated from

Germany to settle in Cleveland, Ohio. On October 5, 1878, they had another son, Ernest Albert Faerber, my father. Sadly, the deaths of Luise and her mother in the early 1880s left Herman (formerly Hermann) Faerber unable to care for his four children, which led him to put his youngest child up for adoption. On June 29, 1885, Ambrose and Abbie Andrews adopted six-year-old Ernest Albert, raising him at their home in Hudson, Michigan. In 1912, at age 33, my father moved to Tennessee and met my mom Margarette soon afterward.

Although Dad did not feel as deep a connection to Germany as he might have if had he been raised by the Faerbers instead of the Andrews, the mounting risk of another war with Germany still weighed on him. Already aged 38 in April 1917, he had been a little old to serve as a soldier when America had declared war on Germany in World War I. But if another war against Germany came, his American sons would almost certainly be fighting his kinfolk.

The war begins: August 1939–June 1940

The war my dad feared arrived just after I turned 16. In the late summer of 1939, Hitler was demanding Poland return territory Germany had been forced to surrender under the Treaty of Versailles, which had ended World War I. On September 1, just after I started ninth grade, Germany attacked Poland.

Though the war did not come as a surprise, the speed and violence of the German *Blitzkrieg* (Lightning War) left us stunned. The Poles put up a valiant struggle against the military might of the *Wehrmacht* but were soon overwhelmed. In a vivid depiction of Nazi aggression, my history teacher unfurled a large map of Europe in which Germany was caricatured as a wolf's head swallowing poor Poland.

Shortly after Poland's defeat, I went to see a movie at the theater in downtown Chattanooga. The newsreel before the feature film brought home the dire consequences of the Nazi victory. Watching German soldiers marching thousands of Polish troops toward captivity, I was particularly haunted by the image of a barefoot Pole who seemed to embody the plight of his nation.

How long could he march in that condition until his bloody and blistered feet would carry him no farther? What would happen to him if he fell out of line?

The cruelty of the smiling German soldiers herding along the defeated Poles made an equally lasting impression on me. More generally, the attack on Poland whipped up popular feeling against Germany, dramatically increasing hostility toward the Nazi regime among Americans. While no one wanted the United States to get involved in another European conflict, everyone supported Britain and France's declaration of war. German aggression had to be stopped.

As my ninth-grade year was ending, war news again intruded into our lives. In April 1940, Germany conquered Denmark and invaded Norway in another sudden move. In May, Hitler attacked France, Belgium, Holland, and Luxembourg. Every night, we tuned in to the radio for the latest developments.

On an evening in late June, one of the teachers from the local elementary school was visiting my mother when my dad arrived home from work.

"I have just learned of the fall of France," he announced somberly.

The teacher—a big Francophile—burst into tears. My mother soon joined her. It seemed to me the tears they shed were for more than the French people. They were crying for a world that was collapsing into the brutality of another long, bloody, and uncertain conflagration like World War I.

If the American public's reaction to the German invasion of Poland had primarily been one of anger, the response to Germany's victory over France that summer was more one of profound shock. How could France have been conquered so swiftly after successfully resisting German military power for more than four years during World War I? In some way, France's defeat felt like a negation of the sacrifice of American lives in that earlier conflict.

By the time I turned 17 at the end of July 1940, the Battle of Britain had begun. In the evenings, my family and I would huddle around our radio to listen to live broadcasts from Edward R. Murrow in London as he reported on the German bombing of British cities and the aerial duels between the Royal Air Force and the *Luftwaffe* (German Air Force). I was amazed at the skill, bravery, and fighting spirit of the British airmen. Prime Minister Winston Churchill's stirring and defiant speeches likewise tugged at our hearts.

Despite their heroics, the British were really taking a beating. Newsreels showed five or six-story walls collapsing into rubble, providing graphic evidence of the tragic consequences of the German bombing. Everyone I knew believed what Germany was doing was terrible and that the Nazis needed to be stopped. The question was how and what the public would support.

Most Americans were sympathetic to Britain and had by now come to see Nazi Germany as a real threat that had to be vigilantly monitored. At the same time, Americans remained overwhelmingly opposed to the United States itself becoming militarily engaged in another European war. The conflict was still viewed as a foreign affair that seemed a long way off "over there." There was no real sense that Germany posed an imminent danger to the United States. Meanwhile, millions of mothers and fathers like mine were morally opposed to war on principle. Acknowledging public sentiment, President Roosevelt declared that the United States would remain neutral in the conflict.

Even with all the war news in the summer of 1940, I did not spend much time thinking about the situation in Europe or talking about it with my friends. None of us expected the United States would become directly engaged in the war, at least anytime soon. If America did eventually have to fight the Nazis, it would be sometime a long way off in the future.

High school: August 1940–December 1941

In August 1940, I started 10th grade at Central High School in Chattanooga. Though my academic struggles persisted, high school proved to be far more interesting than my previous years of schooling up on Signal Mountain. There were pep rallies, football games, and basketball games. I also joined the Future Farmers of America and orchestra clubs. The courses became more stimulating as well, with a chance to conduct hands-on experimentation in biology lab and do woodworking in shop class.

Of course, high school was not just about classes, sports, and clubs. All of a sudden, the girls, all neatly made up and attractively dressed, began to catch my attention in the classroom, in the halls, and in the lunchroom. Never previously one to pay much attention to how I looked, I now started caring about my appearance and my clothes. In particular, I wanted to impress one special girl who was in a couple of my classes. On a number of occasions, we made eye contact, but I could never quite muster the courage to speak to her.

Meanwhile, Germany's conquest of France and its attack on Britain the previous summer boosted popular support for a buildup of America's small military forces. Perhaps the clearest indication of the shifting mood was the passage of the Selective Service Act in September 1940 that required all men aged 21 to 35 to register for military training. But the public supported the Selective Service Act as a means of ensuring America's national defense, rather than as preparation for war against Germany.

Increasing numbers of Americans also came to agree that it was in our own national security interest to provide the British with military aid through the new Lend-Lease program. While I personally believed the United States needed to provide Britain with much greater assistance in its struggle against Nazi Germany, I did not favor America's entry into the war in Europe.

However, most people I knew still clung to more isolationist views. They fiercely resisted any deeper American involvement in European affairs and thought the Europeans would eventually come through the current crisis on their own. Though President Roosevelt recognized Nazi Germany posed a grave and immediate threat to the United States, he faced a huge challenge in attempting to convince the American public to confront it forcefully.

In June 1941, a month before my 18th birthday, Germany attacked the Soviet Union. The speed of the German *Blitzkrieg* caused many people to fear Russia might join the long list of countries already conquered by the Nazis. Whatever the outcome, Germany's latest assault greatly enlarged the scale of the war with all its killing, brutality, and misery. The gigantic significance of this invasion was largely lost on me at the time, but, with war news so constant, it was hard to differentiate the most important events.

As I began my junior year of high school in the fall of 1941, there were more and more news stories about a sort of undeclared naval war against the German submarines called U-boats (from the German *Unterseeboot*) that were sinking American ships in the Atlantic. This was particularly ominous since U-boat attacks had been the main cause for America's entry into World War I. Meanwhile, movies like *Sergeant York*, about a heroic Tennessean who had fought in World War I, helped fuel a patriotic anti-German mood.

Yet the expanding conflict still had little impact on our daily lives and things went on as normal. Certainly, Nazi Germany, and to a lesser extent Japan, presented dangerous international threats, but most people I knew continued to hope America would stay out of the war.

America enters the war: December 7, 1941

Even when we reached our late teens, my mother persisted in her efforts to encourage my siblings and me to develop an appreciation for "good" music, especially classical music and opera. While my own interest in opera was never high, I tried to oblige her whenever possible. On many Sundays after church and lunch, I sat with her in our family's living room while the New York Philharmonic Orchestra played on our radio.

As my mother, Bennett, Bill, Peggy, and I were listening to the musical program on the afternoon of December 7, a radio announcer abruptly broke in.

"We interrupt this program to bring you a special report," he declared, switching immediately to a newscaster.

"The nation of Japan has bombed Pearl Harbor in Hawaii. President Roosevelt will address the nation this evening," the newscaster announced.

Instantly, my mother burst into tears at the news. Her strong emotional reaction was at first incomprehensible to my brothers and me, but we later realized she was sobbing for us, knowing her five sons would soon be heading off to war.

My own thoughts at this shocking news were more uncertain. *What does this attack mean for our country? Surely, we will retaliate against Japan, but how? Will I be going to war?*

The following day, my family and I listened to the radio as FDR asked Congress for a declaration of war against the Japanese Empire. On December 11, Japan's ally Nazi Germany declared war on the United States. Within hours, the United States responded with a declaration of war against Germany.

America would be fighting in both the Pacific and Europe, but feelings toward the two enemies were different. The surprise attack at Pearl Harbor had really wounded us, generating popular outrage toward Japan. In contrast, most people thought Germany's declaration of war against the United States was just words on paper that did not amount to much. Personally, I thought Hitler was out of his mind to take such a step, but, if war with America was what the Nazis wanted, they now had it.

In the ensuing days, weeks, and months, the whole American nation and economy began a full-scale mobilization for the struggle. More than ever, people congregated around their radios to find out what was happening abroad. In the first half of 1942, the war news was bad as Japan went on a rampage in the Pacific and Germany advanced deeper into the Soviet Union.

Back in the States, posters encouraging support for the war effort were soon plastered everywhere. Probably the most popular one featured lanky Uncle Sam pointing his long, bony finger at the reader with a caption that proclaimed, "I want you!"

In reality, the public relations campaign was hardly necessary. Following the Japanese attack, Americans strongly embraced the war effort, completely abandoning their earlier isolationism. While the anger and even hatred directed toward Japan did not abate, most people recognized Nazi Germany was the greater threat and understood its defeat had to be the nation's top priority.

During the preceding years, Germany's conquests in Europe had led my older brothers Karl, Don, and Bennett to discuss the possibility they might be conscripted once they reached 21. After Pearl Harbor, it was clear they were going to enter the armed services and that my 16-year-old brother Bill and I would not be far behind them.

My second oldest brother Don was the first to join up. Without informing our family in advance, he volunteered for the U.S. Army paratroopers on January 9, 1942. More gung-ho than the rest of us, Don liked the challenge, ruggedness, and adventure associated with parachuting and fighting behind enemy lines. The spit and polish of the airborne troops and their special cap and boots also appealed to him, as did the prospect of earning a little extra pay for combat duty.

A couple of months later, my oldest brother Karl in Colorado volunteered for the Army. When he came home to see us on a brief leave after his basic training, we were thrilled to learn he had been assigned the rank of second lieutenant. Karl was subsequently stationed at Camp Carson in Colorado, where he served in the quartermaster's office supplying American troops in the Pacific.

Shortly after Karl's entry into the service, Bennett was drafted into the Army from college. A skilled trombonist, he was made company bugler and would later become the jeep driver for his company commander.

As my brothers entered the armed forces one by one, the hearts of my father and mother grew heavier and heavier, though their fears for us were matched by their pride. Their experience was shared by countless other families whose sons were headed off to war.

At school, America's entry into the war brought the conflict more directly into our classrooms. In our civics class, we received a weekly newsletter that provided war updates and taught us to identify Allied and enemy aircraft by their shapes and silhouettes. The teacher put up maps of Japanese-occupied territory and the many Pacific islands where fighting was taking place.

Stories about the war continued to fill the news, but I had only a vague awareness of important military developments such as the American victory over Japan at Midway in June 1942, the Anglo–American landings in North Africa in November, or the crushing defeat the Soviet Red Army inflicted upon the Germans at Stalingrad in February 1943.

When my friends and I talked about the war, it was mostly in the context of what would happen to us after high school. Like just about everybody our age, my buddies and I planned to volunteer for the armed forces, even if we were not drafted. Caught up in the American "Let's go!" spirit, we all wanted to serve, believing it was our duty to help defeat Japan and rid Europe of the Nazis.

But not everyone was so enthusiastic about joining up. I had one friend from Signal Mountain who was haunted by a premonition of what would happen to him if he went to war. One day at school, he told me, "I ain't going to war. I ain't going because I know I'll get killed."

While most guys intended to complete high school before starting their military service, some chose not to wait. The boys who dropped out before graduating usually fell into one of two groups. The first were the more gung-ho types who wanted to volunteer for the paratroopers or Marines and get into action. The second group volunteered for the Navy, Merchant Marine, or Army Air Force to avoid being drafted into the Army, which was seen as less appealing than the other services. Army troops would regularly risk their lives in combat, while also enduring a dismal grind of long marches in all types of weather, inadequate sleep, grubby conditions, and barely digestible food.

With America's total mobilization for war, the public was asked to make various sacrifices on the home front to support the ever-growing number of people serving in the armed forces. For example, I knew women in Chattanooga who took jobs in local industries involved in war production to replace male factory workers who had entered military service. But other less dramatic adjustments permeated civilian life in ways that affected everyone.

Starting in the spring of 1942, every family was issued a monthly U.S. government ration book containing coupons. In order to legally purchase a growing list of items that eventually included gasoline, shoes, sugar, meats, cheese, fats, coffee, and certain other materials and foods required for the war effort, you had to provide the proper ration coupon. Even with a ration coupon, no one could buy a tube of toothpaste at the drugstore unless they had the old empty one to exchange because aluminum was needed for military equipment.

Citizens were constantly exhorted to respect the rationing limits and to avoid paying more than the maximum ceiling prices for retail items as set by the U.S.

government. Of course, it was possible to obtain additional amounts of these goods on the black market, if you were willing to pay much higher prices. While such activity was illegal and considered unpatriotic, some people nonetheless resorted to it. However, most people I knew believed rationing was necessary, in order to keep the armed forces well supplied, and generally accepted the material constraints on their lives without complaint.

Life at home: December 1941–June 1943

Though the war affected our lives in many large and small ways, things still pretty much went along like they had before Pearl Harbor. Early in 1942, my parents even decided to start building our new house on an empty lot next to our rental home. Despite the wartime shortage of construction materials, Mom knew a contractor who wanted to build the home for her and her family, appreciating the fact she had several sons who were entering the armed forces. To help our folks pay for the house, my brothers and I each agreed to send a portion of our pay back home once we began our military service.

Meanwhile, my academic struggles had not abated. However, late in my junior year of high school in the spring of 1942, an event took place that changed my whole outlook on school. One morning in English class, my teacher, Mrs. Nelson, gave us 15 minutes to write a poem demonstrating meter and rhyme.

Upon completing the assignment, we all took turns reading our poems aloud. After I finished a perfunctory reading of what I had written, Mrs. Nelson exclaimed, "Ernest, your poem is near perfect. Please come to the front of the class and read it again, just like you feel it."

> The mountain waters clear and cool,
> Held a trout within its pool;
> I thought if I had hook and line
> that trout would surely soon be mine.

When my classmates applauded my composition, a feeling of euphoria came over me that I had never before experienced. It was the first time I had ever received praise for any of my academic work. I was on top of the world.

Mrs. Nelson's encouragement completely turned my thinking around about education. Whereas I had previously considered dropping out of high school at the end of my junior year to volunteer for military service, I now decided to graduate and possibly go on to college after completing my military service.

When not at school, I continued hunting and fishing whenever possible, but also helped my dad at his new print shop, worked a part-time job at a miniature golf course, and mowed yards. Outside of school and work, the youth group at Signal Mountain Presbyterian Church was also a big part of my life.

At one of our youth group's regular Saturday night cookouts during the spring term of my senior year in 1943, a beautiful new girl named Margaret caught my eye. In talking with her, I learned she had recently moved to the Mountain with her family and wanted to meet new people her age. Feeling an immediate connection, I invited Margaret to go with me to the next night's youth group meeting. That marked the start of my first real relationship.

From that point, Margaret and I were together at just about every church function and many other social activities. Walking her home in the evenings, we usually detoured to Signal Point, a perfect spot for romance. Our rambling conversations there about church, faith, family, interests, future plans, and all kinds of other things lasted for hours. But when the cool night breezes required us to snuggle up, the talking ended and the smooching started. We remained at the Point until the big passenger plane came out of the east, which meant it was 11 o'clock and our parents would be expecting us back home.

As *the* blonde bomb of Signal Mountain and truly Miss Everything that any guy could want, Margaret had plenty of other boys asking her out, but she always refused them, telling me she wanted us to date exclusively. At the same time, we never spoke of marriage. Even though I was 19 and she was 18, and we were both about to graduate from high school, we recognized we were still much too young to consider getting married.

My dad had taught my brothers and me that a man needed three things before he became serious about marrying a girl. First, he should get as good an education as he could. Second, he should get as good a job as he could. Third, he should get as nice a home as his income would allow. With my pending entry into military service, all of that remained a long way off.

Following the lowering of the draft age to 18 in late 1942, draft notices began to appear in the mailboxes of the guys in my senior class in early 1943. Our local draft board carried out each new induction of military recruits based on registration numbers that had been selected by lottery under the Selective Service Act. Afterward, the local newspaper printed a list of the names of the new draftees, giving the boys and their families a measure of public recognition before their scheduled departure for basic training. Often, the long column of names stretched all the way down the page of the paper.

My notice from our draft board arrived at the beginning of March in the form of a small postcard, stating that I should report for induction into military service on March 9, 1943. Even though I had anticipated the notification, it was nonetheless an exciting moment. In a short letter to the draft board, I explained I was finishing my senior year of high school and requested a postponement of my induction until my graduation. As was standard practice for all high school students who had not yet graduated, I received a three-month deferment.

About a month before my scheduled induction date, Margaret and I went for one of our romantic moonlit walks to Signal Point. To my utter surprise, she proceeded to inform me of her engagement to another guy she had been seeing. Needless to say, this news brought an abrupt end to our relationship.

Once I got past the initial shock of what had happened, I realized I was better off not having a girlfriend to worry about while I was in the service. If she had been two-timing me while I was still at home, she certainly would have done so once I was off in the Army.

Induction at Fort Oglethorpe and my last days at home: June 8–July 7, 1943

As directed in my deferment, I appeared in front of the Hamilton County Courthouse in downtown Chattanooga early on the morning of Tuesday, June 8, just a week after my graduation from Central High School. About 250 other new graduates from local high schools were there, including just about all my friends. Almost every male in our senior class was a draftee, but then probably 90 percent or more of boys our age were conscripted for military service in 1943.

"Now, we're giving you these papers. We want you here again in two weeks and we're going to induct you into the Army," a civilian official announced when everyone had arrived.

So, we all headed back home to prepare for our induction. The material issued to us described the threat Japan, Germany, and Italy posed to America. We had been called up for military service to protect our country and preserve its ideals, though very few of us needed any convincing about the justice of the cause for which our nation was fighting.

At 1:30pm on the afternoon of Tuesday, June 22, I returned to the Courthouse accompanied by my family, who came down from Signal Mountain to see me off. By the time I arrived, most of the other guys were already there with their families. Within an hour, we eagerly boarded a dozen canvas-topped U.S. Army trucks and set off for Fort Oglethorpe, Georgia, located about 20 miles south of Chattanooga, just across the state line.

Upon our arrival, we received a very basic physical and psychiatric examination to confirm that we met minimal height and weight requirements, had adequate eyesight with correction from glasses, and possessed at least half of our teeth. A prospective soldier also had to be able to read and write and could not have been convicted of a crime. Those of us who met these requirements were fingerprinted before supper.

At the conclusion of our first day at Fort Oglethorpe, a sergeant led a group of us to our sleeping quarters in one of the barracks, a wooden building with one long room containing perhaps 20 individual cots. The latrine was located in a separate, block-long building nearby. Containing a series of unpartitioned commodes situated about 18 inches apart, the latrine facilities came as rude awakening for me. As a more modest person who had never had to use a toilet in public, the sudden comprehension of my total loss of privacy came as the biggest shock of my entry into the Army. Quite some time would have to pass before I got used to this particular aspect of military life.

Following breakfast the next morning, we signed our official induction papers, which marked the start of our active military service as GIs. A sergeant then called out our names as he issued each of us dog tags inscribed with our U.S. Army serial number. Henceforth, I would be identified as 34737645. It was immediately drilled into us that we had to memorize this number and be ready to provide it on request.

Afterward, all 250 of us were ushered into a big hall for a short ceremony.

"Hold up your right hand," the presiding officer ordered. A solemn mood fell over the room as each of us raised our right hand and repeated in unison the words of the Oath of Enlistment.

"I, Ernest Albert Andrews, Junior, do solemnly swear that I will support the constitution of the United States. I, Ernest Albert Andrews, Junior, do solemnly swear to bear true allegiance to the United States of America, and to serve them honestly and faithfully, against all their enemies or opposers whatsoever, and to observe and obey the orders of the President of the United States of America, and the orders of the officers appointed over me."

"Welcome! You are now a soldier in the greatest organization in the world, the United States Army!" the officer declared.

At that, all of us clapped, hollered, and tossed our caps into the air. We had willingly pledged to defend our country with our lives. Seeing the war as a fight for freedom, we wanted to be a part of it. Our enlistment was for the duration of the war or other emergency, plus six months, subject to the discretion of the President or otherwise, according to law.

Of course, the Army now had to figure out how best to employ our talents, which inevitably meant lots of paperwork. Taking seats at a table, we filled out a four-page questionnaire designed to probe into a recruit's background.

Upon the form's completion, we were directed to an Army clerk. Seated behind a small table, the soldier reviewed the information we had provided before conducting a brief interview with each of us.

"What do you like to do?" he asked me perfunctorily.

"Well, I like hunting, fishing, camping, and hiking," I answered without giving the question much thought.

"Infantry for you," he declared, scribbling down the information.

Although I had requested a photographic unit in the questionnaire, my reply to the clerk's simple question had made my assignment to an infantry unit practically inevitable. However, I felt a sense of pride rather than disappointment on learning I would be a foot soldier.

As an outdoorsman who knew how to handle a rifle, and long-time Boy Scout, I was confident the infantry would be a good fit for me. At the same time, I could not help speculating where the Army would have placed me if I had indicated sewing, knitting and cooking as my hobbies. It might have meant a nice billet with good food, hot water, and fresh sheets.

When it came to where I would be fighting, I was relieved the Army had granted my request to serve in an outfit destined for the struggle against Nazi Germany in the European Theater, rather than for the battle against Japan in the Pacific Theater. By that time, I had heard too much about the vicious nature of combat against the Japanese. In contrast, my impression was that the German soldier fought hard, but generally respected the basic laws of war, despite the brutalizing influence of Nazi propaganda.

At the end of our two days of processing into the Army, we were trucked back to Chattanooga for a dozen days of leave with our families. The furlough gave us time to put things in order before reporting back to Fort Oglethorpe.

In the mornings, I got up early to have breakfast with my dad. There was not much conversation between us, but I just wanted to spend a little time with him before I left. Two of those days, I went to work with him at his shop, helping to fold the print jobs and deliver them to his customers around Chattanooga.

In the evenings, I enjoyed suppers with my family, where there was lots of discussion of what basic training would be like. For one meal, my mom cooked up squirrel, which I had freshly shot. It would be my last chance to get out in the woods with my gun for a while.

Return to Fort Oglethorpe: July 7–12

On the morning of Wednesday, July 7, the other newly minted soldiers and I reassembled at the Hamilton County Courthouse. Loading aboard the waiting Army trucks, we motored back to Fort Oglethorpe in an excited mood.

Upon our arrival, we headed to a long barn-like structure where we stood in line to receive our first issue of Army clothing. It included several matching pairs of green shorts and shirts, underwear, socks, and shoes in which we could exercise and practice marching.

A sergeant next herded us directly to the base barbershop, where we queued up like sheep preparing for a shearing. Our wait was not long.

"You got mighty pretty hair, soldier," a barber with a menacing grin observed as I took a seat in his chair. Clearly, he took great pleasure in his work.

To his frustration, my extremely thick black hair proved so resistant to his electric clippers that he ended up having to use thinning shears to cut it. But in less than five minutes, my hair was completely shorn, leaving a bristled look just more than stubble.

Before we left, I overheard the barber saying he was going to sweep up all the hair on his floor and take it to a wigmaker to see if he could sell it. "Red hair, black hair, and brown hair should make good wigs," he quipped.

The Army-issued clothing and our new "burr-head" haircuts made the fact we were in the Army more real to us. Step by step, the U.S. Army was transforming us from civilians into soldiers.

Following lunch, we spent the afternoon of that first day in a small theater at Fort Oglethorpe watching Army training films which introduced us to a variety of weapons and equipment. Afterward, we headed outside for calisthenics directed by a sergeant standing atop a small platform. When he had finished demonstrating the proper way to conduct each exercise, he led us through them. Invigorated by the calisthenics, we returned to the theater for more training films before supper and an early night's sleep.

Our acclimation to the basics of Army life over the next several days included the regimentation of sleeping, meals, and every other aspect of our daily existence. Awakened about five just after dawn, we hurriedly dressed. Heading outside, we completed our calisthenics before a quick breakfast. Army chow was not anything special, but we were all so hungry that the food tasted better than it was. This was a good thing since the Army required us to eat everything we put on our plates.

Once we had downed our breakfasts, shaved, and used the toilet, it was time to learn how to stand erect, salute properly, and march. Our introduction to close order drill initially involved learning to stay in step with the fellow in front of us, with much of our marching taking place in the wide open fields of Chickamauga National Battlefield Park, which abutted Fort Oglethorpe. At first, it felt a bit strange tramping around the old Civil War battlefield where my brothers and I had played soldier as kids, but I soon grew used to it.

After lunch, there was more marching and exercising in the hot, humid summer afternoons. Following a shower and supper in the evening, we watched more training films before getting to sleep, which always came swiftly given our state of exhaustion.

On our second or third day back at Fort Oglethorpe, we returned to the tables where we had recently completed the questionnaires so we could write a letter home to our folks, sharing anything we wanted about the start of our training. The Army recognized that keeping us connected to our families was vital for our morale as well as that of the public.

Our training schedule was broken again that Sunday morning when we attended a worship service conducted by the base's Army chaplain. At about this time, we received word we would shortly commence our basic training at Fort McClellan, located just outside of Anniston, Alabama. Now introduced to the essential routines of Army life at Fort Oglethorpe, all of us were anxious to get our real training underway.

CHAPTER 3

Fort McClellan:
July 12–Early August 1943

First days at Fort McClellan: July 12–July 15

On the morning of Monday, July 12, trucks delivered our roughly 250-member training company to a train station near Fort Oglethorpe for the 125-mile rail trip down to Anniston.

From the moment we boarded, elderly Black porters dressed in white jackets waited on us, providing first-class service. "We're gonna stay on this train. We ain't goin' to war like you," they told us.

Upon our arrival in Anniston that afternoon, we transferred back to trucks for the short drive to Fort McClellan. Once there, we immediately assembled for roll call, moving smartly to take our places on a large parade ground.

As all of us sweltered in the muggy heat, still dressed in our civilian clothes, I surveyed the base where we would be training. Located in Alabama's red clay foothills, Fort McClellan was made up of a mix of large drill fields, a few big buildings, and closely packed rows of small, square, tin-roofed wooden huts elevated a foot or so off the ground.

Following roll call, our training company was divided into smaller training platoons of 36 men. While four sergeants would oversee our newly created platoon, Sergeant Marbury had the primary responsibility for turning us into soldiers in the ensuing months. If his five-foot-nine-inch height seemed a bit short for a platoon leader, the sergeant's gravelly tone, barrel chest, and tanned, rugged-looking face made him perfectly cast for the role of drill instructor.

After assigning our platoon to a set of six-man huts, Marbury dismissed us to our quarters to select a cot for ourselves and await further orders. Our hut's spartan furnishings included six cots, a large clothing rack, and footlockers, with a latrine in a separate building next door. As air-conditioning was still a rare luxury, the hut offered us no real refuge from the summer's oppressive heat and humidity.

Fortunately, I was already somewhat acquainted with several of the other recruits billeted in my hut. In addition to a guy who I knew from my high school, I had started to get to know two of the other fellows back at Fort Oglethorpe. Wayne Newsome was from Tennessee and Lincoln Welser was from Ohio.

When Sergeant Marbury visited our hut a short time later to check on our progress, he pointed out the broom and dustpan, stressing we had to keep our quarters spick and span. After showing us how to make up the sheets on one of the cots, he took a quarter from his pocket and bounced it off the cot.

"That's what I want. The quarter has to bounce," he instructed

With the basics out of the way, he announced that he and our training company's commanding officer, Lieutenant Hendren, would make frequent but unannounced inspection visits to our hut.

"It damn sure better be neat and clean!" Marbury warned. "Okay, stow your gear under your bunk. You've got one hour before we call everybody together," he concluded before heading out the door.

Following an hour of calisthenics late that afternoon, we showered and marched to the mess hall. Re-energized with a hearty supper of Army chow, we were shepherded to another building to watch a couple of hours of Army training films before returning to our huts. The lights went out shortly after dark.

Roused by Sergeant Marbury's whistle just before dawn the next morning, everyone hurriedly dressed and assembled outside for roll call and calisthenics. Afterward, we grabbed a fast shower and shave before breakfast. At the mess hall, we hustled through the chow line to load up on food and all the coffee we could drink. So far, Army chow was proving to be better than advertised.

At the end of the hastily consumed meal, our platoon went to get "fitted" for a uniform and boots at the quartermaster, which was located in a long concrete building. On entering, we were ordered to shed our civilian attire.

"We're going to send you through this line and give you Army clothes," Sergeant Marbury informed us as we stood there in our underwear.

My first stop on the assembly line made it clear the Army way was to speed the soldier through the process as rapidly as possible.

"What shirt size, soldier?" the Army clerk demanded impatiently.

"I don't know what size," I replied, unsure of Army sizes.

"Well then, here," he responded, sliding over several olive drab shirts from the stacks of uniforms on the floor behind him.

The next clerk inquired, "What size pants you wear?"

"You've got me," I answered, not knowing what to tell him.

"Well, here's a pair for you," he declared after a quick estimation of my measurements. If the uniform did not fit, a soldier simply had to make do.

"What size shoe do you need?" the following clerk asked.

"I think a 7 or 8," I told him.

"Alright, I got you close to it. Here you go," he said, passing across a pair of shiny new black leather boots.

When another fellow in my platoon complained his boots were not the proper size, the clerk's retort nicely epitomized the Army's SOP.

"Well, Mac, these boots may not fit, but they're yours."

Over the course of an hour, clerks proceeded to issue us underwear, undershirts, socks, raincoats, jackets, and all the other basic gear for a GI. In contrast with the articles of clothing, the Army's helmet truly came in only one size. Made of steel and manganese, it served as the protective outer shell. A separate hard-hat liner inserted inside of the helmet contained an adjustable suspension system that allowed it to be configured to the size of a soldier's head. Altogether, the helmet, liner, and chinstrap weighed about three pounds.

When I later tried everything on, most of the items fit me reasonably well. With some folding over and tucking of excess clothing that I wedged snugly under a belt, I was able to make do until we received better-fitting clothing.

As soon as we reached the end of the line, we were ordered to take our new uniforms to our huts, strip out of our clothes, and put on our raincoats. Wearing only these raincoats and our underwear, my platoon headed for a large multipurpose building where the base's medical staff awaited us. Inside, sunlight shining through high windows amplified the sultry heat, which large fans did little to relieve.

Over the next couple of hours, we experienced a full-scale assault by syringe, enduring eight injections, with four jabs in each shoulder. While the typhus shot took the longest and stung the most, it was the repeated stabbings with needles that made the process so unpleasant. By the end of the inoculations, my shoulders were so sore I was barely able to raise my arms.

Although it seemed to me the immunizations against typhus, smallpox, typhoid, tetanus and a bunch of other terrible-sounding diseases must have left us well protected against just about every conceivable microbe and virus, these were only the first of many rounds of vaccinations we would receive in the months to come. Rather than focus on diseases most likely to affect a particular body of troops heading for a particular area, the Army simply threw the kitchen sink at a problem by requiring inoculations against everything.

After the battery of shots, Sergeant Marbury ordered us to strip out of our underwear, put on our raincoats, and queue up for a comprehensive physical inspection that lasted half an hour. When my turn came, I stood there sweating in my raincoat and feeling awkward while a series of Army doctors probed my "privates" for venereal disease in a manner that made me feel I was some type of livestock. For good measure, the doctor finished off the exam with two injections in my butt which he administered with an oversized syringe, so that my rear now hurt nearly as much as my shoulders. By the time he was finished, perspiration was dripping off the bottom of my soaked raincoat.

With everyone aching from the immunizations, we were spared from exercise and close order drill for the rest of the day. Instead, an officer ordered us to head back to our huts and neatly store our new clothes and other equipment in our footlockers.

Following supper at the mess hall and another evening of training films, we settled down for our second night at Fort McClellan.

Still sore from the previous day's immunizations, we began our third day at Fort McClellan with roll call, calisthenics, a shower and shave, and breakfast before returning to our quarters. After a rapid cleanup operation, a hulking captain from another training unit conducted a 15-minute "hut inspection." Although we had failed to pull the sheets on our cots tight enough for his quarter to bounce, his evaluation was surprisingly positive. We were given a few days to correct the problems in our quarters before the next inspection.

"Outside! Now!" Sergeant Marbury barked in his booming foghorn voice immediately after the hut inspection ended. As our platoon was assembling, we began speculating and joking quietly about what lay ahead.

"Line up and shut up!" Marbury ordered in a dire tone that instantly silenced us. About the only thing that could be heard was the dust settling.

Now commanding our full attention, the sergeant continued, "Welcome to the United States Army's basic training. The reason we have basic training is because you don't know shit about the Army or being a soldier. And speaking of shit, we're going to teach you when to shit, where to shit, and how to shit!"

Almost everyone at least snickered at these words, but one of my friends from home and I made the mistake of laughing out loud. Somehow, Marbury heard my laugh, while my friend's evaded detection. Stomping over with a threatening grimace, Marbury halted in front of me, getting up right in my face.

"You can go start cleaning out the shithouse!" he angrily bellowed. Yanking me by the arm, Marbury led me off to the latrine located next door to our hut. Much like the facilities back at Fort Oglethorpe, the latrine at Fort McClellan contained about a hundred unpartitioned commodes installed along the walls of a cinderblock building at least half the length of a city block.

"Why don't you go in there and wipe all the crap off of them?" he instructed before returning to the platoon. I could not believe it, only my third day on base and I had been banished to the latrine. My task for the next three hours was to clean the white porcelain toilets with a mop, bucket, and brush until they gleamed like ivory thrones. If I learned anything, it was the need to avoid the wrath of Sergeant Marbury. This meant doing everything he ordered, doing it right, doing it right away, and always doing it with a straight face.

When I rejoined the rest of my platoon a few hours later, it was time for lunch. Later that day, another big part of our training was introduced.

"We're going on an afternoon hike through a creek. When you come out the other side and get back, your boots will fit better," Marbury explained.

Taken to a foot-deep creek, we began stumbling over the uneven stones and mud on the creek bed at a pace somewhere between a walk and a jog. After splashing along for five miles, Marbury ordered us to exit the creek and hike another five miles back to our huts, where we could dry out our boots.

By the time we got back, everyone was exhausted and most of us had developed blisters on our feet due to the poor fit of our boots. Thankfully, medics came to our huts to treat our feet. In the meantime, just as promised, the pliable boot leather had shrunk or stretched to better conform to the shape of our feet.

Following supper at the mess hall, we turned out for an evening class on the Browning Model 1917A1 .30-caliber water-cooled machine gun. This was an hour-long introduction to the machine gun that would eventually move to the center of our training. After more training films, we collapsed into our cots back in our hut, utterly spent and savoring the thought of sleep. But a full night's rest was not included in the Army's training manual.

"Get your asses outta bed! Get your asses outta bed!" shouted Sergeant Marbury, as he strode into the center of our hut in the middle of the night.

Alarmed we were under attack, we tumbled from our cots not knowing what to expect. Hastily tossing on our uniforms and boots, our platoon groggily set off on a 10-mile hike through the darkness less than a half a day after our five-mile hike. So much for allowing time for our blisters to heal.

Class, Close Order Drill, and Physical Training

The next day initiated a routine that varied little over the ensuing weeks. Every morning, Sergeant Marbury would enter our barracks at five o'clock sharp, yelling for us to fall out into the dark for roll call. We then had five minutes to form up outside for roll call, which included an inspection of our uniforms once a week.

On a few occasions, someone in our platoon would fail to show up.

"Johnson? Where's Johnson?" Marbury would thunder.

Everyone would remain standing at attention until Johnson was located. Needless to say, the sergeant made sure Johnson suffered a bad day to help encourage him to be on time in the future.

Roll call was immediately followed by what started off as half an hour of calisthenics but eventually expanded into a full hour of rigorous morning exercises. Closely scrutinized by Marbury for any slacking, the calisthenics did a good job of waking us up and building a big appetite for breakfast.

With our morning exercises done, Marbury gave us 15 minutes to "shit, shower, and shave" before our platoon breakfasted at the mess hall. After a half an hour of stuffing our mouths full of chow, most of the rest of the morning was spent either marching at close order drill or learning in the classroom.

Although Sergeant Marbury served as the lead drill instructor for our platoon, he managed our training in tandem with a couple of other drill instructors. This group included First Sergeant Whittle, who oversaw the training when all our company's platoons were drilling together. While Sergeant Marbury operated under Whittle's immediate supervision, Marbury was also acting under the watchful eye of Lieutenant Hendren, who had overall command of our training company.

A young but sharp officer who was always in good spirits, Hendren stood about six-feet tall and was a little bit on the heavy side, something that he joked about with us. In his frequent appearances at our morning lineups for roll call, he urged us to perform well and learn as much as we could during our training, stressing we would need these skills when we went into combat.

In our classes, we were taught the nomenclature of the rifle, pistol, grenade, mortar, and machine gun and watched more training films on various topics. But the Army also made a special effort to scare the living daylights out of us about sexually transmitted diseases by showing graphic films on gonorrhea and syphilis. The gruesome footage of men and women with these venereal diseases was so disgusting some guys actually puked, while others had to be helped out of the room. Most swore off sex right then and there.

During our close order drills on Fort McClellan's parade grounds, we continued to learn to march as soldiers. Even if marching in tight cohesion was of no practical utility on the modern battlefield, close order drill instilled important qualities like teamwork, camaraderie, discipline, and soldierly bearing.

"Straighten up! Pull your stomach in! March!" Marbury would shout.

Directed through a series of twisting turns, our platoon worked on learning how to march forward in formation, turn right, turn left, march to the rear, and halt on a dime without running into the guy ahead of us. We had a long way to go. The first time we heard the command "About face!" half of us immediately collided with the other half in an ugly tangle of bodies.

Correcting our inept execution would not be easy, but it was a challenge for which Marbury seemed exceptionally well-suited. Getting right up in our faces, the sergeant would shout at us with the same deafening gusto that he would have used if he had been standing two dozen yards away.

Even then, Lieutenant Hendren would urge, "Louder, Sergeant, louder!" Hendren's main concern was to keep the cadence steady and our gait lively.

Starting as a confused mess, our platoon of 36 men steadily improved and came to view close order drill as one of the most enjoyable aspects of basic training. By the end of the third week, we were already developing a unit pride as we learned to sharpen our step.

Of all the officers and NCOs who oversaw close order drill and other aspects of our basic training, Second Lieutenant Aubry was the one who did the most to make our training fun. A tall, fit, tanned combat veteran of World War I, Aubry was in charge of all physical exercise and occasionally worked with each platoon to assess its progress in close order drill.

Along with an easy-to-follow singing cadence count, Aubry had a sense of humor and way with words that made him popular. On one occasion, he marched us right into a wall because he forgot to order "To the rear, march!" Everybody laughed when he apologized for the mistake by explaining he had had sex on his mind.

Once all of the platoons in our training company had learned to march together in a single unified formation, our company began competing against other companies in a series of contests that lasted for the duration of our training. In order to help us further enhance our performance, Aubry invited our company to meet with him on the drill field at midnight for additional practice. While none of us wanted to miss out on sleep, everyone agreed to join the lieutenant for four of these midnight drill sessions under the floodlights.

Thanks largely to Aubry's intensive work with our company, we achieved a crisp performance that earned us victories in two of the monthly marching competitions against other companies. Our company even won the final competition for marching precision at Fort McClellan, which was held in front of the base commander in early November just before the end of our basic training.

While close order drill absorbed two or three hours of most mornings, the focus always remained on physical training. At least one morning a week, Sergeant Marbury or another noncom led our entire company on a five-mile hike with all our gear and full packs. Conducted under a blazing sun that heated the humid air into a sauna, we trotted and ran most of the route, passing through creeks, larger streams, dense brush, and thickly wooded areas. Exhausted and drenched in sweat, most of us were gasping for air by the time we finished.

The sweating never ceased, but our muscles gradually ached less as our endurance improved in the ensuing weeks. Always seeking to challenge us, our drill instructors tested our growing strength with more frequent hikes, some of which went for 10 miles and passed through streams that came up to our knees. The primary objective of our physical training was to make us fit and build up our stamina. Though never much of an athlete, I enjoyed these drills and liked getting into shape. Training also brought out my competitive side, a part of my personality about which I had been unaware.

About once a week, our platoon headed to one of McClellan's several obstacle courses after breakfast. The courses were distinct in terms of their specific layout and drills, but generally involved a couple of hours of stepping through tires, crawling through pipes, and jumping over low barbed wire fences to help prepare us for the physical challenges we might face on the battlefield.

On a few occasions, Lieutenant Hendren joined us on the obstacle course and our long hikes. Despite his rather large stomach, he was plenty able to keep up. His close involvement with our training, as well as his obvious concern for us, won him our admiration and respect as a leader.

Much to my chagrin, there was one part of the obstacle course I failed to master. Running up to a vertical, eight-foot-high wooden wall, each soldier was supposed to jump up, grab hold of the top, and pull himself up. Standing only five feet and six inches, a couple of inches shorter than most other guys, my height proved a real disadvantage when I tried to surmount the wall.

After I failed to get over the wall that first day, Lieutenant Aubry pushed me to complete the drill successfully.

"Okay, try again!" he shouted.

"No thanks, I'm going around," I responded, interpreting his words as encouragement rather than an order. He could shoot me for disobedience, but there was no way I would ever be able to climb that wall.

Some of the other guys figured out that teamwork was the key to overcoming this obstacle. One man would run up and place his boot into the clasped hands of another soldier waiting at the wall. This boost would lift him high enough to grasp the top of the wall and haul himself up. Once atop the wall, that fellow could then reach down and pull the "booster" up and over. Somehow, this solution did not occur to me at the time. In multiple tries on several different occasions, I never succeeded in getting over that wall.

Weapons training

One morning, about a week and a half after our arrival at Fort McClellan, our company began its weapons training under the supervision of Sergeant Burke. A big, red-faced, tough-as-leather Irishman, Burke was an older NCO who really knew his business. In recognition of his competence and long experience, he had received a promotion from the rank of corporal to "field sergeant" from Lieutenant Hendren, making him the lieutenant's top field leader among the noncoms.

Among the enlisted personnel, Sergeant Burke was famous for a recent fistfight at the base's barbershop that had taken place on a rainy day. Burke had knocked another new sergeant through the shop's door and out into the mud. No one knew the cause of the fight, but everyone knew Burke had won it.

Our trip over to the firing range with Burke came sooner than we had anticipated, but most of us were anxious to start shooting. Upon our arrival, each of us was issued an M1 Garand rifle, which we had to return at the end of the drill. After hunting squirrels and other animals for years, I was an experienced shooter, though that had been with a much lighter shotgun.

Ordered to lay on our stomachs and aim at the target, I took up my firing position, looked down over the top of the rifle, and carefully drew a bead on the bullseye at the center of a four-foot diameter target at the far end of the range.

"Fire when ready!" Burke called out.

Just before I squeezed the trigger, the guy next to me fired his weapon first. Unprepared for the amazingly loud report produced by an Army rifle firing, his shot momentarily scared the life out of me.

Quickly growing accustomed to the noise at the range, I again zeroed in on the bullseye and gently squeezed off a round at the target. Attached to a pulley system, a target that had been hit would be lowered by soldiers positioned down in a pit at the far end of the range. When the target popped back up, it would have a red dot marking the spot where the bullet had hit.

My first shot struck dead center of the target.

"That's pretty good, soldier. Keep going!" Sergeant Burke shouted.

Increasingly confident, I began blazing away with my rifle, going through one eight-round clip after another. My lifetime of experience with guns had made me a crack shot, so the drill was pure fun for me.

Within 10 minutes, Burke came up behind me and kicked my boot heel.

"Andrews, you can get up and leave. You're too good … and you're using up too much ammo!" he barked.

If my weakest performance came at the obstacle course's wall, my strongest came during our twice weekly visits to the firing range, but I was far from alone in my shooting skills. After our first day on the firing range, First Lieutenant Hendren expressed his admiration for our company's marksmanship.

"Let me tell you guys something. The reason I'm glad to be head of this outfit is because most of you were squirrel hunters and know how to shoot. And I like leading a company that knows how to shoot."

Not surprisingly, our company always did well in subsequent inter-unit shooting competitions. At the end of basic training, about three-quarters of the men in our company were awarded the sharpshooter ribbon.

For the first month of training, we continued to shoot Garand rifles. I was fascinated with the size and weight of the nine-and-a-half-pound Garand and its accuracy at great distances. In the latter part of our training, I switched to drilling with a lighter five-pound M1 carbine at the firing range. It was also an excellent weapon, though not quite as accurate as the longer-barreled Garand.

About two months after our first visit to the firing range, Sergeant Burke issued each of us a Colt .45 pistol.

"Take care of it, soldier, it'll save your life someday," he told me as he handed over the Colt. Unfamiliar with pistols, the weapon's two-and-half pound weight (three pounds loaded) and the size of its bullet surprised me.

Following Sergeant Burke's instructions, I shoved a seven-round magazine into the grip, aimed at the life-sized enemy dummy crouched about 20 feet in front of me, and squeezed the trigger.

Just two feet in front of me, the ground erupted, throwing dirt in every direction. Simultaneously, the force of the pistol's recoil sent my right hand arcing violently back to strike the right side of my face and knock my glasses off. Some of the others laughed at my embarrassing start, but many of them experienced similar trouble mastering the pistol and its recoil.

On my second attempt firing the .45, I managed to hit the dummy. What particularly amazed me was the size of the hole the bullet blasted in the concrete wall behind the target.

Through several practice sessions with the pistol on the firing range, we learned how to hold the weapon, aim it, fire it, and control its recoil. As I became comfortable with the .45, my accuracy rapidly improved. While managing the pistol's kick would remain a challenge, I quickly came to appreciate its heft in my hand.

In the combat to come, the Colt .45 would prove to be a reliable and powerful killing tool. When a firefight erupted, having a loaded .45 pistol in easy reach on my hip was tremendously reassuring, particularly when we came into close contact with the enemy. Even when the barrel grew hot from repeated firing, the weapon would not jam. While freezing weather might cause misfires in other weapons, the Colt .45 always operated perfectly.

At the end of our first month of basic training, our entire training company assembled for an important announcement.

"Today is payday. You will enter the commander's office one by one, giving your name, rank, and serial number. But don't forget to salute first. The officer will return your salute. After you are dismissed, return to your hut and prepare for hut inspection. That's all," First Sergeant Whittle declared.

Since we were lined up alphabetically, my turn to enter the office and receive my pay soon came. Seated at a desk next to Lieutenant Hendren was another young first lieutenant who I had not met.

Coming to attention, I stood up straight and saluted the officers smartly.

"34737645, sir!" I announced enthusiastically.

"Very good, soldier," the unfamiliar lieutenant said. "Now would you mind telling me your name."

"Private Ernest Albert Andrews, Junior, sir. 34737645," I replied, trying to hide my embarrassment at neglecting to begin with my name and rank.

"Very good, Private Andrews. What did you say your full name was?"

"Ernest Albert Andrews, Junior, sir," I repeated.

Regarding me, the officer reflected for a moment. "Ernest Albert ... Ernest Albert, hmm? That's gonna be a helluva name for me to remember. From now on, I'm gonna call you Andy. Do you understand me?"

"Yes, sir. Whatever you say suits me just fine," I responded, thinking that I rather liked the name.

"Okay, Andy. Next man!" the lieutenant said as he passed me my pay.

Up until that time everybody had called me Ernest, but my new name stuck. Before long, everyone at Fort McClellan was calling me Andy.

Christian faith in the Army

What most distinguished me from the other fellows at Fort McClellan was my Christian faith. While perhaps half of the guys would have considered themselves as church-going Christians, only about one-quarter were committed to living out their convictions in a way that really shaped their behavior.

During our first week of basic training, an announcement was posted on the Company Bulletin Board that directed all soldiers who wanted to attend church on Sunday to drop by headquarters for an official pass. This printed slip gave us legal permission to be off the base if we ran into an MP (Military Police).

On my arrival, I noticed a box of condoms had been placed at the front of the desk of the officer who was filling out our passes.

"Here's your pass, Andrews, and take a couple of condoms," he offered.

I explained condoms would not be necessary since I had made a commitment not to engage in sexual activity until I was married.

He congratulated me on my decision but stated that Army regulations required a soldier to take at least two condoms any time he left the post, even to attend church. So, that was that.

Many of the other fellows in our training company were unable to understand why those of us who were committed Christians did not cuss, drink, gamble, or engage in sexual promiscuity. They would often ask me, "What's wrong with you?" This gave me a chance to share my Christian faith, but most were not interested in what I had to say.

Although my faith separated me from many of the other guys when they were involved in behavior that went against my convictions, those of us training at Fort McClellan actually had a lot in common. Almost all of us were Southern boys who had grown up in the mountains of Tennessee and northern Georgia.

Perhaps the most unique members of our training company were eight recruits from Minnesota. How they got mixed in with a bunch of Southerners was a total mystery. But while these Midwesterners never understood many of our Southern ways nor our Southern slang, we generally managed to get along fine and there were never any real problems among us.

However, these eight Minnesotans were without a doubt the crudest men who I ever encountered. Every time they opened their mouths, they spewed an incredible number and variety of obscenities, which regularly included taking God's name in vain. Hoping to reach out, I attempted to share the Bible's instruction concerning how people should live, but this was completely foreign to them. When I explained their cursing was a direct violation of the one of the Ten Commandments, "Thou shalt not take the name of the Lord thy God in vain," it made no difference. They had been cursing and swearing their entire lives and knew nothing else.

Ironically, two of these same Minnesotans declared themselves to be conscientious objectors and refused to take part in the weapons training.

Acting under the orders of the base commander at Fort McClellan, First Lieutenant Hendren rejected their self-proclaimed conscientious objector status. As punishment for their unwillingness to participate in weapons training, he ordered the two men to put on jackets and then pull overcoats over the top of these. Bundled for winter weather and wearing their helmets, the men were directed to dig a large hole in the steamy, hundred-some-degree summer heat.

The base commander apparently believed such measures would convince the two to back down, but they refused to alter their stance. Deeply disturbed by their harsh punishment, I felt compelled to do something before they died from heat exhaustion. As they were digging, I approached Lieutenant Hendren.

"Lieutenant, do you think I could go to the base commander and ask him if I could take the place of one of those guys to give them a break?" I inquired.

"Hell no! I would shoot you first!" Changing his tone, he confided, "I appreciate your feelings, Private Andrews. I'm sensitive to that too, but these are the commander's orders."

Realizing any further effort to challenge their punishment would risk insubordination, I walked away deeply saddened. It was the only instance where I felt the Army acted unjustly toward the troops. We received no official announcement as to the fate of the two men, but they were eventually removed from our training company, perhaps for reassignment to non-combat duties.

Chow and training films

The U.S. Army was not known for its food, but we lucked out. Because the mess sergeant at Fort McClellan had previously worked as a chef at a big resort, the chow we received during basic training was far better than anything we could have hoped for. In fact, it was absolutely delicious. On top of that, every meal was an all-you-can-eat feast. You just had to make sure you could gulp down everything you put on your plate within the prescribed time limit.

Our standard breakfast was a hearty meal of scrambled eggs with bacon or ham, grits, and a couple of large biscuits with jelly, honey, or gravy. Everything tasted like something you would eat in a really fine civilian restaurant. And there was orange juice and lots of coffee to wash it all down and wake us up.

Our lunch and suppers sometimes approached gourmet cuisine. For lunch, the mess might serve up a thick meaty stew with cornbread. Supper was often a choice cut of chicken, pork, or beef and, occasionally, even steaks. The meat was typically served with baked or grilled vegetables and white bread. Gorging on such fare assuaged even the biggest appetites.

At these suppers, the mess sergeant would always do something special for Lieutenant Hendren. Once he even crafted a salad for the lieutenant in which the peach in the middle of a bed of lettuce had been artistically sliced to look like a blooming flower.

"I can't eat that. It's too pretty," Hendren told him.

"You've got to, sir. It's my way of appreciating you," the mess sergeant protested.

Listening to this exchange made me wonder just what the mess sergeant hoped to gain. But putting up with such behavior was a small price to pay if it meant the rest of us could continue eating so well.

To be fair, the mess sergeant's thoughtfulness was not limited to Lieutenant Hendren. When anybody had a birthday, he would bake a small cake. Everyone in the mess hall would sing the soldier "Happy Birthday," a celebration I experienced myself upon turning 20 on July 27.

Though all of us enjoyed the fine food, none of us wanted to serve on KP (Kitchen Police) duty, a punishment meted out to anyone who was late lining up for morning calisthenics or committing other similar infractions. In one instance, when I failed to polish my boots, I earned KP duty and had to peel potatoes.

Between the excellent and abundant chow and the tough exercise regimen, we could feel ourselves growing stronger by the day. Like all the other guys, I took tremendous pride in my improving fitness and stamina.

Three or four evenings a week, a couple of hundred of us gathered to watch training films after supper. These covered a wide variety of topics ranging from basic infantry tactics, to the nomenclature of various weapons, to the uses and hazards of artillery fire. A few of the films described how German troops trained for combat in order to give us a better understanding of the enemy we would be fighting.

While our training films largely ignored the terror, horror, and brutality of warfare, they were still of educational value. In order to drive home particular points, the instructors often followed up the movies with a period for questions and discussion, a dialogue that was at least as valuable as the films.

Perhaps once a week, we got the chance to watch a more entertaining Hollywood picture as well as short newsreels. The newsreels gave us a sense of the larger developments in the war during the second half of 1943, including the Allied invasions of Sicily in July and the Italian mainland in September as well as the progress of the campaign in the Pacific against the Japanese. They also covered the tremendous American effort to ship men and equipment across the Atlantic to Great Britain, always a risky operation because of German U-boats.

When we watched these films, the air in the room would usually become so thick with tobacco smoke that it became difficult to breathe. On a few occasions, smoking was prohibited until after the show, but, as soon as the film was over, the place turned into a smokehouse. While I never smoked, probably 75 percent of the guys did and would light up a cigarette at the first opportunity. It was almost treated as the official way to relax in the Army.

Healthier forms of relaxation included games of baseball and basketball, which would spring up in the rare instances where we had any free time for recreation during daylight hours. However, most of our free time came during the hour or so before the lights went out. While some played cards and gambled, just about everyone enjoyed listening to the radio, which played the latest swing music hits performed by popular big bands like those led by Benny Goodman and Glenn Miller. Once the lights were flipped off, most of us were so dog-tired that sleep came instantly.

Assignment to night-time sentry duty was an honor. Each night, one man from our company was entrusted with guarding one of the entry gates to Fort McClellan. The soldier would challenge anyone who approached by shouting "Halt" and demanding that day's password. Thankfully, my turn on sentry duty passed without incident.

A big announcement: early August

One evening about three weeks into our training, First Lieutenant Hendren assembled our training company for an important announcement.

"Okay, guys. We want to tell you something that's been a secret up 'til now ... All of you fellas are going to be heavy machine gunners!" he enthusiastically proclaimed. As he spoke these words, a big picture of a heavy machine-gun crew in action was displayed up at the front of the room.

Immediately, a spontaneous roar erupted as a couple of hundred guys began clapping, shouting, hooting, howling, and hollering in celebration.

Most of us in the company had already heard we were likely to be assigned as machine gunners, but Hendren's announcement made it official. Just out of high school, the prospect of serving as machine gunners with all that awesome firepower struck us as the most thrilling assignment imaginable.

CHAPTER 4

Training as Machine Gunners: Early August 1943–January 17, 1944

Preparation for machine gunner training: early August

The day after our company learned we would be training as machine gunners, all of us had to undergo a battery of vision tests. Unsurprisingly, my attempt to read the eye chart without my glasses only confirmed my nearsightedness, though my vision was worse than most. During the subsequent testing, the officer conducting the exam ordered me to keep my glasses on.

Seated at the end of a long table, I was directed to observe two small pegs. The officer explained he was going to move the pegs back and forth inside two slits cut into the table in order to evaluate my depth perception.

"I want you to call a halt when these pegs come together," he instructed. Tugging on strings, he slowly moved the pegs closer together in the slits.

"Halt," I declared when it appeared to me the pegs were side-by-side.

The officer informed me the pegs were still at least three feet apart, revealing my depth perception was way off.

"You'll never pass this test, but you're okay to be a machine gunner," the officer proclaimed with a friendly laugh.

Why did I have to do this? It seemed like an utter waste of time to take a test if a poor result made no difference. As I was rapidly learning, the Army simply followed standard operating procedure. Vision testing was a procedural formality for men assigned to train as machine gunners. In wartime, the Army was far less concerned with the practical implications of any results.

The next day, our entire company marched out to the main firing range at Fort McClellan. Ordered onto wooden bleachers built into a hillside, we took our seats to watch a demonstration of the firepower of various weapons.

"We're going to show you what a water-cooled .30-caliber machine gun will do," First Lieutenant Hendren announced. This would be a more dramatic exhibition of the gun's capability than the initial display we had witnessed a couple of weeks earlier in our training.

On cue, a machine-gun crew began blazing away, targeting some old refrigerators 80 yards downrange. Their fire was absolutely devastating, especially when they switched to armor-piercing rounds. In seconds, there was almost nothing left of the refrigerators. Since we were about to begin training as machine gunners, the weapon's power made a tremendous impression on us.

Before the next display of firepower, one of the instructors reviewed the different types of artillery shells and their uses in combat. Most importantly, he stressed that taking cover below ground could save our lives.

"While you're in these bleachers, we're going to show you what artillery shells do. The first artillery shell is going to be a standard high-explosive round."

A minute later, an artillery round whooshed through the air overhead and detonated with a loud explosion a hundred yards away, creating a large cloud of dust and flinging small shell fragments out at least 20 yards in every direction. As the shrapnel struck the ground, it spawned a wide arc of smaller gray dust clouds around the central explosion. It was terrible to imagine what would have happened if human bodies had been anywhere near the point of impact.

After the first round had gotten our attention, the instructor warned us, "Now, the next three rounds that come over together are anti-personnel rounds. They're going to detonate about 30 feet above the ground. You'll see the dust and the tightly packed shrapnel hitting the ground."

Sounding like a freight train, the incoming shells passed just over our heads. When the three rounds burst, countless small clouds of dirt sprung from the ground as shrapnel lacerated an area about 50 yards in diameter. It was stunning, terrifying, and unforgettable, as if a thousand rifles had simultaneously fired at the ground.

The artillery fire ended the exhibition. It had indeed hammered home to us the urgency of digging a foxhole in combat. There was no way to avoid the hailstorm of steel shrapnel if an anti-personnel round detonated directly above your hole, but entrenching gave you the best chance of survival on the battlefield.

While the point had been made about the hazards of artillery fire, it might have been beneficial for us to observe mortar fire as well, given its frequent use in combat. But we never received any training with mortars at Fort McClellan. In fact, I did not even see a mortar during basic training.

Machine-gun training: early August–mid-November 1943

From this point onward, our training focused on the Browning Model 1917A1 .30-caliber water-cooled machine gun. A vintage weapon that had been introduced during World War I, it would prove to be as good or better than any of its contemporaries. The U.S. Army was determined to make sure we would learn everything there was to know about this weapon: how it worked, how to maintain it, how to fire it, and how to deploy it in combat.

For machine-gun training, our platoon broke up into separate seven-man squads. It was through these drills that I really came to know three members of my machine-gun squad who would become long-term buddies of mine.

My hut-mate Wayne Newsome and I had hit it off from the moment we first met back at Fort Oglethorpe. Aside from being a head taller than me, Wayne and I had a lot in common. Lincoln Welser was another member of my squad who I had met back at our induction at Fort Oglethorpe. About my height, Lincoln was a little on the chunky side, but possessed great physical stamina. A good-natured, jovial fellow, he was an optimist about everything and always knew when to crack a joke to lighten the mood. Hector Gonzalez was the third member of my squad who stood out. With high cheek bones and a tanned, lined face, he had a rugged appearance. Quiet but funny, Hector found many opportunities in the Army to deliver his favorite line, "Who gives a damn?"

With the start of our machine-gun training, all seven of us in the squad would be working together much more intensively than in previous drills. Individually, each of us needed to know everything about the machine gun and gain experience firing the weapon. Collectively, the key objective was for us to learn how to work together efficiently as a team.

Our machine-gun training typically took place in the afternoon following lunch. Welcoming us to our first day of instruction on the weapon, Sergeant Burke did not pull any punches.

"Listen up, guys! The reason you are getting this good training is because a machine gunner has an average life expectancy in combat of seven minutes."

As intended, this really got our attention. Until this moment, we had not fully comprehended the extent to which the machine gun's firepower would make us the enemy's primary target in combat. Indeed, it seemed almost as if the Army had issued us a death sentence by assigning us as machine gunners.

Sergeant Burke began our training with a thorough but rapid demonstration on how to disassemble and reassemble the various components of the Browning Model 1917A1 machine gun. Over the next few days, our squad repeatedly practiced breaking down and reassembling the machine gun in order to master the procedure. Fully broken down, the machine gun had only a small number of component parts, reflecting a simplicity of design and maintenance that was part of the beauty of the weapon.

Upon the conclusion of about four days of drilling on the assembly and disassembly of the gun, our squad moved to the firing range. Sergeants Burke and Marbury detailed the Browning machine gun's firing procedure and basic shooting techniques. Marbury showed us how to squat or lay behind the gun so as to present a minimal target to the enemy in combat. We then received a further display of the machine gun's rate of fire, accuracy, and range, which left us even more in awe of its devastating firepower.

Following this instruction, our squad began to practice setting up and firing the gun. Before the drill, more than 150 pounds of equipment were laid at our feet: the 33-pound, three-foot-long machine gun, comprising the receiver housing the firing chamber and the barrel encased in a stovepipe-shaped water jacket; the 53-pound tripod with an attached gun cradle; one seven-pound, six-quart water chest; and four 22-pound metal ammo boxes.

At the sound of Sergeant Burke's whistle, each member of our squad grabbed his assigned components of machine gun off the ground and scrambled to assemble the weapon at a spot about 50 yards away.

The first soldier sprinted the short distance with the tripod slung over his shoulders, using his hands to grip two legs in front of him while the third longer leg hung down his back. This man lugging the tripod was designated to serve as the gunner. On reaching the specified location, he flipped the tripod over his head and took up position behind it.

The next squad member carried the gun. Running up, he jammed the weapon into the socket on the tripod's cradle. As he did so, the gunner pulled back the gun pintle latch lever to secure the machine gun in its cradle atop the tripod. The tripod allowed the gunner to swivel the machine gun right or left, while the cradle allowed him to raise or lower the barrel.

As the gun was being locked into place, the guy carrying the water chest dashed up on the right side. The water chest was attached to the gun by a rubber condensing hose that snapped onto the water plug at the end of the water jacket just under the barrel's muzzle. The water chest was left upright under the barrel.

While the hose was being hooked up, the squad member with the ammunition hustled forward to the left side of the gun, attached the ammo box and flipped its lid open. The gunner raised the receiver's cover with his right hand, grabbed the 250-round ammo belt with his left hand, pulled the belt through the receiver with his right hand, and then closed the cover with his left hand. Pulling back and releasing the bolt, the gunner lodged the first round in the firing chamber.

With his left hand on the gun's handle and his right hand on the aiming wheels at the back of the gun cradle, the gunner aimed at the target and squeezed the trigger with his left forefinger. As the machine gun started clattering away, a torrent of bullets poured out of the muzzle while the spent shell casings spewed out to the right of the gun.

During our first firing drill with the machine gun, we all had a chance to shoot the weapon. If drawing down the trigger and seeing that ribbon of fire blazing out of the muzzle was exhilarating, watching the various targets blasted from their supporting stands was just plain inspiring. It was a surefire method of confidence-building in our training.

Because my pre-Army experience with guns had been limited to taking single shots with hunting rifles, I found the machine gun's firepower awesome to behold and almost impossible to believe. Using the same .30-caliber bullet as the Garand rifle, its ammo belt filled with these brass-tipped rounds was a thing of shining beauty that belied the gun's formidable capacity to wreak destruction.

Firing the standard M2 ammunition, the Browning Model 1917A1 water-cooled machine gun possessed an effective range of about 1,100 yards (.625 miles). It had a maximum range of about 3,000 yards (two miles) but was not very accurate beyond 2,000 yards (a little over a mile). The weapon's nominal rate of fire was 450 to 600 rounds per minute, but that rate was not sustainable for a prolonged period.

When the machine gun was fired, the seven pints of water in the water jacket circulated around the barrel, transferring the frictional heat caused by firing to the liquid in order to cool the gun. But even with this cooling system, the barrel would grow hot after only a dozen rounds were fired. To avoid the danger of the barrel ever overheating, we learned to shoot in intermittent bursts.

If the machine gun was fired for more than a brief period, some of the water circulating around the hot barrel turned to steam. Escaping under pressure through the rubber condensing hose attached to the water plug under the muzzle, the steam traveled down into the water chest, where it cooled back into water. The condensing system both prevented a cloud of steam that would reveal our machine-gun position to the enemy and permitted the recovery of the water that would otherwise be lost to evaporation. If the gunner ceased firing the weapon for an extended period, the steam in the water jacket would cool back into water, creating a vacuum that drew the water back up the hose from the water chest. Alternatively, the water jacket could be refilled manually.

In the event the rubber condensing hose was ever severed and too much water escaped from the water jacket as steam, the gun barrel was certain to overheat and warp, even under the most restricted firing of the weapon. If the barrel did warp due to overheating, it could be replaced, but this procedure was not something that could be done safely during combat. This danger made the rubber hose that ran down to the water chest critically important. Unfortunately, we later discovered this hose was highly vulnerable to enemy fire.

Over the next couple of weeks, our squad drilled with the machine gun three or four times a week, which rapidly enhanced our speed and execution. We also watched training films on the weapon dating from World War I as well as combat footage from that conflict. Despite changes in the machine gun's tactical role, it turned out there was still a lot we could learn from these old movies.

In early September, competitions in setting up and firing the machine gun were introduced as a regular part of our training, giving all of us added motivation to enhance our performance. Matched against four other machine-gun squads at a time, our squad competed against others in our own company as well as against those from other training companies. With points awarded to squads based on their speed in getting the machine gun into action, everyone in our squad was gung-ho to win these races.

Our squad triumphed in the first competition by having the machine gun deployed and firing in 30 seconds. This time was way down from the minute and a half it had taken us on our first attempt four weeks earlier, but still left a lot of room for improvement. In a half-dozen subsequent contests, our squad came out on top about half of the time. More importantly, we won in the final competition just before the end of basic training, having whittled down the amount of time it took us to ready and fire the machine gun to a mere 10 seconds.

Entrenching, camping, and building gun emplacements

If drilling with the machine gun and other firearms was essential in preparing us for combat, learning to properly entrench ourselves was of equal if not greater importance to our survival. This part of our platoon's training began on a nearby hillside one afternoon about a month and a half into basic training.

After receiving a lesson in entrenching, we practiced digging foxholes with our spades. Its small metal shovel blade was hinged to a sturdy wooden handle about 14 inches long. The entrenching tool also included a separate metal pick which could be used to loosen hardened soil or break up frozen ground.

During our first entrenchment drill, Sergeant Marbury ordered us to get down into our foxholes as soon as we had them dug. While we crouched down in the holes, so that our entire bodies were below ground, he began shooting rifle rounds into the dirt bank just inches above our heads. My initial reaction was intense panic, but I quickly grew accustomed to the gunfire.

At the next entrenching drill, a couple of weeks later, Marbury announced a far more severe test of the quality of our foxholes and our nerves.

"This afternoon, you will have a tank drive over your foxhole with you in it." Crouching down in our foxholes with bullets whizzing close overhead was serious business, but having a tank come clanking over the top of our small holes was something else altogether. All we could do was dig deep and wait.

Huddled as far down toward the bottom of my hole as possible, the awful rumble of the tank's approach caused me to try to hunker down even lower and start wishing I had dug deeper. I was absolutely petrified.

A moment later, the tank was passing over the top of my hole, blotting out the sun and inducing a deep sense of claustrophobia. As its treads churned a steady cascade of dirt down on top of me, the bottom of the tank's chassis passed literally inches above my head, bringing the scorching heat of its engine so close I thought it would singe me. The deafening noise and the violent shaking of the ground made it feel as if an earthquake was sweeping through.

It was all over in a matter of seconds but would be one of the most terrifying ordeals we had to endure in our training. However, the experience assured us we could survive if a tank ran over our foxholes in combat. Whatever the danger, a good foxhole could make a life-or-death difference.

On two or three occasions, our platoon went on three-night campouts, where we learned to construct machine-gun emplacements under the guidance of Sergeant Burke. As always, he "showed us by doing," in this case by helping us to build our gun emplacement. While we worked, he gave us reasons for everything that we were doing, whether it was situating the gun's position to provide an optimal field of fire or constructing the emplacement so as to provide ourselves with a measure of protection from enemy fire. Knowing he spoke from experience, we listened attentively to every word.

Naturally, our instructors ordered competitions among the squads to see which of us could build the best gun position, something that turned out to be one of the most fun parts of our training. While four of our squad members chopped down small trees, the rest of us used the freshly cut logs to build the "walls" for our gun emplacement. Employing a skill picked up from my time in the Boy Scouts, I lashed the ends of the logs together with rope to connect the walls. Since none of the guys in the other squads knew how to lash logs, our squad regularly prevailed in these competitions.

Although there was not a lot of time to share my knowledge with the other members of my squad at that moment, I later tried to teach them some basic rope lashing techniques. I likewise attempted to pass along other useful skills I had learned in the Boy Scouts, such as how to build a fire from a pile of small twigs that would create only a minimal amount of smoke.

Breaks from our training were few, but I was issued a three-day pass and, later, a four-day pass that allowed me enough leave time to make the three-hour bus trip from Anniston to Chattanooga and return to base by the following Sunday evening. During these brief visits to Signal Mountain, I could sense my parents' pride as well as their concern, especially after they learned I was training as a machine gunner. While these two short trips home recharged me, I was ready to return to Fort McClellan when my leaves ended.

Gas, grenades, and bayonet training

One morning a couple of months into basic training, our platoon headed out to a weapons range, where Sergeant Burke gave us our first instruction in the art of safely handling and throwing hand grenades.

A surprisingly powerful and highly effective infantry weapon, the grenade was a hand-sized, pineapple-shaped oval with a lever on the side and a large ring-shaped wire pin at the top. The lever served as a safety mechanism. Even when the grenade's pin was pulled, the explosive would not be triggered as long as the lever was held down.

Once a soldier yanked the pin and released the lever, there would be a popping noise followed by a hiss as a spark raced down a short fuse. A GI had less than five seconds to get rid of the grenade before its explosion would spray deadly metal shrapnel in every direction.

"Okay, there's a great big hole out there. You pull that pin and you throw that grenade in the hole as fast as you can. Let's practice. If you don't throw it far enough, you're going to kill a bunch of us," Burke coolly explained.

When the first man in line stepped up to take his turn, he heaved the grenade into the pit 50 feet away where it loudly detonated down in the hole.

I was the second man up. "Okay, Andrews, here's your grenade, throw it!" Burke commanded. Pulling the pin, I easily hurled it into the pit.

For the next few guys, the drill went on uneventfully. About halfway through the queue, a new recruit was up. A late entrant to basic training, this recruit was a timid, milquetoast-type fellow.

"Okay, your turn to throw the grenade," Burke told him.

"I ... I just don't think I can throw a grenade," he whined.

"Well, I tell you what we're going to do, sonny boy," Burke replied. Yanking the pin from a grenade, the sergeant stuck the weapon in the guy's hand. "When I turn loose of this, you got five seconds to decide what to do."

Overhearing this exchange, the rest of us in line scattered like frightened quail. But our fear proved unfounded. Never in my life did I see a grenade go farther. It looked like this fellow was a major league baseball pitcher. The grenade actually landed in the secondary pit 50 feet beyond the first hole.

Clapping this fellow warmly on the shoulder, a grinning Sergeant Burke congratulated him. "You're gonna be fine, soldier! You're gonna make a good soldier!" No one else had any problems throwing a grenade after that.

That same morning, after we finished the first of several drills with hand grenades, Sergeant Marbury oversaw our one and only drill with tear gas. This was designed to prepare us to deal with poison gas, a weapon that had been regularly employed during World War I. For this exercise, each of us was issued a gas mask that had two big glass plates through which to see out. Pulling on the ill-fitting, hot, and generally uncomfortable mask, I entered a large gas chamber with five or six other guys.

Within seconds of the drill's start, tear gas began to seep up under my mask. Immediately, I felt an intense burning sensation in my eyes, mouth, nose, and throat and headed for the gas chamber door in a panic. By the time I emerged into the fresh air seconds later, I was struggling to breathe and unable to see clearly. Several others also had problems with their masks, causing them to suffer similar ill-effects from the gas. Full recovery took about half an hour.

To avoid problems with our gas masks in combat, Marbury directed us to make sure we always fully tightened the straps, but all of us doubted the masks would ever work well. It was alarming to think what might happen if the enemy were to attack us with poisonous gas, instead of just tear gas.

A little later, we also received three sessions of bayonet training at Fort McClellan. Attacking dummies which hung down from poles, we were instructed to aim our rifle bayonets at the stomach. While this skill might be useful to the infantry in certain close-combat situations, it seemed to be of limited utility to us as machine gunners.

Learning to crawl

One morning soon after our introduction to grenades and gas, Lieutenant Hendren made an announcement before our company marched off for training.

"We want you to learn how to crawl with all your pack on." It sounded simple enough but proved to be our most psychologically demanding drill yet.

Wearing our backpacks, we crawled down several long, closely spaced trails that had been laid out in a roughly 100-yard-wide field. After this initial 15-minute practice crawl in three inches of dust, the rest of the exercise was conducted as a series of competitions among our training company's squads in an effort to motivate us to move at maximum speed.

On our second crawl, powerful explosive charges started going off all around us without prior warning, simulating what we would experience in combat during an enemy artillery barrage. With detonations as close as five yards away, the crawl was an unnerving experience. The choking clouds of dust kicked up into the air quickly coated everyone in a layer of thick rust-colored dirt, leaving us indistinguishable from the surrounding Alabama soil.

"Okay, guys, we've got a 20-minute rest," Sergeant Marbury declared after we had repeated this drill three times. Enjoying the respite, we paid little attention to the arrival of several water trucks. As the vehicles drove parallel to the trails, sprinklers under their water tanks thoroughly saturated the ground, transforming the dry dust into a thick, gooey sludge.

"Now you can learn to crawl through mud," Marbury proclaimed.

But that was not all. To go along with the mud and explosive charges, our instructors would add live machine-gun fire in order to more closely replicate battlefield conditions. While the detonating charges would be flinging out muck in every direction, two machine gunners would be firing bullets just a couple of feet above us. Their field of fire would be marked out by intermittent tracer rounds, which used a brightly burning pyrotechnic material like phosphorus to make the trajectory of the bullets visible.

The gauntlet turned out to be even more miserable than I had anticipated. With the machine-gun tracer rounds passing just above my backpack, I pressed my body into the soft earth as deeply as I could. Slithering forward like a giant earthworm, I struggled to keep the mud out of my mouth.

Meanwhile, the series of explosive detonations hurling muck over us kept splattering a slimy film of mud across the lenses of my glasses. Blinded, I was forced to cease crawling in an effort to wipe off my lenses as best I could with an already grimy sleeve. Over and over again, I had to stop to clean my glasses, much to the consternation of the men crawling behind me.

Had we actually been under fire, such halts in our forward movement would have allowed the enemy to zero in on us as a target. If dealing with my glasses was a headache for me, it could potentially be deadly for everyone else once we got into combat.

When our first passage down the muddy trail was completed, we queued up to repeat the crawl a couple of more times. In order to ensure the earth remained saturated under the blazing summer sun, the water trucks returned every hour or so to give the trails a generous soaking.

Quickly coming to loathe these muddy crawls, we simply looked at the drill as an unpleasant part of our training that had to be endured. Though everyone was glad we had only one day of the crawling drill at Fort McClellan, it did help prepare us for what lay ahead. Indeed, its close approximation to the reality of the battlefield made it perhaps more valuable than any other exercise.

Strangely enough, basic training up to that point had largely been a fun experience, almost like summer camp. There was a sort of collective refusal on our part to come to terms with the fact we were headed for combat. This state of denial existed despite the constant admonitions of our drill instructors and officers to treat our training as the deadly serious preparation for war it really was, rather than as just a bunch of games designed for our amusement.

"Now the reason that we're doing this is because you're going to be in combat in a few months. What we are trying to teach you will save your ass, so you better try hard to remember this stuff. It's all important," Lieutenant Hendren kept repeating. "You fellas damn sure better get it right in this 17 weeks, because that's all you got."

One of our officers who was of German heritage employed humor in an effort to make us focus on the vital purpose of our drilling.

"Mein kousins ere vating fur yowh. Zey vill keel yowh iv yowh don git zis rite!" he quipped.

For a long time, we had dismissed these warnings as a scare tactic. But as the training became increasingly realistic, our mood grew more serious. Somehow, the war seemed to be coming closer.

"You know, this is not kid's stuff. We must really be going to war," we began to acknowledge.

Last days at Fort McClellan: early November–November 13

In early November, a week or so before graduation from basic training, our training company assembled for important news.

"You are assigned to the 1st Infantry Division," an officer announced.

If all of us felt relief at finally receiving our assignment to a unit of the U.S. Army, we were thrilled our assignment was to the 1st Infantry Division, the famed "Big Red One." During the past year, the 1st Infantry Division had distinguished itself in the Allied campaign to defeat Germany's *Afrika Korps* and its Italian Axis partner in North Africa. It had also played a critical role in the invasion of Sicily in July, which had helped force Italy out of the war. Few of us knew much about the Big Red One, but we had heard enough to be greatly honored by our assignment.

On reaching the 1st Infantry Division, we would help bring its component units up to full strength after the losses sustained in the earlier fighting. Though it was not public knowledge, the division had just been transferred to England to prepare for the invasion of France, the timing of which remained a closely guarded secret. It would take several weeks for us to ship over there, but all of us immediately had the Big Red One's shoulder patch sewed onto our uniforms, proud to display the large red number "1" insignia.

A short time later, we received more details on our specific unit assignments inside the 1st Infantry Division. Everyone in our training company at Fort McClellan would be dispersed among the division's three regiments as replacement machine gunners. All the men in my machine-gun platoon were assigned as replacements for H Company in the 2nd Battalion of the Big Red One's 16th Infantry Regiment. While the 2nd Battalion's E, F, and G were rifle companies, H Company was the battalion's heavy weapons company, which included two machine-gun platoons and a mortar platoon.

Upon concluding our 17 weeks of basic training in mid-November, the Army officially declared our company ready for combat. Our graduating class included about 225 men, roughly the same number of raw recruits who had arrived with me at Fort McClellan back on July 12. Our training had provided both essential weapons skills and a rigorous physical and mental toughening to prepare us for combat. A trim, but untoned 160 pounds on my arrival at Fort McClellan, my physique had been transformed into 185 pounds of rock-hard muscle. And I had undergone a psychological hardening inside to match it.

Just hours ahead of our graduation ceremony on Saturday, November 13, Lieutenant Hendren delivered a brief address to our company prior to the start of the public proceedings. Congratulating us on our successful completion of the training, he urged us to look out for each other and take care of our weapons.

"There's one thing we need to tell you guys that we have not shared until now. You're going to assault a beach somewhere in France and this is what you can expect. Some of you are going to be killed," he warned. "A machine gunner's life expectancy in actual combat is seven minutes," he added, reinforcing Sergeant Burke's stark warning. "Do not stop to help the wounded. Keep moving forward. That is the only way a unit can be successful in battle."

In contrast to our celebratory reaction to the original announcement of our assignment as machine gunners several months earlier, Hendren's remarks about what lay ahead of us were met with subdued silence. Still, his words seemed more meaningful than his past speeches, as if we had finally earned a candid assessment from him. But whatever dangers awaited us, we believed our training as machine gunners had made us ready for the harsh reality of combat.

With our minds sobered, the ceremony got underway. While my parents had not been able to afford the trip down to Fort McClellan for my graduation, many of the men's families were sitting in the stands to watch as we marched in crisp precision around the central parade ground, demonstrating our hard-earned proficiency in close order drill. In a short address, the base commander thanked the parents and all of us for our good effort during basic training. Like most of the other graduates, I was now officially a Private First Class.

Just after the graduation ceremony ended, all the members of our training company received military travel papers and an extended two-week leave that would last through Thanksgiving. The orders required everyone in the company to report back for duty at Fort Meade, Maryland, in late November.

A final furlough with my family: November 13–November 26

Catching a bus in Anniston, I made the now familiar trip back to Chattanooga to see my family on Signal Mountain. Although three of my brothers were away from home in the service, I wanted to spend all the time I could with my parents, my sister Peggy, and my younger brother Bill, who was a senior in high school. Concerned he might be drafted into the Army, Bill had already stated his intention to volunteer for the Navy as soon as he graduated.

In the mornings, and in the afternoons after Bill and Peggy got home from school, my family worked in our vegetable garden, which was sort of a model wartime Victory Garden in the neighborhood. The freshly harvested carrots, beans, and other produce went straight into that night's supper. Following the meal, we spent the evenings talking together like during earlier years.

With a longer break from Army life, I fell back into the routines of civilian life in a way I had not during my brief leaves at home during basic training. I slept late, ate whenever and whatever I felt like, did some fishing, and hiked solely for pleasure, visiting my favorite spots. I also did a little hunting, which provided squirrel meat to further supplement our family's meals. On my two Sundays at home, our family attended services together at Signal Mountain Presbyterian Church, which allowed me to say my goodbyes.

Thanksgiving fell on Thursday, November 25. The holiday gave me the chance to be together with my family one last time before I reported back for duty. While my thoughts naturally drifted to what lay ahead, I did not want to discuss the prospect of combat. I also kept quiet about my imminent departure, not wishing to upset my mother. With three other sons serving in the armed forces and another planning to join up, my parents were burdened enough.

As I prepared to leave the next morning, the hands of the kitchen clock raced faster than I could ever recall. My dad normally left for his print shop at six o'clock, but this Friday morning he opted to catch the eight o'clock bus in order to see me off. When he had to leave, I walked with him to the door of our house. Giving me a hug, my dad spoke in as strong a voice as he could muster.

"Goodbye, son. I may never see you again. May God keep my dear boy." With those parting words, my dad left without looking back.

A thousand times afterward, I wished I had walked the quarter of the mile to the bus stop with him. It was something I should have done, just to be there, just to share some silent companionship, just to wave him goodbye and give him a smiling thumbs up as his bus pulled away.

Two hours later, I hugged my mom goodbye before I caught the bus down to the train station in Chattanooga. Placing her hand on my shoulder, she looked into my eyes. Tears were running softly down her cheeks as she whispered in a voice choked with emotion.

"I just want you to remember Psalms 91:7: 'A thousand shall fall at thy side, and ten thousand at thy right hand; but it shall not come nigh thee.'"

In the difficult days ahead, I drew great comfort from this scripture as well as my mother's love and prayers. She would unceasingly ask the Lord to watch over my four brothers and me. Just as I was certain her faith in our safe return would never waver, I knew God would indeed keep us all in His care on the distant battlefields ahead.

Fort Meade to Camp Shanks: November 26, 1943–January 17, 1944

Dressed in my uniform, I met up with about 30 other local members of my training company at the train station in downtown Chattanooga late that Friday morning. On boarding our train, we received the same congenial welcome from the white-jacketed Black porters as we had enjoyed during our rail journey from Fort Oglethorpe to Fort McClellan back in July.

"You guys are getting ready to go to war. We gotta take care of you," the porters declared, reflecting the American public's support for the troops. True to their word, they delivered top-notch service throughout our overnight train trip up to Fort Meade in Maryland, located about 550 miles northeast of Chattanooga.

Upon reaching Fort Meade on Saturday morning, we were taken to our barracks, which housed about 50 men. Fort Meade itself was a large base with many buildings spread across flat terrain. As the major troop depot on the east coast, it served as a temporary staging area for replacement troops preparing to ship across the Atlantic to Great Britain.

Of course, the Army did not permit us just to sit around at Fort Meade while we were awaiting our departure. A couple of days after our arrival, we commenced an advanced training program under a new cadre of officers and NCOs who replaced those we had left behind at Fort McClellan. Designed "to tone us up" physically with intensive exercise, the new regimen proved to be even more rigorous than our basic training.

In the morning, we performed an hour of calisthenics. In the afternoon, there were five-mile hikes with full packs and all the components of the machine gun, a drill that proved to be of great practical benefit later. Beyond the physical exercise, there was also work with weapons designed to build upon the skills we had learned during basic training, such as the maintenance and care of the machine gun. Our squad also continued to drill on deploying and firing the machine gun, though we were now expected to do everything faster.

About a week after our arrival, a captain explained we would remain at Fort Meade until a troopship to Britain became available, warning us to refrain from sharing this information with anyone. Because we had to be ready to depart Fort Meade on short notice and needed to keep our orders secret, we would be strictly confined to base.

Everyone hoped our stay would not last more than a couple of weeks, but, in the meantime, we followed our new training routine. One upside to our time at Fort Meade was the chow, which turned out to be even better and more plentiful than at McClellan. On Christmas Day, the chef served up a real feast, which included turkey with all the trimmings and pumpkin pie with ice cream. Adding to the festive mood, a local choir came to sing us Christmas carols.

The next day, the alert order arrived for our company to ship overseas. The first stage would be a 200-mile trip from Fort Meade up to Camp Shanks near Orangetown, New York, close to New York City. After a brief stay at Camp Shanks, we would travel to New York City's harbor to board our troopship.

Before departing Fort Meade, we received what was called a total physical exam to check for any unidentified problems that might prevent a soldier from shipping overseas. During my physical, I complained that my eyeglasses were not a good fit and requested a new pair. After a thorough eye exam, the Army optometrist told me the prescription of my lenses was correct, but that the lenses were not properly fitted into the frame. He wrote out an order to have this problem fixed when we reached Camp Shanks. A short time later, our company caught a train from Fort Meade to Camp Shanks.

The following day, we completed the processing required of all troops headed overseas. The first step was an inspection of our uniforms and equipment, which included a check of our personal possessions to determine if there were excess items to be discarded. Next, we all received a laughably cursory physical, which this time consisted of little more than checking whether each GI had the requisite number of eyes, ears, arms, and legs.

With these checks out of the way, I visited the optometrist at Camp Shanks to pass along the order for a new eyeglasses frame. After reviewing the information and listening to my description of the problem, the optometrist agreed to my request for another eye exam. Contradicting the optometrist back at Fort Meade, this doctor concluded I needed both a stronger prescription for my lenses as well as a new frame before I could go overseas.

Because I had to await their delivery, I was forced to remain behind at Camp Shanks when the rest of the guys from my company boarded trucks to travel to New York City's harbor the next day. Though I was deeply disappointed not to sail to Britain with my company, there was nothing I could do about it. It was just one of the many times my glasses would prove inconvenient, but I would certainly be useless without them.

Following their departure, I was sort of left on my own until my glasses arrived. In an effort to stay fit, I exercised and ran around the track at Camp Shanks. In the evenings, I mostly read. To my surprise, the wait for my new glasses ended up lasting a couple of weeks. Fortunately, when I finally received them, the revised prescription improved my vision and the new frame fit well.

Upon their delivery, I was temporarily reassigned to a company waiting to ship out for Britain. Though stuck with a bunch of strangers for the trip across the Atlantic, I was just glad to be on my way at last.

On the morning of January 16, 1944, an officer announced a 12-hour alert, which signaled we would depart for the harbor later that day. Loaded aboard trucks that evening, we made the two-hour drive to New York's docks, where we joined more than 10,000 other newly minted GIs who were queued up to board the HMT *Île de France*. A one-time luxury liner converted into a British troopship, the gigantic *Île de France* was among the largest ships afloat.

After ascending a long wooden gangplank that extended up from the dock, I stepped aboard and then descended several flights of stairs to the cramped troop quarters far below. Settling in for the voyage, everyone appeared to be struck with a mix of excitement and anxiety as each of us came to terms with an awesome reality.

We were sailing for Europe and would soon be in the war.

CHAPTER 5

England:
January 17–June 1, 1944

Ocean crossing: January 17–January 24

Hoping to evade the notice of any U-boats that might be prowling off the coast, the *Île de France* slipped out of New York City's harbor shortly after midnight on January 17. As we got underway, loudspeakers were barking a steady stream of instructions about what to do in the event we were torpedoed. Everyone had been issued a life jacket, but the thought of jumping into the frigid waters of the North Atlantic was a nightmarish prospect.

All 11,000 of us on board had heard that the ocean was full of German subs. Operating alone and in Wolf Packs, U-boats had already sunk hundreds of American and British ships, causing the loss of thousands of lives and many thousands of tons of supplies. While most Allied ships sailed in convoys protected by armed escort vessels, we were told our ship would be crossing the Atlantic alone in order to take advantage of her speed. By traveling fast and adopting a zigzagging course, our ship would be able to evade any U-boats that might attempt to track us. This seemed to make sense, but none of us really knew whether sailing alone was the better option.

As far as the *Île de France*'s previous service as luxury liner, no hint of this past opulence was evident down in our dimly lit, austere accommodations. With every available space on the vessel filled to capacity, we were jam-packed together. Having claimed an empty berth in a set of bunks stacked six high, I was squeezed into a narrow space that left my nose practically rubbing against the bottom of the sagging canvas bunk above me.

Despite the best efforts of our British crew to make the voyage comfortable, conditions on the overcrowded ship rapidly deteriorated once we were at sea. An indescribably foul odor emanating from the puke of countless seasick GIs soon permeated the air. The nauseating stench grew far worse when the commodes near our quarters overflowed, making each breath a barely endurable experience.

Mercifully, the company to which I was temporarily assigned received "deck duty" a couple of days after we sailed, allowing us to escape the noxious conditions below deck. Deck duty involved continually walking the deck as we scanned the ocean's surface for any sign of a U-boat periscope or the bubbles marking a torpedo's trail.

This was a challenging task in the rough seas of the North Atlantic, but escort planes flying overhead reassured us a German sub would have a hard time approaching the *Île de France* without being spotted. In addition to reporting any and all suspicious sightings in the water, our orders also required us to question any soldier found out on deck after dark.

At the conclusion of our company's first couple of shifts on deck duty, we had to descend to our foul-smelling quarters to rest. But, on the third day, we received sleeping quarters on the ship's top deck closer to our assigned work. Meanwhile, the weather conditions deteriorated. After a few days of beautiful weather, it turned cold and windy and the seas grew rougher. Yet whatever the weather and the tedium of deck duty, all of us remained grateful for the fresh air.

The days were enlivened by regular evacuation drills as well as by more conventional forms of recreation and entertainment. These included games of badminton and horseshoes, movies shown in one of the ship's several theaters, and concerts given by professional entertainers and some of the more musically talented soldiers aboard. Though I did not gamble, a lot of GIs passed the days playing poker or other card games, something I found interesting to observe.

However, most of my free time on the ship went into studying a small Army-issued booklet which presented information about the English, Scots, and Welsh and their distinct customs. The voyage itself offered an introduction to the English diet, permitting us to sample such unfamiliar fare as kidney stew and cold beef heart. Unlike many of the other guys, I found the chow on board to be pretty decent. Even better, we could buy all the candy bars we wanted.

"We are in Scotland," the captain announced when the British coast first came into view. Though we still had a little more sailing to reach our destination, the flat monotony of the preceding 3,200 miles of open ocean was replaced by a spectacular vista of green meadows beneath snow-capped mountains.

On the morning of January 24, after seven days at sea, the *Île de France* anchored off the neighboring ports of Gourock and Greenock. Located on the southern bank of the River Clyde two dozen miles downriver from the city of Glasgow, the ports served as a major disembarkation point for arriving American GIs. I thanked God for our safe voyage—and our exit from the ship.

Before long, tugboats began pulling up alongside the *Île de France* to ferry the thousands of troops on board to the harbor. Once ashore, we took trucks to the nearby rail station to board waiting trains for the trip south to our various destinations in England.

As pretty female Red Cross workers handed out donuts, coffee, candy, and gum, our train began its journey through magnificent Scottish countryside. Rolling slopes were laced with low stone fences that appeared to trail endlessly up and over hill and dale. In the pastures, sheepdogs enthusiastically raced around herding their flocks under the watchful eye of their shepherds. Observing such peaceful scenes made it hard to believe the world was at war.

Bridport: January 24–25

Following a long, 450-mile rail trip down through Scotland and then England, I finally reached my assigned destination sometime late that night. The only light shining in the station illuminated a sign that read "BRIDPORT."

A small market town of a few thousand people, Bridport is located in the county of Dorset in southern England, roughly 125 miles west-southwest of London. Bridport served both as the base for H Company as well as the headquarters of the 2nd Battalion of the 16th Infantry Regiment. The 2nd Battalion's three regular infantry companies were based nearby.

The 30 or so of us who disembarked at the train station in Bridport hauled our gear to the areas of the building designated for our specific units. A sergeant named Huber met the dozen of us assigned to H Company and ordered everyone onto an Army truck for a short ride through Bridport. Upon arriving at our quarters in a set of long, one-story buildings, Huber ushered us into a large room where each of us chose a cot and stowed our gear.

Returning outside, we lined up for roll call and instructions. Huber welcomed us to Bridport and provided directions to the mess hall, the Army commissary, and the building serving as headquarters, facilities that were all confined to a few blocks of the town. The sergeant explained that on most days H Company would march out to drill at nearby training grounds, but that we would occasionally travel to more distant locations for specialized training. Last, we received a local map and a sheet of paper with Bridport's stores, restaurants, movies, churches, and the like. It also included a few details on English customs as well as the rules of conduct for our dealings with the civilian population.

The next morning, a lieutenant in H Company spoke to all of us who had just arrived as replacements.

"We're gonna show you how to really train now. We're gonna give you combat training." Our "severe combat training" in England was designed to toughen us to a physical peak, while also improving our handling of weapons and teaching us advanced infantry tactics.

Information about the specific target and timing of the coming invasion of France remained top secret, but much was also done to conceal even basic information about the location and movement of military units in England. To hide our unit identity, all newly arriving 1st Infantry Division replacements were instructed to remove all Big Red One shoulder patches from our uniforms.

To support the training of replacement troops, all units were leavened with 1st Infantry Division veterans who had fought in North Africa and Sicily. Garrisoned in

Bridport since early November 1943, H Company's veterans had been conducting regular and specialized training for a couple of months prior to our arrival, exercises which had further honed their combat skills. While veterans may have made up less than half of H Company's roster after the arrival of all the replacements, they provided most of the officer and NCO cadre. Interspersed throughout the company's platoons, sections, and squads, these veterans shared combat experience that would be invaluable to our training in England.

Viewing themselves as members of an elite American infantry outfit like the paratroopers or the Marines, the 1st Infantry Division's veterans had a pride that made them stand out from other U.S. Army troops. Naturally, these H Company veterans often treated us replacements as if we knew nothing and they could do everything better. Typically in their mid-20s, the veteran sergeants and junior officers were also a bit older than most of us, which further reinforced their sense of superiority. In short, they could not help looking down on us until we proved ourselves as worthy members of the Big Red One in combat.

Despite the inevitable tensions between combat veterans and freshly arrived replacements, the rapport between us was actually excellent. Because we looked up to them, we would listen carefully when they applied lessons from their previous battles that helped make our exercises more useful and realistic. Whatever feeling of superiority the veterans possessed, they sincerely wanted to help us to avoid mistakes that would get us killed in combat.

Training in Bridport: January 25–March 6

From day one, we late-arriving replacements jumped into the existing training program. In the mornings, a sergeant from H Company rousted us from bed at 5am with his whistle and shouts, sometimes lifting the end of our cots and then dropping them back to the floor for added urgency. After roll call, we had an hour of calisthenics out in front of our quarters, 30 minutes for breakfast at the mess hall, and 15 minutes for personal hygiene back in our quarters.

By 7am, our second machine-gun platoon was trucking out to an open area near Bridport. The day's training usually commenced with an hour of bayonet drill, something we had done little of back at Fort McClellan. After jabbing stuffed dummies, we held out our rifles with the attached bayonet, maintaining that back-breaking pose until our instructors released us.

After bayonet drill, we typically carried out some type of strenuous physical exercise before lunch. Usually, this meant one of H Company's sergeants leading us on five-mile and ten-mile "fast hikes." Unlike our hikes during basic training, we always lugged backpacks stuffed full of at least 50 pounds of gear. Occasionally, our hikes lasted several hours and covered closer to 20 miles, more than twice the distance of our longest march at Fort McClellan.

With winter temperatures hovering in the 40s, hiking in southern England was a big improvement to exercising in the blazing heat and humidity of an Alabama summer. But now, we often trekked under cold, drenching rains, through creeks that left us sopping wet, and across a very rough terrain of fields and woods broken up by downed trees. Constantly required to hit the dirt, crawl, get up, walk, run, hit the dirt, get up, walk, and run, we finished muddy, dog-tired, and chilled to the bone. Designed to "harden" our bodies, build our stamina, and prepare us for combat, these fast long-distance hikes achieved their purpose.

On a few of these hikes, our instructors had each man carry half of the equipment needed to assemble a tent. On reaching our assigned destination, we would pair up with another man and set up a tent for the night. Camping was something I enjoyed, but tents were far too visible a target to risk using them on the front line. Once we were in combat, the only tents I ever saw were those utilized at the company kitchen, first aid stations, and rest areas in the rear.

Sometimes, the day's physical exercise involved a trip to the obstacle course. Although it included more obstacles and was more difficult than the courses during basic training, I was thrilled to discover there was no flat wall climb, the one feature that had given me so much trouble back at Fort McClellan.

To train us how to stay low, one of H Company's veteran sergeants would order us to switch to a crawl on our hands and knees for what was probably 50 yards. It felt like a mile.

"Get down! Get down!" he chided throughout the crawl.

After learning our names, the sergeant put the information to good use. Whenever a soldier failed to keep his butt down during the crawl, the sergeant liked to lean down close to the offending man's ear to deliver his message.

"Andrews, get your ass down!" he barked at me more than once, shouting at a volume that left my ears ringing.

Following a brief lunch break for sandwiches, our platoon would usually march over to a firing range for an hour or so of intensive target practice with our carbines and pistols. There were also exercises on the same range with grenades as well as with gas. The tear gas always left us with irritated eyes, despite our best efforts to adjust our gas masks in order to prevent any seepage.

Everyone who had been assigned to one of H Company's two machine-gun platoons spent most afternoons training on the guns at the weapons range. During these drills, each of us was placed in one of the seven-man machine-gun squads in his assigned platoon on a provisional basis. With two squads in each of the 15-man sections and two sections in each of the two 36-man machine-gun platoons, H Company possessed a total of eight machine-gun squads.

However, our permanent assignment to a specific squad was not immediate and only took place over a couple of weeks. As a lieutenant evaluated our performance, he also determined who would best fulfill the various roles—the "order of service"—within each of the eight-gun squads in the two platoons.

"Andrews, you are the number one gunner in the number two squad of the second section of the second platoon," the lieutenant announced one day, a decision based mainly on my accuracy with the machine gun in our firing drills. Before long, everyone was assigned to a spot in one of the machine-gun squads.

Because replacements from our old training company at Fort McClellan formed the bulk of H Company's two machine-gun platoons, we already knew a good number of the other members of our new squads. After training together in Alabama, we shared a bond that would have been absent if we had been thrown together with a bunch of strangers. While I knew Wayne Newsome, Lincoln Welser, and Hector Gonzalez from my old machine-gun squad at Fort McClellan, our new gun squad included an H Company veteran and a couple of other recently trained replacements who I did not know before arriving in Bridport. However, the four of us soon became buddies with the other three GIs.

My designation as our squad's primary machine gunner meant I would also be the one who would carry the 53-pound tripod. Though excited to be named the main gunner, I knew this would also make me the primary target of enemy fire once we went into combat. None of the other members of my squad complained when I received the assignment.

Since Wayne was especially strong, he would lug the 32-pound gun with its stove-piped barrel. Because Lincoln was quick as a flash with the tricky task of securing the rubber condensing hose to the water plug under the barrel's muzzle, he would carry the seven-pound, six-quart water chest and rubber hose as well as ammunition. With Hector being highly adept at loading the ammo belt into the gun, he would serve as an ammo carrier. Along with two other guys, Hector hefted a couple of 22-pound ammo boxes, each of which contained 250-rounds of belted .30 caliber ammunition. The final squad member was assigned as our squad's "chauffeur" to drive our jeep, which hauled our supplies in its trailer.

While each of us had designated roles in the squad to fit with our individual abilities, we cross-trained in order to be ready to carry out the other tasks as well. In combat, a squad member might need to serve as the tripod carrier and gunner one day, lug the machine gun the next day, carry ammo boxes the following day, and then haul the water chest the day after that. We also had to be ready to operate with fewer than our normal complement of seven men, though it took a minimum of four men to fulfill the squad's critical functions.

Our drilling was rigorous. In one exercise, our squad practiced running for 50 or 100 yards with all of our equipment until we heard the sound of machine-gun fire. Dashing along with the tripod bouncing on my shoulders, I would flip it over my shoulders and hit the ground at the moment the gunfire sounded. The others would come up an instant later to assemble the gun.

To further enhance our speed and performance, our instructors continued to hold occasional contests among squads to determine which of H Company's eight gun squads could set up the machine gun the fastest and achieve the most hits on short-range and long-range targets. Our squad's regular victories in these contests were a great source of pride that brought us closer together.

A couple of times a week, we received instruction in the tactical deployment of the machine gun to maximize the effectiveness of our fire. On several occasions, our two machine-gun platoons practiced moving with, and operating in close support of, the 2nd Battalion's rifle companies. This more active training was balanced by regular practice in the disassembly, cleaning, and reassembly of the machine gun as well as our carbines and pistols.

On perhaps half a dozen occasions, all of H Company marched to a steep hillside some distance from our usual training area. Perforated with numerous holes, the hill appeared to be home to a colony of oversized groundhogs.

"You've got 15 minutes to get into a hole before we cover that field with live machine-gun fire!" the NCO in charge, Sergeant Gentry, shouted when we reached the foot of the hill on our first visit to the site.

At the sound of a whistle, we all hollered at the top of our lungs as we charged up the slope to the foxholes 25 yards away. By the time the second whistle blew, everyone was hunkered down deep in a foxhole.

When the machine gun began raking live fire just inches above my foxhole, the bullets striking the sloping ground above me produced a miniature landslide of muddy earth and pebbles that bounced off the top of my helmet. If coming under fire still remained somewhat unnerving, I was gradually getting used to people shooting at me.

Several afternoons were reserved for the far more hazardous drill of crawling down trails under live fire. It would be a much more intense version of what we had endured back at Fort McClellan.

At a gesture from the officer, the machine-gun crews on either side of the field let off a few bursts so we could see what we faced. Just like during basic training, their field of fire passed a couple of feet above the two trails, a crossfire marked out by bright tracer rounds that made the trajectory of the bullets visible.

"Okay, guys, you're going to crawl under this gunfire. There will also be explosions on your right and left, pretty close to you," the officer announced. "Now listen, I need to tell you something. Most of you guys are going to get wounded. And do you know where you are going to get wounded? You're going to get wounded in the butt because you can't keep it low enough to the ground. So, when you go through this mud, I want your butt down."

With this warning in mind, our platoon began crawling down the trails, which were left dry for the first couple of passes. While the machine guns swept fire back and forth just above us, explosives were detonated about 30 feet away, providing a good incentive to stay low and finish the drill as fast as possible.

After two "dry" runs, an Army truck equipped with a water sprinkler thoroughly doused the trails, transforming them into cold, muddy slime. On our next crawl, the explosives steadily showered muck onto us as we slithered forward down the trail. In the chill of the English winter, crawling through the mud was an even more miserable experience than during basic training in Alabama, where at least we never got cold.

When we repeated this same exercise a couple of weeks later, a terrible tragedy occurred in one of the 2nd Battalion's rifle companies as the outfit was training on the second trail a few yards away from us. Apparently unable to cope with the psychological strain of making the crawl with bullets whizzing overhead, two GIs suddenly stood up and tried to make a run for it. Caught completely off guard by their impulsive act, the machine-gun crews were not able to cease firing in time. The men were cut down before they could take a step.

Focused on our own drill, several minutes elapsed before we became aware of what had happened. Only when they carried away the bloody, mangled corpses did we realize what had taken place. Seeing dead men for the first time, I was very saddened that two of our fellow soldiers had lost their lives so tragically. But our drill did not halt. Instead, the calamity was used as a warning.

"See, guys, this is what you get if you stand up. This is what you get if you don't keep low," declared the officer in charge.

With their fate in mind, we strove to keep even lower in our subsequent crawls. Wriggling through the frigid mud like slugs, our bodies literally carved out a trench in the earth. Again and again, I was forced to stop and wipe the accumulated mud from my glasses, delaying my completion of the crawl. Though exasperating, there was nothing I could do but push through the drill.

While these live-fire exercises were designed to accustom us to battlefield conditions, it remained impossible for me to truly imagine myself ever coming under hostile fire. But perhaps those who have never been in combat cannot really conceive what it is like until they experience it firsthand.

Our training at Bridport also included new drills not conducted at Fort McClellan. On several afternoons, we traveled to a location about five miles from Bridport to practice assaulting a specially built, full-scale mockup of a French village. Our attacks on this "village" of about a dozen clapboard houses gave us valuable experience in house-to-house fighting with live ammunition. With our platoon divided into dozen-man assault teams, the instructors kept our groups spread out, so we would not accidentally kill each other.

Kicking in the doors, our team burst into a house. Suddenly, an armed dummy soldier in a German uniform would swing down from a hidden opening in the ceiling or spring out at us from closets and kitchen cabinets. Reacting to the threat, we blasted and bayonetted our enemy attacker. Despite his ill-treatment, the almost lifelike rubber dummy would still be standing there staring back at us when we ceased shooting and stabbing. It was a bit eerie.

Once the structure was cleared, we headed to the next house to repeat the exercise. When confronting a fortified "enemy" position in a house, dummy grenades were employed to reduce the defenders inside before we attacked. As with all elements of our training, these actions were thoroughly scrutinized and critiqued afterward in order to improve our subsequent performance.

"You guys need to be serious about learning all this stuff because we're going to be in combat," our officers continued to warn. If such admonitions had once been dismissed, we grew more serious as our training became more real.

Training films, night problems, and amphibious exercises

At the end of a long day of drilling, we headed back to our quarters in Bridport for a quick shower before supper and our evening activities. About every other night, H Company assembled to watch training films on various topics. Covering advanced tactics and skills, these films somehow seemed more realistic in their portrayal of combat than the ones shown back at Fort McClellan.

Many of the movies were periodically paused for officer-led discussions, which often dealt with the machine gun's tactical employment in combat. Tactics had evolved from those used a quarter century earlier during World War I, when machine-gun crews had deployed their weapons in a fixed position. Firing from the security of their entrenchments, gunners had devastated the enemy's infantry when it attacked across the No Man's Land separating the trench lines.

In the modern war of movement for which we were training, our heavy weapons company would advance right along with the rifle companies. As soon as our outfit met strong German resistance, we would deploy and fight alongside the infantry. Our primary mission was to provide heavy fire support for our attacking troops, but we were also available to help repulse any enemy force that attempted to counterattack.

Once discussion on a subject ended, we would resume watching the movie. When the film finished covering a new topic, such as creating a secure gun emplacement, the officer would again turn off the projector to offer advice based on his experience fighting the Germans in North Africa and Sicily.

"This is a way you can put your machine gun behind dirt, if you've got time and if you know you're gonna be there overnight. You need to protect that gun. So push some dirt up around it or put some logs in front of it. Use something to hide it!"

A couple of nights later, we might watch a film about a mortar squad in action, a subject very relevant to us since H Company included a mortar platoon with six 81-millimeter mortars. Dashing to a safe firing position, the mortar crew would plant the weapon in the ground and go into action. If the first mortar rounds were not on target, they would adjust the mortar tube. If the mortar's range needed to be reduced, the crew would remove one of the four propellant bags attached to the mortar round's fin assembly.

Even though we were H Company machine gunners, our officers wanted all of us to know how to operate a mortar in an emergency or at least to have a basic understanding of the weapon. However, I never received any hands-on instruction with mortars during my period of training at Bridport.

Just as at Fort McClellan, newsreels were screened to keep us abreast of developments in the war. The ones that covered combat in the Pacific against the Japanese always made me glad I had opted for the European Theater.

On several occasions, a special Army instructor presented lectures using what could be described as "hate tactics." In an effort to inculcate a deep animosity toward the Germans in us, he described the terrible atrocities Nazi Germany had perpetrated against Jews, civilians in occupied territories, and its own political prisoners. Though it was all true, this approach did not appear very successful in persuading American GIs to adopt more hostile attitudes toward our German enemy. Most were young, easygoing types who just did not get worked up about what they heard.

To me, hate tactics were utterly alien and very disturbing. Because my grandfather was German, I did not and could not feel that hatred in my heart. As far as I knew, killing Germans might mean killing family. More fundamentally, my Christian faith commanded me to follow Jesus's teaching to love one's enemy, even if it might be necessary to fight against them. As a result, I never developed any personal feeling of animosity toward the young German soldiers we were preparing to fight. To me, the real enemy was the Nazi regime and its evil ideology, not the German people who were in its grip.

While many nights were devoted to watching training films and related discussions, we sometimes engaged in more active training. Three or four times, a group of H Company sergeants burst into our room in the middle of the night.

"The enemy's here! Let's go!" they shouted, flipping on the lights. Aware that the Germans remained safely on the other side of the English Channel, we would happily have gone back to dreaming, but that was not an option.

Some nights, our rousting from sleep was followed by a "midnight hike," a five-mile or ten-mile trek often conducted under a cold English rain. Other times, our mission involved "night problems," where our second machine-gun platoon practiced infantry operations. Once our scouts discovered an "enemy position," flares were fired to illuminate the battle space for a simulated firefight. Using only hand signals, we carried out flanking maneuvers in strict silence. Conducting these exercises in the darkness on little sleep made everything harder.

Our night-time activities also included more drilling in urban combat at the mock French village. Having absorbed the basics of this type of fighting, we now received training from a pair of American and British instructors in soundlessly approaching enemy positions under the cover of darkness. Sneaking up on dummy sentries from behind, we tightly covered their mouths while slashing their throats with our bayonet knives. Entering the village's clapboard houses, we slit the necks of sleeping dummy troops with surgical precision. Caught by surprise, those poor rubber dummies suffered greatly at our hands.

Most of H Company's training took place near Bridport, but our company also participated in a major regimental level exercise outside of Dorset a couple of weeks after my arrival in England. On the morning of February 8, H Company traveled to the U.S. Army Assault Training Center at Braunton in Devon, located about 70 miles west-northwest of Bridport.

From February 9 to 25, the 16th Infantry Regiment practiced beach landings in cold, wet weather. Conducted under simulated fire against fortified enemy positions, the landings were meant to be as realistic as possible. In addition to focusing on individual and boat team assault tactics, we also received specialized instruction in clearing mines and the use of demolition charges. Though the amphibious exercises employed LCVPs (Landing Craft, Vehicle, Personnel), Higgins boats, I retained little recollection of this element of our training four months later.

Over the course of our regular drilling in Bridport and the training exercise at Braunton, we developed a positive impression of H Company's commanding officer, Captain Robert M. Irvine. Standing about six feet tall, our captain was a college-educated soldier from Massachusetts in his mid-20s. A tough, no-nonsense veteran of the outfit's earlier battles in North Africa and Sicily, he had already proved himself to be a gutsy and competent commander.

Of course, most of our interaction was with our NCOs, the sergeants assigned to oversee our training duties. The one most closely involved in our machine-gun training at Bridport was Sergeant Gentry. A short guy who always seemed in need of a shave, he was quiet, steady, and very accurate with the machine gun. Having served with H Company since late 1942, Gentry's extensive combat experience gave him a higher than usual sense of superiority but also made him very knowledgeable. He would later be our squad sergeant.

Sergeant Carpenter had served in the prewar Army and worked as a drill instructor before going overseas. Standing about five-foot-nine-inches tall, slender, and very agile, he was businesslike but friendly. Heavily involved in our training at Bridport, he would later be one of our platoon's NCOs.

Working closely with Carpenter, Sergeant Carter was an experienced veteran and former drill instructor who assisted in training our platoon and would later help lead us in combat. Short but muscular, he was highly capable and quick-thinking. Whatever the situation, he always saw the bright side.

The only NCO who I got to know outside of those involved in our training was H Company's First Sergeant William Huber, who had met us at the train station when we arrived in Bridport. Serving as the company quartermaster, he handled all the nitty-gritty bureaucratic paperwork that kept our outfit supplied with equipment and other vital items.

Off duty

During the occasional breaks in our rigorous training regimen, the Army sometimes organized recreation for us, mostly games of football, basketball, and baseball. In addition to playing a little baseball, ping-pong, and badminton, I sometimes shot pool with a few of the other guys at an Army club for enlisted men in Bridport. We also took in several intramural boxing bouts arranged by the 16th Infantry Regiment as well as a few more elite matches in which the fighters were drawn from all three regiments of the 1st Infantry Division.

On rare occasions, Hollywood feature films were screened to provide us with entertainment. When movies like *Tarzan*, a Roy Rogers western, *Treasure Island*, or *Gone with the Wind* were shown, there was plenty of audience participation with lots of clapping, yelling, whistling, and booing, depending on the scene. In one of the more memorable events, we saw Jimmy Cagney's Yankee Doodle Dandy show. The USO (United Service Organizations) also sponsored a performance by Gypsy Rose Lee, another star of the day. While her sort of burlesque song and dance routine dazzled many of the men, it failed to captivate me and I left the show before it ended.

Just as at Fort McClellan and Fort Meade, we again lucked out as far as the chow. Thanks to three professional chefs who had earlier worked at fine dining establishments back in the States, H Company troops enjoyed truly exceptional cuisine throughout our training in England. While the food served in our earlier training had been excellent, our meals at the mess hall in Bridport were a step above with attention to small details like an appetizing presentation of the meals. Our chow also seemed more nourishing, with lots of vegetables and less starch.

"Eat up men, the folks back home don't have it this good," our company cook Steve often told us, though such encouragement was hardly necessary.

Even with the outstanding fare available at the mess hall, most of us still ate out on Friday and Saturday nights when we had the chance. My buddies from the squad and I patronized an English pub in Bridport that served up a big platter of fish and chips that we washed down with tea. Literally dripping with grease, the deep-fried cod and thick French fries were delicious, filling, and cheap. An American dollar went a long way in England.

With London only a couple of hours from Bridport by bus, most GIs used a weekend pass to visit the British capital at least once. Though the city remained a target for sporadic air raids by the *Luftwaffe*, few of us wanted to miss out on seeing the sights. During my two leaves in London, my buddies and I used the time to wander through English shops, try out different restaurants, and take in a movie. One trip included an overnight hotel stay, which allowed me to spend the night in a real bed and sleep late in the morning. Around us, life in wartime London went on at a brisk pace, but I was struck by the piles of rubble from ruined homes and businesses, a sad legacy of the years of German bombing.

Back in Bridport, I continued to spend most of my off-duty hours with my buddies from the squad. In comparison with our training company at Fort McClellan where most of us had been Southerners, H Company included a far broader cross-section of Americans. Naturally, there were some cultural differences as we mixed and mingled with guys from different parts of the States, but these regional distinctions were treated with good humor. Yet, despite the overall harmony, a wide gulf existed when it came to the matter of race relations, specifically on views relating to Black troops dating the local girls.

While our training left little spare time for regular dating, a few GIs gave it their best effort. Interestingly, I noticed the English girls seemed to prefer, and often dated, the Black American soldiers. It was not uncommon to see these interracial couples together out in public, especially on trips to London. Being from the American South where such interracial relationships were absolutely taboo, I found the sight extraordinary, but was not bothered by it. As with all matters, my views on race had been deeply shaped by my Christian parents, who possessed a far more tolerant outlook. In contrast, most Southerners were less open-minded and many were profoundly offended by interracial dating.

Whatever their race, a lot of the GIs dating local girls were looking for sex rather than romantic relationships. As the invasion grew closer, many soldiers in my company expressed mystification at my determination to abstain from sex before marriage when I might soon be killed in combat. However, the approach of combat just made me embrace my Christian faith even more tightly.

Meeting the English

Sundays provided our only regular weekly escape from the regimen of military life. While a soldier could do whatever he wished with the day, Captain Irvine constantly encouraged us to attend local churches.

"Guys, go visit a local church if you want to meet some English families. They are very cordial and would like to host you in their homes. They want you to feel at home away from home."

A printed announcement inviting American soldiers to attend local church services and meet English families had caught my eye on my first day in Bridport. For no special reason, I chose to attend services at an Anglican church in Yeovil, Somerset, a town located about 15 miles north of Bridport.

Just as back at Fort McClellan, Army regulations required each soldier be issued a pack of condoms every time he received a pass. But with my firm commitment to remain celibate until I married, the rule still seemed pointless and annoying to me, so I decided to tell the officer in charge how I felt.

"Listen, I don't need those things," I objected when I picked up my pass.

"I don't give a crap what you don't need, you take 'em!" he ordered.

"Okay. Yes, sir! Whatever you say," I relented, knowing not to argue.

The following Sunday morning, a dozen of us who were visiting churches outside Bridport set out aboard an Army truck. When the driver let me off in front of the church I was to attend in Yeovil, he told me that someone would return to pick me up at 5pm, allowing me to spend the whole day in the town.

The Anglican worship service turned out to be a lot different than services at my Presbyterian Church back on Signal Mountain, but I enjoyed it. At the end of the service, the pastor announced, "If any U.S. soldier would like to visit a local home, we have families who would like to 'adopt' you. They will be waiting to meet you in the vestibule after the service."

Minutes later, a woman came up and introduced herself as Mrs. West.

"Would you like to come to my home this afternoon for high tea?" she asked. Despite having only a vague idea what "high tea" meant, I accepted.

After introducing me to her two daughters, Gill and Cathrene, Mrs. West added, "My husband is a captain in the British Army and is training for deployment overseas." Even from this brief encounter, it was already apparent the Wests were part of the upper crust of English society.

A short trip in the family's car brought us to their home on the outskirts of Yeovil at around one that afternoon. The dining room table was quickly set with a silver pot of hot tea, milk, sugar cubes, and a plate of freshly made crumpets, bite-sized English muffins that reminded me of small doughnuts.

At my first opportunity, I hungrily dug into the crumpets. Breaking one in half, I dipped a piece into my cup of tea.

"Andy! What are you doing?" exclaimed an appalled Mrs. West.

"I'm dunking my muffin. This is a custom in America," I explained, hoping to excuse my apparent faux pas.

"Well, it isn't a custom in England," she declared. Dunking anything at high tea clearly violated English rules of etiquette.

Despite my miscue, we enjoyed a pleasant afternoon and they invited me back to their home for lunch the next time I was able to attend their church.

Before my second Sunday trip to Yeovil, H Company's mess sergeant urged those of us who would be visiting English homes to come by the mess hall in order to procure a few items as gifts for our hosts. Due to wartime rationing, even better-off English families were enduring an extremely tight food situation, so this was a chance to share from our abundant stocks to help them out.

Stopping off at the mess hall's pantry on Sunday morning, I filled a large canvas sack with cans of beef and gravy, Spam, soups, potatoes, fruit, tomatoes, beans, corn, peas, and pumpkin. I even slipped in a canned ham. By the time I was done, the sack was almost too heavy for me to carry.

When I unloaded this bounty at the Wests' home that afternoon following the church service, the family could hardly believe the quality and quantity of the canned goods. After years of wartime austerity, the food seemed to mesmerize them. Their gratitude was overwhelming.

"Oh, this is enough for a week!" Mrs. West proclaimed as she dumped the cans into big bowls. Now fully aware how much this additional food meant to them, I planned to bring more on all of my future visits to their home.

While Mrs. West prepared our meal in the kitchen, I helped set the dining room table and mingled with the daughters. During the ensuing lunch, we conversed about wartime life in Britain, my family back home, our training, politics, and the latest war news. Afterward, Mrs. West served tea and dessert.

On a Sunday visit a couple of weeks later, I was finally able to meet Captain West. While his towering height was a little intimidating, it was his personal warmth that stood out. Shaking my hand heartily, he could not have been more gracious as he thanked me for being in England and helping them in their fight.

Like the rest of her family, 17-year-old Gill West was a really wholesome sort of girl with a pretty face and sweet disposition. During our strolls along the narrow country lanes and through the fields of flowers near her home, we developed a friendly mutual interest. Even if there was not time for it to develop into anything more, I still enjoyed our hours alone together.

Over the course of a half-dozen visits, the Wests proved to be just the opposite of the aloof and reserved English stereotypes. The family really made me feel at home, like I was their adopted son.

Through the same church in Yeovil, I was also later invited to visit the home of the Chapman family, which was a bit awkward since Mrs. Chapman turned out to be the full-time servant of Mrs. West. But while the Chapmans might have been several ranks down in the English social hierarchy, the couple and their two kids were the most wonderful, humble people imaginable.

The readiness of both of these English families to open their homes and extend me their friendship was a genuine kindness I would never forget.

Chaplain's Assistant: March 6–May 13

On the morning of Monday, March 6, First Sergeant Huber informed me I had been summoned to report to H Company's new chaplain.

Why would the chaplain want to see me? Had I done something? Had something happened to one of my brothers or someone in my family?

When I arrived at his small office after a short walk through Bridport from our quarters, the chaplain was sitting behind his desk, obviously impatient for me to appear. Inviting me to take a seat, he got right down to business.

"Private Andrews, I see on your poop sheet here that you play the piano."

"Not very well, sir," I responded hesitantly, unsure where he was going.

"Well, you're a good pianist now. You're going to be my assistant. Do you understand that?" he announced. After noting that he had asked around to confirm I was a committed Christian, he explained I would be playing a portable organ at worship services, doing some typing, and assisting him with other aspects of his work.

"Yes, sir, but you've got the wrong man here. I don't play the piano very much. I only know about nine or ten hymns," I protested, adding that I was unable to read music. I also pointed out my complete lack of any typing skills. Having already concluded that I had little desire to work with this chaplain, I was hoping to disqualify myself from the position.

But the chaplain dismissed my reservations, making it clear the issue was not up for further discussion. Since he held the rank of captain, I had no choice in the matter. So, with a handshake, I was reassigned as his assistant.

At just that moment, Captain Irvine entered the office. The chaplain and I stood up and saluted. Both men were captains, but Captain Irvine held seniority.

As the chaplain stretched out his hand to introduce himself, it became apparent to me this was the first meeting between the two men.

"Glad to meet you," responded Irvine, shaking his hand.

"I can tell we're going to get along real good," the chaplain declared.

"You're damn right we are—and you're going to do the gettin'!" Irvine retorted, setting the record straight without a hint of a smile. Seeing the crestfallen look that came over the chaplain's face, I struggled not to laugh.

After Captain Irvine left the room, the chaplain informed me my first task would be to assist him in preparing for a special Easter worship service that would take place a month later on April 9. This service would be held for troops not participating in special training exercises scheduled for that date.

When Easter arrived, we had an enthusiastic group of GIs and everything went off without a hitch. Of course, that was just one of the many worship services in which I assisted the chaplain. My regular duties included helping him plan the scripture reading, prayers, and hymns for worship services, preparing the communion wine and bread, and joining him on visits to troops in the hospital. However, my main job was to provide the musical accompaniment for the two worship services he conducted each week.

In our ministry, we primarily served H Company troops in Bridport, holding worship services for soldiers of any Protestant denomination. However, the chaplain also occasionally helped out other company chaplains by conducting Protestant services for the 2nd Battalion's other three companies and for widely scattered outfits in the 16th Infantry Regiment's other two battalions.

For each worship service, I took along a lightweight portable "organ" which folded up into a sort of oversized suitcase with a wooden handle. Once unfolded, the organ's keyboard was supported by the case's two side pieces. Pulling a chair up to the keyboard, I pumped the pedal with my foot, forcing air into the instrument's bellows in order to generate an accordion-like sound at a fairly decent volume. Unfortunately, my inability to read music meant I was playing the same few hymns during all kinds of services, whether it was a celebratory service or a more somber occasion. The chaplain complimented my playing, but I am sure he grew just as tired of hearing these songs as I did.

Though I joined the rest of H Company on Bridport's cricket field when General Eisenhower delivered an address and carried out an inspection of our outfit on April 2, my participation in combat training had completely ceased after I started working for the chaplain. Because my assignment as his assistant seemed increasingly likely to be permanent, missing out on these drills caused me no concern. Indeed, I was enjoying a far less strenuous duty.

But whatever the advantages of my new assignment, these were balanced by the fact the chaplain turned out to be a real jerk as well as a very odd duck. While I learned to work with him, his religious convictions remained unclear to me. Based on my conversations with him, it seemed to me he lacked both a basic Christian faith and any spiritual passion. Because his own faith was so ambiguous, it was not surprising his preaching failed to offer spiritual inspiration and moral strength to soldiers preparing to go into battle.

Beyond my responsibilities tied to the worship services, the chaplain also attempted to delegate the typing to me, despite my protests that I could not actually type. The work mostly involved typing up detailed reports on the chaplain's activities and three letters of condolence to the parents of soldiers who had been killed in various accidents. Lacking any knowledge of shorthand, it took me forever to copy down what he dictated to me. Once that was done, I laboriously pecked out the text of the letters on the typewriter with my two index fingers. Unimpressed with my typing, the chaplain eventually informed me he would get another assistant to handle any future correspondence.

Even though I was no longer training with H Company, I continued to reside in my original quarters in Bridport and spend much of my limited free time with my old buddies from the machine-gun squad and the cook named Steve. I also got to know a fellow named Jesse Beaver, a new H Company replacement from Illinois who had been assigned to the next room over from me after his arrival at Bridport in April.

Standing only a little over five feet tall, Jesse was even shorter than me, but what most stood out about him was his age. A married man in his early 30s, he had somehow been assigned to the infantry, which was unusual for a GI of his years. More than a decade older than most of us, he naturally caught a hard time for being an "old man," but despite the difference in our ages, he and I shared a lot in common and quickly became buddies.

Once I began my assignment as the chaplain's assistant, there were few opportunities for me to travel to Yeovil, but it finally worked out for me to visit the West family for supper on a Sunday evening in early May. As we were enjoying tea and crumpets after our meal, a siren sounded outside. This signaled the start of a German air raid, one of a series of *Luftwaffe* attacks on England carried out that spring during the "Baby Blitz."

"Let's go down to the basement," Mrs. West directed in a calm voice that indicated a practiced routine. Ten minutes after we reached the basement, an unbelievably loud roar marked the arrival of a fleet of German aircraft.

"Andy, you need to go see our girls operating the searchlight," Mrs. West urged. I enthusiastically agreed, excited to get my first look at the enemy.

Gill, Cathrene, and I walked a block up the street to a spot where we could observe a crew of three English girls operating a searchlight. Expertly, they spun the control wheels that oriented the huge light, the face of which measured several feet in diameter. Directing a shaft of light up into the night sky, the girls worked with other searchlight crews hunting for German bombers.

Momentarily caught in the beams, the planes glistened like giant stars. Despite only intermittent illumination of the bombers, nearby antiaircraft gun crews relentlessly hounded the enemy through the sky. Their tracer fire leapt up in narrow streams of light that joined the thicker beams of the searchlights in a fantastic visual spectacle, with the thudding guns and the low buzz of the aircraft supplying the auditory accompaniment. Amazingly, only one of the German intruders was hit in the dense barrage of fire. Falling from the sky in a fireball, the plane crashed somewhere off in the distance. No parachutes were visible.

When the fleet of enemy aircraft was out of range, we returned to the Wests' home. Ten or fifteen minutes later, booms off in the distance confirmed the German planes had reached their target. Tuning into the radio, we grimly listened to BBC reports on the bombing before I left. My first direct exposure to the war provided a memorable finale to my last visit with the Wests.

One morning a week or so later, as I was sitting at my desk in the chaplain's office, he called me over to him.

"Andrews, the Army does funny things. This afternoon you are to report back to H Company. They must be getting ready to invade Europe."

Though I had thought my assignment as the chaplain's assistant was permanent, the Army was urgently calling back all clerks, assistants, and other GIs who had been assigned to "nonessential duties" in order to bring infantry units up to full strength before the invasion of France.

The order to report back to H Company after a two-month absence was unexpected but came as a great relief. In the first place, I had never wanted to leave my outfit. Serving as the chaplain's assistant had been a lot easier than training, but I felt like I had been drafted to serve in a combat unit and was glad to be rejoining my buddies in the machine-gun squad. In the second place, I had never grown comfortable working with the chaplain. Of course, my assignment might have been a bit more enjoyable if I had been a better pianist.

Soon after my departure, the chaplain was replaced by another man far better suited to the position. Although my interaction with the former chaplain had not been positive, I would later come to know other chaplains who were very decent men offering real spiritual comfort to the troops they served.

H Company at Camp D-8: May 13–June 1

My return to H Company came just days before all three battalions of the 16th Infantry Regiment were repositioned to D-Camps on May 17. These pre-invasion marshaling camps were located about 15 miles east of Bridport, placing the regiment just a few miles north of the port of Weymouth on the English Channel. H Company was assigned to Camp D-8, a marshaling area located at Down Wood, just north of the village of Bincombe in Dorset.

Only the top Allied brass knew exactly when the invasion would come, but it was no secret the operation was now imminent. Two days after H Company's arrival at the D-Camp on May 17, General Clarence Huebner, the 1st Infantry Division's commander, gave a pep talk to several hundred of us. In a frank address about the invasion, he inspired us to feel like we were truly part of something heroic and historic, while also warning us to keep our butts down.

Since I had left combat training to serve as the chaplain's assistant back in early March, the daily regimen of intensive physical drilling had grown even more rigorous. After a couple of months on soft duty, these drills at first proved extremely challenging for me, especially the five-mile fast hikes with full packs. Fortunately, the resumption of regular exercise swiftly restored the muscles of my five-foot-six-inch, 185-pound body to peak physical condition.

In addition to the long hikes, the obstacle course, bayonet practice, and other basic infantry drills, our machine-gun squad also trained intensively at the D-Camp. Despite my lengthy separation from the squad, I immediately resumed the role of tripod carrier and primary gunner as if I had never left. Our live fire drills with the weapon were limited, but we regularly rehearsed the rapid deployment and disassembly of the machine gun, with a special emphasis on keeping it clean and in perfect working order.

Though it did not seem particularly important to me at that moment, my stint with the chaplain had caused me to miss out on most of the 16th Infantry Regiment's amphibious exercises in which the troops had extensively drilled with landing craft. During loading drills, the men had practiced climbing down the rope scramble nets hung over the side of the troopship to board the Higgins boats waiting in the sea below. In this crucial element of the forthcoming amphibious operation, I would have no training at all.

On May 25, the D-Camps were sealed off from contact with the outside, preventing anyone from entering or leaving. Now all of us knew for sure we would be moving to the disembarkation ports for the invasion in no more than a few days. The next day, we received the first of a series of briefings on the plans for the operation, making us privy to the great secret.

The D-Day landings in France would take place on the coast of Normandy in less than two weeks. Our 16th Infantry Regiment would form a major part of the American spearhead assaulting Omaha Beach, the Allied codename for one of the five invasion beaches in Normandy. The other major American landing zone was Utah Beach to the west of Omaha. Gold, Juno, and Sword Beaches to the east of Omaha would be assaulted by Anglo–Canadian forces.

Using detailed relief maps of the beaches, aerial surveillance photographs, and recently collected intelligence, Captain Irvine and Sergeant Carpenter explained H Company's mission to our machine-gun platoon. Our 2nd Battalion would lead the way on to Easy Red Beach, a sector of Omaha. H Company was slated to land on Easy Red during the assault's first hours. Arriving in the third wave just behind the 2nd Battalion's E, F, and G Companies, our company would provide heavy fire support. The three battalions of 16th Infantry would be rapidly reinforced by the 18th and 26th Infantry Regiments of the 1st Infantry Division, which formed part of V Corps of the U.S. First Army.

The briefings gave us a clear picture of what we would encounter when we hit the beach. On top of the several million landmines and other obstacles planted along the beach and further inland, German troops defending the coast possessed up to 80 machine guns to cover each mile of beach. We were also shown photographs of huge bunkers with thick concrete walls that protected the enemy's feared 88-millimeter guns and even heavier artillery pieces.

While such formidable enemy defenses would pose a daunting challenge, our orders were to run for the dunes as soon as our landing craft reached the beach and then push inland as fast as possible.

"Do not stop to help the wounded. Keep moving forward!"

The objective was to expand the beachhead inland as far as possible before the *Wehrmacht* could bring up reinforcements in an effort to drive us back into the sea. To speed our advance, we were directed to kill as many German troops as possible and generally discouraged from taking prisoners, though certain other units were assigned to seize prisoners for intelligence purposes. We were told any captured Germans would serve as grave diggers for us, information that did not necessarily provide much encouragement.

Among the other replacements and me, there was a sense of pride that we would form part of the invasion spearhead. But for our veterans who had fought in the invasions of North Africa and Sicily, the prestige of this assignment was balanced by a feeling the Big Red One had been selected for special missions too often.

At the end of May, the Camp Finance Officer distributed a small amount of "invasion money" in French francs to each soldier. Everyone joked that it looked like play money, but we were glad to have a little French currency in our pockets. In fact, some even used American money from their pay to buy more. To aid us in our dealings with the French, the Army also supplied us with a French language phrasebook and a pocket guide to France, which offered a brief description of the culture and people.

Alongside the issuance of such items and the briefings, our drilling persisted without pause through the end of May. Rather than feeling tense, our mood was more "matter of fact" as we prepared for the invasion. Being a pretty quiet bunch, not a lot was said, but each of us wondered how we would handle ourselves in combat. *Would we measure up?*

All of us knew hard fighting and the sacrifice of many lives would be required to win the upcoming battle and the war, but we believed our training, our equipment, and our will to get the job done would see us through.

Okay, guys, we're ready! Let's go! We can do this! was the general feeling. In just days, our confidence in victory would face the ultimate test when we went up against Hitler's battle-hardened troops.

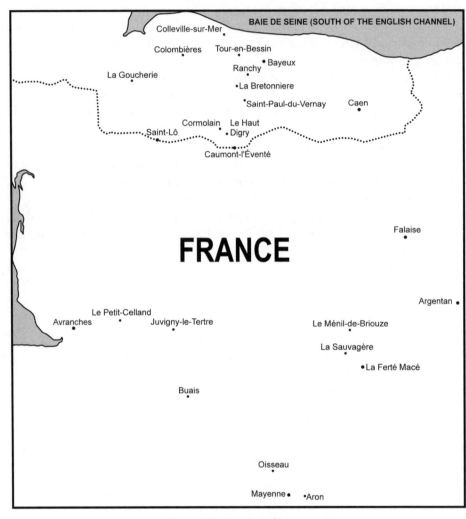

Map 1: The Battle Of Normandy

The Battle for Normandy:
June 7–July 27, 1944

Colleville: June 7/8

As the sun first began to color the thick clouds over Normandy early on the morning of June 7, most of the men around me were already awake, alert for any sign of a possible assault on our position by German troops. None of us had gotten much sleep during the short summer night after D-Day.

Following the delayed landing of a large part of our second machine-gun platoon on Omaha Beach the previous evening, we had joined the other guys from our Higgins boat for the slow climb up to the high ground above the beach. Claiming abandoned enemy foxholes, we halted for the night, dispersed among a few dozen GIs from a mix of outfits. Our position on the ridge was a hundred yards behind the forward-most posts held by American troops in this sector.

When our jeep and trailer reached us about three hours after our arrival, both squads in our section of the platoon had immediately deployed the machine guns. Anticipating an enemy counterattack at any moment, the other members of my squad and I took turns on watch behind the machine gun. With the almost constant whistle of naval artillery shells hurtling through the sky above us, the crackle of gunfire around us, and the rumble of explosions in the distance, it was clear the battle for the beachhead was raging through the night.

By the time sunrise came at 4:45am, I had managed only a brief catnap, but adrenaline left me feeling wide awake. Just as I was starting to think about breakfast, a whispered order, passed from foxhole to foxhole, reached me.

"Let's go!"

A moment later, our squad and the other troops on the ridge began advancing through the morning mist toward the forward-most American positions with our jeep and trailer following a short distance behind us. Moving cautiously through territory that had already been taken but not yet secured, we saw nothing of the enemy. In fact, things were calm enough that we were able to snack from our rations as we continued inland.

After pushing beyond the forward-most American positions, we began to move up a gently rising slope of sand and grass. Our objective was a wooded area a half-mile ahead where intelligence indicated an enemy unit was still encamped. Expecting to come under hostile fire at any moment, everyone spread out to avoid offering the Germans an inviting target.

Despite the absence of enemy shelling or small arms fire, our progress was slowed by the danger of German antipersonnel mines. Before each step, we carefully inspected the ground ahead of us in the dim morning light, looking for any disturbance in the earth or other sign that might hint at an enemy mine.

Widely dispersed and cleverly concealed throughout Normandy, the most common and most feared of these German mines was the treacherous S-mine, better known as the "Bouncing Betty." The weight of a soldier's boot would trigger a three-second fuse on a charge located under the mine. When this small charge ignited, it propelled the main explosive canister upward. Detonating three to five feet in the air, the canister spewed hundreds of deadly ball bearings outward at high velocity for up to 40 yards.

Roughly an hour after setting out from our foxholes, we all reached the tree line without incident. Entering the woods, a group of us immediately came upon a small clearing among the trees. In its center, charred wood was smoldering in a fire pit, sending small spirals of smoke drifting upward. On the ground nearby lay an abandoned mess kit with a Nazi swastika imprinted on its canvas covering. The ripe odor of unwashed bodies still hung in the air, a particular smell we soon recognized as distinctive to German soldiers.

Surveying the site, it was obvious the enemy had bivouacked here the night before and had just hightailed it out of the place in a big hurry. Like hound dogs hot on the scent of an escaped convict, everyone's blood was now up, filling us with an overpowering, primal urge to chase down our German prey.

"Golly, these guys couldn't be very far away. Let's get after 'em!" Lincoln Welser exclaimed, vocalizing the thought on all our minds. It was the first but not the last time war felt more like a game than the lethal business it really was.

Just as we were about to set off in pursuit of the Germans, the command came down to hold up where we were. Within an hour, those of us in H Company's second machine-gun platoon received new orders. Along with troops from a rifle company, we were to proceed to the nearby village of Colleville-sur-Mer, one of the main D-Day objectives for troops landing at Omaha Beach. Once there, we would link up with H Company.

When we reached our outfit later that morning, it had been more than 24 hours since we had last seen the other men aboard the USS *Henrico*. While our own boat team had come under sporadic enemy artillery fire during our delayed landing on Omaha Beach the previous evening, the rest of H Company had a far rougher time of it. When the company came ashore early on D-Day, operating in support of other elements of the 16th Infantry Regiment pushing inland, they had engaged in bitter fighting against stiff German opposition.

By the morning of June 7, Colleville had been largely secured. H Company and other troops in the 16th Infantry's 2nd Battalion were now tasked with eliminating any German troops still holding out inside the heavily damaged village. Filled with solid stone buildings, it provided the enemy with lots of readily defensible positions.

As our section of the platoon entered the outskirts of Colleville, the sound of small arms fire ahead put everyone on alert. Making our way down a side street, we came to a junction with another road, one so narrow it would not even accommodate a tank.

Suddenly, a shot rang out from nowhere. Ten feet away from me, a guy in our section's other machine-gun squad cried out as he spun to the ground with a shoulder wound.

Instantly, our squad scrambled for cover behind a wall, while the other squad took refuge in a cemetery located beside the road. Under direct enemy fire small arms fire for the first time, a momentary wave of fear passed through me. But, thanks to our months of training with live-fire exercises, I experienced no sense of mind-numbing panic or terror.

As the German continued sniping at us, all of us scrutinized the surrounding buildings to determine his location. Within about 10 minutes, we spotted him in the second-story hayloft of a barn halfway up the street.

Operating from a superior position in the cemetery off to our right, the other squad targeted the sniper with heavy machine-gun fire, which tracer rounds marked out as brilliant streaks of light. As their gun blazed away, it was hard to imagine anyone surviving such a fusillade. Indeed, the intensity of the gunfire was so great it looked as if the tracers might ignite a fire inside the barn.

A couple of minutes later, a German helmet tumbled from the window, bouncing noisily off the stone street below. This seemed to indicate the sniper's demise, but we took no chances. After cautiously advancing up the street, one of our guys lobbed a grenade up into the hayloft to make certain he was dead.

While most of us started to make our way further up the road to continue clearing the town, a couple of fellows ventured up to the loft. A moment later, they tossed the body of the dead German onto the street. We had been fortunate to escape with only a single wounded man in our initial encounter with an enemy sniper, but it would only be the first of many.

After our advance had pushed a little deeper into Colleville, we received orders to deploy the machine gun to resist a possible German counterattack. Within 10 seconds, our squad had the gun ready for action. The noise of nearby fighting increased the tension as we waited for the enemy to appear.

But the anticipated counterattack never came. Instead, we saw a group of about 15 German prisoners being led off to the rear, which signaled that enemy resistance in the town was ending. Before long, an officer arrived with the "all clear" and orders for us to move out.

Following the completion of our mopping-up operation inside Colleville, H Company took up a defensive position a half-mile south of the town and roughly a mile and a half inland from the beach. That night, our platoon slept in the basements of local homes, spreading hay on the floor as bedding.

On the morning of June 8, we were treated to a hot breakfast of eggs, grits, biscuits, gravy, bacon, and coffee. All of us thanked the kitchen crew for their effort, knowing we would be eating mostly cold rations in the coming days.

Resuming our mopping-up operations outside of Colleville, we searched the surrounding farm fields and along the edges of woods, where we encountered three small groups of German soldiers. Instead of shooting at us, these troops identified their positions by waving small white surrender flags. Most were teenagers who had never experienced combat and simply wanted to end their part in the war. Happy to oblige them, we took their weapons and sent them to the rear under guard for processing as prisoners.

During this time, the 1st Infantry Division's 18th and 26th Infantry Regiments passed through the lines of our 16th Infantry Regiment to take the lead in the division's advance into Normandy. Because our regiment had suffered substantial casualties in spearheading the assault on Omaha Beach, we were now assigned to be the Big Red One's regimental reserve.

The 16th Infantry's three battalions would support the attacking 18th and 26th Regiments and secure the division's flanks and rear area, dealing with bypassed German strongpoints and snipers. In this mission and all future operations, H Company's two machine-gun platoons and mortar platoon would provide heavy fire support for E, F, and G Companies, the rifle companies that made up the rest of the 16th Infantry's 2nd Battalion.

Of course, down at the level of our seven-man second machine-gun squad in the second section of H Company's second machine-gun platoon, we knew little about the overall military picture. Our squad was simply one small cog in the vast and expanding Allied military machine in France.

Through the hedgerows: June 8–June 13

On the evening of June 8, our company left its position near Colleville and tramped southward a couple of miles to our next objective, where we assumed a secondary defensive position in support of the 18th Infantry Regiment.

The following afternoon, we moved out again, advancing with the other squad in our machine-gun section in support of a small detachment of riflemen from an infantry company. Strung out in single file, we proceeded warily, having received a warning that enemy rearguard forces were in the vicinity.

About an hour after we had set out, bullets suddenly began whizzing through the air. Though most of the rounds passed above our heads, all of us immediately dove for cover. Hitting the ground, I raised my carbine and squeezed off a dozen shots toward the German position, which was located behind a four-foot-high concrete wall in front of a deserted French home.

Recovering from our surprise, our squad quickly readied the machine gun for action. As I waited behind the gun to see whether its firepower would be needed, all the guys in our two machine-gun squads began shooting with their carbines, joining the riflemen who were already blazing away at the enemy.

The limited return fire coming from the Germans behind the wall indicated we were up against a small rearguard that had been left behind to slow our progress. Though our rifles and carbines were doing a fine job suppressing the enemy's resistance, I decided the machine gun might help deliver a stronger message to the Germans—that their situation was hopeless.

When I opened up, it felt a little odd to me to be shooting at a wall instead of German soldiers, but my fire soon blew off a chunk of concrete. This seemed to serve as a signal to our section's other machine gun, which now added the weight of its fire to the fight.

With the torrent of rounds coming from our two machine guns and about two dozen rifles and carbines, it sounded like a major battle was underway. Under this relentless fire, the concrete wall crumbled over the next 10 minutes.

Realizing the game was up, the Germans hoisted a little white flag attached to a rifle. A moment after we ceased our fire, five scared soldiers who must have been around 50 years old emerged from behind the ruined wall with their hands raised high in the air. Hoping for gentle treatment, one of the Germans told us in broken English they had purposely fired above our heads because they did not want to kill anyone.

The age of these troops revealed how desperate Germany must be for manpower. But these middle-aged men certainly looked just as relieved to be out of the war as the surrendering teenaged German soldiers had been the day before. As I thanked God none of us had been killed or wounded, it struck me that this small skirmish would have turned out a lot differently if we had run into a larger force of Germans who had been intent on killing us.

At the end of our four-hour advance on the afternoon of June 9, we took up a defensive position close to Tour-en-Bessin. This placed us around five miles southeast of Colleville-sur-Mer and three miles west-northwest of the important Norman city of Bayeux. The following day, H Company pushed three miles further south, where we assumed a secondary defensive position near Ranchy.

On the evening of June 11, we carried out another three-mile march southwest to La Bretonnière, where we took up a secondary defensive position less than half a mile from the highway linking Bayeux with the city of Saint-Lô to the southwest. Early the following afternoon, our company was again on the move. Trekking about five miles in two and a half hours, we arrived at Saint-Paul-du-Vernay, located three miles south-southeast of our previous position at La Bretonnière. Here, we again adopted a defensive posture.

As our 16th Infantry Regiment conducted this series of short advances inland behind the 18th and 26th Infantry Regiments, we entered Normandy's *bocage* (hedgerows), an extensive network of earthen walls that was as unexpected as it was daunting.

Ranging from six to eight feet in height and from ten to fifteen feet in width, these hedgerows flanked the region's network of narrow, sunken roads. Built up over centuries by generations of French farmers who had piled their plowed-up stones at the boundaries of their property, the hedgerows were now overgrown with a dense foliage of bushes, briars, and trees. The root systems of these shrubs and trees reinforced the structure of the earthen banks, making them nearly impenetrable. Meanwhile, the hedgerow's canopy of overhanging trees kept the roads shrouded in dark shade, even in broad daylight.

The *bocage* thus afforded the Germans an extensive network of ramparts ideal for defensive operations. Beyond providing natural fortifications, the hedgerows also shielded enemy movement from observation and isolated us from our own units, even ones nearby. Lacking any type of specialized training in how to fight in this difficult terrain, it was only through trial and error that we gradually adapted our tactics to respond to this unforeseen obstacle.

However, it fast became apparent the Germans had been preparing for a battle in the hedgerows. Although we were on the offensive, it was the enemy who held the tactical initiative in deciding when and where to engage us. While the troops advancing ahead of us in the 18th and 26th Infantry Regiments bore the brunt of the Big Red One's hedgerow fighting, plenty of concealed German troops remained behind to keep our own regiment busy in its mop-up role. As the *Wehrmacht* increasingly deployed more battle-hardened troops to confront us, the easy surrenders of the first few days became far less common.

During the advance of our 2nd Battalion, 16th Infantry Regiment, each of H Company's two machine-gun platoons was typically attached to one of the battalion's three rifle companies. Normally operating in a two-squad section rather than in the larger four-squad platoon formation, we pushed forward just behind the infantry. Moving on foot through the narrow confines of the dark, hedgerow-bound country lanes, the tension in our two gun squads was palpable. Eerily, nearby firefights produced an almost continuous din, while remaining invisible to us. Sometimes, we would come across the bodies of GIs killed moments earlier when we had been just 40 or 50 feet away.

While German infantry hiding in the brush atop the hedgerows posed a danger to us on the road down below, most of our casualties came when we crossed intersections. Concealed enemy machine gunners, snipers, and mortar teams struck with devastating effectiveness, often acting in concert with other nearby German troops to create a murderous crossfire.

Adding to our problems, pockets of enemy resistance were just as likely to be encountered beside or behind us as ahead of us. In many places, the Germans had dug eight-to ten-foot-long tunnels inside the hedgerows through which they could sneak around us or fire out at us. As a result, a firefight could erupt at any moment from any direction.

In an effort to prevent ambushes, we constantly scrutinized the brush and scouted every road junction. But spotting the enemy's carefully camouflaged positions was almost impossible, especially if our movements took place at night. When confronting the thickest foliage in the hedgerows, we did not even risk investigating it for an enemy position. Instead, we simply threw grenades first and then searched the brush. Often, we found dead Germans who had been preparing to ambush us.

At other times, our infantry would be moving along one side of the hedgerow, while the Germans would be shadowing our men on the other side in a sort of deadly game of cat and mouse. But once the enemy's fire exposed their location, our infantry would climb over the hedgerows and cut across the fields in an effort to outflank their position.

Even if only a few enemy troops were involved in these skirmishes, the process of clearing them out was a bloody and time-consuming process that relied on grenades, flamethrowers, and firepower. While many Germans were killed in these engagements, others escaped to fight again at the next ambush.

Our machine-gun squad

In the hedgerows, combat typically involved short sharp firefights at close range or even hand-to-hand struggles where our squad could not effectively bring the machine gun to bear. However, our weapon remained integral to the tactical operations of the rifle companies and we operated in close support of them during larger or longer engagements. While the riflemen could handle lightly armed enemy opposition, our heavier firepower was available to deal with stiffer resistance, such as a German machine-gun emplacement or a larger force of a half-dozen or more enemy troops.

Ready to go into action in support of the infantry at a moment's notice, our seven-man squad advanced close behind them, carrying all the various components of the machine gun. Apart from hauling the gun's components, each of us in the squad also holstered a .45-caliber pistol in our belts. As the designated gunner lugging the tripod, I did not regularly carry a carbine, but most of the other squad members also had a carbine slung over one shoulder.

While we had plenty of gear weighing us down, our burden would have been much greater without the extra storage space provided by our squad's jeep and its attached trailer. Driven by our squad's designated "chauffeur," the jeep and trailer followed our advance on foot but stayed back a hundred yards or so in the rear. Before long, we nicknamed our jeep "Little Joe," feeling it was practically another member of our outfit. Of course, unlike the rest of us, Little Joe never complained or grew tired.

Although there was some trading off among us as far as who would carry the tripod, gun, water canister, and ammo boxes, each of us tended to stick to our routine roles. Perhaps 90 percent of the time it was my job to lug the machine gun's steel tripod, which meant I was almost always the gunner when we became engaged in combat.

While I was glad to serve as our squad's primary gunner, the tripod's 53-pound weight and three legs made it an awkward burden. To carry it, I rested the two shorter legs of the tripod on my shoulders with the feet positioned at chest height where my hands could hold on to them, while the longer leg hung down behind my back.

Carrying the tripod in this way became uncomfortable after a while, but this was true of all the gun's components. The man hefting the 32-pound machine gun itself also had to struggle with an unwieldy load, and our squad members who lugged the dead-weight of a 22-pound, 250-round ammo box in each hand for a couple of hours did not have it any easier.

Strung out in single file, each member of the two machine-gun squads in our section kept about 20 feet of separation from the man ahead of him in the column in order to reduce our vulnerability if we ran into an ambush or came under artillery or mortar fire. When we were ordered into combat, speed was of the essence. Soldiers who could quickly establish a secure firing position would usually survive the engagement.

From our training, all of us were well aware the machine gun's firepower made the man serving as the gunner a priority target for the enemy, just as their machine gunners would be a priority for us. Even when crouching low on my knees behind the machine gun so as to present the minimal possible target, I still remained vulnerable to enemy fire. Naturally, the machine gunner's stated average life expectancy of seven minutes in combat was something I tried to block from my mind.

Even knowing the risk, I loved the weapon. While few of the regular riflemen would have wanted to trade jobs with me, I would never have traded my assignment as a machine gunner to serve in their role. Barely a year out of high school, I found the opportunity to control the machine gun's devastating firepower and blow a target to pieces too alluring and exhilarating.

But the gunner was not alone in a firefight. Our squad was a team and we all depended on one another in combat. Once we had set up the machine gun, I counted on all the other members of the squad to protect my flanks with covering fire from their carbines. I also needed to know there was a squad member ready with another ammo belt close behind me, who would come up and reload the instant I ran out of ammo.

Though we were all primed for action, there were few opportunities for us to apply our training during our first days in Normandy. While the 2nd Battalion's rifle companies to which we were usually attached were skirmishing with German troops two or three times a day, our machine-gun section only deployed for action in about half of these engagements.

But even when our squad deployed the gun, there was seldom a need for me to fire off more than a short burst or two before we were again advancing through the hedgerows. More often, as soon as I had taken up my position behind the gun, we were disassembling it to resume our advance without firing a single round. Setting up the machine gun, waiting to see if we were needed, and disassembling the weapon became our routine.

As our section was following an infantry company through a small village several days into our advance through the hedgerows, two French farmers approached our column. Obviously excited to share some type of intelligence with us, they spoke at a speed we found difficult to comprehend with our limited command of French. But by scratching the number "25" on the dirt road and pointing, the farmers were eventually able to convey to us that a force of 25 to 30 Germans were holed up in a barn about a mile ahead.

When we reached the place, the barn turned out to be a long two-story stone building with a square opening on the ground floor and two rather large square openings on the second floor, spaces that presumably once had held a door and windows. The area around the barn was clear of brush, but the well-worn wagon road leading up to it was bordered by clusters of tall, thick weeds.

Suddenly, a German on the barn's second floor opened fire at us with his burp gun, sending everyone darting for cover as submachine-gun rounds from the MP 40 kicked up dust and gravel all around us.

"That place is full of Germans, cut it down," a captain from one of the rifle companies shouted. Instructing our section's two squads to deploy the machine guns about 30 yards apart, he directed our gun to target the second-floor openings and the other squad to focus its fire on the ground floor opening.

The command to go into action triggered an adrenaline rush that heightened all my senses. Finding a spot behind some brush about 40 yards away from the barn, I flipped the tripod off my shoulders as the rest of the squad hustled to help me set up the gun. Assuming my position as gunner, I crouched down low behind the weapon.

Within 10 seconds of the captain's order, both of our machine guns began spraying the barn with long bursts of fire. As we raked our fire back and forth across the barn's stone walls, the powerful .30 caliber bullets generated a cloud of dust and debris.

With every fifth round in the ammo belt a tracer that blazed a brilliantly lit path to the target, I was able to direct highly accurate fire into the barn's second floor through the openings. Observing the trajectory of my tracer fire, I could see that the bullets passing through these openings were glancing off the stone wall in the rear of the building before ricocheting wildly in every direction. On both floors, the barn's interior had become deadly, but the Germans held out.

Thinking the barn was likely to be full of dried animal fodder, I continued to target as many rounds as I could through the openings in the second story. If ricocheting pyrotechnic tracer rounds set the hay ablaze, the ensuing conflagration could force the Germans to evacuate the building.

Although I failed in my effort to ignite whatever hay was inside, the fire from our two machine guns and our small arms totally suppressed the enemy's ability to shoot back, allowing several of our infantrymen to crawl forward toward the barn. About 20 minutes into the engagement, three or four GIs crept close enough to toss grenades inside, each of which detonated with a loud thud.

A moment later, a German burp gun was tossed out of one of the second-story openings. As it clattered to the ground in front of us, a white flag started waving from the same opening. The other gunner and I both instantly ceased firing. The captain with us then shouted for the Germans to come out.

Immediately, a number of mostly older enemy soldiers began exiting the barn with their hands up. At final count, we took 32 prisoners. Unfortunately, there were no officers among the surrendering troops, so none of us had a chance to claim one of the prized Luger pistols.

The main lesson our two machine-gun squads drew from this action was that the aid tracer rounds provided in aiming our fire had to be balanced against the fact they also clearly revealed our positions to the enemy, making us easy targets. If we had received heavier return fire during this engagement, our use of tracers might really have endangered us.

As a result, our squad decided to remove the tracer rounds from a portion of the ammo belts and replace them with standard .30 caliber ammo. From this time, we normally used ammo belts with tracers during night fighting and for engaging more distant targets, some of which might be as far as 2,000 yards away. When shooting at closer range targets in daylight, tracers were usually unnecessary for directing the gun's fire since the .30-caliber bullets caused easily visible destruction.

More broadly, the one-sided firefight at the barn had given our section's two squads the first chance to use our machine guns to support an infantry assault as we had been trained. Having experienced our most intense combat since arriving in France, we felt like we had fought in a great battle. Later, we would realize the action had only been a large skirmish.

However, this skirmish proved to be our most significant engagement with the enemy during the early fighting in France. For the majority of the time, our squad was simply slogging through the hedgerows in a mop-up role. One step at a time, we expected to plod forward all the way to Germany.

Stalemate in Normandy: June 13–July 21

Early on June 13, H Company set out southward on a roughly seven-mile foot march from Saint-Paul-du-Vernay toward the village of Le Haut Digry. Late that hot morning, as our two machine-gun squads were heading along a dirt trail parallel to the main route of the advance, we crested a hill and saw a small, isolated wooden shack about 30 yards off to the right. Located above the trail, it appeared to be some type of storage shed for a farm and did not at first attract much attention.

"Yoo-hoo!" a sweet female voice called down to us from the shack as we were passing below it a few moments later.

"Wow! Hey, look at that!" one of the guys in my squad hollered excitedly, pointing up toward the shack. To our utter astonishment, there in the doorway stood a topless young woman, dressed only in a skirt and waving enticingly.

"Yeah, look at her, but don't go up there!" another GI cautioned, suspicious that this seductress was bait intended to lure us up to the shack.

Disregarding the warning, the soldier who had first spotted the woman left the trail. Heading straight up towards her, he ignored our shouts to return.

Just before he reached the shack, the girl disappeared behind the door. At the same moment, a hail of submachine-gun fire from inside tore into the GI, killing him instantly.

As all of us hit the ground, the lieutenant in command yelled for our machine-gun section to go into action. While most of the men stayed down, our two gun squads deployed our weapons and opened up.

Under the hail of machine-gun fire, boards began ripping away from the shack. But before the demolition had proceeded very far, our tracer rounds caused the structure to burst into flame. We saw no sign of the woman or any Germans, but there was little doubt anyone in the shack would perish in the blaze, if they had not already been killed by our guns.

When the flames died down a few minutes later, a number of us gathered around our squad member who had fallen into the trap. I had not been close to this fellow, but the tragic sight of his bullet-riddled corpse still deeply affected me. Two medics soon took his body back to the rear in our squad's jeep.

The episode dramatically reinforced our training about the enemy's use of various tricks to lure us into an ambush. We left the burned shack behind, but the horrible image of the GI's shredded corpse revisited me when I tried to sleep.

By the time we reached Le Haut Digry to take up our new defensive position just after noon on June 13, we were more than 15 miles south of our starting point at Colleville. This placed us just a couple of miles northwest of Caumont-l'Éventé, a vital hub in Normandy's road network that had just been seized by other elements of the 1st Infantry Division.

During our series of short advances through the hedgerows, all of us in the enlisted ranks were vaguely aware that some military logic was directing our movements, but we remained ignorant of our location on a map and the larger operational strategy behind these shifts in our position. At most, we knew our 16th Infantry Regiment was pushing forward in a mop-up reserve role behind the Big Red One's 18th and 26th Infantry Regiments.

After breaking through the tough German beach defenses at Omaha on D-Day, the 1st Infantry Division and other American units had made rapid progress, but that ended in mid-June when higher quality enemy troops appeared. As these German units were digging in, setting up strongpoints, and planting mines, the worsening weather in the latter half of June limited the use of Allied aircraft, allowing the enemy to bring up additional artillery and reserves.

While our company had no contact with the enemy during our five days at Le Haut Digry, German resistance continued to mount ahead of us. By the time we departed our position at Le Haut Digry on the evening of June 18, the front line was stalemated. As a consequence, our two-hour, three-mile march that night was not really an advance but rather a shift to a front-line defensive position a couple of miles northeast of the small town of Cormolain, a move which placed us about five miles north of Caumont.

The day after our arrival, a major storm rolled into Normandy, battering the area with high winds that caused the heavy downpours to blow in sideways. Penetrating our raincoats and soaking into our clothing, the water ran down into our boots. Soon, several inches of cold water puddled at the bottom of our foxholes. Drenched and chilled to the bone, we experienced an unwelcome reminder of the trenches in World War I. More disturbingly, we heard that the rough weather was making it difficult for our ships to unload supplies.

During these four or five days of intense storms, we kept our machine gun at the ready and maintained a constant lookout for the enemy. In fact, the pouring rain made our squad even more vigilant because the storms furnished the enemy with especially good cover to try to sneak up on us undetected. Leaves and branches moving in the wind might well conceal the approach of a small German detachment sent forward to reconnoiter our position or even the vanguard of a large-scale enemy counterattack.

On several occasions, small German scouting parties were observed and taken under fire. Meanwhile, our company's mortar platoon also regularly engaged the enemy. Even the worst weather did not stop the war.

June 24 brought another shift of our position. All of us were glad to leave our muddy, rain-saturated foxholes and needed to walk a bit in order to give our clothes time to dry. After trekking a couple of miles, we assumed a new defensive position. Though still northeast of Cormolain, we were now a mile or so closer to the small town, a location where we remained until the end of June.

On the afternoon of July 1, we moved to a secondary defensive position a couple of miles northeast of Cormolain, placing us close to the spot we had held from June 18 to June 24. In sum, these shifts in our position within the same small area reflected the ongoing deadlock of the military situation in Normandy.

With German artillery fire only occasionally targeting us at this new location, we received our first opportunity to bathe since landing in France. To rig up a hot shower, the kitchen crew heated up a large pot of water, which was then dumped into a big waterproof canvas bag. Hung from a three-pole tripod, the bag had a nozzle with a cutoff valve attached at its bottom. A little water was first released for each of us to soap up. More water was released when we were ready to rinse off. It felt good to get clean, even if the feeling did not last long.

On the afternoon of July 6, we carried out a two-and-a-half-mile march to a front-line defensive position a couple of miles southwest of Cormolain. Our squad was glad to get the order to "dig in," since it indicated we would remain posted there for at least that night. In a couple of hours, Hector Gonzalez and I had our foxhole shoveled out, though the rocky soil prevented us from digging it as deep as we would have liked.

Trying to establish a position amid the hedgerows was a dangerous and often deadly business. As soon as we arrived, H Company began aggressively patrolling the surrounding hedgerows in an effort to gain intelligence and try to determine the actual location of the "front line." With the Germans also conducting patrols, firefights and mortar strikes were frequent.

At night, all of us tried to get a little shuteye down in our foxholes, which were spread along the front line amid trees and brush. Of course, it was impossible to ever fully relax with the Germans so close. Warned to remain alert for enemy infiltrators, everyone was extra vigilant during his two-hour shift on sentry duty.

On our sixth night at the position, my turn on watch began at midnight. Roused from my slumber by someone repeatedly shaking my shoulder, I was still feeling a bit groggy when I poked my head out of the foxhole and started scrutinizing the ground ahead of us. No movement was discernible, but that provided little reassurance in the almost pitch-black darkness.

A few minutes later, a soft but distinctive noise like sticks crunching under boots drew my attention. Misjudging the direction from which the sound had originated, I looked to my left. Almost immediately, noise from movement on my right caused me to turn my gaze in that direction.

While my head was still swinging to the right, all at once I saw a muzzle flash, heard the loud report of a rifle shot, and felt a sharp, stinging pain at the left corner of my mouth. As I raised my hand toward my mouth to check the wound, I caught sight of the dark silhouette of the enemy infiltrator who had fired the round at me from some bushes a few yards away.

Rising up to his full height, the big, tall German started to charge toward me with his rifle's bayonet extended out in front of him like a spear.

Reacting instinctively, I reeled backwards down into my foxhole. But before my assailant had even taken a full stride, gunfire cracked.

Luckily for me, Hector was patrolling only a couple of dozen yards away when he heard the shot. Spotting the German starting his charge toward my position, Hector fired a bullet into the man's back that passed through his heart.

Now mortally wounded, the German still somehow managed to stagger the few strides to my foxhole before his lifeless body tumbled down on top of me. Knocked back to the bottom of my hole under the dead man's weight, I struggled futilely to shift his heavy corpse off of me.

"Hey, get this big guy off of me! He's bleeding all over me!" I implored.

Laughing at my predicament, Hector, Wayne Newsome, and Lincoln Welser displayed little haste in lifting off the body.

"He's too big! He's big and heavy!" my three buddies joked as they half-heartedly tugged at the dead German.

Only after a long moment did they finally drag the corpse off me. Brushing the dirt from my jacket, I used a handkerchief to try to wipe off the dead man's blood, but it had soaked into my uniform in a couple of places.

Though the German's shot had been fired at such close range that it had left a powder burn on my face, the bullet had fortunately just nicked the left corner of my mouth. When a medic examined my face, he concluded the wound was slight and told me to keep pressure on it to stop the bleeding.

While the superficial wound radiated a painful sting, it emitted only a slow trickle of blood. Dabbing it with a handkerchief, I thanked God for sparing my life. Turning my face toward the noise on the right at the precise instant I did had probably saved me from taking a bullet in the side of my head.

When I thanked Hector for shooting the German before he could bayonet me, he downplayed his action. "What the hell, Andy, you'd do it for me!"

A couple of nights later, H Company was pulled out of its front-line position southwest of Cormolain after another division arrived to relieve our 1st Infantry Division. Boarding trucks, we motored off on a long, slow trip through the darkness. After all of our footslogging in recent weeks, it was a nice change to ride aboard trucks.

About 3am on the morning of July 14, we dismounted in a rest area well to the rear of the front. Located just west of the small village of Colombières, the rest camp was about 15 miles north-northwest of our previous position near Cormolain and roughly eight miles west-southwest of Colleville.

Over the following week, all of us enjoyed what we felt was a well-deserved period of R&R (Rest and Relaxation). Billeted in tents, we had a chance to eat hot chow, take showers, wash our clothes, and write home. There was also time for horseshoes, softball, footraces, and movies. Just about everyone attended church services.

On a couple of afternoons, a GI from Texas nicknamed "Quick Draw" McGraw put on a show for us. Amazingly, he could whip out his .45 pistol and hit a target 40 yards away in one rapid motion. We gave him a standing ovation.

Of course, we did not totally escape our regular duties. When our squad was in combat, the machine gun was cleaned about once a week. Our downtime at the rest area permitted us to carry out a more thorough cleaning and oiling of the weapon as well as our pistols and carbines.

We also received our first replacements at the rest area. Each of us in the squad spent time showing the new guys our equipment and explaining some of the basics, like how to get the machine gun set up in a hurry. Everyone wanted to make sure these guys were ready for action the next time we saw combat.

Toward the end of the week, it became clear an infection had developed at the left corner of my mouth where I had been nicked by the bullet. Though the wound had bled only a little at the time, the spot had never formed a scab, even after I had stuck a small piece of paper over it.

With the infection now visibly spreading through the blood vessels in my left cheek like tendrils of poison ivy, I visited H Company's aid station. After carefully examining my face, a medic issued me a jar of medicinal ointment, telling me to apply it daily and return to see him if the infection grew worse.

Our days at the rest area near Colombières passed swiftly. For the 1st Infantry Division as a whole, the break served as an operational pause to reorganize, re-equip, and receive replacements before a new offensive operation.

Scheduled to jump off from a front-line sector near the city of Saint-Lô in a few days, Operation *Cobra* was intended to smash southward through the German defensive lines which had so far bottled up American forces in Normandy, enabling the U.S. military to exploit its armored and mechanized capability. In combination with other planned Allied operations, it was designed to help bring about the destruction or surrender of Germany's military forces in Normandy.

Preparing for Operation *Cobra*: July 21–26

Shortly after midnight on July 21, our company boarded trucks at our rest camp near Colombières and headed west through rain on another long, slow trip. Arriving at the 2nd Battalion's assembly area late that morning, H Company joined other elements of the 1st Infantry Division, which was one of several American divisions assembling in preparation for Operation *Cobra*. Located three-quarters of a mile west of the village of La Goucherie, H Company's new position was about nine miles west-southwest of the rest camp and nine miles north-northwest of Saint-Lô.

Under a persistent downpour, we set up camp and ate a hot meal. At this time, we learned of the failed assassination attempt on Hitler by a group of German officers on July 20. While we were too focused on our own situation to pay much attention to this news, all of us were certainly sorry the effort had failed. Nobody would have minded if the war had ended that day.

With heavy rains saturating the ground and thick cloud cover limiting air operations, the military brass postponed the start of the operation by several days. While we waited out the bad weather, our main concern was simply to keep dry inside one of the tents or covered trucks, though hot chow made the situation more bearable. We also used the delay to rearrange and replenish the equipment stored in our jeep's trailer, loading it up with new crates of grenades and new boxes of ammo belts for the machine gun.

To open the way for the breakout of VII Corps, Operation *Cobra* would commence with a gigantic air attack against the German forces concentrated on our front. The primary target of the carpet bombing would be a four-mile stretch of line held by the elite *Panzer-Lehr* Division in a sector located three miles west of Saint-Lo and a little south of the Saint-Lo-Periers Road.

After some limited bombing on July 24, the main air assault finally began on the morning of July 25. Down in foxholes at our assembly area a few miles north of the target zone, everyone in H Company stared up at the sky as an armada of more than a thousand American bombers passed overhead in a spectacle that was even more impressive than what I had witnessed on D-Day.

Flying at a low altitude for heavy bombers, the massive formation of aircraft was so large and thick it literally darkened the sky, producing a steady hum that must have been ominous for those enemy troops about to suffer bombardment. Taking it all in, I was thinking that American airpower was really going to help our forces on the ground.

Despite the continuing cloud cover, we were able to observe much of the ensuing action from our location. Though it was impossible for us to see the bombs dropping from the planes, we saw the smoke rising from their explosions as the ground shook around us.

The first couple of waves of bombers ran into furious resistance from German antiaircraft guns, which filled the sky with flak that burst in puffs of black smoke all around the planes. When hit, a few of the bombers exploded in fireballs from which no one appeared to escape. Several other damaged planes briefly remained in formation pouring smoke before they broke away and careened wildly down to earth in a blaze of fire and smoke.

Luckily, some of the crews managed to bail out after their bombers had been hit. We saw about a dozen white parachutes open up as airmen floated down to earth. In a horrific and heartrending sight, a few of the chutes caught fire from the burning fuel raining down from the damaged planes. Sadly, it turned out most of the parachuting airmen who made it safely to the ground landed in German-occupied territory and were taken prisoner.

Once the third wave of bombers arrived, the enemy flak guns were no longer firing, their gun crews either out of ammunition or dead. When the bombing ended a short time later, the Germans to our front could still fight, but they had suffered severe losses. Tragically, we later found out some of the bombs had also caused casualties among the forward-most American troops.

The conclusion of the morning's bombing mission signaled the start of Operation *Cobra*'s ground operation by VII Corps. As other American infantry divisions pushed into the now devastated German lines, the Big Red One readied itself to join the attack the next day, July 26. However, stiff enemy resistance delayed the start of our 2nd Battalion's advance until July 27.

Medical evacuation to England: July 27

By now, I had grown extremely concerned about my worsening medical condition. Since my first visit to H Company's aid station about a week earlier, the spidery web of infection had spread aggressively outward from the original wound at the corner of my mouth. It now completely covered the left side of my face, reaching almost up to my eye. It was clear the medicinal ointment provided by the medic had done nothing to halt the infection's advance.

Early on the morning of July 27, as H Company was making its final preparations to join the Operation *Cobra* offensive, I headed back to H Company's aid station to see the medic who had previously examined me. Shocked by the infection's rapid progress, he did not mince words.

"It looks like leprosy to me. We've gotta send you back to England."

After H Company's platoon sergeants and officers approved the medic's judgment, I was issued the necessary orders for my evacuation to England for medical treatment.

"We have arranged a flight for you," an officer informed me.

Up until this time, I had fully expected to participate in the coming big offensive, just sort of ignoring the worsening infection in my face in the hope it would improve. Though hating to leave my buddies just as our part of the operation was getting underway, I now acknowledged the severity of the infection urgently required more advanced medical care. My fear was that once I was healed and ready to return duty, I would be assigned to another outfit in which I did not know anyone, but there was nothing I could do about that.

With my evacuation orders in hand, I was driven by jeep to a field hospital a couple of miles away. In order to conceal the facility from any prowling enemy aircraft, the facility was camouflaged under netting interwoven with cloth strips of multiple earth-tone colors. Numerous doctors and nurses were scurrying among the tents where the wounded were being treated.

Despite the hectic conditions at the hospital, I was immediately taken to see an Army doctor. Following a 10-minute examination, the physician confirmed the diagnosis of H Company's medic and my evacuation orders.

"You need to go back to England. That's where you'll get the best treatment."

My fate now determined, I was directed to a large tent about 20 feet square. Smelling strongly of medicine, the tent provided an enclosed space to leave stretchers while the wounded awaited transportation further to the rear. Nearby, three Army ambulances were parked under the spreading branches of young trees to hide them from enemy observation.

Three wet, muddy soldiers with slight arm wounds waited alongside me as medics loaded two men on stretchers in the rear of an ambulance, fastening the stretchers onto the side of the vehicle. When the medics were finished, they directed the other three men and me to board the ambulance, where we took seats on a wooden bench that folded down from the side of the vehicle opposite the stretchers.

Within a half-hour of my arrival at the field hospital, we set off in the smelly, stuffy ambulance for a nearby airfield. The four of us on the bench in the back held on as best we could as the driver picked his way down what appeared to be a lightly traveled dirt path in a thickly wooded area.

When we reached the rudimentary airfield about an hour later that morning, a large transport plane was waiting on the runway. After the wounded on stretchers had been loaded, the four of us who could walk climbed aboard the aircraft, which was already occupied by about two dozen other wounded GIs. Placed along both sides of the fuselage, several were laying on stretchers and many of the guys appeared to be in really bad shape. Three Army nurses were working to make these men as comfortable as possible before the plane took off.

The rest of us were ushered forward to the closely spaced passenger seats at the front of the plane. Even knowing that my infection required urgent medical attention, it was hard for me not to feel a little out of place among these seriously wounded men as I claimed one of the cushioned seats. Leaning back, I instantly fell into a deep slumber before the plane was even off the ground.

Though the day's date never crossed my mind, July 27, 1944 marked my 21st birthday. At that moment, a flight back to England for medical treatment was the best gift the Army could have given me. Indeed, the trip might just have saved my life.

At that same moment, Operation *Cobra* was already achieving a breakthrough, ending the weeks of stalemate in Normandy. With the imminent collapse of the *Wehrmacht*'s defensive position in France, its military situation on the Western Front looked hopeless. Nazi Germany's defeat appeared close at hand, but it turned out the war was a long way from over.

CHAPTER 7

Victory in Normandy:
July 27–August 25, 1944

Recovery and return: July 27–August 2

Fingers gently massaging the left side of my face slowly brought me back to consciousness on board the now airborne plane, even as the sweet aroma of perfume made me wonder if I was dreaming.

Opening my eyes, I found myself looking up into the smiling face of a beautiful blonde, blue-eyed Army nurse. With my head cradled in her bosom, she was gently rubbing a medicinal salve into my infected left cheek. An angel sent by Heaven could hardly have performed the task better.

"Now you'll be okay, soldier. Just stay right here and I'll help get you well," her comforting voice reassured me.

If this is what a wound means, I might just go back to the front line and get wounded again, I mused.

The length of time that had elapsed since our boarding of the aircraft back in Normandy was unclear to me, but we landed at a military airfield in southern England only a short time after I awoke. Those of us who could walk were directed to an ambulance bound for an American military hospital near London.

When we arrived at the facility, I was shepherded into a long room with beds arranged along both walls. Within an hour of claiming one for myself, a couple of doctors came to evaluate me. Expressing deep concern over the spread of my infection, they immediately ordered a nurse to start applying a multitude of specialized ointments to my face. In the meantime, I got busy praying.

Under sustained assault from these almost hourly treatments, my condition rapidly began to improve. Within three days, the spidery web of infection that had enveloped my left cheek began to disappear.

As my face began to heal, I became more aware of the gravely wounded soldiers occupying the beds around me. Many had their heads thickly bound with bandages, while others had arms and legs that had been amputated.

During my third day at the hospital, a group of three or four nurses congregated around the bed of a soldier across the room from me. After examining him with all kinds of instruments for any sign of life, they sorrowfully shook their heads.

Pulling the sheet up over his face, the nurses rolled his body away on a gurney to make space for someone else.

How horrible. Somebody's mother and dad will be receiving the terrible news of their son's death, I sadly reflected.

By the sixth day, my face was fully healed. After evaluating me, a doctor announced, "Okay, soldier, you're well enough. You can go back to combat."

On learning of my imminent return to the front, I experienced the same intense foreboding I had felt just prior to D-Day. After several weeks in combat, I found it very hard to think about returning to the battlefield, but my anxiety was outweighed by a deep sense of duty and my hope of reuniting with my buddies.

By mid-morning of the next day, August 2, I was flying back across the English Channel on a transport plane packed with troops returning to Normandy. When it landed at a small airfield around noon, many of us immediately boarded a two-and-a-half-ton Army truck headed for a replacement depot.

While most GIs arriving at a replacement depot did not know the unit to which they would be assigned, I had learned I would be returning to my original outfit. No soldier wanted to be put with a bunch of strangers, so the news that I would be rejoining my buddies in H Company came as a big relief.

Because the roads between the airfield and the replacement depot were crowded with tanks and other military vehicles motoring toward the front, our trip in the canvas-covered rear of the truck was a slow one. Bouncing down the road with a dozen or so other guys seated on the truck's wooden benches could not be described as a pleasant experience, but it was a lot better than slogging the same distance on foot.

During these truck rides, we were at the driver's mercy as far as the timing of the stops for us to relieve ourselves. "Piss call!" one of the men would eventually plead, banging on the rear of the cab to get the driver to pull over.

The drivers of these unglamorous trucks were Black soldiers who had been assigned to service units in the segregated U.S. Army. While racial tension existed among American troops, it was almost completely absent aboard the trucks. On the contrary, we developed a friendly camaraderie and often joshed with our drivers, which helped to lighten everyone's mood.

"I'm gonna take you guys back to where the Germans are gonna shoot you," the driver would shout back at us with a wide grin.

"Oh yeah, well, we'll flatten your tires so you'll have to stay and fight with us," one of us would respond, as we ribbed the driver about how safe and easy he had it.

In truth, the skill of these overworked truck drivers never ceased to impress me. They expertly handled the big vehicles in all types of terrain and weather conditions, whether we were traveling along cratered roads, around boulders and over logs, or across muddy quagmires and swollen creeks. When winter arrived, we learned they were just as proficient driving on roads slickened by ice and through white-out blizzard conditions.

Suddenly, the war intruded into what had so far been an uneventful trip from the airfield to the replacement depot.

"Strafer!" our driver yelled as he slammed on the brakes. Alerted to the danger of a German fighter overhead, we all hastily spilled out of the rear of the truck and took cover in the drainage ditches that ran beside the road.

After a moment, the enemy aircraft flew off. We had been lucky. Despite Allied dominance of the skies, the *Luftwaffe* remained active. Even a lone German plane carrying out a strafing attack upon road traffic could be deadly.

Later that evening, just as it was starting to get dark, our truck finally pulled into a replacement depot close to the front line.

"All out!" the driver hollered. The six of us from the 1st Infantry Division who were returning to duty from medical treatment in England were met by guys from our various companies.

"Welcome back, Andy!" a familiar voice called out. Sitting in a jeep, Sergeant Carpenter was waiting to give me a lift back to the front. Tossing my gear in the back, I swung into the passenger seat.

During the short drive up to H Company's position, Carpenter brought me up to speed on the progress of Operation *Cobra* since my departure. In several days of hard fighting, American forces driving south had broken through the German lines in western Normandy, creating a fluid situation on the front that set the stage for further rapid advances. While Sergeant Carpenter's knowledge was largely limited to our company's immediate situation, wider military developments would shape all of our subsequent movements.

Exploiting the Allied breakthrough, a larger follow-on operation was just now getting underway. As the U.S. First Army advanced toward the southeast around the left rear of the German position, the newly activated U.S. Third Army was to swing further eastward through open country. If this thrust by the Third Army succeeded in linking up with an Anglo–Canadian force swinging around behind the Germans from the eastern end of the Normandy beachhead, the Allies had a chance to encircle the entire German Seventh Army.

In this operation, the 1st Infantry Division would be on the First Army's right flank, advancing beside the Third Army's left flank. Our 16th Infantry Regiment would serve as the covering force for the 1st Division's right flank at the junction of the First and Third Armies. As the 16th Infantry Regiment pressed forward, H Company would continue supporting the 2nd Battalion's infantry.

"We're doing mop-up operations. We lost some good men in the hedgerow country, but, thank goodness, we are moving out of that mess into more open country where our tanks can operate," Carpenter told me.

But this positive news was balanced by recent intelligence reporting a build-up of German heavy tanks, tank destroyers, and artillery in our sector of the front for an anticipated counterattack. We would have to stay alert.

Carpenter explained that, due to losses suffered by our company's first machine-gun platoon, our second platoon had "loaned" it a couple of men, leaving us a bit short on manpower. With our reduced numbers, I could expect to take a turn on the gun as soon as we arrived at our front-line position.

Le Petit-Celland: August 2/3

By the time Sergeant Carpenter and I reached H Company about half an hour after departing the replacement depot, it had already bivouacked for the night. Halted near the village of Le Petit-Celland, our outfit was now roughly 37 miles south of La Goucherie, the company's assembly area prior to the start Operation *Cobra*.

After passing company headquarters, Carpenter stopped the jeep about a hundred yards from the front line. Shouldering my pack, I walked the remaining distance to our squad's position, where Wayne Newsome was manning the gun.

"About time you came back, Andy. In about 10 minutes, it'll be your turn on the gun. With all that rest you've had, I'm sure you can handle a two-hour shift," he announced.

Hector Gonzalez was the next of my buddies to greet me from out of the descending darkness.

"Did they get that little spot on your face healed up?" he asked. The other squad members were already asleep beside their foxholes.

After setting down my gear and retrieving my .45 pistol, I claimed my old post behind the machine gun and studied our position in the fading daylight.

Situated on a slight rise in the ground, our gun emplacement was surrounded by low bushes, making it very difficult for any enemy observers to spot. Out in front of our position lay a somewhat lower open area about 50 yards wide. A clump of bushes off to the right marked the edge of the field of fire for our section's other machine gun. Supported by several riflemen from one of the 2nd Battalion's infantry companies, our two machine-gun squads held a strong position in the event of an enemy attack.

Late in my two-hour turn on gun duty, a German plane appeared in the night sky. At the sound of its engine, at least a half-dozen searchlights popped on and began tracking the intruder. Shimmering in the blue-white beams, the aircraft looked like a silver bug trying to flee into the darkness.

Roused by the lights, everyone in our squad got up to watch the spectacle playing out overhead.

"Good glory, what a sight!" Lincoln Welser exclaimed.

"Somebody sure as hell ought to hit that little guy!" commented Hector in his slow Southwestern drawl.

Abruptly, the still mostly black night became bright as day as more than a dozen antiaircraft guns opened up. Like some spectacular fireworks show on the Fourth of July, a brilliant barrage filled the horizon as the gunners chased the lone plane across the sky. The noise was no less mind-boggling.

The display was all the more amazing to me because I had no idea so many antiaircraft batteries were stationed around us. The demonstration of our strength was a revelation that instilled a powerful sense of comfort and confidence.

Ironically, even with all of our antiaircraft guns blazing away, the pilot somehow managed to evade the intense fire and buzz off to safety. With the night's entertainment over, everyone else got back to sleep.

Early the following morning, I went back on duty behind our gun. Still anticipating a German attack, I instead saw three American Sherman tanks come clanking slowly over a little rise about 200 yards in front of our position, moving from right to left. The lead tank had its turret rotated away from our location and began blasting round after round at an enemy target beyond my view.

At nearly the same instant, I heard the unmistakable bang-zip of a German 88-millimeter gun. A split second later, one of the Shermans cresting the small hill burst into flames with an ear-splitting blast.

Reacting to the threat of the unseen German 88, the two other Shermans immediately reversed gear in an attempt to retreat back the way they had come.

But just seconds after the first tank's destruction, an 88 round struck a second Sherman in the side, annihilating the tank in another fiery explosion.

Meanwhile, the third American tank managed to race away, escaping certain destruction. Behind it, the wrecks of our two Shermans were burning fiercely, emitting thick black clouds of smoke. It was gut-wrenching to think of the poor tank crews. I could only hope they had died instantly.

By now, everyone in my squad was staring at the burning tanks. Recovering from our immediate shock at what we had just witnessed, we began scrutinizing the area around us, searching for the source of the devastating fire.

To our utter surprise, just 30 yards to the right of our gun emplacement sat a massive German Tiger tank, with smoke still drifting from the muzzle of its long-barreled 88-millimeter gun. Nestled beneath small trees with low-hanging branches, the tank had been superbly camouflaged, leaving us completely oblivious to its presence during the preceding night.

Apparently, the Tiger's crew had not caught sight of us either as they lay in wait to ambush any American tanks venturing into the area. However, in the daylight, it seemed likely the enemy tankers would spot us at any moment.

Fortunately, a bazooka man had been assigned to our position for just such an eventuality. With a roughly five-foot-long metal tube that fired a rocket-propelled, cone-shaped projectile, the bazooka mainly served as an anti-tank weapon. And we had a bazooka man who really knew his business.

Emerging from a position a couple of dozen yards away from me, the bazooka man and a lieutenant sprinted toward a spot behind the Tiger. When they were about 20 yards from the rear of the tank, the men crouched down on their knees and the lieutenant loaded a rocket into the back end of the bazooka.

Seeing the two head for the tank, our entire squad and the nearby infantry charged forward a moment later. Though armed only with pistols, rifles, carbines, and grenade launchers, all of us wanted to help take down the Tiger.

But before we could go into action, the bazooka man fired off a rocket that blasted the tank at the base of its turret, right at the juncture where the turret rotates on the hull. While not penetrating the Tiger's thick armor, the explosion produced enough intense heat to melt the metal at this spot, sort of welding the turret in place. Although the tank's crew was now unable to traverse the turret, none of us knew what to expect as we approached the damaged vehicle.

An instant later, a small white flag popped up from the turret hatch, waving back and forth. To our astonishment, the tank's crew was surrendering without a fight. Excited to take the enemy tankers captive, all of us gathered around the Tiger, among the biggest battlewagons that Germany possessed.

The tank commander emerged first, followed by two other crewmen, which was fewer than the normal crew of five. Climbing down from the tank, the three men kept their hands high in the air. All were neatly attired in clean battle dress uniforms adorned with Nazi shoulder emblems and other insignia.

Speaking excellent English, the tank commander politely requested permission to remove his Luger pistol from his belt, which he presented to the lieutenant. While this act demonstrated a fine respect for military protocol, it was a disappointment to the rest of us who would have loved to have claimed that beautiful pistol for ourselves.

Military courtesies out of the way, the tank commander proceeded to inform us his crew had been watching as our squad had set up the machine gun the previous day. Rather than firing on our position, he instead decided to lie in wait for a larger target, which he had found when the three American Shermans had arrived on the scene that morning.

The commander next explained why he had decided to surrender to us without putting up a fight. First, in addition to having his turret disabled by the bazooka round, his tank had run out of fuel and could not move. Second, he told us he had experienced enough killing and simply wanted out of the war.

The German officer went on to share a little more about his background and how he had acquired his language skills. Raised in the port city of Hamburg, he had studied English in high school and college. Afterward, he had taken a job as a high school English teacher before entering military service.

At this moment, a second, much smaller German tank cranked up its engine and emerged from concealment about 40 yards from us. Incredibly, we had remained totally ignorant of the presence of this enemy tank as well.

Once again, our bazooka man and the lieutenant sprung into action, running across the field to take up a position behind the fleeing German tank.

As the rest of us looked on, the bazooka man crouched on one knee and took careful aim as the officer reloaded the weapon. A second later, the bazooka man fired a rocket smack into the tank's left tread.

With its tread blown off, all the tank could do was to drive around helplessly in a circle. After spinning around a couple of times, the tank's crew shut off their engine. When the two German tankers climbed out of the turret hatch with their hands up, they looked really scared. Although neither man spoke English, they relayed their thanks to us for not blowing them up.

By this point, Captain Irvine, H Company's commanding officer, arrived in his jeep to see what the commotion was all about. The destruction of the two Shermans was shocking, but two enemy tanks had also been knocked out and we had captured their crews. A lot had happened in a short time.

After the five Germans were sent to the rear for processing as prisoners of war, we had a chance to study the Tiger up close, which was a sight never to forget. Examining the heavily armored monster, I was amazed there could be an engine powerful enough to carry a vehicle of this size and weight at a decent speed.

As we had witnessed firsthand, the Tiger also possessed a deadly 88-millimeter cannon that was capable of punching a hole right through the armor of a Sherman. With its thick armor and powerful main gun, a Tiger completely outmatched a Sherman in any direct engagement. But whatever the relative advantages of the best German tanks versus an American Sherman, our side made up the difference in numbers.

"The trouble with the Americans is that every time we knock out one of your tanks, seven more come over the hill," one captured German told us. With the number of American tanks growing fast, we were beginning to win the day.

However, on this morning, our bazooka man was the hero. His fast action and skilled handling of his weapon had made the difference.

Of course, not all bazooka men were so competent. On another occasion, a German tank appeared nearby just as our machine-gun squad was moving into a new position. During the encounter, I was close enough to the GI with the bazooka and the officer in command to overhear their conversation.

"Kill that tank with your bazooka!" the officer shouted at the soldier.

"I don't know how to work it," he replied.

"There's a little gizmo that you pull," the officer instructed.

When the soldier finally managed to fire his bazooka, the rocket sailed right over the top of the German tank. Fearing he would be targeted by the tank after he missed, the bazooka man took off running.

Even if a bazooka man succeeded in hitting a German tank, its thick armor often protected the vehicle from any significant damage. We had indeed been very lucky that morning to have a bazooka man with us who really knew how to handle his weapon.

Juvigny: August 3–6

Later that day, we began cleaning our gear in preparation for the next mission. In the first phase, the Big Red One was given the assignment of seizing the commanding high ground near the key road junction at Mortain. For the 16th Infantry Regiment's part of this operation, the 2nd Battalion attached our second machine-gun platoon to E Company. Our specific objective was to secure an area near the just captured town of Juvigny-le-Tertre, located about four miles west-northwest of Mortain and about nine miles east of our current position at Le Petit-Celland.

While having no knowledge of these larger operational details or even the name of our next objective, we had heard that our intelligence on German troop strength in that sector was poor. However, the speed of the enemy's retreat from Normandy caused us to expect little in the way of significant opposition.

As our squad loaded our machine gun, tripod, ammo, and other gear into "Little Joe's" trailer that afternoon, we were excitedly anticipating the trip to the next town. To "save our strength," a tank commander had invited a portion of our second machine-gun platoon to ride aboard three Shermans waiting in a wooded area nearby. Though no enemy contact was anticipated, we slung our carbines over our shoulders and grabbed a few grenades from a crate in the trailer.

A dozen infantrymen from E Company had already claimed spots on board the lead tank, so those of us from the second machine-gun platoon and the remaining riflemen began boarding the other two tanks. Climbing up on a bigger-than-life Sherman is not the easiest thing to do, but we managed it with a boost from guys still on the ground and a tug from our buddies already aboard.

Late that afternoon, the three Shermans moved out with all of us clinging on for dear life. Leaving the wooded area, the tanks followed a slightly worn path to a gravel road about 50 yards away, where they turned east.

As I surveyed our small column from my vantage point on the third tank, the thought hit me that we offered a perfect target for an enemy anti-tank gunner. With the racket the engines and tracks were making, any Germans positioned along our route would certainly hear us coming.

While we had to struggle a bit to hold on as the tanks sped down the bumpy, narrow roads, the exhilaration of riding along in the open air made it easy to forget about any possible danger. But that complacency was soon shattered.

Just as the lead Sherman reached a road junction, there was a sudden blinding flash of an explosion that hurled bodies in every direction.

As the other two tanks jerked to a stop, all of us riding on board slid down from the vehicles and darted for whatever cover we could find. None of us wanted to meet the fate of the other GIs as we looked in horror at the blood and body parts scattered on and around the lead tank, which was emitting smoke.

When everyone had dismounted, the two remaining Shermans sped forward to the road junction. From there, the tank commanders quickly spotted a German 88-millimeter artillery gun among the trees ahead. In quick succession, the Shermans blasted four rounds at the enemy position, killing the gun's three-man crew and flipping the gun on its side.

In the meantime, my squad and I grabbed our machine gun from the jeep trailer and deployed it at the intersection to handle any German follow-up attack.

Once it became clear no attack was coming, we helped our medic with the grim task of collecting and stacking the bodies of more than a dozen men who had been riding atop the lead Sherman. Meanwhile, a crew member from one of the undamaged tanks managed to put out the blaze inside of that tank with a fire extinguisher. Miraculously, only two of its five-man crew had been killed. Later, a somber bunch of soldiers listened as Captain Irvine warned us we should never again ride on board a tank. As far as I know, no one in H Company ever did.

When the column of trucks carrying the rest of H Company reached the battered town of Juvigny about 11pm, the 2nd Battalion moved into position for a night attack near the town, with our second machine-gun platoon supporting E Company, the first machine-gun platoon supporting F Company, and the mortar platoon operating with G Company. Other than enemy mortar rounds falling to our front, there was not much opposition at first.

However, following our advance on foot to a location about half a mile north of Juvigny, we came under German small arms and machine-gun fire. As my squad deployed our machine gun in the darkness, I asked our gun carrier, Wayne Newsome, to stay close to me and be prepared to change locations quickly as directed by Sergeant Gentry, our squad's NCO. With fires in Juvigny lighting up the horizon behind us, our squad had to keep down to avoid the enemy bullets whizzing through the air, especially each of the three times that we had to reposition our gun during the course of that night's brief but sharp firefight.

By early that morning, our 2nd Battalion's initial objectives were achieved, but fighting against scattered pockets of enemy resistance persisted over the rest of August 4. Throughout the day, German artillery periodically targeted our positions in and around Juvigny. Meanwhile, our mortar platoon fired on a detachment of enemy troops and vehicles that was spotted on the move.

In the midst of that day's operations to secure the area around Juvigny, I had my first chance to observe a Sherman tank that had been modified with a sort of plow. Because standard Shermans could make little dent in the thick hedgerow walls, the Army had introduced what it called the "Culin hedgerow cutter" in July. Fitted with what resembled a fixed bulldozer blade mounted on the front of the hull, a Sherman could punch a gap in a hedgerow with repeated ramming, allowing other tanks and infantry to get off the dangerous roads.

When we observed these modified Shermans, it was apparent just how sturdy these hedgerows could be. Even with a steel blade up front, a charging Sherman would sometimes still bounce off a hedgerow's earthen walls, which was a pretty funny sight. However, by repeatedly running its blade sideways along the edge of the hedgerow, the tank could scrape away some of the outer layer of earth, rocks, and roots. After a few passes, the Sherman had gnawed away enough material to allow it to successfully smash through the hedgerow.

As the sun was setting that evening, Lieutenant Sutton informed our gun section that just-collected intelligence indicated German infiltrators would attempt to break through our lines in a particular sector. A good leader who knew his business, Sutton immediately pointed out two spots on "high ground" where he wanted our section's two machine guns mounted. Located about 40 yards apart, the assigned posts on the crest of a hedgerow would give each gunner an ideal vantage point from which to keep watch over the area's only open ground, a small field bounded by dense woods.

Darkness was fast descending as our two machine-gun squads moved into position. Once our guns were anchored amid the brush atop the hedgerow, the other gunner and I "zeroed in" our field of fire by shooting off a 30-second burst. In the darkness, we opted to use tracer rounds, which showed our fire crisscrossing 50 or so yards ahead. From our elevated gun positions we could see the other members of our squads down in foxholes where they could also take any enemy force under fire. Nearby, at least a dozen riflemen from E Company provided further support for our position. We had a perfect defensive setup.

With orders to "let the lead fly" if we saw any movement whatsoever, everyone remained on high alert as the night fell faster and darker than usual. Gradually, a fog rolled in to shroud the landscape, making us even more apprehensive. Staring into the darkness, we imagined movements and sounds that were not there. My finger rested on the trigger, ready to squeeze off a burst.

Perhaps a half-hour after we had taken up our posts, the shrill, unmistakable voice of a German soldier began repeatedly shouting the word "*Kamerad!*"—an obvious ruse he hoped would make us hold our fire.

Instead, all of us instantly opened up, with our machine guns delivering a withering stream of bullets from two angles. As our tracer fire crisscrossed, it illuminated the field to the extent that we could see enemy troops darting to the right and left and falling to the ground. Others fell back into the thick woods. Little return fire came our way.

In a few minutes, it was all over, though the rancid smell of cordite still hung heavy in the air. My first experience working with another gunner to hold off an enemy attack had happened fast and ended quickly. Despite the absence of any sound from the spot where the Germans had come, everyone remained wide awake, vigilant for another attempt to break through our lines. But the enemy must have recognized our sector was well defended and made no further effort.

When daylight finally came, two medics accompanied by two volunteers walked into the field to check for any survivors. Fifteen German troops had been killed, perhaps half of those who had carried out the attack. On receiving this news, I felt no immediate remorse for the enemy dead. Our mission had been a success.

Though German artillery continued to shell our positions in and around Juvigny on the morning of August 5, the firefight at the hedgerow turned out to be our last engagement near the town. Ordered to pull back from our front-line position to the vicinity of H Company's main command post, we wolfed down a hot meal and waited to redeploy to another part of the battlefield that was rapidly widening as American forces pushed out of Normandy.

By six that evening, our company was motoring slowly southward in a convoy of trucks. In every French village along the way, overjoyed civilians were enthusiastically celebrating the end of the Nazi occupation. After a couple of hours, we reached the 16th Infantry Regiment's assembly area near the just liberated town of Buais, roughly 11 miles south of Juvigny-le-Tertre.

Our orders to shift southward proved fateful. If the 1st Infantry Division had not been ordered out of the Juvigny/Mortain area, we would have been right in the teeth of a major German counterattack toward Avranches, which jumped off on August 7. In fact, the 30th Infantry Division, which had just relieved us, would play a critical role in the quick defeat of this enemy counterattack. But the Big Red One had an important mission of its own to complete as VII Corps pressed southeast into the left rear of the enemy position in Normandy.

Mayenne: August 6–13

When H Company set out from Buais for its next objective on the morning of August 6, we rolled up the canvas side curtains of our truck, not wanting to miss out on the joyous revelry in the newly liberated French communities along our route. As we waved at the residents of these towns and villages, they cheered and threw flowers. Our passage through these communities was brief, but the festive welcomes were emotional, thrilling, and unforgettable.

Following a 35-mile, four-hour trip, we arrived at the town of Mayenne, roughly 22 miles southeast of Buais. Situated astride the Mayenne River, the town had been taken by another American outfit the previous day. Crossing the river, the 16th Infantry Regiment established a defensive perimeter east of Mayenne, placing the 3rd Battalion in the north, the 1st Battalion in the center, and our 2nd Battalion on the south side of a semi-circle. With the Germans holding the town of Aron just three miles east of Mayenne, our regiment faced the danger of a counterattack from an enemy force seeking to regain lost ground.

Attached to F Company, our second machine-gun platoon and part of the mortar platoon took up a position east of Mayenne. Soon afterward, a couple of German tanks opened fire on our troops nearby. We could not see the action from our location, but we certainly heard it. We did see two American aircraft swoop down to tree level and release a couple of bombs. Later, we found out the bombs and an American tank destroyer had finished off the enemy attack.

Throughout our time at Mayenne, the *Wehrmacht*'s intentions in our sector remained uncertain. The Germans hit our front line with intermittent mortar and artillery fire and our artillery retaliated. The enemy also sent out patrols that attempted to penetrate our lines, while our patrols similarly probed their positions. However, intelligence reports about enemy troops and tanks concentrating for a large-scale assault, as well as the frequent alerts for German paratroopers and infiltrators, turned out not to amount to much.

Yet, there was occasional excitement on the front line. On August 10, a German smoke shell landed on our second platoon's position. Figuring the shell might have been targeted to mark our location for an imminent enemy artillery barrage, we immediately pulled back a short distance. When nothing happened for an hour or so, we returned to resume our original positions.

Meanwhile, the *Luftwaffe*'s raids at night accomplished little. Though a few bombs landed in the vicinity of our position near Mayenne, these enemy sorties were more of a nuisance than a real threat, thanks to the protection we received from the hardworking crews manning our antiaircraft batteries.

But a special sort of anxiety came over us whenever our ears picked up the distinctive sound of the unmanned, pulsejet-propelled German V-1 (Vengeance Weapon 1) missiles, which made an odd noise like a sputtering engine. Commonly known as "buzz bombs," these were part of Hitler's so-called "Wonder Weapons." We had first heard of the V-1 in the second half of June, but at first had no real idea of the destructive power of its warhead.

Launched from inside German-occupied France, a couple of dozen of these buzz bombs had flown over us as they traveled toward England. Packed with a ton of explosives, a V-1 would plunge to earth when it ran out of fuel, reaping destruction on some random location in London or another city in southern England, targets big enough for the highly inaccurate weapon to hit.

On really clear days, we could observe the buzz bombs up in the sky, but most passed over our lines at night. If a V-1's sputtering motor stopped because it had prematurely run out of fuel or experienced some type of malfunction, the anxiety produced by the weapon turned into real fear.

One night in mid-August, a buzz bomb's motor cut off almost right over our position, causing a mad scramble for cover in any hole available. Its subsequent explosion a mile or so away was as loud as anything I ever heard.

The next morning, several of us obtained permission to borrow our squad's jeep "Little Joe" to search for the spot where the V-1 had struck. It did not take us long to locate a smoking crater perhaps 50 feet or more across with an even larger blast radius. The French living nearby told us the explosion had destroyed a farmhouse, killing everybody inside. The obliteration was so complete that no recognizable debris from the home remained visible.

Climax of the battle of the Falaise Pocket: August 13–18

By August 12, the German troops in Aron were withdrawing. While we had maintained a defensive posture during the week-long standoff near Mayenne, events elsewhere were moving fast. After racing eastward toward Paris, the U.S. Third Army had swung northeast toward Argentan. Meanwhile, British and Canadian units were driving southward toward Falaise, a dozen miles northwest of Argentan. This steadily narrowing gap between the two Allied forces provided the *Wehrmacht's* only escape route to the east.

As part of the U.S. First Army's VII Corps, the 1st Infantry Division would now press north-northeast behind American tank units, moving parallel to the advance of the Third Army further east. Within this larger operation, the objective for the 16th Infantry Regiment would be the high ground near the village of La Sauvagère, located about two dozen miles north of Mayenne.

As always, we knew next to nothing about the big picture when H Company departed our position near Mayenne early on the morning of August 13. Less than two hours later, our truck convoy halted a half-dozen miles north-northwest of Mayenne at a location near the town of Oisseau, where we were given an opportunity to rest and wash. After a hot supper that evening, we boarded trucks for a further 15-mile, three-and-a-half-hour ride toward our objective before halting for the night.

On the ensuing evening of August 14, our second machine-gun platoon loaded aboard trucks with E Company, while the first platoon traveled with G Company. After motoring another 11 miles, we disembarked a little north of the town of La Ferté-Macé and then proceeded northeast on foot for another three miles. By 9pm that night, we reached our initial objective a couple of hundred yards southeast of La Sauvagère, a town taken earlier that same day.

On August 15, our second platoon pressed forward a bit further with the infantry before halting. After supper, we boarded jeeps and drove the last couple of miles to our assigned front-line position, which we reached a little later that night. Now roughly 18 miles south-southeast of Falaise and 18 miles east-southeast of Argentan, we were posted at the southwestern edge of the Falaise Pocket from which the Germans were attempting to break out to the east.

When the 2nd Battalion's assault kicked off early on the morning of August 16, our second machine-gun platoon advanced in support of E Company. With only limited and disorganized enemy resistance to our front, we pushed forward rapidly, but claimed only a few German prisoners in the process. Within a short time, our battalion seized the attack's main objective, the small town of Le Ménil-de-Briouze, located three and a half miles north of La Sauvagère.

On August 17, as German artillery and mortar shells continued dropping around us, British units coming down from the north reached our lines as part of the linkup of Allied forces. That afternoon, a small party of British soldiers halted on the side of the road just yards from our squad's gun position.

"I say there, Yanks, we're having a spot of tea. Come on over," one of the men shouted across to us.

Strolling over, we joined half a dozen Brits in a small circle, savoring the freshly brewed tea. Amazingly, these fellows had even scrounged up a few of the delicious muffin-like crumpets to make it a proper English tea.

Despite the German artillery rounds exploding nearby and enemy aircraft buzzing overhead, the British troops retained their relaxed carefree manner. During the next several hours, we inspected each other's weapons, swapped battle stories, and talked of home. It almost seemed like a victory celebration.

Fighting in the area had not completely ended, but our part of the battle of the Falaise Pocket concluded on August 18. Though many of the retreating Germans had managed to escape to the east before the pocket was sealed, the *Wehrmacht*'s Seventh Army and Fifth Panzer Army had been shattered. Beyond the tens of thousands of German troops killed or taken prisoner, an enormous quantity of enemy equipment had been destroyed or abandoned. With little organized German resistance left, France was now there for the taking.

But our great triumph in Normandy had come at a terrible price in Allied and civilian casualties. The fighting had also forced thousands of French refugees onto the roads. Elderly men and women, babies cradled in the arms of a parent, crippled children barely able to walk, and sick people transported in wheelbarrows flowed away from the battlefield like a swollen river. Because many of the young children were too tired to walk but too heavy to carry, their parents had to tug them along by an arm or hand as their heels dragged in the dirt. Utter exhaustion and despair marked every face.

How would these refugees keep warm? What would they eat? Where would they find shelter?

Their plight was heartbreaking. Hundreds would likely die. Thousands would never go back home. If they did eventually attempt to return home, many would find only ruins in the wake of the fighting.

War left a bleak scene of utter desolation. The huge artillery barrages and aerial bombardments had reaped horrible devastation upon the French countryside, obliterating houses, barns, fences, trees and every other landmark. Sometimes, the fires ignited by these barrages were still burning days later when we passed what had been farmhouses and villages. Solitary chimneys, collapsed walls, and piles of brick offered the only evidence of prior human habitation.

The battlefield was littered with bloated corpses of unburied German bodies and still-smoldering smashed vehicles and equipment. The erect legs of toppled cattle and swollen horse carcasses stood out above the flat wasteland. Rotting in the summer heat, the dead exuded a nauseating stench worse than anything I had ever imagined. The tragic, grisly aftermath of the fighting reinforced the urgency of bringing the war to a victorious end.

Rest area near Le Ménil-de-Briouze: August 18–25

On August 18, with the fighting in our sector over, the three regiments of the Big Red One received a week-long break from combat operations. Arriving at H Company's bivouac area just east of the newly won town of Le Ménil-de-Briouze, we took up temporary quarters in tents.

At two that afternoon, our company's paymaster began shelling out each GI's monthly salary from the stacks of American currency piled beside him. During combat, we would be ordered to the rear a few at a time to receive our money, but the absence of any fighting meant everyone queued up to get paid. It was a fun time with lots of joking about what we would do with our money.

As an unmarried Private First Class serving overseas, my annual salary while in combat was about $900, which meant a monthly paycheck of about $75. However, because I had directed that a portion of my pay be sent home to my parents on Signal Mountain to help them out financially, I received a smaller amount of cash on paydays. Quite a few GIs wanted their full pay so they would have cash to gamble or spend in other ways, but I did not gamble. Most of the time, I only carried around a few bucks. Indeed, I had my D-Day "invasion money" stuffed in my pocket for months.

War souvenirs were about the only items on which I was tempted to spend my cash. In particular, I was very interested in buying three mint-condition, 16-inch-long daggers from a guy in our platoon who had liberated them from captured German troops. With beautiful ribbon-wrapped handles and an engraving of Hitler's signature, they were a really unique war trophy. The soldier refused to sell his prized daggers, but soon lost them in a game of poker.

"I don't want these things," the winner announced when he claimed the daggers. Relaxing nearby, I saw my chance.

"Well, how much would you charge for them?" I inquired.

"I'll give 'em to you for a hundred bucks a piece," the GI responded. His price was steep, but my desire to acquire the three daggers led me to agree to an amount equal to four months of my combat pay before deductions. I also had to toss in a large carton of cigarettes, which was easy for me since I did not smoke.

After the distribution of our pay, most of the rest of August 18 and the next morning were spent putting our equipment in "apple pie" order for a weapons inspection at 11am on August 19. Once that was over, a ration of champagne was issued to each man in honor of our victory in Normandy. The war might not yet be won, but we all celebrated like the hard part was already over. Not a drinker myself, I happily sold my glass and made a quick five bucks.

Following a surprisingly large turnout for an outdoor worship service on Sunday, August 20, the remainder of our week of R&R included a mix of training and leisure. Our morning and afternoon drills mainly involved physical exercise to keep us fit for a return to action. During this period, I interacted with a couple of teenaged kids who had been assigned to H Company's other machine-gun platoon just prior to the start of Operation *Cobra*. Though I had only turned 21 less than a month earlier, these younger replacements jokingly called me "Pop," which made me sound like some old, grizzled veteran. For the rest of the war, that remained my name among the younger guys in our outfit.

As soon as we had free time, bathing in makeshift showers was the first priority, but washing our clothes ran a close second. After laundering items in large Army-issued wash tubs, we hung everything out to dry, which took a while since sunshine was in short supply. Rain kept us stuck in our tents for part of the week, but that gave us the chance to catch up on much-needed sleep. For recreation, I competed against some of the other men in horseshoes and watched movies. If we wanted something to eat outside of our regular Army chow, the Red Cross was on hand with donuts, coffee, and small chocolates.

On an outing from our rest area near Le Ménil-de-Briouze, a group of us from H Company ran across a large party of soldiers from a Canadian armored outfit. We approached them just as they were preparing to chop down a big tree for use in a construction project back at their encampment some distance away.

To carry out the task, one of their officers selected a short, but tough-as-iron former lumberjack. Picking up an axe, the soldier cautioned the other troops.

"You fellas better move your equipment. You just need to move your equipment a little, because this tree's gonna fall about five feet from where you're sitting. As soon as I fell this tree, I'll have a beer," he announced.

While we looked on in amazement, the guy proceeded to chop through the foot-thick trunk in a matter of perhaps 60 seconds. His well-aimed blows toppled the tree exactly where he had indicated.

"Hey, Mac, you want that beer?" one of the Canadians asked afterward.

"I believe I'll have a glass," the soldier responded, happy to quaff down a small reward for what seemed like an almost superhuman feat.

In the meantime, several of the Canadian soldiers speedily stripped the branches off the fallen tree and hefted the trunk up onto the side of a bulldozer to haul it back to their camp. With the show over, we headed back to our rest area.

Our brief encounters with the British and Canadian troops left me with a positive impression of our Allies, who possessed a military professionalism equal to our own.

Likewise, I did not observe any distinctions in the fighting quality of American soldiers from different parts of the United States. Most GIs were fighters and in it to win, even as their units suffered casualties.

As we were preparing to return to action at the end of that week, BBC radio reports of Allied advances boosted everyone's spirits. The *Wehrmacht* was now in a rapid, general retreat eastward through France toward Germany.

Believing we faced a largely beaten enemy, it seemed all that remained was a sort of giant mopping-up operation. Anxious to get on with the big drive toward final victory, we were as eager and optimistic as any soldiers could be. If everything went as hoped, the war might even be over before Christmas.

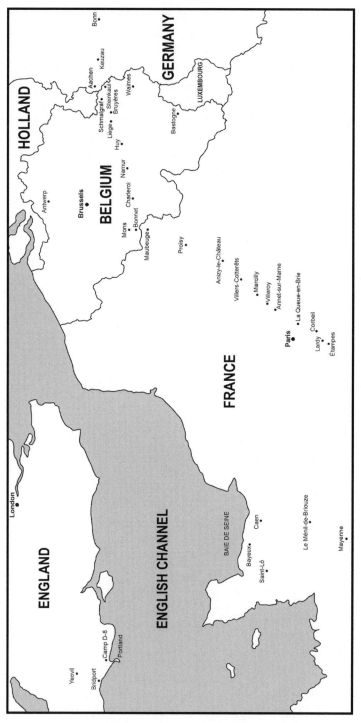

Map 2: The Campaign to the German Frontier

CHAPTER 8

The Race across France: August 25–September 7, 1944

Chasing the Germans: August 25–September 3

Early on the morning of August 25, H Company motored out of our rest area near Le Ménil-de-Briouze in a column of trucks. As we traveled eastward, our initial enthusiasm, sparked by the rumor we were headed for Paris, was quickly replaced by a mounting impatience to get the trip over. Jammed together in the canvas-covered truck bed, we soon began sweating heavily in the summer heat. Far worse were the exhaust fumes and constant dust that severely irritated our eyes and throats and left all of us feeling half-sick.

The end finally came 11 hours and 162 road miles later when we reached the 1st Infantry Division's assembly area that evening. Located about a mile north of the town of Lardy, our new bivouac area was roughly 120 miles east of Le Ménil-de-Briouze and two dozen miles south of the center of Paris. After the long, hard-fought slog through Normandy, we had leapt a third of the way across France in just a single day's drive.

As we downed a hot supper after setting up camp, all of us were convinced our outfit would be the first into Paris. Despite our expectations of a difficult battle for the French capital, there was a lot of excitement at the prospect of seeing the famous city. Naturally, everyone was upset to learn we would not be entering Paris, which had, in fact, been liberated that same day.

While we continued to remain ignorant of the larger military developments, our arrival south of the city was one small part of a gigantic shift eastward by the Allies. With *Wehrmacht* units in the west in disorganized retreat, Allied forces were preparing to advance on a broad front across eastern France and Belgium. The new campaign's objective was to breach the *Westwall* defensive fortifications running along Germany's western border and push to the Rhine beyond.

In this offensive, the U.S. First Army would drive northeastward from its position south of Paris with the dual mission of intercepting German troops retreating through northern France and preventing the establishment of a Meuse River defense line by the enemy. The First Army's VII Corps would advance with the fast-moving 3rd Armored Division out front, the 9th Infantry Division on the right, and the

1st Infantry Division's three regiments on the left. Operating on the far left of the Big Red One at the boundary between the First Army's VII Corps and V Corps, our 16th Infantry Regiment's assignment was to push forward as fast as possible, mopping up any pockets of German resistance bypassed by our armor.

Leaving our position near Lardy late on the afternoon of August 26, H Company set out on a 10-mile trek in the sweltering heat. With sweat stinging our eyes and soaking our clothing, a lot of guys were grumbling and cussing, while some struggled to keep up. Four hours later, we reached our assigned objective, roughly nine miles northeast of our jumping-off point and about 17 miles south of the center of Paris. Three miles to the east of our new position was the town of Corbeil, a vital crossing point on the Seine.

The following afternoon, our second platoon moved out aboard jeeps, advancing in support of G Company. Though trucks typically conveyed us over longer distances, jeeps were our preferred mode of transportation since they allowed us to ride in the fresh air. While men from our platoon's four machine-gun squads could cram into the four jeeps assigned to our squads, these jeeps also had to pull trailers. With the limited space on our existing complement of jeeps, additional vehicles were required in order to transport the entire platoon.

Crossing the Seine, we sped north. Covering 23 road miles in three hours, we reached our objective that evening without encountering enemy opposition. Halting a couple of miles north of the town of La Queue-en-Brie, we were about 16 miles north-northeast of our last position and less than a dozen miles east-southeast of the center of Paris.

Led by tanks, the 2nd Battalion resumed its rapid drive northeast early on the afternoon of August 28, with E and G Companies and our company's two machine-gun platoons flanking the advance. On reaching the outskirts of Annet-sur-Marne 10 miles northeast of our last position, a portion of our platoon entered the town and was ambushed by at least a couple hundred enemy troops. The encircled men were rescued when the 2nd Battalion's infantry and supporting tanks punched a gap through the German lines, but the episode was a sharp reminder of the ongoing danger posed by the enemy.

Proceeding another five miles northeast from Annet-sur-Marne, we halted for the evening in the village of Villeroy, located roughly 15 miles north-northeast of that day's starting point at La Queue-en-Brie. Despite little sign of the enemy, we dug out foxholes for the night. This was probably a good decision as a couple of German tanks were reported to be in our vicinity on the morning of August 29.

By noon that same day, we were again advancing northeastward. Covering about 15 miles on foot and aboard vehicles, we arrived at Marcilly, a town on an important east-west highway. Situated about five and a half miles northeast of Villeroy, we were now 27 miles east-northeast of the center of Paris.

Getting back on the road early on the morning of August 30, we made a further big leap, with our second machine-gun platoon attached to F Company. A couple of hours later, we reached the town of Villers-Cotterêts, an important crossroads located roughly 18 miles north-northeast of Marcilly.

Searching the forest around Villers-Cotterêts, we came across a sprawling enemy supply dump that must have been one of the *Wehrmacht's* major depots for the western front. Gear and ammo had been stockpiled in what seemed to be an endless number of wooden storage huts constructed along a network of narrow access roads concealed in the woods.

During the middle of the night, a series of explosions erupted in the forest. In the morning, we discovered the storage huts had been systematically obliterated by German demolition experts. Only rows of craters remained.

Later that same morning of August 31, H Company was again on the move. As we rode through the Soissons area on our way to our next objective, we were reminded that the 1st Infantry Division had fought in this same spot in 1918 during World War I. The contrast between our own rapid advance and their bitter struggle for every inch of ground could not have been starker.

After motoring some 35 miles, we halted late that afternoon at Anizy-le-Château, located roughly two dozen miles northeast of our previous position at Villers-Cotterêts and some 67 miles northeast of the center of Paris. Following the series of big leaps over the preceding five days that had carried us some 85 miles northeast of our starting point at Lardy southeast of Paris, we bivouacked at Anizy-le-Château for a couple of nights, which permitted us to enjoy a brief rest.

Campaigning through France

Each day of the three months since D-Day was different in its details, but every day seemed much like the last, so that days and times largely lost their meaning for us. Every aspect of our lives was dictated by the Army: when we slept, when we woke, and when and what we ate. We simply followed orders, moving when directed and fighting where we ran into the enemy.

Though we had spent a lot more time advancing on board jeeps and trucks since leaving Normandy, most of the past three months had involved us trudging forward on foot, strung out in columns with two men abreast on either side of a road. We were footsloggers and no name better described life in the infantry.

Often advancing miles on foot for several days in a row with little sleep, we halted only for brief breaks every couple of hours. No matter what the weather that summer, there was no let-up in our advance whenever the enemy was in retreat. With the sun beating down on us, maintaining a swift pace was a real trial. Perspiration ran into our bleary, sleep-deprived eyes and poured down our backs. The heat sapped our strength, magnifying the weight of our gear. At times, the steel legs of the 53-pound tripod I lugged on my shoulders caused my sweat-soaked jacket to chafe against my neck until the skin was raw.

When rain fell, our dusty treks turned into slogs. Eventually, I grew inured to the sensation of water oozing between my toes inside my waterlogged leather boots. If we had to cross muddy ground, I chided the guys carrying the gun and ammo to make sure to protect their equipment, fearing that failure to do so might cause the machine gun to jam the next time we went into action.

During a rapid advance on foot, it was hard to find a spare moment for even the most basic task, whether that was retying my laces before a boot became too loose, clearing the stinging sweat from around my eyes, or wiping the fogged-up lenses of my glasses, something that was a constant problem for me. Mounting exhaustion left my muscles and bones screaming for a longer rest that would allow me to put down the tripod down for even a few minutes.

Even a simple misstep by just one soldier could throw off the pace of the entire squad. Trying to regain your balance after stumbling on a rock or root required a lot more energy because of our heavy gear. Yet whether our pace temporarily slowed due to a stumble or our sheer fatigue, there was no stopping outside of the 20-minute rest breaks which were all too rare and all too short compared to the hours of marching. These halts gave me only a moment to relieve myself and try to wipe the dust or mud from my glasses with grimy hands and fingers. In no time, we were on our feet striding forward again.

Each day now took us through a succession of French villages and towns that erupted in spontaneous celebrations when we arrived. Emerging from their cellars, jubilant and boisterous residents poured into the streets loudly singing France's national anthem "The Marseillaise." Weeping with joy and wearing big smiles, everyone shouted in English, "Thank you! Thank you!" Several in the ecstatic crowds even waved small American flags they had somehow acquired.

When we were on foot, adults and children would trot alongside our column, often throwing flowers at us. Occasionally, the women and kids would press forward to insert flowers into our jacket pockets, plant a kiss on our cheeks, or throw their arms around us, an embrace which we awkwardly accommodated, encumbered as we were with all our gear. Accepting their gifts of homemade cookies, pastries, and other tasty delicacies particularly tested my dexterity, since I had to keep my hands clenched around the front legs of the machine gun's tripod balanced on my shoulders. Realizing my difficulty, one elderly lady with tears streaming down her face slipped a little loaf of cinnamon bread into my jacket pocket, saying "Thank you!" in my ear as she did so.

Though the residents offered us food or wine, their own condition was often as miserable as that of the refugees who filled the roads. Yet the preceding years of hardship under German rule seemed only to swell their outpouring of gratitude. These emotional spectacles left me with a deep affection for the French and, later, the

Belgian people. Of course, such a sentiment comes easily when people are shouting their gratitude, throwing flowers at you, hugging you, and generally lauding you as a hero.

Surprisingly, before the start of our campaign in Europe, we had not really thought of ourselves as "liberators" or anticipated the response we would receive from people who had suffered under four long years of Nazi occupation. Our focus was on defeating the Germans, but the unbounded joy displayed so passionately and eloquently in the faces, words, and tears of the liberated made a lasting impression on us. The experience imparted real meaning to freedom and reaffirmed the justice of our cause in a way nothing else could have.

Leaving behind a French village, we continued to plod forward in an endless, wearying series of advances. Our extreme exhaustion and discomfort made our progress through the gauntlet of minefields, snipers, enemy machine-gun nests, and mortar and artillery fire all the more grueling and treacherous. By distracting us, our weariness caused us to pay inadequate heed to the enemy, who were well hidden in the brush or in earthen dugouts.

The mind-numbing fatigue left me apathetic to what might be happening around me, even when we came under enemy fire. In this dog-tired state, I experienced the true exhilaration of real war, the high-stakes game of it all. It was us against the enemy with no one knowing when his number was up. Feeling the contest and competition, I fell into a sort of fearless fatalism.

To hell with the whiz and zing of enemy bullets flying near my head! To hell with hitting the ground, getting up, and hitting the ground again and again to avoid bullets and shell shrapnel!

Encountering the enemy

Trekking along the path to one small French village, we passed the lifeless body of an American infantryman lying face down where he had been shot. Still wearing his glasses, he looked fresh and alive. The rifle gripped in his hands made it appear as if he was awaiting orders to go into action. He served as another reminder that, despite the speed of our advance and the German retreat, we were still in a war. If you take ground, somebody pays for it with his life.

Though many soldiers fell victim to cleverly planted enemy mines, the German snipers were our most dreaded foe and killed many an American GI. Combat always triggered a certain level of fear, but nothing provoked as much anxiety as our encounters with a well-hidden enemy sharpshooter.

Ever since our first run-in with the sniper back in Colleville, a particular trepidation would descend upon us whenever we entered a recently captured village, town, or city. The fear produced by an invisible marksman who could deliver death with such precision was worse than what we experienced when confronting a tank. On hearing the creaking approach of a tank, you could hide or even try to ambush it. A sniper usually only made his presence known when someone in our outfit was hit.

That first shot marked the start of our hunt for the sharpshooter. Whether he was concealed up in a hayloft of a barn, behind the shattered window of a building, or amid the foliage of a tree, this single soldier could potentially stall our advance for an hour or more. If we were lucky, one of our guys would eventually spot a wisp of smoke rising from the muzzle of his rifle. However, most of the time, the German snipers remained undetectable. In this situation, our tremendous advantage in firepower was of limited utility. We could only saturate the most likely enemy positions with heavy fire and hope to see a lifeless body appear or some other evidence of the sharpshooter's elimination.

Attached to the 2nd Battalion's rifle companies, we often joined in sweeps of villages for enemy troops. Though rarely encountering significant opposition during these searches, we always had to remain alert. In a flash, a routine inspection of a home could abruptly break out into a skirmish.

At times, our advance ran headlong into a rearguard of a dozen or so enemy troops, bringing on a sharp engagement. In other instances, we unknowingly bypassed a hidden enemy force, which would then ambush us from the rear. Ordered into action, our section's two-gun squads would come together from our strung-out column of march. As we deployed our machine guns to support the infantry, the size of the enemy force confronting us was rarely clear. But whatever the number of troops, the Germans typically put up a hard fight.

Sergeant Gentry would direct each of our two squads where to place our guns, posting us behind brush, rocks, or whatever nearby cover was at hand. By coordinating our positions at right angles about 40 yards apart, we achieved crisscrossing fields of fire over a large zone. Throughout the firefight, Gentry would move continuously between our guns, hollering commands and ordering us to shift to a new firing position as necessary. We respected this willingness of our NCOs to be right there with us in the thick of combat, likewise exposing themselves to enemy fire.

While German rearguards or even localized counterattacks took a small but deadly toll on us, most of these skirmishes did not involve a heavy exchange of fire and lasted less than 30 minutes. Once the enemy had retreated, surrendered, or been eliminated, our infantry would resume advancing. If our company's machine guns and mortars were unable to overcome the German resistance, we would request artillery fire to destroy the enemy's position.

In one instance, G-2 intelligence informed us a particular swathe of trees concealed a German rearguard.

"Set up these two machine guns and tear those woods apart!" the sergeant ordered. As soon as our guns were deployed, we blasted the thick foliage. Within a couple of minutes, the Germans came out with their arms raised in surrender.

Another time, Captain Irvine directed us into action after receiving word an entire company of German troops was assembling in a boulder strewn field a couple of hundred yards from our position. Opening fire with both of our section's machine guns, we could see our tracer rounds glancing off the huge boulders the Germans were hiding behind. At 200 yards, it was difficult for us to observe the enemy troops, which allowed them to crawl among the boulders and escape to the rear. Though we were not organized for an attack to take advantage of their retreat, the threat had at least been driven off.

Occasionally, the Germans engaged us with their own famous machine gun, the MG 42 (*Maschinengewehr 42*). With a sound that resembled a greatly amplified ripping of paper, the rate of fire of the MG 42 was so high it was impossible to distinguish the individual rounds. It was a real terrorizer that would undoubtedly cut a man in two if he was caught in front of it.

Though our M1917A1 .30 Caliber Water-cooled Machine Gun possessed a rate of fire less than half that of the MG42, our weapon was extremely accurate and utilized a powerful bullet. Perhaps it is normal that a soldier comes to believe his weapon is the most wonderful piece of equipment in existence since he depends on it, but even captured Germans told us they considered our machine gun to be a harder-hitting weapon. They also stated our bullets were more durable than their own, enabling our rounds to hold together longer without fragmenting. If we targeted a dozen rounds into an area concealing the enemy, we were confident our gun would wipe out the target.

In one incident, Captain Irvine received a report that a German machine-gun unit very similar to ours was concealed among a cluster of small trees very near where we had halted for the night. Quickly assembling our section's two machine guns, we began blazing away at the forest. Our bullets struck the trunks about three feet from the ground, speedily felling the trees with chainsaw-like precision. After about five minutes, the Germans raised a white flag to give up. Our prisoners told us they had been lying on the ground awaiting the signal to attack but were glad to surrender after coming under heavy fire.

On yet another occasion, we learned that a group of German soldiers were gathered inside a small frame house. As soon as I had claimed my spot behind the gun, a German *Kübelwagen* (the *Wehrmacht*'s equivalent of a jeep) appeared behind the house, where the driver parked the vehicle so that its front half was visible from our position. Opening up with my gun, I targeted the exposed portion with three or four long bursts. As the hood of the *Kübelwagen* flew up in the air, the engine caught on fire and both front tires were blown out, leaving the vehicle a total wreck. My machine-gun fire must have caused the Germans inside the house to retreat, since we saw no further sign of them afterward.

Of course, the threat posed by our firepower always made the machine gun a top target for the enemy. Beyond a concern for my own physical safety, my chief apprehension was for the rubber condensing hose, which led down to the water chest. If the hose was severed by a bullet or shrapnel and I continued to fire, the water circulating inside the barrel's water jacket would rapidly evaporate away, producing a cloud of steam that would reveal our gun position to the enemy. More importantly, the gun would quickly overheat without water, possibly warping the barrel and rendering the weapon useless.

German fire severed the hose once in France and a couple of more times later in the war. When this happened, I was forced to cease firing almost completely. Within a minute, another member of our squad crawled forward to attach a replacement hose. But because I was unable to fire our machine gun, the enemy's fire on our position was always exceptionally heavy during this interval, making the installation of a new hose an especially terrifying ordeal.

Even with the water circulating properly, the machine gun could still overheat if the gunner failed to monitor the weapon carefully. Just squeezing off three long, 30-round bursts would cause the water inside the gun's jacket to begin boiling noisily, but we had learned how to cope with this danger during our training in Alabama and England. By tapping the gun's trigger in three to five second bursts, the gunner could minimize the risk of the weapon overheating as well as conserve ammo. These short bursts of fire allowed the gun a few seconds to cool, while still forcing enemy troops to keep their heads down. This firing technique was standard practice, unless the fighting grew extremely intense, which was seldom the case in France.

While we occasionally ran into German tanks in France after leaving Normandy, they did not generate the same degree of terror as they had during our first encounters. Tanks were fearsome machines, but, once they had fired and exposed their location, we could take evasive action and request artillery support to counter them, assuming we survived that first round.

While our artillery provided most of the heavy fire support for our infantry operations, the speed of the recent phase of our campaign across France did not always allow the gun crews adequate time to set up their batteries. In this situation, our forward observers could call in close air support, which would arrive swiftly when the sky was clear. Within minutes, several P-38 Lightnings, P-47 Thunderbolts, or P-51 Mustangs would sweep in low to wreak terrible havoc on enemy troop concentrations and strongpoints with bombs, rockets, and strafing, sometimes hitting targets just 50 yards ahead of us.

Because of the dominance of Allied airpower, the *Luftwaffe* possessed only a very limited ability to threaten us in the same way, but German artillery presented a real and ever-present danger. After the first few weeks in combat, I developed a knack for deciphering the various noises of the battlefield, staying particularly alert for the thump of artillery firing in the distance.

Within a couple of seconds, the whistle of an incoming round became audible. If the whistle grew louder, I automatically darted for cover in the ditch beside the road or a natural furrow in the ground. If an artillery barrage caught us out in the open where there was no cover, I threw myself flat against the ground, pressing my body into the earth.

If the initial round struck somewhere in the distance, I figured I was safe. If the first shell landed within 30 yards of me, I knew I would be in danger if further rounds followed—and they usually did. On more than one occasion, members of our machine-gun platoon were killed by artillery fire. But, like all aspects of combat, shellfire was something to which we grew accustomed, though the fear of getting killed never disappeared.

War meant digging in just as much as it meant attacking. Any time we came under artillery or mortar fire, or a firefight was anticipated, everyone entrenched. We quickly learned how to dig a foxhole while lying on our stomachs under fire. Shoveling out one hole after another along our route of advance, we came to know more about European soils than any county agricultural agent in America would ever learn about the local soils back home.

That summer, we were often digging in under a driving rain that turned the earth into a muddy quagmire. But the weather did not matter. Our exhaustion did not matter. Whatever the difficulties, a soldier does anything he can to escape below ground when bullets or shrapnel are whizzing through the air. Your survival often depended on digging out a foxhole that was large enough and deep enough to offer you a measure of protection.

A footslogger's life

Death usually came suddenly. A moment before, we had been cheerfully joking together about our shared hardships. An instant later, the other guy was gone, his blood mixing with the ground under his body. Whether a close buddy or a stranger, the death of a fellow GI affected all of us powerfully, perhaps because we knew it could just as easily have been our turn. The loss of a man in our squad was always deeply felt, but there was little time for us to mourn.

Our squad would usually receive a replacement within a few days. But even with the steady arrival of replacements, there were many times that we had to operate at less than our full strength of seven men. Most of the time our squad had between four to six men, though sometimes we got down to just three.

As fast as new men joined the squad, they were often killed or wounded after only a few days in combat. Whatever prior training these new replacements had received, their inexperience left them far more vulnerable than the veteran members of our squad or the experienced replacements who transferred in from another outfit. Because the green troops got killed and wounded so fast, I never really made much of an effort to get to know them. But while their high casualty rate made it difficult, if not impossible, to develop a deep bond with any of the replacements, we generally had a good working relationship with everyone assigned to our squad and called each other by our first names.

Our limited relationship with these replacements contrasted with the close camaraderie among those of us in the squad who had fought together since Normandy. We cared about, and looked out for, each other. Still, even among us veterans, there was a certain purposeful distance in our relationships. We were fully aware any of us might be wounded or killed in the next engagement.

Wayne Newsome, Hector Gonzalez, and Lincoln Welser remained my three closest buddies in the squad. My best friend Wayne continued to carry the machine gun most of the time. A tough soldier, he was always alert, always ready for action, and always in the middle of the fight. When we went into combat, he looked out for me.

Though Hector possessed a relaxed demeanor, his dark eyes always remained vigilant and he was quick to notice the slightest movement around us. As soon as he finished helping to load the ammo into the machine gun, he took up a position protecting my left flank with his carbine. Like Wayne, Hector was always in the thick of the action and had a real talent for killing the enemy.

Lincoln Welser also proved to be reliable in combat. Despite carrying a few extra pounds, he never seemed to grow tired lugging the water chest and an ammo box during our long slogs, even as the rest of us were dragging our feet. In combat, his normal job was to attach the hose that ran down from the gun barrel to the water chest. But whenever our squad's jeep's regular "chauffeur" was unavailable, Welser loved to get behind the wheel of "Little Joe."

Our squad's jeep and trailer always stayed as close to the action as was safe, so we had ready access to critical supplies. These included our backup machine gun; carbines; extra boxes of machine-gun, carbine, and pistol ammo; spare rubber hoses; crates of grenades; a mortar; and extra water chests, in case the existing one was pierced by an enemy bullet. In addition to these combat supplies, the jeep and trailer also held our food rations, a length of rope, and a canvas tarpaulin, which we used to camouflage our gun emplacement as well as to cover it in the event of rain. At rare times when the risk of combat was minimal, we temporarily dumped the tripod, gun, ammo boxes, and other gear in the jeep or trailer and advanced largely unburdened.

We also used the jeep and trailer to haul various other items we collected along the way. On several occasions when our guys found bicycles abandoned beside the road or on the porches of empty homes along our route, they stored them in the trailer to ride later when it was safe to do so.

Any time a stream, a well, or other relatively safe source of drinking water was available, we always filled up our canteens, so thirst was rarely a problem. While there may have been a risk of imbibing some water-borne disease, the battery of immunizations we had endured at the start of basic training seemed to protect us from just about everything. When winter weather later arrived, I became convinced these shots even acted as a sort of human anti-freeze, somehow preserving us against the icy cold.

As we advanced, all of us looked out for opportunities to supplement our regular rations with fresher fare. Though most wild game had cleared out ahead of our passage through an area, we seized any chance we had to shoot at nearby pheasants and rabbits with our pistols. In a couple of instances when we halted near a stream, I used the opportunity to fish, but failed to catch much.

The most common means of augmenting our rations involved foraging on abandoned farms, either during a halt or by briefly breaking away from the advance. Typically, "foraging" meant chasing down chickens, which is harder than it sounds. When one of us captured a bird, we would bind its feet together and toss it into the trailer.

The next time we halted out of sight of enemy observers, we roasted our freshly killed wild game, fish, or foraged chickens on an open fire. Because I knew how to build a small fire that would not produce a lot of smoke from my time in the Boy Scouts, it often fell to me to prepare the cooking fire.

While we occasionally supplemented our regular chow with fresh meat and vegetables acquired along the way, we were never short of Army-issued rations. Our standard C-ration meals consisted of one 12-ounce can that contained a meat entree and one 12-ounce can that included several dense crackers and items like jam, a packet filled with coffee or some other powdered beverage, and a chocolate bar for dessert.

More interesting to me were our "meals-on-the-run" K-rations, which came packed in three-pound cardboard boxes. Looking inside the K-ration box reminded me of a kid opening up a new box of Cracker Jacks, anxious to see what the surprise would be. In truth, there was no real suspense since the K-rations contained a basic set of foods.

The main component of both C-rations and K-rations was a can of meat, which might be mixed with beans, vegetables, or noodles. Just as with the second can of our C-rations, the K-ration box also typically contained a package of three thick crackers as well as a three-inch chocolate bar, a bar of processed cheese, and a thin round tin of jam. Usually orange marmalade, the "jam" in our rations might best be described as a sort of revolting orange slime.

Other standard K-ration items included an envelope of soup, four bouillon cubes, a bag of peas, packets of salt and pepper, a couple of pieces of candy, a cough drop, a salve for hands, a candle, and a box of matches. The K-ration box also sometimes held three cigarettes, which I always traded away for an additional chocolate bar.

Our supper K-rations were pretty much identical to the breakfast or dinner (lunch) versions but would have a different kind of canned meat. However, the supper ration contained a box of raisins or prunes, or a bar made of compressed raisins and peanuts. While the cheese and chocolate bars at breakfast and lunch would act to help clog our bowels up so we could walk during the day, the raisins and prunes at supper helped free things up in the evening to keep us regular. The Army was thoughtful that way.

Perhaps half of the time we got to eat hot chow cooked by H Company's kitchen crew, who somehow managed to keep up with us and prepare meals. Whenever our squad halted for any length of time, we would take turns on gun duty at our front-line position, while the other squad members would hurry a mile or so back to the rear for a hasty hot meal, perhaps stew and cornbread washed down with a mug of coffee.

If there was a longer lull in a battle or we held a stationary defensive position, the kitchen crew would cook up a really good meal. This might be beef, chicken, or pork, mashed potatoes and gravy, green beans, biscuits, and usually applesauce or apple pie. Proud of his culinary creations, our company cook Steve would break out in a big smile whenever anyone complimented his efforts.

Following the 1st Infantry Division's passage through the Soissons area, we had a rare opportunity to sample captured German rations. H Company's kitchen served up real ham, noodles, and a very hard bread with jelly.

"You're eating Heine chow, fellas," one of the mess sergeants informed us. The supply did not last long, but we appreciated any break in our routine diet.

When ordered to halt for the night, we usually dug our foxholes just off the road. After a quickly eaten supper, sleep came the instant I shut my eyes. In good weather and mild temperatures, a few hours of rest curled up in our field jackets down in our foxholes was not too bad, but a cold wind or rain—and later snow—prevented anything like a good night's rest. If the rain was heavy, we simply got drenched to the bone and froze, though I said a prayer of thanks that my blessed helmet at least kept my head dry.

"That's okay. You'll walk it off. You'll get warm," Sergeant Carpenter would inform us in the morning when we awoke stiff and chilled. He was right.

Every now and then, we sheltered for the night in a barn or the ruins of a home, which seemed like a real luxury after sleeping out in the open. But although such accommodations promised a relatively good night's rest, we were always a little skittish about entering buildings, aware that an enemy machine-gun nest might be waiting inside to greet us. Eventually, a brave soul among us would venture into the structure to conduct a search. Even if he found nothing, we remained apprehensive that some German armed with a burp gun remained hidden inside, waiting to ambush us once we let our guard down.

In a wrecked home, it was safest to sleep under a supporting arch in the cellar. Rubble from the collapsed floors above also helped offer protection in case of an enemy artillery strike. The downside of sleeping in a barn or home in whatever condition was that any structure presented a more obvious target.

While a good night's sleep was as prized as a hot meal, it was rarer. Despite our complete exhaustion, few of us ever had more than about four hours of sleep a night, which was typically broken up by a turn on gun duty. I soon grew accustomed to waking up half-slept and feeling tired all day.

When the order came to resume the advance, an almost hopeless feeling often came over me. Even if I was chilled to the bone and miserable down in a foxhole filled with three inches of cold muddy water, it was still safer than the alternative. Advancing always meant putting one's life in jeopardy.

The battle of Maubeuge-Mons: September 2–5

If a soldier almost never feels completely safe from danger, none of us anticipated a major engagement lay just ahead when H Company set out from Anizy-le-Château on the morning of September 2 after our two-day halt.

At the end of a long 35-mile, nine-hour trip by truck, we pulled into the village of Proisy, some 30 miles north-northeast of Anizy-le-Château. As usual, H Company's machine-gun platoons were supporting the 2nd Battalion's infantry companies, with our second platoon attached to G Company. There was not much in the way of enemy activity that night, but that was about to change.

While we had been racing northeast through France from just south of Paris, the *Wehrmacht* was in rapid retreat eastward toward the *Westwall*, Germany's extensive frontier fortifications more commonly known as the Siegfried Line. On the last day of August, the U.S. First Army's VII and V Corps received the mission of cutting off the retreat of the German Fifth Panzer Army in the corridor between the cities of Maubeuge, France, and Mons, Belgium.

In this operation, VII Corps's 3rd Armored Division thrust forward and entered Mons on September 2, with the 1st Infantry Division arriving close behind. Leading the Big Red One into action, the 18th and 26th Regiments collided with and engaged large numbers of enemy troops. But as our 16th Infantry Regiment came up behind the other two regiments, it was not expected we would encounter a significant enemy force when we reached the area.

On the morning of September 3, H Company departed Proisy aboard a convoy of trucks headed north-northeast toward Maubeuge, about 28 miles away. Following our arrival that afternoon, part of the 2nd Battalion proceeded north toward Mons with the 16th Regiment's 3rd Battalion. The rest of our 2nd Battalion was to check for the enemy in the sector northwest of Maubeuge.

Continuing forward cautiously, our convoy soon approached France's border with Belgium near the village of Goegnies-Chaussée, located four miles north of Maubeuge and eight miles south of Mons. Just ahead of us, perhaps two dozen American P-47 Thunderbolt fighters were swarming through the sky, swooping down toward German targets on the Bavay–Givry highway that ran east-northeast along the Franco-Belgian frontier. Moments later, we heard the explosion of bombs and rockets and the chilling staccato fire of their strafing.

Contrary to our earlier intelligence, it was now clear a significant German force was present in this sector. Ordered to take up a blocking position on the highway where it ran through the Bois (Wood) des Lanières near Goegnies-Chaussée, our machine-gun platoon moved forward through the woods, advancing with G Company and armor from the 745th Tank Battalion.

When we reached a point about 500 yards short of the highway, the American fighter planes flew off, enabling us to safely proceed. Dismounting from our trucks, we advanced on foot down a tree-lined service road for the last couple hundred yards. Armed with our carbines and pistols, none of us knew what to anticipate when we reached the highway.

Emerging from the trees, our eyes took in a truly hellish spectacle of devastation. Mindboggling in scale, the carnage almost defies description.

Around us lay mounds of shattered German military equipment, much of it still burning. There were gutted trucks, overturned tanks, and upended half-tracks. *Kübelwagens* and command cars riddled with bullets had flipped over. The destruction of the enemy column created a giant roadblock that stretched along the four lanes of the highway for several hundred yards.

Among the most pitiful sights were the dead horses still harnessed to their wagons, which carried small bales of hay, water cans, boxes of German Army rations, ammunition, and first-aid kits. Despite having grown accustomed to seeing dead and swollen cattle in pastures, this was the first time I had witnessed beautiful horses with 50-caliber bullet holes extending along the length of their bodies. Already, some of the animals had bloated to half again their original size.

Yet, more horrible still was the condition of the German dead. Some of the men had been blown apart, their bodies ripped open and still spilling blood. Adding to the vile, unforgettable odor of death, cordite from all the expended ammo hung over the area like a malevolent pall.

While it was shocking to look upon the vast swathe of desolation, my reaction to death and destruction had hardened over time. Maybe a soldier's desensitization is inevitable and even necessary if he is to maintain his sanity in the midst of such killing, but it also eats away at his soul.

A moment later, I was yanked away from my contemplation of this terrible panorama by the renewed sound of strafing as a P-47 started another pass down the highway. Knowing that bullets do not discriminate between enemy and friendly troops, I reflexively lunged for cover. Like a baseball player sliding for a base, I skidded across the pavement on my side toward the drainage ditch that ran alongside the highway.

Coming to a halt down in the ditch, I was shaken to find myself staring straight into the face of a dead German. Beneath a helmet that remained tightly strapped under his chin, the man's eyes and mouth were wide open as if he was screaming in pain. His badly burned clothing gave evidence of an agonizing death, as did the sickening stench of his charred flesh.

Never had war's terrible reality confronted me so intimately. Only the strafing on the highway above prevented me from instantly bolting from the drainage ditch. Instead, I was forced to remain in this horrifying position, trying to stay motionless in order to avoid drawing fire.

By now, the sound of the P-47's strafing had merged into the wider noise of combat. All along the highway, sharp firefights were erupting as GIs began encountering German troops in the undamaged portion of the enemy column.

After about five or ten minutes, my ears picked up the distinctive rumble of an approaching motorcycle coming from further down the highway. The sound of its engine grew louder and louder until the vehicle was passing almost directly above my location down in the ditch. Probably seeking to escape the area by weaving through the wreckage, this lone motorcyclist apparently had no idea a Thunderbolt was still prowling above in search of new targets.

The abrupt return of the plane an instant later spelled certain doom for the German. A short burst of machine-gun fire from the P-47 was followed by a deafening explosion just above me. Hunkered down in the drainage ditch, I felt a wave of intense heat and a sharp change in air pressure that stung my ears.

Once the strafing finally ended a few minutes later, I cautiously raised myself up enough to peer out onto the highway. Just 10 feet away, a German soldier sat upright on his motorcycle with his hands still clutching the handlebars. Caught in this riding position, the motorcyclist's charred, still-smoking body had literally been roasted in place, as if incinerated by a flamethrower. I could not be sure of the cause of the explosion, but it seemed likely a bullet from the P-47 had penetrated the motorcycle's gas tank and ignited the fuel.

This grotesque monument served as a further grim testament to the horror of war and the suddenness of death. While the gruesome image of the motorcyclist as well as the ghastly screaming face of the soldier in the ditch stood out for me among the enormous carnage on that highway, the whole terrible scene would remain indelibly etched in my mind.

When I rejoined my squad a few minutes later as it was growing dark, they were setting up our machine-gun position among the trees of the Bois des Lanières, locating it within sight of the highway. At first, there was still some small arms fire in the vicinity as our troops continued to engage the dispersed and thoroughly disorganized German troops, but the shooting soon died down.

Throughout a mostly quiet night, we remained alert, listening for the approach of enemy soldiers who wandered into the woods from the highway. As small groups of frightened and utterly dispirited Germans reached our position, we simply motioned them to toss their weapons into a pile and sit down.

By night's end, our squad had taken two dozen enemy prisoners. With nobody immediately available to accept custody of them, they sat and waited. However unfortunate their circumstances, they were just lucky to be alive.

Around sunrise, the remaining German forces in our sector accepted a general capitulation, apparently oblivious to the fact that these thousands of troops confronted only a battalion-sized American force. To carry out this surrender, German officers were assigned the task of conducting their troops to the temporary prisoner of war pens in the rear of our battalion. Since the officers retained their side arms until they reached the rear, it marked yet another lost opportunity for me to acquire a Luger pistol.

Following that morning's surrender, our machine-gun platoon spent the rest of September 4 helping the riflemen clear the Bois des Lanières of Germans who had not yet given up.

The next day, H Company was relieved by another unit and shifted just across the Franco-Belgian border to the small community of Bonnet, Belgium, located about a mile and a half northeast of Goegnies-Chaussée and a half-dozen miles south of Mons. Although we were still conducting patrols and operating roadblocks, the situation rapidly calmed down after the German surrender.

Later, we learned our 2nd Battalion had captured more than 3,000 Germans during the engagement in the Bois des Lanières. As a whole, the 1st Infantry Division claimed several thousand prisoners, suffering only very light casualties in the process. In the end, the wider battle of Maubeuge–Mons achieved the destruction of almost five *Wehrmacht* divisions, troops Germany would not be able to use to man its Siegfried Line fortifications.

Whatever challenge Germany's *Westwall* defenses might pose to our advance, our morale was sky high at the end of our week-long race across northeastern France and the total rout of the retreating enemy forces on the Franco-Belgian border. The surrender of thousands of German soldiers who had lost the will to fight reinforced our belief we were winning the war, further boosting our hopes that final victory might come by Christmas.

CHAPTER 9

To the German Frontier: September 7–14, 1944

Crossing Belgium: September 7–12

After a couple of days spent regrouping and resupplying in the vicinity of Mons, Belgium, the Big Red One resumed the offensive on September 7. Pivoting from its previous northeasterly route through France, the U.S. First Army's VII Corps now headed due east directly toward Aachen, the westernmost city in Germany. In this advance, our 1st Infantry Division would push forward on the northern left flank of VII Corps, while the 3rd Armored Division occupied the center, and the 9th Infantry Division proceeded on the southern right flank.

As always, we knew nothing of the larger operational picture when H Company and the rest of the division's 16th Infantry Regiment set out aboard trucks for a long leap eastward through the Belgian cities of Charleroi and Namur toward the town of Huy. In each community along our route, the newly liberated citizens greeted us with the now familiar clamorous reception. But in contrast with our prior experience, the Belgian crowds welcoming us also often included members of the local underground, anti-German resistance forces who had rarely been on hand during the liberation celebrations back in France.

On finally reaching our destination just north of Huy, H Company took up a defensive position some 57 miles east-northeast of our jumping-off point back at Bonnet, south of Mons. With almost no German opposition to check our progress through Belgium, logistical issues proved to be the biggest obstacle to our advance. Since the victory in Normandy, the speed of the Allied campaign and the ever-growing distance from the coastal ports had made it increasingly difficult to maintain a steady flow of supplies, particularly gasoline. When the fuel shortage reached a crisis at Huy, there was little for us to do but wait.

Passing through the beautiful Belgian countryside on the way to Huy, we had been impressed with the neatly maintained farmhouses and barns and the carefully marked out property boundaries, features that had been less visible on French farms. Stables on these farms often housed huge Clydesdale-sized horses, which were considerably larger than the horses we had seen back in France.

Many of the Belgian farms also contained large pens in which chickens foraged for food. At one such farm near our stopping point, the chickens were ranging quite far from the farmhouse. After many days of consuming regular Army fare, an irrepressible urge for a hot chicken supper came over me.

Spying a rather fat hen, I started chasing her around the yard, unprepared for the long pursuit that ensued. Squawking loudly and flapping her wings like a wounded goose, the hen repeatedly darted away. By the time she finally gave up, both of us were thoroughly winded and had our tongues hanging out.

Soon after my successful capture of our squad's supper, the first sergeant announced that Captain Irvine wanted to see me. Excited to have earned his notice, I anticipated a special assignment. Instead, the captain informed me that a local farmer had sought him out in his squad car, complaining a GI from our outfit had chased down and killed one of his prized chickens. The farmer's description of the chicken thief fit me to a tee.

My "special" assignment was to go see the farmer, apologize, and pay him five dollars in U.S. currency for the hen. In truth, I felt a little ashamed about what I had done and was happy to make amends. Fortunately, the farmer was thrilled to receive American money as compensation. Pleased with the matter's positive resolution, Captain Irvine joined our squad for a hot chicken supper.

By the end of our third day at Huy, a prodigious effort had delivered us enough gasoline to enable another leap eastward. Setting out on September 10, our convoy soon passed through the Belgian city of Liège, where we received an especially rapturous reception. Welcoming crowds with faces radiating joy rushed into the street to kiss us and hang flower garlands around our necks. Women pushed forward to ply us with cookies and cakes. Along the street, small ensembles of musicians gathered spontaneously to offer instrumental accompaniment for the ongoing celebration. Other locals who lived in the buildings along the street were hanging out of second and third story windows, frantically waving Belgian and American flags. It was a wonderful time to be a soldier, but such warm welcomes were about to come to an end.

Once past Liège, forces at the vanguard of our advance encountered the first German resistance since Mons. Though the enemy's defensive screen was rapidly pushed back, our easy drive to the east was over.

Our company's new bivouac in the Belgian village of Les Bruyères lay some 25 miles east-northeast of our previous location at Huy, a mile or so south of the 16th Infantry Regiment's headquarters in the town of Herve, and three and a half miles northwest of the 2nd Battalion's headquarters in the city of Verviers. More significantly, Les Bruyères was only 16 miles southwest of the center of Aachen and about 55 miles from the Rhine.

This put us at the western boundary of "new" Germany, a disputed border region that lay between Belgium and Germany. Following Germany's victory in 1940, the

Nazi regime had annexed this strip of land to the *Reich* (Empire), a portion of which was former German territory that had been awarded to Belgium after World War I in the 1919 Treaty of Versailles.

Just beyond this narrow strip of "new" Germany lay the Siegfried Line fortifications that ran along the pre-1940 Belgian-German border. Although the *Wehrmacht* lacked adequate troops to fully man its concrete pillboxes and other defenses, the Siegfried Line still posed a barrier to our advance into Germany. Even if it proved possible to breach the outer belt of the Line along the border that protected the city of Aachen (the Scharnhorst Line), we would still have to deal with the main inner belt of Siegfried Line fortifications just east of Aachen (the Schill Line).

Taking a German village: September 12

The 1st Infantry Division's probing attack through "new" Germany toward the Scharnhorst Line got underway on the morning of September 12, led by the 1st Battalion of the 16th Infantry Regiment on the right southern flank and one battalion of the 18th Infantry Regiment on the left northern flank. When this force ran into German opposition, our 2nd Battalion received orders to join the 16th Infantry Regiment's attack that afternoon.

With the resumption of combat operations, H Company proceeded on foot from Les Bruyères, deployed for action. By this time, a new lieutenant had been put in charge of our second machine-gun platoon. Called "a damn Yankee" by some of my fellow southerners in H Company, this roughly 30-year-old Midwesterner had been assigned to replace Lieutenant Sutton just after our victory in Normandy. Rather than identify our platoon's new commanding officer by name, I will hereafter refer to him as Lieutenant "Yankee."

In general, we considered our junior officers and NCOs to be capable leaders who commanded our respect. In combat, these junior officers and sergeants were right up front with us getting killed and wounded, suffering about as high a casualty rate as we did in the enlisted ranks. But this high regard for our junior officers did not extend to Lieutenant Yankee. From the moment he took command of our platoon, we knew it portended nothing good for us.

Perhaps Lieutenant Yankee's poor reputation was partly due to his lack of military bearing. Short in stature, he was regularly unshaven and unkempt, an impression reinforced by the frequent presence of straw in the netting of his helmet. Because the lieutenant carried all kinds of nonessential items in his overstuffed backpack—a lot more than any GI needed—he bore the look of a packrat, reinforcing his shabby, unsoldierly appearance.

Far more concerning was Lieutenant Yankee's recklessness. The field telephone was normally carried by an enlisted man in our platoon, but the lieutenant decided to carry the phone himself. He then turned it off to avoid receiving Captain Irvine's instructions so that he could act as he wished, displaying his insubordinate attitude toward his superiors. This lack of respect for authority was especially dangerous since the lieutenant lacked sound tactical judgment, which he exhibited in his ill-judged placement of our machine guns and in other ways. With his obvious lack of fitness for command, it was a great mystery to us how such a jackass had ever become an officer.

Given our deep mistrust of Lieutenant Yankee, I immediately experienced a sense of foreboding when he called me over to his jeep a short time after we had set out on foot from Les Bruyères.

"Andrews, get in the jeep. We're going to take a town," he ordered.

"Don't we need a platoon to take a town, sir?" I protested, wondering what crazy scheme he had concocted.

"No, you and I will be alright," he responded without explaining his plans. While his reassurance did little to diminish my unease, I had no choice but to climb into the jeep's passenger seat and hope for the best.

After traveling down the road for some distance without encountering either German or American troops, we entered a small German farming village and drove to the central square, stopping at the foot of a set of stairs that led up to a large stone monument commemorating soldiers killed in World War I.

Grabbing a carbine from the back of the jeep, the lieutenant handed it to me. "You get out and sit on those steps with your carbine. I'll be back soon."

"Well, what are you going to do?" I anxiously inquired.

"I'm going back and check my map. And I'm bringing up the rest of the platoon," he answered. I was not at all thrilled with his plan to leave me behind.

When the lieutenant sped off, a wave of apprehension passed through me as I pondered waiting alone for the arrival of the rest of my outfit. Still, for the moment, I did not particularly sense I was in any danger as the village appeared to be completely deserted. Not even a stray dog was in sight.

As my eyes wandered across the buildings around the square in search of some sign of the community's inhabitants, a small face appeared in a basement window of one of the homes. After we had gazed at each other for a long moment, another face popped up behind the same window. A minute later, yet another face showed up in a different window of the home. Only then did I realize these faces belonged to children.

Our staring contest went on for a long while. Setting my carbine aside, I began smiling and waving at the children. After a couple of more minutes, I gestured to the kids to come outside. Perhaps feeling afraid, the children ducked out of sight, but their faces soon reappeared.

Finally, the basement door of the house opened. Three little kids stepped outside, clinging to each other for mutual security. Their curiosity about this foreign stranger was clearly in close competition with their trepidation.

As these three children stood there studying me with wide eyes, several more kids emerged from other homes around the square, all of them ranging from about five to seven years in age. After looking at each other and at me, the small crowd of children collectively started toward me, advancing right up to the bottom of the stairs where I sat.

"*Guten tag!*" I said in my best German, offering my warmest smile.

Uncertain grins appeared in response.

"*Kommen Sie hier,*" I invited, patting the steps beside me.

Growing a bit more confident, the children congregated around me in a small semicircle at the foot of the stairs.

"*Was ist dein Name?*" I inquired in my rudimentary German, nodding my head toward one of the boys.

"Heinz," he shyly replied.

"*Was ist dein Name?*" I asked another boy.

"Henri."

The first thing I knew, the boys and girls were coming up the steps. Claiming seats around me, they packed in tightly. One little girl boldly plopped down in my lap, announcing that her name was Heidi. Smiling ear-to-ear, the other children began telling me their names and talking all at once.

Children are the same everywhere I mused, wishing I had a pocketful of candy to pass out. It is hard to express how deeply moving it was to have these German kids around me after months of fighting German soldiers.

Within 10 minutes, their parents and other adult residents of the village started to filter into the square. Soon, a group of two dozen or more people had gathered around me, comprised mostly of elderly men and women, a few younger females, and the children. While my very limited German made real communication impossible, everyone was trying to engage me in friendly conversation and ask me questions.

At that moment, my eyes caught sight of a wire protruding out of the ground, abruptly jolting me out of my carefree mood. Fearful that it was some type of explosive device, I panicked and yelled, "Look out! Look out! Look out!"

Though no one in the crowd understood me, they all comprehended that there was some sort of danger. Tension filled the air.

Then one elderly man casually reached down and pulled up the wire.

Nothing happened.

Everyone laughed and I shouted, "Boom!"

"*Nein! Nein! Nein!*" the crowd light-heartedly responded.

With the cordial atmosphere restored, our muddled babble of words and gestures resumed. Several of the men seemed to be trying to tell me their sons were also soldiers. After perhaps half an hour someone thoughtfully brought me a glass of water, which I gladly drank.

While I was thoroughly enjoying myself, my inability to speak German was immensely frustrating. I knew if we could really talk with each other about our lives, we could make a deeper connection. The people of this village were the salt of earth, just like the good folks of Signal Mountain where I had grown up.

About three hours after he had dropped me off, Lieutenant Yankee reappeared, motoring up to our little assembly at the war monument in a column of three jeeps filled with men from my platoon.

"I see you've taken the town," he observed in a congratulatory tone.

"I sure have and I love all these people," I announced.

"What are you talking about?" he objected, apparently unable to view the Germans as anything other than the enemy.

"I love these people," I declared, meaning every word.

"Andrews, you're a case, boy. Get in the jeep."

As we departed the village to continue our advance, the residents were waving me goodbye like I was an old friend. It was a heartwarming scene, a remarkable moment made all the more powerful because it took place amid the war's brutality, death, and tragedy.

My Christian faith and German heritage had given me a different attitude toward German people than that held by most of my buddies, but my encounter with these friendly German villagers had firmly cemented my belief people everywhere are pretty much alike if they are free.

Tragically, much of the German population had fallen under Hitler's spell, forging a bond that had yet to be broken. Driven by an evil ideology, the Nazis had led Germany into its ruthless attempt to conquer and enslave Europe. But though I loathed the Nazi dictatorship and its teachings, I never felt hatred toward individual Germans or the German people as a whole.

Misled into disaster: September 12

Advancing on foot late that same afternoon, our two machine-gun platoons came to the edge of a wood, where Captain Irvine ordered a halt. Beyond the line of trees lay a wide pasture and, past that, a farm at the outskirts of a village. Arriving at this spot near Schmalgraf in "new" Germany, we were now roughly 10 miles east-northeast of our jumping-off point at Les Bruyères and just over half a dozen miles south-southwest of the center of Aachen.

By this time, those of us who had joined H Company back in England had seen plenty of our company commander in action. A gutsy officer who always led from the front, Captain Robert Irvine was well-regarded by everyone and had a good working relationship with the other officers in our outfit. However, it was apparent to us that the captain may have shared some of our misgivings about Lieutenant Yankee as he issued instructions to our two platoons.

"Okay, guys, now listen up. I'm going to take the first machine-gun platoon across this open field to that farm and reconnoiter the area. The enemy's observers are going to see us, so don't you all follow 'til I radio back to you," Irvine ordered, looking directly at Lieutenant Yankee as he spoke.

While the captain's scouting party stood a fair chance of making it across the meadow without drawing the enemy's fire, he knew their arrival at the farm would make the Germans aware of our presence. Once alerted, the enemy's forward observers would be primed to target any further movement across the field with their artillery. Until Irvine notified us of the withdrawal of the German rearguard, it would be too risky for the rest of us to follow him to the farm.

His orders delivered, the captain headed off with more than a dozen guys from the first machine-gun platoon, leaving behind about two dozen of us, mostly men from my second machine-gun platoon.

After 15 minutes with no word from the captain, Lieutenant Yankee became visibly agitated, obviously chomping at the bit to get into action.

"C'mon, let's go!" he finally exclaimed, too impatient to wait any longer.

All of us knew the captain had still not radioed back on the field telephone to authorize our advance, but it fell to an NCO to point this out.

"The captain hasn't called us yet," Sergeant Carter objected.

"That's alright. I'm saying let's go," Lieutenant Yankee responded. While he was blatantly disregarding the captain's explicit orders, we had no way to challenge his decision. He was now in command and orders were orders.

Leaving our concealed position in the woods, all two dozen of us set off at a trot across a flat pasture in which a few cows were grazing. Although the farm lay only a couple of hundred yards away, everyone knew we stood little chance of making it safely across the field if the enemy's forward observers spotted our movement. Yet despite my desperation to get to the farm, the weight of the tripod on my shoulders prevented me from proceeding with any real speed. At each stride, my pace grew slower as my load seemed to grow heavier.

Less than halfway across the field, my legs involuntarily slowed to a walk. With sweat from the exertion stinging my eyes like some kind of acid, I glanced around me and discovered the other guys had quit running too. After expending all the energy we had, a passive resignation had set in.

"To hell with it, we're just gonna walk. We can't run any farther," seemed to be our shared attitude. Not for the first time, war felt like a game of chance. Your fate is not in your hands, so you almost become indifferent. Once fired, bullets and shells inflict injury and death with a random mindlessness. If your name is on one, you will get it. If not, you will survive.

As our party reached the middle of the pasture a hundred yards from the farm, an eerie silence fell over the whole area, a quiet broken only by our heavy footfalls, deep breathing, and racing heartbeats.

At that moment when we were most vulnerable, the faint boom of artillery resounded from somewhere ahead of us. Throwing myself flat against the ground, I pressed my body into the spongy earth as my ears tracked the spine-chilling whine of the incoming shells. The few seconds that elapsed between the firing of the artillery rounds and their arrival were agonizing.

Almost simultaneously, three shells detonated 20 yards away from me, their explosions hurling jagged shards of lethal shrapnel through the air in every direction. In the ensuing moment I wondered whether any of my buddies had been killed. But even if we had all survived this first volley, I knew the German artillery had now zeroed in on us. We were not safe yet.

Less than a minute later, the German guns boomed another three times, a salvo I both heard and felt as the ground trembled under me. Once more, incoming rounds whistled toward us for terrifyingly long seconds. Even with my body pressed deeply into the soft surface of the field, death seemed imminent.

"Please God, cause that artillery crew to stop firing," I prayed aloud.

With tremendous force, the three shells exploded only 10 yards away.

The enemy artillery fire then ceased as abruptly as it had begun. Sensing it was over, we rose to our feet and headed toward the farm at as fast a pace as we could manage. During our trek across the rest of the field, the initial euphoria we felt at our own survival soon turned to sorrow. Of the two dozen of us who had departed the woods, three men had been killed. Though I did not know any of them well, two were from my section of our platoon.

Based on the short duration of the enemy's artillery fire, it was painfully clear to us the German rearguard had just fired off a few parting rounds to hold us back as they completed their retreat from the farm. If we had only waited in the woods for another five minutes, the Germans would have finished pulling out and Captain Irvine would have signaled that it was safe for us to advance.

Instead, three of our buddies lay dead because of Lieutenant Yankee's impatience. The fury we felt toward this incompetent officer for his rash decision to lead us into the open field against orders was beyond words. After we reached the farm, Captain Irvine rebuked the lieutenant for disobeying orders, but it fell to my buddy Wayne Newsome to give him the chewing out he truly deserved.

Seething with grief and rage over a friend he had just lost in the field, Newsome stomped right up to the lieutenant. With the rest of our squad standing behind him, Newsome got up in the officer's face and proceeded to cuss him out in some of the most crude and abusive language I had ever heard.

"Why the hell did you take us out into that open field against the captain's orders? You worthless son of a bitch!" Newsome exploded.

Staring blankly at his accuser, the lieutenant remained mute. For a moment, I really thought that Newsome might shoot him then and there. A brief pause ensued as Newsome seemed to be weighing his final words.

"You'd better keep a sharp eye out over your shoulder. One of these days, one of us might put a bullet through your no-good ass!" he warned.

Lieutenant Yankee never said a word. Though it was probably a court martial offense for an enlisted man to direct that kind of language toward an officer, the lieutenant knew what he had done was utterly indefensible. Even if I would never have threatened an officer, I felt no sympathy for him. His impulsive disobedience to the captain's orders had gotten good men killed.

A long night: September 12/13

With our objective secured and dusk now falling, we halted at the farm for the evening. After supper, Captain Irvine instructed 15 of us to find a place to sleep in a one-story, cinder-block cattle barn located on the edge of the property.

On entering the barn, Sergeant Carter proclaimed his satisfaction with our accommodations. He particularly appreciated the foot-thick layer of fresh straw on the floor, which promised our most comfortable night's rest in weeks.

Stripping off our battle jackets, ammo belts, grenades, and boots, and stacking our weapons in the corner, all of us quickly settled down to sleep. Despite the emotional burden of the loss of our buddies, sheer exhaustion caused everyone to drop off into a deep slumber almost instantly.

Before I drifted off, my attention was drawn to the barn's lone kerosene lamp. Sitting atop a small barrel in the corner next to the spot where I had bedded down, the lamp still blazed brightly, emitting a thick, smelly smoke. Fearing a stray spark could ignite the straw, I decided to lower the flame in the lamp before going to sleep.

As I reduced the length of the burning wick exposed to oxygen, I expected the flame to diminish or be snuffed out. Instead, the flame followed the wick down into the lamp's small glass reservoir that stored the kerosene.

A split second after a barely audible "pop," the glass reservoir shattered, showering burning oil onto the surrounding dry straw. In a flash, the flames began fanning out across the barn's floor in a widening arc.

"Fire!" I blurted automatically. Instantly, the other guys came awake. Though still in a confused, drowsy stupor, they all instinctively grabbed their weapons before stumbling after me toward the door in a panicked haste.

All of us managed to make it outside without injury, but the flames were hard on our heels. Gathering a dozen or so yards from the barn, we watched as the fire blazed up into a real inferno, causing our rifle bullets inside to begin going off like popcorn.

Everyone just stood there with mystified expressions on their faces. Only a couple of guys had retrieved their boots, so most were dressed only in their shirts, pants, and socks. Nobody had their battle jackets or their helmets. And no one had managed to get any sleep. We were a sorry sight.

At that moment, Henry Spohn, a member of the other gun squad in our section, realized he had forgotten something more valuable than his boots.

"Hey, I left my billfold in there and I got 500 dollars in it! Someone give me a gas mask!" he urgently pleaded.

Even though that amount of money represented a small fortune, the rest of us thought Spohn was nuts to go back into the burning barn. Nonetheless, one fellow who always carried his gas mask handed it over to Spohn.

Yanking the gas mask down over his face, Spohn darted back through the door into the blaze. With all of us fearing that one of the grenades left inside would go off at any second, tense seconds ticked by.

Just when it seemed he was not going to make it back out alive, Spohn bolted out of the barn clenching his prized billfold. As we applauded his dramatic escape, he collapsed to the ground on his hands and knees. Gulping in fresh air, he coughed harshly, trying to clear out the smoke that had entered his lungs as a result of the poorly fitted gas mask he had hastily donned.

Spohn got out just in time. At almost the same moment as he exited the barn, the grenades inside began to detonate, forcing us to move further away from the structure. Meanwhile, the men around me began wondering aloud how far away the Germans were and whether they might mount a counterattack.

With the blaze now lighting up the night sky, Captain Irvine suddenly appeared from out of nowhere with a puzzled, exasperated look on his face.

"This is the most amazing thing that I've ever seen," he announced despondently as he shook his head in disbelief.

"How the hell did this happen?" the captain asked no one in particular as he gestured toward the fire. "Somebody tell me how the hell this happened!" he demanded.

Nobody spoke. Every GI's face bore a grave expression.

"How the hell could this tragedy happen and no one know a damn thing about it?" Irvine angrily repeated.

"Andrews, you're the only one wearing a jacket. What the hell happened?"

"Sir, I think an oil lamp was accidentally turned over," I explained, not wanting to admit my culpability unless the captain asked me a direct question.

"Shit!" was all Captain Irvine could say on hearing my explanation.

Speaking into his field telephone, the captain began requisitioning a long list of items to replace the gear we had lost. "I want 15 pairs of boots, 15 battle jackets, 15 helmets, and a full crate of grenades."

A momentary silence ensued as the captain listened to someone's response on the other end.

"What? I don't give a damn what size; just get 'em up here in a hurry!" he roared into the mouthpiece.

Despite the circumstances, it was impossible for us not to chuckle at the captain's exchange with the quartermaster. It was even more amusing when we later tried to sort out the boots according to foot size. Many of the guys had to take a pair that did not fit well and would be limping around for a while.

As the captain turned to get into his jeep, I overheard him muttering.

"How the hell could such a disaster happen and nobody know a damn thing about it?"

Observing the captain's agitation, I decided it was wiser to say nothing else. After his departure, all of us claimed a spot on the ground to sleep, but no one got the comfortable night's rest that had been anticipated.

Nazi desperation: September 13

During our company's advance to Schmalgraf on September 12, the probing attack into "new" Germany by the First Army's VII Corps had managed to reach the Siegfried Line's outer Scharnhorst Line fortifications running along the pre-1940 Belgian-German border.

On September 13, the push up to the Scharnhorst Line resumed with the 16th Infantry Regiment's 2nd and 3rd Battalions assigned to the northern flank of the 3rd Armored Division. As part of this larger operation, our first and second machine-gun platoons moved out from Schmalgraf in support of the 2nd Battalion's E and F Companies early that morning.

A little later that day, as the GIs at the front of our column were coming over the crest of a low hill, heavy machine-gun fire suddenly erupted, sweeping back and forth across the road. Forced to pull back behind the hill, we searched the thick brush ahead for the source of the enemy fire, but it took some time before we pinpointed the location of the German machine-gun emplacement.

Waving me over, Captain Irvine explained the plan to deal with it.

"Andrews, why don't you go around there through the woods and put a grenade in that machine-gun nest," he directed in what sounded as much a suggestion as an order.

Proud of my selection for the assignment, I enthusiastically set out through the dense surrounding woods. Making a wide loop, I reached a spot on the right rear flank of the German machine-gun position about 15 minutes later.

As I stealthily crept forward through the brush in a low crouch, the machine gun was steadily rattling away, but the weapon and the gun crew were hidden from my view by dirt piled up around the gun emplacement.

When I had come within 10 yards of the machine-gun nest, as close as I dared, I grabbed a grenade from my belt. But just as I cocked my arm and hooked my finger in the ring to pull the pin, the gunfire abruptly ceased.

For a split second, a wave of fear raced through me as I thought the gun crew had heard me. Then, strangely, the unmistakable sound of children crying reached my ears, though it was hard for me to determine its origin.

Keeping my grenade at the ready, I crept a few feet closer. As I approached the gun emplacement, it became clear the crying was coming from down inside the hole. Moving up to the edge of the position, I reached a spot where it was just possible for me to peer down over the rim into the four-foot-deep dugout.

To my utter astonishment, three young German boys sat at the bottom whimpering loudly. Outfitted in military-type uniforms with the *Hitlerjugend* (Hitler Youth) insignia, they were tugging up and down on a rope that was rigged to the machine gun through a pulley system. As they yanked on the rope, the now empty gun repeatedly swiveled from left to right on its pivot.

Shuddering with horror, I realized that only the timely exhaustion of the weapon's ammo had prevented me from killing these children with my grenade.

When the boys noticed me gazing down at them, a look of sheer terror came over their faces. Overwhelmed with compassion, I knew I had to get the kids to safety. Jumping into the hole, I tried to calm them and win their trust.

"Was ist dein Name?" I asked, speaking to each boy in a gentle tone.

"Heinrich," one boy responded, choking back his tears.

"Hans," said another, drawing courage from the first.

The third kid remained too scared to speak.

With only a single stick of chewing gum to offer, I tore it into three parts and presented each boy a little piece. Immediately, smiles lit up their faces and the tension lessened.

When the other men from H Company reached the gun emplacement after I had signaled them it was safe to come forward, I handed the kids up to them one by one and then climbed out of that awful hole.

Over the next few minutes, a German-speaking member of our company interviewed the boys, translating for the rest of us. The kids told us they were all seven years old and lived nearby. Someone in authority had recruited them for this assignment, ordering them to keep the machine gun's fire sweeping back and forth on the road as soon as enemy forces appeared.

"How could anybody do this? How could children be trained to do this?" I angrily demanded. The rest of the guys were just as incredulous and disgusted.

It was simply incomprehensible to us that even the most desperate enemy would cowardly sacrifice the lives of innocent young children to cover their own retreat. The heartless exploitation of these boys did not make me hate the German people, but it did fuel my loathing of the Nazis. They had created a truly wicked regime that lacked any semblance of morality or humanity.

A short time later, a local German civilian was brought to the scene. Captain Irvine asked the man to take the children to the *Bürgermeister* (mayor) of the nearest village. Later, I heard that the *Bürgermeister* immediately recognized the boys and returned them to their parents.

My encounter with these boy soldiers profoundly touched my heart, even more than my visit with the German children the previous day. Together, these two incidents had a lasting impact on my life. Reinforcing my long-held inclination to devote my life to Christian Ministry, they helped me clarify how I wanted to serve.

Not long afterward, I wrote a letter to the East Tennessee Presbytery of the Presbyterian Church, informing them of my intention to pursue a career as a Christian youth director when I returned home. Having witnessed the terrible consequences of the Nazis preaching hate and violence to children, I wanted to dedicate my life to working with youths and teaching Christian values of love and kindness, if I survived the war.

A new hunting rifle: September 13

By the afternoon of September 13, our 16th Infantry Regiment had pushed through the enemy's rearguards and delaying actions and was approaching the Scharnhorst Line near the small town of Steinkaul. Located just south of a major German *Autobahn* (highway), Steinkaul was four or five miles east of our previous position near Schmalgraf and five miles south of the center of Aachen.

Our intelligence informed us a unit of the notorious SS (*Schutzstaffel*) had pulled out just ahead of our arrival after having been stationed in the area for about a year. Since the SS contained the most hardcore Nazi troops, our company commander suspected local German civilians might be particularly sympathetic to the Nazis and could present a security threat to any American forces occupying Steinkaul.

When we reached the center of the town, an American officer climbed up on a monument to issue an announcement through a megaphone. Speaking in German, he ordered the citizenry to come to the town's main square and surrender all of their firearms, knives, swords, and cameras.

Obediently complying, the townspeople soon queued up to turn over the proscribed items. Observing the process from across the square, a group of us commented on their surrender of a large number of magnificent hunting rifles, some with polished stocks crafted from a beautiful maple wood.

Once the collection of contraband items was completed, a couple of GIs started smashing the weapons and cameras and tossing their remnants into a pile. When done, they dowsed everything with gasoline and ignited the scrap heap.

Just as I was reflecting that all of this destruction seemed a bit of a waste, a middle-aged German man furtively sidled over next to me, carrying a long object at his side that was concealed with rags.

"Would you happen to be a sportsman?" he inquired in flawless English.

"I sure am," I replied, my curiosity aroused.

The man proceeded to remove the rags to unveil a beautiful rifle.

"This is a custom-built rifle that I had made for myself," he informed me. "Its specifications are according to what I wanted. It's a double-barreled rifle and very rare. And I want you to have it, if you will take it. I don't want them to tear it up," he explained as he handed the weapon over to me.

"Well, I do, thank you," I responded. Not knowing what else to say, I shook his hand. A big tear rolled down from the man's eye before he walked off.

After he departed, some of the guys standing nearby came over to inspect the .30-30 rifle. They urged me to dismantle the weapon and carry it back home with me after the war, arguing it would not make it back if I shipped it by mail.

GIs could mail items at no cost, but I did wonder whether such a beautiful rifle would make it all the way back to Tennessee. Weapons sent by mail might be confiscated by the Army as contraband or stolen by an unscrupulous worker in the U.S. Postal Service. On the other hand, I expected the rifle would likely be damaged or lost if I kept it with me, so mailing it seemed to be the better option.

Entering a partially destroyed home nearby, I swiped a tablecloth from the dining room. After disassembling the rifle into three pieces, I wrapped them up in the tablecloth and secured the bundle with a rope. After writing my name and home address on the oversized parcel, I dropped it in our company's outgoing mail, hoping that postal workers would respect a foot soldier's effort to send a fine war trophy back home.

By the end of September 13, our forces were in position to support an attack on the first belt of the Siegfried Line fortifications the following day. But whatever happened there, we were already beginning to sense the *Wehrmacht* was not close to giving up and the war was not close to ending. In defending the home soil of their fatherland, the Germans would mount a desperate fight, making us pay dearly for every foot of ground.

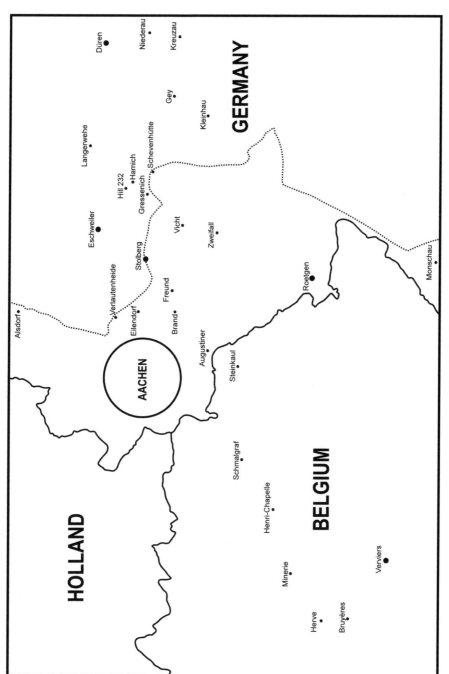

Map 3: Aachen Area

CHAPTER 10

The Stolberg Corridor: September 14–23, 1944

Across the Dragon's Teeth: September 14

After spending the night in a basement in Steinkaul, our squad used the first half of September 14 to clean and check our equipment for the next operation. In the middle of that afternoon, we set out from the town on foot under overcast skies, with H Company's two machine-gun platoons operating in support of the 2nd Battalion's E and F Companies.

Together with the other two battalions of the 16th Infantry Regiment, our immediate assignment was to support the 3rd Armored Division's assault against the Scharnhorst Line, the outer belt of the Siegfried Line's network of defenses. While knowing nothing beyond our current objective, our mission was one small element of a larger military plan.

Once the Scharnhorst Line was breached, VII Corps would enter the "Stolberg Corridor." Starting south of Aachen and running northeast through Brand toward the industrial town of Stolberg, this narrow strip of land was mostly free of the dense forests and other natural obstacles which existed elsewhere in this region of Germany. Though several small communities were located inside the Stolberg Corridor, it presented the best route for our advance.

Rather than aiming for the immediate capture of Aachen, the operation's primary objective was to secure the inner belt of the Siegfried Line—the Schill Line fortifications—that ran along the high ground just east of Aachen. If the Schill Line could be breached before the *Wehrmacht* could rush reinforcements into the area, it would open the way to subsequent American advances further east toward the Rhine.

To carry out this mission, VII Corps would deploy the 3rd Armored Division to batter a path forward in the middle, with our 1st Infantry Division attacking on the northern left flank of the corps and the 9th Infantry Division advancing on its southern right flank.

In this operation, the Big Red One was tasked with isolating Aachen on the south and east. Our 16th Infantry Regiment's specific orders were to push northeast about five miles up the Stolberg Corridor to seize a sector of the Schill Line that ran through the hills just east of the town of Eilendorf, an eastern suburb of Aachen. But first the Scharnhorst Line had be broken.

Advancing with the 2nd Battalion infantry from Steinkaul toward the Scharnhorst Line, our platoon followed the *Autobahn*, an impressive highway that ran northeastward toward the old Belgian-German border. While German artillery shells occasionally exploded nearby as we approached our objective, we met no other opposition. None of the several tanks at the head of our column even fired a shot.

Upon cresting a hill about a mile from Steinkaul, we got our first look at the Scharnhorst Line. Having heard so much about Germany's famous *Westwall*, it was thrilling to finally view these truly awesome fortifications. The most visible feature were the rows of dragon's teeth designed to block the passage of tanks and other vehicles. Pyramid-shaped, each of these three to four-foot-high "teeth" was constructed of reinforced concrete. About five rows of these closely packed teeth made up the line, with land mines filling the gaps between them. A wide moat-like ditch in front of the line of dragon's teeth served as a further impediment to any attacker.

Stretching up and down the rolling hills as far as the eye could see, the Scharnhorst Line's dragon's teeth were secured by concrete pillboxes, smaller bunkers, and hidden artillery batteries. When the advancing Allied tanks and infantry collided with this defensive barrier, the *Wehrmacht* intended to smash the stymied forces with a devastating barrage of targeted fire.

As we were surveying these fortifications from about a hundred yards away, the Germans opened fire with rockets, giving us our first exposure to this weapon. Because these rockets zoomed out of the six-barrelled, 150-millimeter *Nebelwerfer* with a terrifically loud shriek, the weapons were dubbed "Screaming Meemies." If artillery fire was worse because you could hear the shells whining down toward you, the eerie whirring of the "Screaming Meemies" as they launched their rockets was something terrible.

Thankfully, the barrage of enemy rocket fire did not last long. As soon as it ended, our section immediately deployed our two machine guns to support the infantry's advance, but this proved unnecessary. To our surprise, the fighting here was already largely over. Despite the visual impressiveness of the fortifications, the speed and power of our attack had made short work of the enemy in this sector of the Scharnhorst Line.

Following the destruction of the main German artillery positions and other defensive works by American artillery and armor earlier in the day, our infantry swiftly routed the surviving enemy troops. As we watched, Army engineers now swarmed forward to place explosive charges among the dragon's teeth. Before long, we heard shouts of "Fire in the hole!" as they triggered a series of spectacular explosions.

Within a few minutes, Army bulldozers began pushing dirt up over the top of the moat-like trench and what remained of the dragon's teeth, opening several routes across the fortifications for vehicles and infantry. By the time this task was completed, our 16th Infantry Regiment had been relieved by another unit, permitting us to start our drive northeast on the left flank of VII Corps.

Considering the amazing rapidity of our breach of the outer belt of the Siegfried Line, the barrier had proved to be a massive waste of Germany's resources. All of us wondered how Hitler must have felt about his world-famous *Westwall* being so easily overcome. Could Germany's military leadership really have believed it would be effective in keeping a modern enemy army at bay?

Our success here also brought home to us the significance of the destruction of the retreating *Wehrmacht* divisions back at the Franco-Belgian border a dozen days earlier. If Germany had possessed adequate troops to properly man its Siegfried Line defenses, the story might have been different.

Breaking into Germany: September 14/15

"YOU ARE NOW ENTERING GERMANY" the sign read as our outfit marched across the Scharnhorst Line late that foggy afternoon. On reaching the far side, we assisted the infantry in mopping up the enemy troops still holding out inside the surrounding fortifications. Clearing enemy pillboxes and bunkers was always dangerous, but the few remaining Germans quickly gave up, freeing us to resume our advance up the Stolberg Corridor toward Eilendorf.

But only a mile or so beyond the Scharnhorst Line, a sharp firefight broke out near the village of Augustiner. Supported by heavy German artillery and mortar fire, at least 50 or 60 enemy troops blocked our progress for some time. Though our route of attack passed south of Aachen's fortified urban area, it was clear that German units operating on the outskirts of the city's defenses were prepared to put up stiff resistance.

After we had advanced a bit further, Captain Irvine called me over. Pointing toward a yellow, two-story wooden house 75 yards away, he issued my orders.

"Andrews, there's a German machine-gun nest in that house. I want you to go around through the woods, sneak up on the porch, kick open the front door, and throw a grenade inside. Get rid of that machine-gun nest."

"You mean by myself?" I replied anxiously.

"Yeah, by yourself. You did it yesterday. Just take a couple of grenades, get up on the porch, and kick the door in. Throw the grenades in. Simple," Irvine instructed, making it sound like a trip to the store for bread.

My handling of the boys firing the machine gun the previous day had ended well, but that did not make me an expert in wiping out machine-gun nests. And this new job sure did not look as easy as he made it sound. Any German gun crew hidden in that house was not likely to welcome a grenade, but I had my orders.

With my carbine in hand, I circled around through the trees for 200 to 300 yards, trying to stay concealed. On reaching the side of the house a few minutes later, I slipped onto the porch. Ducking beneath the windows to keep out of sight, I silently crawled across the porch's wooden floor toward the front door.

Standing up, I yanked a grenade out from my belt, readying myself to kick open the door and toss in the grenade. Just at that very moment, my ears picked up the unmistakable sound of female voices. Moving up close to the door, I could clearly hear a group of women chatting and laughing inside.

I can't throw a grenade in there. Our intelligence about a German machine-gun nest in the house must have been wrong. After carefully securing the grenade back in my belt, I unslung my carbine from my shoulder, still not knowing exactly what to expect inside.

Kicking the door open, I stepped into a spacious living room. In an almost surreal moment, I found myself staring at a group of eight, nicely dressed German *Fraus* who were seated around a long table sewing. They might have been a group of ladies from back home, except for what they were sewing.

Operating in a sort of assembly line, the women were cutting black fabric into swastikas, stitching the swastikas onto two-foot-wide white fabric circles, and then sewing the completed swastika diadems onto big rectangular pieces of bright red cloth to produce Nazi flags.

For a moment, the women were utterly petrified with fear at my sudden appearance in the room. Each face bore an identical expression of disbelief and alarm as they processed the sight of an armed American soldier in their midst. I was not going to need my carbine with these ladies.

"*Amerikanisch!*" one *Frau* of about 60 years of age finally gasped.

"Yeah, Amerikanisch and I want that flag!" I announced, pointing my finger at a just completed Nazi banner. It would make a fine war trophy.

"*Wir verstehen nicht,*" responded the woman who had first spoken, pretending not to understand me.

"Yes, you do. I want that flag," I insisted. Withdrawing my .45 pistol from its holster, I directed the barrel toward the banner.

"*Ja! Ja! Ja!*" the woman agreed. She had no problem understanding a .45.

"*Herr* Goebbels just said on the radio that the Allies were still in France," the *Frau* informed me in halting English. Even with artillery fire in the vicinity and a GI right in front of their eyes, these women still seemed intent on believing what the Nazi state's chief propagandist had told them.

"Well, no, darlin', we're right here. And I do want that flag," I reaffirmed.

The woman who had done all the speaking hastily folded up the flag and submissively handed it over. After tucking the flag into one of my pockets, I swiped a couple of extra swastika diadems off the table for good measure. These would be added to my growing collection of belt buckles, uniform insignias, and compasses I had already liberated from captured German soldiers.

As I slipped my pistol back into its holster, a collective wave of relief passed over the faces of the women as they realized they would not be harmed. Using the English-speaking woman as our interpreter, we went on to have a pleasant conversation. None of them would know how close I had been to tossing a grenade into the room moments earlier. Just as with the boys operating the machine gun, a real tragedy had barely been avoided.

After I reported what had happened to Captain Irvine, he congratulated me for not killing the civilians, even if they had been sewing Nazi flags.

Upon rejoining my squad, one of the guys asked, "What did you do?"

"I shot 'em all," I told him. As he stared at me in awe, I imitated firing my pistol, reenacting my fictitious assault on the German "machine-gun nest." Once this gullible GI appeared suitably impressed, I revealed the truth.

"I didn't shoot anybody," I confessed. It was hard for me not to laugh at the look of chagrin that came over his face.

When we resumed our advance northeastward along wooded trails to the left of the *Autobahn,* our progress was slowed by enemy artillery fire, felled trees, and a persistent drenching rain that turned the ground to mud. One of our weapons carriers even became stuck in it and had to be hauled out by a tank.

By the time we halted for the night on September 14, H Company had pushed forward another couple of miles. This advance brought us close to the larger town of Brand, roughly four miles north-northeast of our starting point in Steinkaul and three miles east-southeast of the center of Aachen. Sleeping in abandoned homes, we remained alert for enemy infiltrators.

Meanwhile, elements of the 3rd Armored Division spearheading our drive had pressed forward to the outskirts of Eilendorf, a couple miles further north of our location. Our forces were making progress, but German opposition was steadily mounting.

Eilendorf: September 15–18

Early on the morning of September 15, just after breakfast, enemy artillery began hammering our position. There was nothing for us to do but take cover as best we could while H Company awaited orders to resume its advance.

Finally, about two that afternoon, squad leaders, gunners, and assistant gunners set out aboard our company's jeeps, while the rest of the outfit moved out on foot. With the enemy's artillery shells continuing to explode around us, we pressed forward a short distance to the northern outskirts of Brand.

After pausing awhile at this location, our column of jeeps took off in a hurry, hoping our speed would make it hard for the enemy to target us. As we raced the mile or so north toward Eilendorf, German snipers, tanks, and artillery kept us under a terrific hail of fire, directed by enemy observers who had a clear view of the entire area.

Upon reaching our objective on the outskirts of Eilendorf about four miles east of the center of Aachen, we immediately took up a defensive position with orders to remain alert for possible German attempts to infiltrate our lines.

By nightfall on September 15, troops from our 2nd Battalion had entered Eilendorf and captured a number of pillboxes in the Schill Line east of the town. Part of the main belt of the Siegfried Line fortifications, this sector of the Schill Line ran along the Verlautenheide Ridge, the high ground that extended southeast from the village of Verlautenheide down toward the town of Stolberg. While our rapid advance left Aachen surrounded on the west, south, and east, the Germans were putting up stiff resistance and pouring reinforcements into the area in an effort to prevent the city's full encirclement and capture.

On the following day of September 16, 2nd Battalion infantry finished clearing Eilendorf of enemy troops and H Company shifted its command post into the center of town. But while we were working to secure our newly won position, the *Wehrmacht* still possessed one big advantage.

With the Germans still holding the high ground in the nearby village of Verlautenheide, a little over a mile northwest of Eilendorf, and Crucifix Hill (Hill 239) a further half a mile northwest of that, enemy observers possessed superb vantage points from which to monitor our lines, exposing our whole position to highly accurate enemy shelling.

At our machine-gun platoon's new front-line position in the hilly ground just east of Eilendorf, German mortar fire was especially heavy and deadly. Unlike the whistle of an incoming artillery shell that could be heard before it exploded, the hissing sound made by a descending mortar round often came too late for us to take cover.

During a pause in the German shelling, we watched as American and *Luftwaffe* pilots fought running dogfights through the skies overhead, but our interest in the aerial spectacle quickly faded when enemy fire resumed. That evening, brilliant flashes lit the horizon as our mortar and artillery crews engaged their German counterparts in an intense, thunderous exchange of fire.

While our 2nd Battalion was battling the enemy near Eilendorf, the 16th Infantry Regiment's 1st Battalion had been supporting a task force from the 3rd Armored Division that was attacking the neighboring towns of Münsterbusch and Stolberg. Located roughly three miles east-southeast of Eilendorf, the town of Stolberg was a particularly vital objective. Although the assault made some headway, our offensive operations were by now about at their limit as additional enemy forces continued to stream into the area.

Early in the predawn hours of September 17, our lines came under furious bombardment from German artillery and mortar fire. The hurricane of shells during the ensuing hours was like nothing we had ever known, far worse than anything we had endured in Normandy. Hoping and praying it would end soon, we could only crouch in our foxholes to wait it out. As the barrage persisted, we wondered if it was a prelude to a major enemy counterattack to try to regain control of the hills east of Eilendorf and relieve our pressure on Aachen. The counterattack did come, though later than we anticipated.

Late that morning, we received intelligence that German troops were about to launch an assault against our position from woods about 50 yards away.

"I want you two machine gunners to cover that little forest up there, just mow it down!" an officer ordered our gun section, hoping to impede the attack.

Although no enemy troops were yet visible to us, we immediately opened up with our two guns, raking the trees with heavy fire.

Moments later, German infantrymen charged out of the woods, rushing toward us across the open field with fixed bayonets. If they were expecting to mop up American troops dazed by the heavy mortar and artillery fire, we disappointed them. Pounded by our artillery while they were still in the woods and under withering fire from our mortars, machine guns, and rifles, the enemy troops were cut down before they reached us. The carnage was dreadful.

About 15 minutes into the fight, the hiss of a German mortar round dropping toward me reached my ears. In the ensuing split second, I pressed myself flat against the ground, but raised my head to see where the round landed. In that same instant, a terrific explosion five yards away flung debris in every direction, walloping the right side of my face with a big clod of hard earth.

The blow left me unhurt, but badly damaged the frame and one lens of my glasses. With our situation too critical for me to leave the line, I bent the frame back into shape as best I could so the glasses would stay on my face. This was an inconvenience, but I knew I had been extremely lucky not to have been injured as a couple of our riflemen nearby had been wounded in the explosion.

By late that morning, the enemy's first major counterattack was finally driven off under the weight of our firepower. Our machine-gun crews and infantry had suffered casualties, but the Germans had sustained far worse.

Subsequent German attacks fell into a pattern. After heavily shelling our lines for about five minutes, their infantry would surge toward us. The ensuing fighting usually lasted half an hour before the Germans were forced to withdraw to their lines. Then another enemy bombardment of our position would begin.

Following a series of attacks on September 17, the Germans renewed their assault early the next morning. Just as it was starting to grow light, enemy troops erupted from the woods 150 yards to our left. I could not immediately see them, but our section's other machine gun opened up, firing steadily into the darkness.

As the light improved, I spotted German soldiers crawling forward with fixed bayonets. Rapidly rotating the elevation knob to depress the barrel of my machine gun, I began shooting down at them. I could see the bullets kicking up dirt in the area where the force was moving, killing many of the enemy. Under fire from our two machine guns and a good number of crack-shot riflemen, the surviving German troops again retreated into the woods.

While we managed to hold our ground, the succession of repeated barrages and attacks left us exhausted. If the *Wehrmacht* had been able to concentrate a larger force in our sector, we would have been overwhelmed.

The resurgent opposition surprised us and made it clear the Germans were not close to giving up, but we at least knew we were winning. In contrast, enemy prisoners disclosed deep morale problems tied to Germany's ever more dire military situation. While some German troops would fight fanatically and give their lives in defense of their homeland, many more were prepared to surrender once they felt they had adequately performed their duty.

Kitchen duty: September 18–23

After we had beaten back several enemy assaults, I was at last able to head to the rear on the afternoon of September 18 in order to speak with First Sergeant Huber about requisitioning a new pair of glasses. Though I had managed to twist the frame of my glasses so they were wearable, I could not continue fighting with a cracked right lens and a badly mangled wire frame.

Huber was an NCO with whom I had developed a friendship back in England. Standing about six feet tall, neat, and clean-shaven, he looked and acted the part of a first sergeant as he handled various administrative and supply duties for H Company. After ordering new glasses for me, Huber assigned me to KP duty in our company's kitchen while I awaited their delivery.

The kitchen had been established in an abandoned three-story house on the far side of Eilendorf, a mile or so behind the front line. The home's top floor had suffered severe damage in earlier fighting, but the two lower floors were in pretty good shape, offering plenty of space for me and the rest of the kitchen crew to sleep and work.

When I reported downstairs for kitchen duty the following morning, I was instructed to peel and mash a bushel—about 10 gallons—of potatoes for that night's supper. The regulation recipe called for one pound of butter, but I decided the spuds would have more flavor if I instead mixed in four pounds of butter. While this turned the mashed potatoes from white to yellow, my formula proved to be a hit with the guys on the front line and they clamored for more.

My mashed potatoes also drew praise from Steve, a friend of mine who served as company cook. A good-natured, stocky guy, Steve had honed his culinary skills working at a restaurant back in Minnesota. Perhaps because his parents had immigrated to the United States from Sweden, he also had a knack for languages and could speak a little German and Russian.

A couple of days after I had come up with the extra-buttery mashed potatoes, Steve put them back on that night's menu. Unaware of the secret to my recipe, he asked me to whip up another batch the same way.

Sometime after I had begun peeling potatoes in a room on the home's first floor, an attractive blonde in her early twenties entered the house. With sparkling blue eyes and a nice figure, she was the kind of girl who attracted a lot of male attention.

Heading back to the kitchen, the young woman began chatting with the mess sergeant. Because he spoke German, I assumed she must be a local *Fräulein*. Before long, they were joined by a couple of other members of the kitchen staff. Covering their mouths conspiratorially as they whispered to each other, one guy kept pointing toward me as the woman nodded her head.

Just before their conversation ended, I heard her say in German-accented English, "I understand, I understand." Soon afterward, she left the kitchen and the guys who had been speaking with her went back to work.

Returning to my potato peeling, I would not have given their conversation another thought, but my buddy Steve had overheard enough to be suspicious.

"Andy, these guys were talking about you with that German woman," he confided. While it was unclear what exactly that meant, Steve warned it was likely they were scheming up something with me as the target.

About an hour later after I had finished peeling the bushel of potatoes, the mess sergeant came over and told me to grab another bucketful from the storeroom at the rear of the house.

On reaching the storeroom, I began filling the pail with potatoes. Suddenly, the door slammed shut behind me and the lock clicked.

Spinning around, I was stunned to see the voluptuous young *Fräulein* with long golden hair seductively reclining on a sofa just to the right of the door—stark naked. She was definitely the most beautiful naked woman I had ever laid eyes on. In fact, she was the only naked woman I had ever seen.

At that same moment, I heard muffled snickering and scuffling coming from the other side of the door, mixed with demands for silence so as to better eavesdrop. It was obvious these were the same guys who had been talking with this *Fräulein* earlier. They had likely told her that I lacked any experience with women and wanted to test the waters. She may well have consented to their plan without realizing I had no interest in such an encounter.

During our time in England, France, and Belgium, other guys in H Company had often encouraged me to join them in their sexual escapades with young and willing foreign girls. I always refused these invitations, stating my determination to remain celibate until marriage. I was determined to wait for God to lead me to the woman of my dreams who would be my partner for life. The girl on the couch was a knockout, but she was not the woman for me.

Moving up to the door, I spoke in my normal tone of voice to the still whispering and giggling pranksters on the other side.

"You guys, I know you sent me in here for this pussycat, but I came in here for potatoes. I'm going to count to five slowly. If you don't unlock the door by the count of five, I'm blowing the lock off the door with my .45 so you boys need to get out of the way," I announced, withdrawing my pistol from its holster.

Apparently not taking my threat seriously, they were still laughing when "five" came and a bullet from my .45 blasted through the lock. When I kicked the door open, the three guys in the hallway were white with shock and fear.

Grabbing my bucket of potatoes, I was about to step out of the storeroom when I realized I had neglected to pay my respects to the *Fräulein*. Turning my head back into the room, I gave her a parting wave. Only when she cowered in the corner of the sofa did I recall that my hand still wielded the .45.

"I was just waving goodbye to you, darlin'," I reassured her with a smile. No doubt she believed this crazy American was going to shoot her.

"What the hell's wrong with Andrews?" I heard one of the guys grumble as the three plucked wooden splinters from the door out of their faces and arms.

"I told you guys that he didn't want to fool with women until he gets home and is married, so you shouldn't be surprised," the mess sergeant told him.

"Yeah, but he didn't have to be so damn rough about it!" sulked one of the men. It was the last time they would conspire to set me up with a *Fräulein*.

While most other GIs respected my faith, some may have doubted my commitment to adhere to it. Certainly, my persistent refusal to engage in sex, gambling, and drinking was viewed as highly peculiar. Raised in a Christian home, I had taken a vow to live in accordance with my faith back in high school and meant to stick to it. My deeply held convictions about what was morally right defined how I would live my life and behave as a soldier. Whatever its brutality and horrors, war was not an excuse to act immorally.

Preparing to return to the front line: September 23

On the evening of my fifth day on KP duty, First Sergeant Huber stopped by the company kitchen.

"Your glasses are here. I'm sorry you have to go back. By the way, before you go back, what's it like up there at the front?" Huber inquired.

"Like nothing you ever saw!" I said dramatically. "Hey, why don't you come up there and join us so you can see for yourself!" Although Huber served only a mile behind the front line, he lacked any real sense of what combat was like.

With a somewhat chagrinned expression, he handed me my new glasses and walked off, apparently not interested in taking up my invitation.

The Andrews family at supper in 1940 (Andy is seated at the lower left). (From the personal collection of Andy Andrews)

Andy with the West family in Yeovil, England. (From the personal collection of Andy Andrews)

Andy with a buddy from his squad. (From the personal collection of Andy Andrews)

The crew of a German armored vehicle about to surrender. (From the personal collection of Andy Andrews)

Andy with a couple of guys behind signs for II Battalion HQs. (From the personal collection of Andy Andrews)

The Germans surrendering in Czechoslovakia on May 9, 1945. (From the personal collection of Andy Andrews)

Andy and a buddy with the machine gun and jeep. (From the personal collection of Andy Andrews)

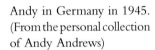

Andy in Germany in 1945. (From the personal collection of Andy Andrews)

Andy's squad with their jeep "Little Joe" (Andy is at the far left). (From the personal collection of Andy Andrews)

Unit photo with a machine gun in Germany, 1945 (Andy is at the far left in the second row). (From the personal collection of Andy Andrews)

Sign at Camp Calas near the port of Marseilles, October 1945. (From the personal collection of Andy Andrews)

Piled helmets of departing GIs, October 1945. (From the personal collection of Andy Andrews)

Andy and First Sergeant Huber aboard the USS *Mount Vernon*, October 1945. (From the personal collection of Andy Andrews)

Soldiers on the deck of the USS *Mount Vernon* after the landmass of the USA first becomes visible, October 12, 1945. (From the personal collection of Andy Andrews)

Andy with his new bride, Hellon Andrews, 1949. (From the personal collections of Al Andrews and Sarah Murray)

Andy and Hellon with their children Sarah and Al at the World Council of Churches in Geneva in the late 1950s. (From the personal collections of Al Andrews and Sarah Murray)

Andy and Hellon with their family celebrating their 50th wedding anniversary in 1999. (From the personal collections of Al Andrews and Sarah Murray)

Andy at the Normandy American Cemetery. (From the personal collections of Al Andrews and Sarah Murray)

Andy with his grandsons Brent and Hunter Andrews at the opening of The National D-Day Memorial, Bedford, VA, June 1, 2001. (From the personal collections of Al Andrews and Sarah Murray)

Andy with his grandsons Scott and David Murray at The World War II Memorial in Washington, DC, in November 2007. (From the personal collections of Al Andrews and Sarah Murray)

World War II memorabilia that Andy brought back from Europe. (From the personal collections of Al Andrews and Sarah Murray)

Andy with his World War II souvenirs in 2012. (From the personal collections of Al Andrews and Sarah Murray)

Andy receiving his honorary doctorate at Montreat College, May 2006. (From the personal collections of Al Andrews and Sarah Murray)

As I prepared to return to the front on September 23, we remained on the defensive. Even if most of us had not been worn down by the previous month of campaigning that had carried us from Normandy to the frontier of Germany, our troop numbers as well as our supply of fuel and ammunition were simply inadequate to maintain offensive operations. Beyond that, the weather had deteriorated, bringing heavy rain and dense fogs that prevented us from exploiting our airpower to provide close tactical support to the ground forces.

Meanwhile, the *Wehrmacht* continued to deploy additional forces into the area as they struggled to reverse our gains around Aachen. Confronted by this German buildup, logistical issues, and bad weather, the U.S. First Army's VII Corps shifted its efforts to further isolating the enemy's garrison in Aachen, while simultaneously resisting German attempts to relieve the American pressure on the city. Working with VII Corps, the First Army's XIX Corps was pushing forward north of Aachen to complete the encirclement of the city.

Still operating on the left flank of VII Corps, the 1st Infantry Division's 26th and 18th Infantry Regiments held the ground south of Aachen, while our 16th Infantry Regiment secured the division's eastern right flank. Settled into a defensive posture, the 16th Infantry Regiment's mission was to resist German attempts to break through our lines in order to relieve their forces in Aachen.

On the right of the 16th Infantry Regiment's line, the 1st Battalion had fought its way into the city of Stolberg, where it remained locked in a bitter house-to-house struggle. In the regiment's center, the 3rd Battalion secured the line extending east-southeast from Eilendorf toward Stolberg. On the regiment's left, our 2nd Battalion held positions in the Schill Line that ran along the Verlautenheide Ridge near Eilendorf, south of the village of Verlautenheide.

Although our battalion had managed to penetrate the Schill Line defenses, this breach of the primary belt of the Siegfried Line remained partial, with some of the fortifications in our hands and others still in German hands. Amid the rain, fog, and bone-chilling cold of that autumn, we would have to hold this position against a series of counterattacks by enemy troops desperate to break our grip on Aachen.

The war was not over.

CHAPTER 11

On the Siegfried Line:
September 23–October 22, 1944

The bunker: night, September 23/24

Later that same night after my new glasses arrived, I caught a lift up to the front line in a jeep. To evade detection by enemy observers, the driver left the headlights off and instead navigated the road with a flashlight held in his left hand. The short ride was a bit nerve-racking, but he managed to get us safely to the Verlautenheide Ridge.

When the driver pulled up at the foot of a hill, the familiar voice of Sergeant Gentry, our machine-gun squad's veteran NCO, greeted me from the darkness.

"C'mon, Andrews, we're going up to the front."

Rugged and war-weary in appearance, Gentry briefed me on our squad's tactical situation in the Schill Line as we climbed a steep grassy slope in the cool night air.

"We are quartered in a German bunker on the far side of this hill that we've just captured. There is a German bunker position about 60 or 70 yards away that we have not captured."

After cresting the hill, we made our way down to our squad's bunker. Built into the slope a short distance from the top of the hill, only about half of the thick-walled concrete bunker protruded above ground. A tree on one side of the bunker and another tree above it helped further conceal the structure from view. Not intended to be a fortified firing position like a pillbox, the bunker had been constructed to provide quarters for German troops.

"Now, there's several guys in there sleeping. You're going to join them. We'll give you a nap and then you go on the machine gun," Gentry whispered. "The door is real low, so you gotta get down on your knees to get inside," he cautioned. When I failed to duck low enough to avoid banging my head, he hissed, "Get lower than that!"

Crawling through the door, I found myself inside a dark, cold, and stuffy room about the size of a one-car garage. With everyone else in my squad asleep, I groped my way through the blackness until I found an empty bunk, comprised of a straw mattress supported by woven wire stretched between the bars of a metal bed frame.

Almost as soon as I fell asleep, Gentry was shaking my leg to awaken me at the end of his shift behind the gun. It was about four in the morning.

"It's your turn on the gun," he whispered. Still drowsy, I followed him outside.

"You sit right here," he instructed. Obediently, I crawled into the five-foot space between the machine gun and the bunker's large steel door that faced the German position.

"I want you to feel this," the sergeant directed once I was in position. With my hands on the machine gun, Gentry swiveled the weapon first one way then the other. "You can go this far or you can go that far," he explained.

"Out there is your field of fire. If you see anything move, cut it down," he instructed before crawling back inside the bunker to get some rest.

On gun duty: night to early morning, September 24

Knowing the Germans were nearby, I kept my head raised just high enough to see over the top of the two-foot-high machine gun, which allowed me a relatively comfortable posture. However, if the enemy began shooting at our position, I would immediately duck my head, crouching low enough so that I could target my return fire by looking down the underside of the barrel. Staying as low as possible during combat was a technique I had learned in basic training. More than one H Company gunner had taken a bullet in the forehead by sighting over the top of the gun during a firefight.

If fighting broke out, a dirt bank on my left offered some protection on that flank, while bushes and a small mound of earth in front of the gun helped further conceal the position, making it less exposed than it at first appeared to be.

In the darkness, no details were clearly visible on the German side of the line, but I could just make out two enemy-held bunkers about 60 or 70 yards away. Situated among trees on the slope of the hill facing us, the bunkers were a little off to my right.

About 40 yards away, below and a little to the left of the bunkers, a bulldozed mound of earth ran from my right to my left. The earthen rampart was almost perfectly flat at its top, perpendicular to my position, and on higher ground, giving the Germans the ability to shoot down at our gun emplacement in the event of any future firefight.

Beneath my position, a gully formed by the juncture of the steep bank coming down from the earthen rampart and the grassy hill sloping down from our bunker marked the midway point of the No Man's Land that separated our gun emplacement from the enemy position. Our section's other machine gun was posted 40 or 50 yards to my left, while another machine-gun crew was positioned perhaps 75 yards to my right.

The proximity of the enemy heightened all my senses. Gazing out into the darkness, my eyes constantly searched for the slightest movement. Meanwhile, my ears remained alert for the faintest stirring in front of me.

When an hour or two went by without incident, I began to hope the night would pass uneventfully. This would mark a change in my fortune. Up to this point in the war, it had seemed to be my fate that everything happened during my shifts behind the gun.

Just before the first light of dawn, when the night is the darkest, my eyes detected the movement of two sets of three very small shiny dots near the German bunkers.

Processing the scene in a split second, I determined that the shiny dots were the glint of brass buttons on uniforms. Straining my eyes, I was just able to discern the shadowy faces and bodies of two German infantrymen. Standing beside a huge boulder, they appeared to be fitting something on to the end of a rifle.

A moment later, one of the soldiers started to raise his rifle with a shiny object on the end. Realizing that he was about to shoot a rifle-grenade right at my position, my reflexes automatically took over.

In one swift motion, I turned the knob to lower the machine gun's barrel even with my target and squeezed the trigger, letting off a short burst of about a dozen rounds. As the gun clattered, a phosphorus tracer round flashed out toward the two enemy infantrymen in a blur of light, marking the path of my fire. It was just a bit low.

Slightly elevating the barrel to correct my aim, I let off a second burst an instant later. The soldier who was targeting me with the rifle grenade tumbled to the ground, while the other man dove sideways for cover behind the boulder.

At the same moment, Gentry emerged from our bunker in a fast, low crouch.

"What the hell are you shooting at?" he challenged.

"I'm shooting at two Krauts over there. One of 'em's dead, but the other one's behind that boulder," I explained, gesturing toward their location.

"Yeah, you got one of them," Gentry acknowledged, peering across toward the enemy position where the body of the dead German was just visible.

"Where's the other one?" he demanded more loudly.

"Behind that boulder," I replied, pointing out the big stone where he had hidden.

"Get out of the way and let me get behind that gun," Gentry ordered.

"Why don't you leave me behind the gun?" I protested, feeling I had already demonstrated my proficiency with the weapon. But he just waved me aside.

Yet despite repeatedly shooting at the boulder, Gentry could not get the German to break cover. For the next 10 minutes, he did not budge.

But as the sky began to brighten, the enemy soldier must have finally decided he had to make a run for it before daybreak. Bolting from behind the stone, he made a mad dash for the nearest enemy bunker a few yards away.

The instant the German emerged, Gentry opened up with the machine gun. Dogging his every step with fire, tracer rounds passed under and over the man's arms, right between his legs, and just above his head. But somehow, miraculously, all the bullets missed and the soldier reached the safety of the enemy bunker.

"You should have left me on that gun. I'd have got that guy," I joshed, good-naturedly ribbing the sergeant as I resumed my post behind the gun for the remainder of my shift. The episode would be a running joke between us for the next few days.

The first day at the bunker: September 24

Following my four-hour shift on gun duty, I turned the weapon over to another man in my squad and snatched a few hours of sleep in the bunker.

Returning outside late that morning, I joined the six other members of my squad and a half-dozen infantrymen who were posted around our bunker to help repel any new German attack. A gung-ho lieutenant crouched among us, watching for any enemy activity. Although the German side of the line was quiet, we observed enemy troops intermittently scurrying back and forth between their two bunkers.

"Let's zero in on that spot where they're moving!" exclaimed the lieutenant after monitoring the situation for half an hour.

As ordered, the gunner squeezed off a quick burst of fire. Tracer fire blazed a phosphorescent arc into the gap between the bunkers.

"That's it! That it!" shouted the lieutenant enthusiastically. "Let's fire a burst when you see another man running between the bunkers!"

A few minutes later, another couple of Germans emerged and began the sprint to the other bunker. Immediately, our gunner opened up. Over the next minute, dozens of rounds poured from the barrel, kicking up the dirt between the enemy bunkers.

"Let up on it! Don't waste all your ammo!" the lieutenant eventually cautioned.

For the rest of the day, the German troops ceased trying to cross between their bunkers. Once it fell quiet, I began to survey our surroundings in the daylight. While the trees around our bunker prevented us from seeing very far to the right or left, a magnificent scenic vista lay in front of us. Behind the German bunkers, thickly wooded rolling hills stretched off into the distance. It was sad we had to fight in such a place.

After a while, I decided to make my way back to our latrine in the rear. After swiftly ascending the ridge behind our bunker, I reached the crest, where I caught a brief glimpse of Eilendorf's sharply sloped rooftops and tall chimneys below the hill. Easing down the steep slope a little way, I found a spot to relieve myself.

As I was preparing to take care of business, a hot breeze whipped past my face as an incoming artillery round whistled through the air past my head. Landing down below the hill, the shell's explosion devastated a house on the outskirts of Eilendorf.

While we knew the Germans had the entire area under observation, I had never imagined they might target us individually. Apparently, an enemy artillery observer had zeroed in on this location after seeing several GIs relieve themselves there.

Not wanting to risk a second shell, I scrambled back up the hill and down to our bunker. On both sides of the front line, any movement during daylight hours was perilous, but even movement at night was not without risk.

A strange incident

Chow at the bunker consisted mainly of our regular Army rations and cold coffee, but our diet was supplemented with sandwiches and an occasional hot meal. For these items, we had to head back to the rear, where our kitchen crew had established a mess area a short distance behind the hill.

On my third or fourth afternoon at the bunker, I noticed most of the other members of the squad had left our position to grab lunch in the rear. Before heading back to join them for a sandwich, I placed one of our new squad members in charge of the machine gun, telling him that I would return in a few minutes.

While eating a sandwich in the mess area a short time later, I was shocked to see the same squad member who I had left on gun duty arrive for lunch. Realizing no one was manning our position, I hustled back over the hill to the bunker.

Luckily, when I reached our gun emplacement, nothing appeared to be amiss. Just to be certain, I decided to check inside the bunker as well.

To my astonishment, an American grenade was sitting in the middle of the bunker's floor with the space around it swept clean. Propped upside down, the grenade rested precariously on its latch with the safety pin removed. If someone accidentally knocked it over, the latch would be released, detonating the grenade. Its explosion would send a cloud of shrapnel ripping through anyone inside the bunker.

Who in the world put this thing here where it would be so easy to trip over and blow everything apart?

My first thought was that a German must somehow have obtained an American grenade and slipped into our bunker unobserved, but it seemed very unlikely an enemy soldier could have infiltrated our position during my brief absence in the rear. Outside of that short interval, it would have been almost impossible for a German to have made his way over to our bunker without being seen.

If a German had not booby-trapped the bunker, then it must have been one of our own guys, as incomprehensible as that seemed. *But who would have done it?*

On the one hand, the grenade might have been rigged by a squad member with a grudge against somebody else in our outfit. Alternatively, it could have been planted by some screwball or by someone who had gone nuts under the strain of combat.

Whoever had rigged the lethal trap, I had to get rid of the thing. Carefully picking the grenade up while squeezing the latch to prevent it from springing off, I took it outside. After making sure none of our personnel were in the vicinity, I threw the grenade over the hill, where it exploded with a terrific bang.

Later, I discussed the matter with Sergeant Gentry but we never figured out who had attempted to booby trap our bunker.

A long night: September 28/29

By the end of September, the weather was turning increasingly cold and storms were frequently rolling through the area. During my fifth night on gun duty at the bunker, another thunderstorm arrived about an hour into my shift.

First falling in a cold, thin drizzle, the rain gradually intensified into a torrential downpour. Lacking any type of tarp to cover our position, I used a poncho to protect the machine gun's firing chamber and hunkered down in my battle jacket.

As raindrops noisily splattered off the gun barrel's stovepipe-shaped water jacket, lightning flashes in the sky reflected off the brass casings of the rounds in the canvas ammo belt, reassuring me I could handle whatever the Germans might throw at us. But apart from the fleeting illumination provided by lightning, visibility was greatly hampered by the heavy rain and a thick fog, so I could only see about halfway across the 60 or 70 yards between our position and the enemy bunkers.

Two hours into my shift on the gun, a voice nearby hailed me from the darkness. *"Kamerad! Kamerad!"*

Spoken in German, the eerie salutation sent a chill up my spine. A familiar enemy ploy, this friendly greeting to a "comrade" was intended to cause me to hesitate for a moment if I observed anyone approaching our bunker. Instead, I swung the barrel in the direction of the voice, scrutinizing the darkness for the enemy infiltrators.

With perfect timing, a bolt of lightning lit up the night at just that moment, exposing the startling sight of two German soldiers who were rising to a standing position just six feet to my left. Taking advantage of the storm and fog, they had managed to sneak right up to our bunker without me noticing them.

At the same instant, I became aware one of them was poised to hurl a "beehive" (a *Hafthohlladung*, also nicknamed the *Panzerknacker* or "Tank breaker"). Resembling an oversized version of the German "potato masher" hand grenade, the beehive was a grapefruit-sized magnetic high explosive shaped charge attached to the end of a three-foot wooden pole. If the soldier succeeded in tossing the beehive in my direction, the "sticky" magnetic charge would readily adhere to the bunker's steel door just behind me. On detonating, it would kill me and leave everyone inside the bunker dead or severely concussed.

In the split second before the enemy soldier could throw the beehive, my hand thrust to the machine gun's trigger and I let off a burst. At pointblank range, the gun's .30 caliber rounds were utterly devastating. Almost as if in slow motion, I watched the stream of bullets ripping through the bodies of the two Germans.

But there was no time for me to think about my close brush with death. With my adrenaline flowing, I immediately focused on the imminent threat of an assault by a larger force. The main attack often ensued close on the heels of a scouting party of two or three troops who were sent forward to probe our position and strike unexpectedly.

The presence of our machine-gun emplacement on the Verlautenheide Ridge presented a major obstacle to the enemy in this sector of the Schill Line. As long as we held this post, they could not penetrate the front at this location. On the other hand, if they managed to breach our line, they had a chance to upend our entire effort to isolate the *Wehrmacht* garrison inside Aachen.

Defending our bunker position

The expected follow-on attack commenced a couple of hours later that night. Though drizzle and fog continued to limit visibility, I spotted five German infantrymen momentarily silhouetted against the skyline as they moved into position atop the bulldozed earthen rampart about 40 yards from my location.

Crouched low behind the machine gun to minimize my exposure, I sighted the weapon from under the barrel, letting off a four-second burst of 16 to 20 rounds toward the enemy troops. From the tracer fire, I could see my aim was a little low, striking the slope just beneath the men.

The split second that elapsed before I could elevate the barrel and fire a second burst gave the Germans a chance to duck down behind the embankment. In the foggy darkness, it was impossible for me to tell whether my second burst had hit any of them, but I saw three German helmets tumbling down the slope of the earthen mound.

This small party turned out to be the vanguard of a larger force that had been brought forward for the attack. Over the next quarter of an hour, what appeared to be at least a couple of dozen German troops spilled out of one of the enemy bunkers off to my right. While one group began blazing away at me from a location near the bunker, another portion took up firing posts along a 50-yard stretch that extended from a position directly across from me to the high ground on the earthen rampart off to my left, with some shooting down at me from an elevation about 20 feet higher.

An uninterrupted hail of rifle and submachine-gun bullets began zinging through the air all around me, with some rounds sinking into the earthen mound piled up in front of me and others striking our bunker behind me. Despite the enemy's overwhelming numerical advantage, my machine gun enabled me to hit back at least as good as I got. Our section's other gun on my left also engaged the German force.

Returning fire in long bursts, I targeted the tiny orange and red muzzle flashes that flickered like fireflies all along the enemy line. While the brilliant tracks of my gun's tracer rounds arcing across the gap helped me target my fire, I knew they also made my gun emplacement visible to the Germans shooting back at me.

Sweeping my fire back and forth along the entire length of the enemy line, I worked to avoid any regular pattern as I shifted my aim from the troops holding the high ground on my left down to the enemy force near bunker on my right and then at the Germans directly across from me. If the enemy infantrymen could anticipate where I would next target my fire, they could use any predictable pause to take careful aim at my gun as well as to creep forward toward our bunker. But despite my effort to avoid any consistent pattern, enemy troops momentarily out of the line of fire still popped up to shoot dozens of rounds at my position. It was a deadly game of cat and mouse.

My extended bursts of fire soon caused the gun to emit a loud hiss as the water circulating around the barrel started to boil, while the cold rain striking the hot surface of the gun's water jacket produced whiffs of steam. Forced to slow my rate of fire so the weapon would not overheat, I knew it was dangerous to risk a pause of more than a few seconds before I resumed my suppressive fire.

Burning through a 250-round belt of ammo every couple of minutes, I repeatedly loaded a new belt into the firing chamber less than five seconds after the previous belt had been expended. Another squad member crawled forward from the bunker to keep me supplied with ammo, but otherwise remained sheltered in the bunker's small doorway where he could observe the fighting and replace me on the gun if I got hit. Unfortunately, the amount of lead flying around our position prevented the rest of my squad from taking up their usual posts on my flanks to provide additional return fire.

About 10 minutes into the firefight, loud popping noises rose above the din of battle as the Germans launched what appeared to be a half-dozen rifle-grenades at my position. One after the other, the grenades whistled through the air, with some passing just over my head and detonating as close as four yards to my left.

When one of these grenades exploded a short distance behind me, a shrapnel fragment slammed into the back of my right shoulder with tremendous force. A sharp jolt of pain was followed by a powerful aching throb, but it was not severe enough to cause me to crawl back to the bunker for medical treatment.

Suddenly, a new concern emerged as I heard the water in the gun barrel begin boiling like a kettle on a stove. Sliding my hand down to the rubber condensing hose, I felt a gap in its side where a German round had pierced it. With water now escaping the gun barrel as steam, I was forced to slow my rate of fire. Luckily, at about this moment, enemy fire began to slacken, allowing me to replace the damaged hose with a spare.

For the first 15 minutes of the firefight, only our section's two machine guns engaged the German force. At this point, two of our company's mortar squads located about 50 yards behind the hill began shelling the enemy lines. The mortar's ability to deliver a plunging fire was particularly effective because it allowed our crews to target the German infantry taking cover behind the earthen rampart.

Soon, screams and yells began coming from the enemy troops as the mortar rounds exploded among them.

Once our mortar crews began shelling the Germans, they, in turn, began to be targeted by enemy mortars and artillery firing from the woods behind the German lines. Just as quickly, our own artillery joined the fight. In the ensuing mortar and artillery duel, the shells whistled overhead in both directions, detonating with thunderous blasts at the end of their trajectory.

Fortunately, none of the German mortar or artillery rounds landed near me, while our own mortar and artillery crews suppressed the volume of enemy small arms fire coming in my direction. Whatever else was happening, my focus remained on defending our position and keeping the Germans across from me under steady fire.

The 20-minute-long exchange of mortar and artillery fire marked the crescendo of the firefight, though the shooting did not end right away. Perhaps an hour after the fighting had started, the firing gradually tapered off just before dawn as the Germans ended their attempt to overrun our position.

Morning after the firefight: September 29

As the day broke, the surviving enemy infantrymen quietly withdrew from their posts atop the bulldozed rampart, carrying away a dozen or so dead and wounded men, but leaving behind at least a couple of their dead. Even with the persistent rain and fog, visual evidence of the intensity of the previous night's battle was abundant. The beautiful woods behind the German bunker position had been transformed into a ravaged landscape filled with trees split in two, jagged stumps, huge shell craters, and a multitude of fires. The expended cordite, burning trees, and dead bodies all combined to create a sickening stench.

Not long afterward, three German soldiers emerged from nearby woods to surrender. Under interrogation, they confirmed the enemy force had suffered significant casualties. Later, more complete after-action reports stated that our section's two machine guns, strongly supported by our mortar and artillery crews, had been decisive in repulsing what had been a company-sized attack on our sector of the front.

Just before I turned over the gun to another squad member a couple of hours after the firefight ended, my eye fell upon one of the unfired .30 caliber rounds in the machine gun's ammo belt. A cartridge just three rounds to the left of the machine gun's firing chamber had taken a direct hit from a German bullet. This had bent the unfired cartridge in half so that it resembled a beckoning forefinger, causing the cordite propellant inside the casing to spill out. Had I fired just one more burst, the machine gun undoubtedly would have jammed, leaving our position completely vulnerable.

At about this same moment, I also became aware that the left lens of my glasses had been scratched during the firefight. Because I had been firing from a crouched position behind the gun, my face had been very close to the damaged round in the ammunition belt. This led me to conclude that the same German bullet that had collided with the unfired cartridge in the ammo belt—or at least some fragment of that enemy bullet—had subsequently ricocheted into the left lens of my glasses. That lens had probably prevented my eye from being injured.

A little later, when I sought to requisition another new pair of glasses from First Sergeant Huber, one of H Company's lieutenants gave me a hard time.

"What the hell have you been doing, Andrews, holding your glasses up out of the foxhole? You were just here!" he grumbled.

In truth, that night's fighting had been the roughest combat I had yet experienced. The storm of enemy fire had nearly taken my life. It was all the more miraculous to me that I had escaped the fight almost unscathed. Saying a big prayer of thanks to God, I switched out the damaged round in the ammo belt for an intact cartridge before the next gunner arrived to start his shift.

On turning to crawl back to the bunker, I was stunned to see hundreds of indentations from German bullets pitting the bunker's steel door and concrete wall five feet behind the gun emplacement. So dense were these impacts that it would have been impossible for me to place my hand anywhere on the door or wall without touching a spot pockmarked by a bullet. God was certainly watching over me.

Back in the bunker, I removed my field jacket so our medic could examine my still aching right shoulder. A big blue welt had arisen where the grenade shrapnel had struck, but, thankfully, the wound did not require medical attention.

As the rush of adrenaline that I experienced during combat faded, my sense of humanity returned, causing me to feel compassion toward the Germans whom I had killed. If I never gave much thought to the enemy dead we passed along the road or on the streets of villages, watching men die at close range in front of my machine gun left an indelible mark on my soul.

The encirclement of Aachen: early October–mid-October

The enemy's assault on our gun position was just one small operation in a relentless series of large and small attacks carried out by the *Wehrmacht* as it sought to counter our effort to isolate Aachen.

At the start of October, the Germans still retained a supply route into the city, but this six-mile-wide land corridor, that extended north from our position near Eilendorf up to Alsdorf, was now starting to come under pressure. On October 2, the U.S. 30th Infantry Division of the XIX Corps began its push southward to link up with our 1st Infantry Division.

As the threat of American encirclement of the city mounted, so did German efforts to breach our lines. While enemy artillery and mortar bombardment was an almost constant aspect of daily life at the bunker, it became especially intense when the enemy staged larger offensive operations.

Around midnight on October 3, German artillery began mercilessly shelling the 16th Infantry Regiment's lines, lobbing round after round at the positions held by our 2nd Battalion and the neighboring 3rd Battalion. Forced to take cover in our bunker, we dragged the machine gun inside with us, both to protect it from destruction as well as to prevent its capture by the enemy if we remained in the bunker too long. With the gun sitting just inside the door and all of us prone on our beds, the bunker felt cramped, but there was nothing for us to do but wait out the barrage. It was a situation to which we soon grew accustomed.

When the German artillery fire ceased, we immediately resumed our posts outside in anticipation of a possible assault, but, in this instance, our portion of the line turned out not to be the enemy's focus. Instead, the attack by enemy infantry and assault guns fell mainly upon the 3rd Battalion's sector. Bitter close-in fighting occurred before the Germans were repulsed with heavy losses.

The next phase of the U.S. Army's encirclement of Aachen began on October 7, when Alsdorf was seized by troops from the American 30th Infantry Division, which was continuing its drive south against fierce German resistance. The following day, the 18th Infantry Regiment of our 1st Infantry Division jumped off from positions near Eilendorf in an attack toward the village of Verlautenheide, about a mile north of us.

Beyond tightening the American grip on Aachen, the 18th Infantry's successful capture of the enemy positions in Verlautenheide, on Crucifix Hill (Hill 239), and on Ravels Hill (Hill 231) had another important consequence. By seizing this high ground that German observers had used to direct artillery fire against the 16th Infantry Regiment, their action also helped secure our front line along the Verlautenheide Ridge.

With Aachen almost completely encircled by October 10, the Big Red One's 26th Infantry Regiment began its assault on the city the next day, advancing from the east rather than the south. Seeking to prevent Aachen's further isolation and capture, the *Wehrmacht* prepared another large-scale operation to breach our lines, massing their forces in the wooded area in front of our positions on the Verlautenheide Ridge.

On October 15, a tank-supported German assault struck the juncture point where the 18th Infantry Regiment's lines linked up with our 2nd Battalion on the 16th Infantry Regiment's left flank. The furious enemy onslaught threatened to overwhelm I and G Companies and also pressed our 2nd Battalion's E and F Companies. If the Germans succeeded in pushing us off the ridgeline and forcing open a gap, our whole position around Aachen would be undermined.

Remorseless American artillery fire, heavy air support from P-47 fighter-bombers, and hard fighting by our infantry inflicted severe losses on the attacking force. By that afternoon, the *Wehrmacht* was forced to break off its attack.

Yet despite suffering heavy casualties, the desperate Germans would not give up their effort to break through to Aachen. Early on the morning of October 16, the enemy renewed its assault on our 2nd Battalion positions. Once again, our artillery, mortar, and machine-gun fire drove them back with severe losses. Further German attacks after dawn met the same result. The enemy failed to rupture our lines.

Meanwhile, following its capture of Alsdorf on October 7, the U.S. 30th Infantry Division had continued to battle its way southward. Overcoming bitter German opposition, it linked up with our 1st Infantry Division's 18th Infantry Regiment late on October 16 to complete the encirclement of Aachen. With the failure of the *Wehrmacht's* subsequent effort to breach our lines on October 18 and 19, Aachen's fate was sealed.

A brass symphony: mid-October

Early one morning in the second half of October, several German soldiers emerged from one of the bunkers across from our gun emplacement, causing us to open fire. Just after the ensuing skirmish ended, a runner delivered a message to Sergeant Gentry, who then came over to me at the machine gun.

"At 10 o'clock, I want you to start firing your gun, just raise hell with it. Fire it everywhere," he ordered.

"What's going on?" I asked, completely mystified by such an unusual order.

"There's an officer coming up to the front line. He wants to hear some battle," Gentry explained.

As it turned out, a lieutenant colonel had been visiting our headquarters back in Eilendorf during that morning's firefight. Hearing almost nonstop machine-gun fire in the distance, the officer had expressed an interest in observing a display of our weapon's firepower. To accommodate his wish, our section's two machine guns were to commence firing in precisely three hours.

Informed of this request, the usual jokes about the "brass" started.

"Yeah, he won't come all the way up to the front line until it's safe." But whatever our ribbing of officers, this one was going to get quite a show.

As scheduled, the lieutenant colonel appeared at our bunker promptly at 10 o'clock to catch the fireworks. By this time our section's other gunner had shifted his weapon to a position roughly 30 yards away from me in order to make the display more entertaining.

As the officer stood watching, the other gunner and I proceeded to blaze away in the general direction of the German lines. Fully embracing our orders to waste ammunition, the two of us had a ball. Directing tracer rounds up into the cloudy sky, we crisscrossed our fire in a spectacular five-minute shooting exhibition.

"Wow! What a powerful weapon!" the lieutenant colonel proclaimed with satisfaction before returning to the rear. It was the only time any of the brass put in an appearance at our front-line bunker.

The capture of Aachen: October 21–22

At 7:30 on the morning of October 21, the Germans surrendered their forces in Aachen, a city Hitler had boasted would never capitulate. On receiving the news over the field telephone at our bunker, all of us celebrated knowing we had played a small part in the operation's success.

Acting in coordination with the 30th Infantry Division and elements of the 28th Infantry Division, the Big Red One had helped achieve an important victory. While troops from the 1st Infantry Division's 26th Infantry Regiment had fought house to house against enemy forces inside Aachen, our 16th Infantry Regiment and the 18th Infantry Regiment had played a critical role in isolating the city and repulsing the *Wehrmacht*'s repeated efforts to break its encirclement.

As the first German city to surrender to the Allies, we knew Aachen's psychological impact on the Nazi *Reich*'s morale would far outweigh the more limited military significance of its capture. Although the month-long stalemate at Aachen had bought the *Wehrmacht* additional time to build up its forces and improve defensive positions in the neighboring Hürtgen Forest, the Germans had suffered the loss of over 10,000 troops who were killed, wounded, or captured during the fighting.

Yet our victory had come at the price of 5,000 American casualties, with about two-thirds from the 30th Infantry Division and a third from our 1st Infantry Division. Even our own company commander Captain Irvine had been wounded in the fighting. All of us wondered whether our future objectives in the rest of Germany would turn out to be so costly.

The day after Aachen's capture, H Company and the 2nd Battalion's three infantry companies were ordered to prepare to pull out of our positions in the Schill Line and rotate to the rear for a few days of hard-earned rest. Welcoming the news after a month of combat at the bunker, we began packing up our gear to leave.

Sometime around noon on our final day at the bunker, one of our sergeants made an unexpected announcement to me during my last turn on gun duty.

"Hell, Andy, I'm going home," he stated flatly, deciding he had seen enough combat. I knew the sergeant had previously fought in North Africa and Sicily and had been wounded twice. However, following the news we were about to rotate to the rear for a rest, I thought he was kidding when he said he was going back to the States.

Even when the sergeant withdrew his .45 pistol from his holster and took aim at his foot, I still believed he was joking. But, as I watched wide-eyed, he fired a round through the top of his right boot into his foot. Stories of soldiers shooting themselves in the foot in order to get a ticket home were common enough, but I never imagined I would witness such an act firsthand.

As the sergeant spun around several times like a chicken with its head cut off, he yelled for our medic who soon came forward to offer first aid. Two of our squad members held the sergeant down while the medic removed his boot and put a temporary dressing on the wound in his foot. The same squad members then assisted the medic in taking the sergeant back over the hill to the rear.

The sergeant did not return to our outfit and I never learned what happened to him or whether he managed to get shipped home. Just after he was taken back for medical treatment, our squad discussed the guts it took to shoot yourself in the foot, but no one was especially surprised by his attempt to get out of the war. During our month of combat at the bunker, we had endured repeated German attacks and the most severe shelling we had so far experienced in the war. Everyone's nerves were severely strained and most of us were suffering from some degree of combat fatigue.

Hunkered down day after day risking your life under enemy fire, a foot wound can start to look like a pretty tempting option as a means of survival. Some guys even tried to stick their foot up in the air as a target, hoping some German would give them a ticket home. Of course, shooting yourself in the foot was a lot more reliable.

However, there was a real danger of getting caught for a self-inflicted wound as a result of the tell-tale powder burns that were left when a weapon was discharged at such close range. From the start, the Army was highly suspicious of any such "convenient" injuries. GIs received a printed warning that any gunshot wounds to the foot would receive special scrutiny. If the Army determined the wound was self-inflicted, the soldier's punishment would be severe.

Yet desperate soldiers still occasionally reached a point where they were simply "used up." Unable to go on fighting, they would do anything to get out of the war, a conflict that no longer seemed so near its end.

CHAPTER 12

The Hürtgen Forest:
October 22–November 18, 1944

A rest at Brand before returning to the front line: October 22–November 9

Despite the surrender of the German forces in Aachen on October 21, the situation at our bunker on the Verlautenheide Ridge near Eilendorf remained tense. Nearby gunfire kept us on high alert for a possible enemy attack throughout the next day and into that evening, even as we went on preparing to turn over our position.

After troops from the 26th Infantry Regiment relieved us on the night of October 22, we boarded trucks for the two-mile ride southwest to Brand, a town we had passed through during our rapid advance up to Eilendorf back in mid-September. Our arrival in Brand marked the start of four days of R&R for H Company and the three infantry companies in the 2nd Battalion, the first of the 16th Infantry Regiment's three battalions to rotate to the rear following a month of front-line combat during the battle of Aachen.

A bit of rest was a much-appreciated blessing and something to write home about. At night, we slept on mattresses scattered across the floor of a damaged German home, free from the prospect of rushing out of the bunker to fight off another enemy attack. While sleep and hot showers were the main attractions, the break from combat also gave us a chance to enjoy hot meals, grab a snack from the donut wagon, attend worship services, watch movies, and visit the small Army PX (Post Exchange), which sold toothpaste and soap as well as gum and candy bars.

The R&R in Brand also allowed us to deal with other basic needs. Removing our boots, we hung them upside down on sticks to dry out them in what little sunlight filtered through the overcast autumn sky. We also requisitioned new socks. By now, the fabric on the bottom of my two pairs of thick, Army-issue socks had completely worn away, leaving only a useless remnant around the top of my foot and my ankles.

During the day, huge armadas of Allied bombers were often visible high up in the clouds, flying eastward toward targets deep inside Germany. Some nights, we gathered outside just to listen to the roar of the massed bombers. They appeared to be an irresistible force, but we knew many of their crews would not make it back home.

Over the preceding months, our seven-man machine-gun squad had periodically received replacements for our earlier losses in order to keep us at or near full strength. One of the recent replacements was Jesse Beaver, a good buddy of mine from our training back in Bridport. Because he had been assigned to H Company's other machine-gun platoon, I had seen him only occasionally during our campaign through France. However, just after we crossed the Franco-Belgian border, Jesse received a transfer to our second machine-gun platoon and then obtained permission to switch to our squad.

Unfortunately, as a new arrival to our squad, Jesse initially had been tasked with lugging two of the heavy metal ammo boxes packed with cartridge belts for the machine gun, each of which weighed 22 pounds. Only a little over five feet tall and in his 30s, Jesse lacked physical stamina and frequently lagged behind the rest of us on the march as he struggled under the combined weight of the ammo boxes and his carbine. As he worked to keep up, he regularly overtaxed himself, growing so exhausted he had to stop and rest. Sometimes, he even became sick and then had to catch up to us. Jesse never asked for help, but I would often grab one of his ammo boxes, hooking its handle on the end of the left leg of the tripod to give him a break for a stretch.

The subsequent arrival of fresh replacements eventually gave Jesse a degree of seniority, lightening the load he had to carry. He told the new guys, "Okay, you're on the tail end with the ammo now and I'm up here close to Andy."

Another replacement was a full-blooded Cherokee Indian from Oklahoma who had acquired the nickname "Chief." To be clear, his moniker did not possess any sort of pejorative connotation. Indeed, none of us would have dared say anything to him that he might find offensive. Short, stocky, strong, and skilled with a knife, Chief was quick in his movements and would prove himself to be a tough, fearless fighter.

Though membership in our squad would remain fluid as men were killed or wounded, I gradually came to know Chief pretty well. If Jesse and Wayne Newsome were my only close friends in my squad, Chief eventually became a buddy of mine like Hector Gonzalez and Lincoln Welser. All of us got along well in and out of combat.

In the latter part of our four days at Brand, a group of about 20 of us from my platoon decided to venture into Aachen on foot to get a firsthand look. Devastated by the recent street fighting and earlier bombing, the city appeared to be a lifeless wasteland, emptied of its civilian population. Nearly all the buildings and houses were scarred, with many now only mounds of rubble, charred wood, and shattered glass.

What made the greatest impression on me was an enormous, four-story concrete building that had functioned as the local center of Nazi power. Looking like an over-sized bunker more than a public building, its walls were reputed to be 13-feet thick. Incredibly, an unexploded American 155-millimeter artillery shell remained visible where it had embedded itself in one of the concrete walls, a testament to the structure's solidity. But this former symbol of Nazi tyranny now served only as a monument to Allied determination to crush that dark empire.

Strolling amid the ruins of a city Hitler had declared to be unconquerable, not a single Nazi flag was in sight. I suddenly comprehended the true meaning of total defeat and wondered about the citizens who remained in Aachen.

Were there even enough locals left to clear the city of debris? What would be their next move? How would they go about rebuilding their city, their lives, and their nation?

Our rotation from the rest area in Brand back to the nearby front line came just after our visit to Aachen. On October 27, H Company relieved a company from the 3rd Battalion of its position near Freund, placing us a couple of miles east of Brand and a couple of miles southeast of our previous front-line bunker position near Eilendorf.

Over the next two weeks, the Germans targeted our new position with artillery fire, but it was nothing like the severe pounding we had endured during the preceding month back at Eilendorf. Though shelling, patrol activity, and enemy infiltration efforts continued, our two weeks at the front near Freund were relatively quiet. For now, our side remained in a defensive posture, while the Germans focused on resisting further American advances. But both sides were building up for the next battle.

Awaiting a new offensive: November 9–16

Over the course of November 8–9, the 16th Infantry Regiment turned over its front-line positions to other American units. H Company briefly returned to Brand, where our platoon cleaned its equipment, received crates of grenades and other supplies, and acquired further replacements in preparation for a new offensive operation. Even with all the replacements, roughly half of the men in H Company had served with our outfit since Normandy, giving us a solid core of tested troops.

On the afternoon of November 10, H Company departed Brand with our two machine-gun platoons riding in jeeps. Motoring southeast six miles, we reached our new position a couple of miles southwest of Zweifall and about three miles southwest of Vicht. Our move was part of a larger deployment of the 16th Infantry Regiment to a wooded assembly area that stretched three miles further northeast from Vicht toward Schevenhütte, placing our regiment a little south of the front line. Extending roughly due east a half-dozen miles from our old position at Eilendorf, the front line cut through the still contested town of Stolberg, ran just south of German-held Gressenich, and then passed just north of American-held Schevenhütte before turning south. Despite our capture of Aachen, the front line had changed little since our advance into Germany back in mid-September, almost two months earlier.

As H Company took up its new position in a thickly forested area southwest of Zweifall, we were not exactly sure how close the Germans were. We only knew we were waiting for the start of the next offensive and might have to remain at this spot for several days. Soaked by an icy mix of rain and snow that left us half-frozen, our section of the platoon got busy building two machine-gun emplacements. Knowing our stay might last for a few days, we constructed roofed dugouts, a project for which my knot-tying and log-lashing skills really came in handy.

First, our two squads dug large holes and piled the excavated dirt up around them to create small earthen walls, leaving the space immediately in front open for a firing port. Taking advantage of the young evergreens that carpeted the surrounding area, we next cut down lots of saplings and stripped them of their branches. Lashing the resulting wooden poles together in a lattice, we placed the rudimentary "roof" over each of the dugouts. We then covered each roof with about four inches of freshly dug earth, some flat stones, and lots of small branches, which gave us a measure of protection from shrapnel and wooden splinters if our sector of the woods came under German artillery fire. After a dusting of snow that night, our gun emplacements were nearly invisible.

But while these roofed shelters were well-camouflaged and somewhat protected from artillery fire, they failed to block out the cold rain that seeped into our clothes, dripped down into our boots, and generally left us miserable. Indeed, I was amazed no one in our section reported sick or came down with trench foot. Fires would have kept us warm but would draw unwanted attention from enemy observers.

Shortly after our arrival, a medic passed along the welcome news of Lieutenant Yankee's transfer out of H Company. It was his rash decision to cross that open field in willful disobedience of Captain Irvine's orders that had gotten three of our buddies killed by German artillery fire. Rumor was that H Company's higher-ups had learned there were men in our outfit who wanted to take revenge on the lieutenant and decided to order his reassignment to another unit before something bad happened.

Of course, those tragic deaths back in September were only the most glaring example of Lieutenant Yankee's reckless incompetence, so it was unclear whether he was transferred out of H Company due to his repeated failures as an officer, out of concerns for his safety, or for some other reason. Whatever the cause of his departure, we were simply glad to be rid of him. Wayne Newsome best expressed our feelings on the matter when he remarked, "Well, he won't bother us anymore."

The new lieutenant who replaced him was a far more competent officer. None of us had ever previously served under this lieutenant, but we immediately liked his gung-ho attitude and his aggressiveness. With these leadership qualities, we were willing to follow our new officer anywhere.

One morning a couple of days later, during a break in the rain and snow, a dozen of us from H Company watched four American Sherman tanks begin construction of a new firing position about 20 yards away from our machine-gun emplacements. The sound was deafening as the tanks clanked back and forth to clear the area of small trees.

About a half-hour into this clearing operation, a German Tiger tank suddenly burst out of the thick undergrowth 40 yards to our left, pushing aside branches as it charged directly toward our detachment from H Company. Having somehow gotten behind the American front line further north, the Tiger's approach had been concealed by the brush and masked by the noise of the Sherman tanks. Now, it looked set to wipe out both us and the Shermans, whose crews appeared to be oblivious to the threat.

Rather than opening fire, the Tiger abruptly halted about 50 feet in front of us. As the German tank commander surveyed the situation from his perch in the turret hatch, his face bore an utterly baffled expression. At this same moment, having now caught sight of the Tiger, two of the Shermans spun to face the enemy. Stunned by the rapid turn of events, all of us expected a fierce tank battle to erupt at any second.

However, instead of fighting, the Tiger's commander raised his arms in surrender, apparently concluding the odds were against him. Under gestured directions from the commander of one of the Shermans, the German tank pulled off to the side of the road near the clearing so it would not block traffic. With numerous weapons trained on the Tiger, its commander climbed out of the turret hatch and crawled down the side of the tank as the rest of his crew emerged with their hands raised. Meanwhile, the crews of the Shermans also crawled out of their tanks and walked over to the Tiger.

Then another surprising thing occurred. With the English-speaking commander of the Tiger acting as translator, everyone began warmly shaking hands like old buddies as we shared our sandwiches, apples, chewing gum, and candy with the German tank crew. Before sending them off to the rear for processing as prisoners, a friendly exchange of tank inspections was carried out. The Germans all seemed genuinely glad to be out of the fight, as if they had decided, "Well, we surrender. That's all for us. This is the end of our part in the war."

The plan for Operation *Queen*

Though we knew nothing about the plan for the impending Allied offensive called Operation *Queen*, the strategic objective of the U.S. First and Ninth Armies was to break through the German defenses west of the Roer River. This would set the stage for a further drive to the Rhine, some two dozen miles beyond the Roer.

As part of the First Army's VII Corps, our reinforced 1st Infantry Division, supported by the 104th Infantry Division and the 3rd Armored Division on its left flank, was assigned the task of capturing the Hamich Ridge, which extended northwest from the vicinity of Schevenhütte for about four miles toward Eschweiler. Once the ridge was secured, the 1st Infantry Division would have to fight its way a half-dozen miles further eastward to the Roer.

In the 1st Infantry Division's operational planning, it fell to our 16th Infantry Regiment to take a strategic height known as Hill 232 and the Hamich Ridge. Our regiment was also tasked with capturing the village of Hamich, located a mile northeast of Gressenich, a mile north of Schevenhütte, and a half mile southeast of Hill 232. While a frontal attack on Hill 232 would be difficult, it could be flanked from Hamich, so that was the initial objective.

To reach Hamich and Hill 232, we would first have to fight our way through the northwestern corner of the Hürtgen Forest. A 20-mile-long, 10-mile-wide stretch of dense woods, the forest formed the southern boundary of the Stolberg Corridor. Rather than a natural growth woodland, the Hürtgen was a man-made forest that had been designed under the direction of the *Wehrmacht*. As intended, it thus presented a formidable defensive barrier in this part of Germany's western border.

With trees planted to take full advantage of the terrain, the Hürtgen Forest sprawled across rolling hills broken up by numerous deep ravines and streams. Closely resembling a "wilderness" area near my hometown of Signal Mountain, the Hürtgen's rugged beauty reminded me of places where I had spent my youth hunting, hiking, and camping. Yet whatever recreational diversions its woods might have offered in peacetime, the Hürtgen presented an incredibly difficult environment for combat operations. Based on the bitter experience of American troops who had fought in other parts of the Hürtgen earlier in the fall, ground taken here came at a very high price.

Like them, we would have to fight in the dark shadows of trees that ranged from towering evergreen firs to spruce and balsams with limbs reaching down to the ground. Not only was visibility limited, but the lack of any main roads meant all vehicular traffic had to travel on narrow secondary roads and fire trails, routes made nearly impassable with mud caused by the continual autumn rains. With most of the trees arranged in neat rows like tombstones in a cemetery, German machine gunners in concealed bunkers had ready-made firing lanes to target any movement inside the Hürtgen. Huge, moss-covered boulders provided more cover for the enemy defenders.

Opposing our attack would be well-prepared *Wehrmacht* units. Dug in behind barbed wire and minefields, the German troops were backed by a couple hundred artillery pieces. As we knew from recent experience, soldiers defending their homeland would fight fiercely, even fanatically, to resist our advance.

Operation *Queen* begins: November 16–17

On the morning of November 16, the weather cleared after two weeks of almost constant rain and snow. Sometime just before noon, the low rumble of approaching aircraft rose in the distance. Moments later, a gigantic wave of American bombers and fighters swept through the sky to strike the German lines ahead of us, bringing an end to our week-long wait for the start of the offensive. Although targeting a more widely dispersed area further away from our front line than the bombing that had preceded Operation *Cobra* back in July, the air attack was still unbelievable to behold.

At the end of the aerial bombardment an hour or two later, our artillery took over, battering the enemy positions for perhaps another hour with a barrage that was as powerful as any that I could recall. It was difficult to imagine that the German troops in front of us could survive such a storm of bombs and shells, but the enemy was still there waiting for us and the rest of VII Corps.

Early that afternoon, the 1st Battalion started the 16th Infantry Regiment's ground operation, assaulting the German positions in the Hürtgen Forest north of Schevenhütte. Running into strong enemy opposition, the battalion succeeded in advancing a mile or so northward to the edge of the woods just south of the village of Hamich by dusk, but its further progress was stymied by fierce small arms fire as well as mortar and artillery fire directed by German observers on Hill 232.

Later in the afternoon, orders came for the 3rd Battalion to move up on the 1st Battalion's left flank. While our 2nd Battalion remained the 16th Infantry's regimental reserve, we also repositioned forward. Leaving our staging area about five that evening as the sun was setting, H Company began a slow five-mile trip by jeep to our new position two-thirds of a mile east of Vicht, which we reached in a couple of hours.

Halted for the night in a thickly forested area, our squad set up the machine gun behind a hastily constructed log wall. After establishing our position, one member of our squad went on sentry duty behind the gun while the rest of us slept.

Awakened for my turn on gun duty in the middle of a cold, black night, I kept watch through an uneventful two-hour shift as another light snow dusted the area. But just as my new buddy Chief was preparing to relieve me on the gun, a shot rang out from the darkness, striking the tree about three feet from his head.

Instantly, we both dropped into a low crouch behind our log walls, fearing we were under fire from a German sniper. About 15 minutes later, another round snapped off a small limb just above where we were kneeling. Neither of us had been hit, but it was only a matter of time before someone in our squad caught a bullet.

"Hell, Andy, I'm gonna go kill that sonuvabitch!" Chief announced, snatching up his razor-sharp knife in a lightning-fast movement. He favored his non-regulation, eight-inch folding knife, but was able to wield any knife with deadly effectiveness. At 10 or 20 paces, Chief could pin a pack of cigarettes to a tree.

To prevent anyone from mistakenly firing on him when he made his way back from his self-appointed mission to take out the sniper, Chief indicated his return route.

"Stay low, guys. I'll be back in about half an hour," Chief concluded, his words distorted by the knife clenched between his teeth. In case he ran into trouble, another fellow in our squad passed Chief his .45 pistol. Sliding the weapon under his belt, Chief slipped into the darkness, moving silently over the damp ground.

Knowing someone had to man the gun, I remained on duty, but the two or three of us who were awake all listened intently for any sound of Chief's return.

Blessed with the best hearing in our platoon, my ears were the first to pick up a slight rustling in the woods half an hour later as Chief made his way back toward our gun emplacement along the path he had pointed out. When he reached us, his hands and one sleeve of his field jacket were stained with blood.

"This is German blood, Andy. That sonuvabitch won't bother us no more," Chief whispered in a low voice. After wiping the blood from his hands and knife with tree leaves, he told me to get some rest and took over behind the gun.

Defying an order: morning, November 17

It was overcast and misty the next morning as we pushed deeper into the Hürtgen Forest. Advancing with an infantry outfit, we soon approached a spot thick with trees and brush that provided ideal concealment for enemy troops.

Deploying for action, I took up my post behind the machine gun. Meanwhile, the rifleman on point fired a volley toward the foliage, sort of prodding a hornet's nest.

Sure enough, the unseen enemy began shooting back, sparking a sharp firefight. While our infantry steadily blazed away at the woods, I added a few short bursts from my machine gun to their fire. Within minutes, we started trading grenades with the Germans as the fighting intensified.

To our surprise, a white flag abruptly appeared on the enemy side. When we stopped shooting, 10 Germans emerged from the trees to surrender.

As they approached us with their hands held high, the insignia on their uniforms caused us to believe they were SS. Especially with the more fanatical SS troops, we were always a little suspicious a surrender might be some type of ploy. Remaining crouched behind my machine gun, I kept the barrel trained on the men.

The ranking American officer on the scene was an unfamiliar lieutenant who led the infantry unit to which we were attached. When the 10 surrendering Germans were about 50 feet away, the lieutenant unexpectedly appeared right beside me.

"Get that machine gun going, soldier. Kill those bastards!" he suddenly barked.

Hearing the order, I could not believe my ears. *What's the matter with this guy? This is a war, not a turkey shoot. We are not going to start murdering unarmed enemy troops*, I thought to myself, deeply disturbed by the command.

But the lieutenant was just getting warmed up. Furious as all get out, he began cussing up a storm in an attempt to bully me.

"Kill 'em! Kill 'em!" he roared at me amid a tirade of vulgarities.

"I can't shoot those unarmed men … I won't do it!" I yelled back, standing up behind the machine gun to make clear my refusal.

"That's a direct order, soldier," he declared.

"You can go to hell … You can get someone else to do your dirty work for you. Damned if I will do it!" I angrily retorted.

Not really knowing the lieutenant made it easier to tell him off. While this meant disobeying a direct order, there was no way I was going to gun down 10 unarmed men trying to surrender. In fact, my rebuke was so adamant that the lieutenant may have believed I would shoot him if he persisted in pressuring me to carry out his command.

Still hoping to find someone who would shoot the surrendering Germans, the lieutenant began badgering the other nearby GIs to execute the order. But they also refused to go along, defying the officer with similarly strong language.

Once the enemy troops reached us, the lieutenant regained control of himself and detailed a couple of men to guard them. When we reached a spot where it was possible to set up a command post, he contacted headquarters about sending back the prisoners.

Only at this point did I learn the lieutenant had been infuriated by a shrapnel wound to his arm that he had suffered during the firefight. Though this injury in no way justified his order to shoot unarmed troops who had already given up, it did help explain his shocking behavior. The fact the surrendering troops appeared to be members of the hated SS may also have played a role in his actions.

The incident presented one of the first real ethical challenges I had faced in combat, but I knew I had a higher moral obligation that superseded this lieutenant's authority. Equally disgusted by his criminal order to murder the surrendering Germans, the other men later thanked me for my refusal to obey it. In the end, I think our rejection of the order shamed the lieutenant and helped bring him to his senses.

In my experience, this episode was an aberration. Generally, both sides respected attempts to surrender, but that does not mean the taking of prisoners always went smoothly. In the heat of the moment when buddies have been killed and emotions are running high, soldiers sometimes did things they would not normally do.

Hell in the Hürtgen: late morning to afternoon, November 17

As that morning's advance into the Hürtgen Forest continued, our machine-gun section entered a roughly two-mile-square grove of young fir trees, most of which were fully mature. As we cautiously proceeded down one of the narrow dirt fire trails that cut through the firs, our boots churned the path into gooey mud. A hundred yards in, the closely planted trees gave the whole place an unusual darkness.

At this point, the GIs at the head of our column spotted a well-hidden enemy log bunker 50 yards ahead of us. Part of a dense network of strategically situated and skillfully camouflaged German machine-gun and artillery bunkers that defended the routes through the forest, this one sheltered an 88-millimeter artillery gun that was aimed right down the trail along which we had intended to advance.

Unable to move forward, we indicated the enemy position to the crew of a nearby Sherman tank. With amazing daring, the tank sped off down a service road that ran parallel to the one that led to the bunker, racing past huge firs that made the Sherman look like a toy. Crashing through a bunch of trees, the tank maneuvered into a firing position just 20 yards from the right flank of the bunker.

At almost pointblank range, the Sherman blasted three rounds in quick succession into the log wall on the bunker's right side, probably concussing anyone inside. Within seconds, five shaken German soldiers emerged waving a white flag.

After sending the enemy prisoners to the rear, we deployed our machine gun to resist a possible counterattack. Gathering some of the thick green moss that was scattered around the wrecked bunker after its pounding by the Sherman, we used it to camouflage our gun position. When no counterattack came, we resumed our advance.

Early that afternoon as our attack drove deeper into the rough, densely wooded terrain of the Hürtgen, we became entangled with the German infantry along the front line. Enemy troops seemed to be lurking all around us, lying in wait to ambush us. Forced to take cover among the trees, we struggled to move forward. Close combat in the shadowy forest made the fighting chaotic and desperate. Then it got worse.

With sudden fury, an intense German artillery bombardment began crashing through the dense forest canopy 80 to 100 feet overhead. Many of the incoming artillery rounds passed through the trees to explode at ground level, spewing out shrapnel in every direction and gouging deep craters in the earth. Other shells detonated among the tree trunks and branches, sometimes causing the whole tops of trees to disintegrate. Every tree burst sent a lethal hail of jagged metal shrapnel and foot-long wooden splinters knifing toward the ground to shred anything in its path. Next to a sniper, it was the most terrifying thing we had yet encountered.

Instantly, everybody in our squad dropped to the needle-covered ground and began digging, hoping to burrow out a foxhole where we could wait out the artillery barrage. Even if a hole would not protect us from the shrapnel plunging down from the trees overhead, it was safer than just staying out in the open above ground.

Lying flat, I furiously shoveled out muddy earth, working in tandem with Hector Gonzalez. A GI who loved fighting, Hector was particularly irritated by artillery fire against which he could not hit back, but there was nothing for us to do but dig.

Yet, as fast as the two of us could remove a shovelful of mud from the saturated ground, watery sludge oozed back to refill the hole. After a quarter of an hour, the hopeless nature of our effort left both of us exhausted and utterly dispirited.

"What the hell, Andy, let's just let it fill back up. If it's our time, it's our time," Hector exclaimed, glumly tossing aside his shovel.

With no better place to go, we lay there resigned to our fate in the gloom of the cold, dark forest as German artillery rounds continued to plaster the area, periodically bursting up in the trees. Amid the tangy aroma of burning pine cones and the earthy smell of freshly uprooted moss, we could only pray and await whatever was to come.

By now, men were getting hit all around us. A moment after we gave up on digging out a foxhole, one of the shells passed through the trees unscathed to come whistling in right next to us. The tremendous blast 50 feet to our left hurled huge clumps of earth and shrapnel through the air.

A second later, a guy nearby let out a piercing shriek at the top of his lungs, causing me to look over in that direction. A GI from our company I barely knew had been struck by a large shard of shrapnel, which had deeply gashed his shoulder to open a gaping wound.

"They're coming! They're coming!" he yelled, terrorized by some unseen enemy.

"Mother!" the man cried out a moment later.

Then more quietly, "Mother?"

And then more softly still, "Mom."

They were his last words and the most heart-wrenching plea I ever heard a man make. Before a medic could reach him, he had suffered a fatal loss of blood.

Overwhelmed with emotion, tears flowed from my eyes until I could no longer see. Death was no stranger but witnessing a sad end like his was just hard to bear.

Brushing away my tears with a muddy sleeve, I caught sight of what appeared to be a small hut made of pine branches about 20 yards away. Hoping it would offer some protection from the ongoing enemy barrage, I dashed toward it.

Crawling through a narrow passage into the hut's cramped four-by-four-foot interior, I plopped down on the dry floor in relief. Only at that moment did I realize the pine branches covering the hut's exterior camouflaged an ammo dump of dozens of German 88-millimeter artillery shells. Neatly stacked with their tips pointed inward, the rounds formed igloo-like interior walls that gleamed so brilliantly that myriad distorted reflections of my face appeared on their protruding curved surfaces.

As I was still absorbing my ominous surroundings, the pounding footfalls of someone fast approaching the hut reached my ears. Squeezing back out of sight of the hut's opening, I withdrew my .45 from its holster as the runner entered the shelter.

Still breathing hard from his sprint and unaware of my presence, a German soldier sat down heavily two feet away from me, relieved to have found a refuge. At that same moment, he suddenly sensed he had company and spun his head toward me.

His eyes and face displayed utter astonishment as he stared right into the muzzle of my pistol. Unarmed, the German was terrified. Sensing he presented no threat to me, I had no desire to shoot him.

"Hi there!" I said, with a friendly wave.

Instead of returning my greeting, the German jumped up and fled. As I watched from the hut's opening, he darted through the incoming artillery fire into the forest.

But I knew it was not safe for me to remain where I was. Fearing a stray bullet or piece of shrapnel might detonate the shells around me in a gigantic explosion at any moment, I departed the hut immediately after the enemy soldier.

With no real safe place to take cover from the barrage, I squeezed into the narrow space between two tree trunks as my best chance of gaining some protection. Fifty yards away, I could see the German from the hut surrendering to a GI. Watching him led back to the rear as a prisoner, I reflected how lucky he was to be out of the fighting.

About an hour after it began, the enemy artillery barrage finally ended, allowing us to resume our advance that afternoon. But the long day in the Hürtgen drove home to me the essential truth underlying war's brutality, horror, tragedy, and insanity. When one side is resolutely determined to defend a piece of ground against an enemy that is equally determined to seize that ground, people are going to suffer and die.

Our arrival at Hill 232: November 18

While we had been pushing toward the northern edge of the Hürtgen on November 17, other American forces had taken Gressenich, but the 16th Infantry Regiment's 1st Battalion was still engaged in a fierce battle for the village of Hamich. In the face of stiff German resistance, the 16th Infantry's 3rd Battalion had been ordered to reinforce the 1st Battalion. With the 1st and 3rd Battalions committed to the effort to capture Hamich, our 2nd Battalion would now be on its own in trying to seize Hill 232.

Unaware of any change in the 2nd Battalion's plans, our platoon received orders about noon on November 18 to proceed to a particular point on a map in support of E Company. Warily pushing forward along a very narrow, seldom used fire trail that wound through a particularly thickly wooded area of the Hürtgen, our detachment of 30 or so men was on high alert for an ambush or another artillery barrage like the one we suffered the previous day. To our surprise, we encountered no significant enemy opposition, perhaps as a result of other recent American advances in this sector.

About two o'clock that chilly autumn afternoon, an hour or two after setting out, we reached the edge of the forest at a spot a couple of miles northeast of the previous day's jumping-off point. Hamich was located a short distance off to our right but was not visible from our location among the trees. What drew our attention was the large hill that loomed less than a half mile away on the far side of a wide, grassy farm field. Only at this point did someone identify this high ground as Hill 232.

Taking its name from its 232-meter (261-foot) elevation above sea level, Hill 232 was the highest point in the Hamich Ridge. Rising about 200 feet above the local terrain, it provided a strategic observation point from which German artillery observers were targeting movement in the Stolberg Corridor, the narrow strip of land that was free of the forests and other natural obstacles that existed elsewhere in this part of Germany. The capture of Hill 232 and the Hamich Ridge was thus vital to open up the planned route of advance that ran northeast of Gressenich and Schevenhütte.

About 500 yards long with slopes covered by trees and brush, Hill 232 plunged steeply into a ravine on the left. Though a natural formation, it appeared to be some huge man-made rampart pushed up by bulldozers. Occupied by an unknown number of German defenders, such valuable high ground was bound to be heavily fortified.

As we stared up at our objective, it was hard to imagine how any attacking force could capture that hill without taking heavy losses.

Hill 232:
November 18/19, 1944

Seizing the hill: afternoon, November 18

Shortly after our arrival at the side of the field across from Hill 232, an officer started issuing orders to the four squads in our second machine-gun platoon.

"Put your machine guns down here and cover this hill!" he directed, indicating four spots spaced 20 yards apart along the edge of the woods. All four of our machine guns were speedily made ready for action, with me posted behind our squad's weapon.

"You guys with the machine guns spray the top of that hill with crisscross firing for the next 10 minutes. Riflemen will advance under your fire, so be damn sure you keep it high!" a sergeant ordered just before the 2nd Battalion's infantry companies started their attack at 2:15pm.

When we opened up, tracer fire revealed my first rounds were striking too low on the hill, so I corrected my aim. Working with the other gunners, I helped lay down a heavy crossfire that raked the German positions along the top of the hill.

A minute after we commenced our suppressive fire, two dozen or more riflemen from our 2nd Battalion bounded out of the woods off to my right, charging toward Hill 232 at a run. As we continued scouring the hill with an almost liquid fire, it seemed impossible any of the enemy troops posted there could possibly survive to resist our assault.

Yet it took only moments for the Germans on the hill to retaliate with a ferocious return fire against our machine-gun positions, which had been exposed by our tracer fire. As enemy bullets buzzed all around me, some snapped off twigs and small branches from the dense brush in which I was concealed. Other rounds smacked into the wet ground in front of me, kicking up small geysers of mud.

Ten minutes after we began taking fire from Hill 232, a German mortar shell struck the ground five feet away from me before I was even aware of an incoming round. Miraculously, the shell failed to explode, but its impact splattered mud all over me, adding to the thick layer of grime already coating the lenses of my glasses.

Forced to spend a minute trying to wipe mud off the lenses with my dirty sleeve, I was unable to continue providing fire support for the advancing infantry at a critical moment. It was incredibly frustrating, but I was useless in combat without my glasses.

Some 10 to 15 minutes after I was able to resume shooting, enemy fire from Hill 232 gradually began to subside.

"Cease fire!" the officer in command yelled. Our four-gun squads were immediately ordered to disassemble our weapons and get ready to run.

"Okay, let's haul ass!" the officer shouted a moment later.

As he led our machine-gun platoon across the 500 yards of open ground that separated us from the hill, everyone spread out to minimize ourselves as targets. We tried to move at a quick trot, but the burden of our equipment and backpacks made our pace frustratingly slow.

Still under sporadic but persistent enemy rifle fire from the hill, I was praying hard as bullets whizzed by my ears every few seconds with a sharp clapping noise. But though nerve-racking, the enemy's shooting was not well-aimed and only one member of our party was hit.

Once we made it three-quarters of the way across the field, the enemy fire ceased completely. Roughly 15 minutes after setting out, we reached the base of the hill and began ascending a gently sloping narrow dirt road that led up the hill's left side.

When we reached the top around 3:30pm, our infantry informed us the Germans defending the hill had either surrendered or retreated. The relative ease of our capture of such a formidable position surprised us. At this time, we remained unaware that American artillery had heavily bombarded Hill 232 before our arrival in the area. This prior artillery barrage against the enemy force defending the hill explained the light opposition to our attack as well as our numerous German prisoners.

The top of the hill was made up of a flat level area about 30 yards long and 20 yards wide that dropped off sharply to the left and a mound on the right which rose some 30 feet above the plateau. Exploring the site, we discovered several enemy machine-gun emplacements and a small cave. Behind the cave sat an abandoned German Panther tank with its whole chassis and turret dug in evenly with the slope of the hill to conceal it. Apparently knocked out by our artillery, the tank's 75-millimeter gun might otherwise have inflicted a devastating fire against our forces below.

Looking out through the leafless trees, we had a spectacular view of the surrounding countryside in every direction. For an artillery observer, Hill 232 served as an ideal vantage point from which to monitor and target any enemy movement in the area. Now this high ground was in our hands, if we could hold it.

Preparing for the German counterattack: twilight, November 18

"Everybody be alert, there's going to be a counterattack," the officer in command warned a half-hour after we reached the top. A German attempt to regain Hill 232 was nearly inevitable and almost certainly imminent. To defend against the expected assault, our platoon's gun squads were ordered to set up four machine-gun positions on the northern side of the hill facing the enemy's new front line off to the northeast.

The placement of our machine guns was overseen by Sergeant Carpenter, who always had a reassuring calmness about him. Having served with H Company since England, Carpenter was well liked by everyone and was a buddy of mine. Aside from First Sergeant Huber, he was the NCO closest to our company's commanding officer.

Two of our machine-gun emplacements, designated Posts "Number One" and "Number Two," were established in the narrow roadway that ran along the north side of Hill 232, roughly halfway down from the plateau on top. Sergeant Carpenter assigned our gun squad to Post Number One on the lower left flank of our battalion's position on the hill, about three feet back from the edge of a sheer bluff that plunged 30 feet straight down. At the bottom of the bluff, a wide field stretched 500 yards or so northeast to a road, beyond which lay woods held by the Germans.

Post Number Two was occupied by our section's first machine-gun squad. Situated about 40 yards to our right, it was more vulnerable to a German attack. Instead of the sheer cliff face protecting our gun position at Post Number One, Post Number Two was located at the mouth of a gently sloping trail that led down to the ground below.

The platoon's other two gun squads at Posts Number Three and Number Four were located 30 yards behind us and at least 20 feet higher up at the edge of the plateau atop the hill. These gun crews could offer fire support for our gun emplacements lower down and were tasked with holding Hill 232 in case we were overrun. Our company's mortar squads were stationed further back to provide additional support.

Meanwhile, medics had established an aid station in the small cave on the hill, roughly 30 yards behind our Post Number One. It would initially treat any of our wounded, who would subsequently be transferred to a larger aid station in the rear. Though we had suffered amazingly light losses in seizing Hill 232, the aid stations prepared for heavy casualties in the event of a German counterattack.

With darkness rapidly descending, there was little time to improve Post Number One beyond digging a shallow foxhole in the rocky soil of the roadway. As I assumed my usual spot behind the gun, Carpenter advised the other members of our squad where they should position themselves to help protect my flanks. Another half-dozen 2nd Battalion riflemen took up supporting positions on either side of our squad.

While Wayne Newsome, Hector Gonzalez, and Lincoln Welser were posted off to my right, my friend Jesse Beaver claimed what had become his regular spot just off my left shoulder, protecting that flank with his M1 carbine. Whenever we went into action, he would try to reassure me by regularly repeating, "Keep firing, Andy! They ain't gonna get you. They ain't gonna get you."

A crack shot with his carbine, Jesse backed up his words with his weapon and had picked off a lot of the enemy in combat. Of course, in bravely providing this covering fire, he made himself vulnerable. Luckily, his small stature was an asset in this situation since it made him a more difficult target.

Waiting for the enemy: night, November 18/19

When the last light of day faded from the sky a little after five that evening, it quickly turned colder. As during our past nights in the Hürtgen Forest, we made the best of our light battle jackets in an effort to stay warm, while wishing we had been issued the heavier overcoats now worn by some of the infantry.

Accompanying the darkness was an eerie mist that added to the chill and further fed our anxiety. Even though I felt sure we were prepared for whatever the Germans might throw at us, my confidence in our readiness did not alleviate an underlying apprehension about an enemy counterattack.

Since our seizure of Hill 232, we had come under intermittent German artillery fire, with more shells falling a couple of hours after dark. The rounds exploded on the hill behind us and somewhere off on our flank, but none struck our position at Post Number One. Our focus remained on the threat of an enemy infantry assault.

About 10:30pm, two back-to-back rifle shots rang out not far to my left.

"Hold your fire!" Sergeant Carpenter hollered. Everything fell quiet. Five or ten minutes passed without any further gunfire.

Anxious to find out what had happened, I slipped out from behind the machine gun and joined several others making their way through the darkness toward the spot where we had heard the shooting. About 30 yards away, we found the bodies of two very young German soldiers sprawled backward, barely visible in the blackness.

A sentry told us he had heard the approach of the intruders in the night and challenged them to provide the password. When they failed to respond with "Ship Ahoy" the sentry had opened fire, cutting them down just 10 feet in front of his foxhole. From experience, it was clear to us this had been an enemy scouting party sent forward to reconnoiter our position on Hill 232.

"We're gonna catch hell because these two guys are supposed to go back to their unit and report. When they don't go back, they're gonna attack," Sergeant Carpenter declared with an almost fatalistic certainty.

With nerves on edge, none of us could relax enough to sleep as we braced ourselves for the impending counterattack. Every GI was in position. Each Garand, carbine, and Browning Automatic Rifle had been checked and rechecked for readiness. Our machine gun's ammo belts had been carefully straightened out to prevent any jamming. Our mortar squads had dug in and stacked rounds to drop down the tubes. Now, there was nothing for us to do but await whatever was to come.

No moonlight brightened the night, leaving us in pitch-black darkness that made it impossible even to see your hand right in front of your face. Other than the sporadic explosions of incoming German artillery rounds behind us, the only things audible were the chirping of a few crickets, the flutter of an occasional night bird, and the tree leaves brushing against each other in the breeze.

My thoughts turned to Exodus 10:21 where God is preparing to bring down the Darkness Plague on Egypt at the behest of Moses. The Bible passage describes "even darkness which may be felt." On this night too, the darkness was a physical presence that could be felt. It carried something sinister and full of foreboding.

Hours passed. No German counterattack came.

Long before dawn, the intermittent enemy artillery fire finally ceased. Everyone tensed, anticipating a follow-on attack at any moment, but nothing happened.

Only silence filled the darkness. Even the crickets had grown quiet and not a sound disturbed the night.

A furious battle: before dawn, November 19

Just as we were beginning to hope we would make it through until morning without a counterattack, it came. At 5:30am, a roar erupted out of the darkness from the field in front of us as what must have been hundreds of Germans began shouting in unison at the top of their lungs. Whooping like a bunch of Indians on the warpath in some Hollywood movie, their spine-chilling battle cry left the hair on my neck standing on end. Fear is normal before a battle, but what I was experiencing was outright terror.

As the hollering grew louder, I began blazing away at the dark field with my machine gun, using the tracer rounds to crisscross my fire with the other gunners on the hill. In moments, the enemy force surged toward the far right end of the hill, heading directly for our gun squad and riflemen over at Post Number Two.

Over the next half-hour or so, the fighting raged 40 yards off to our right with repeated grenade explosions and heavy machine-gun and rifle fire. At any moment, we knew the Germans were likely to extend their attack to our sector of the hill.

With the first pale light of day barely brightening the horizon, I was just able to discern three or four dark silhouettes climbing into the upper branches of several tall pines in a stand of trees about 50 yards away from our position at Post Number One. In moments, the Germans would gain a perch at the same height as our ledge from which to shoot across at us, just as Sergeant Carpenter had warned they might try to do.

Before they could reach these firing positions, I let off a short burst of eight or ten rounds from my machine gun, sending a brilliant stream of tracer fire into the treetops. The enemy soldiers instantly plummeted from the trees, while their rifles momentarily dangled among the limbs. Slowly tumbling down from one branch to the next, the weapons also eventually fell to earth.

A minute later, three or four more Germans followed the first group up into the pines. When I also blasted these men from the branches, the enemy ceased their effort to climb the trees. But my tracer fire had given away our gun position.

By this time, Germans had reached the ground 30 feet below us and were shooting up at our position on the bluff. While it was impossible for me to depress the barrel of the machine gun down far enough to target the enemy troops at the bottom of the bluff, the other members of my squad and the riflemen on either side of me were firing down at them with their carbines and rifles. Despite it still being too dark to see much, the shooting was fierce with our guys aiming at the enemy muzzle flashes and the Germans targeting ours.

Roughly a quarter of an hour into this firefight in the lingering pre-dawn darkness, I spotted fingers coming over the edge of the bluff three feet in front of me. Frantically, the German soldier's hand began feeling around for a grip on the rocky ledge so he could haul himself all the way up.

Filled with terror and exhilaration, my actions were now guided more by instinct than calculation. As a rush of adrenaline sharpened my senses to a peak, time seemed to come nearly to a standstill, slowing all movement to a series of snapshots.

Unable to use the machine gun at such close quarters, I whipped my .45 pistol from its holster as a German helmet popped up over the ledge in front of me, just seconds after the fingers had first appeared. Taking aim, I fired a single bullet into the crown of the soldier's helmet. Instantly, the attacker dropped back behind the ledge, plunging to the ground 30 feet below.

As one helmeted head after another came into view over the edge of the bluff, I squeezed off a single round into each new target before the enemy soldier's face was even visible. Shooting at pointblank range, it was impossible for me to miss.

When I inserted a new seven-round ammunition clip, my pistol had grown hot from repeated firing. I knew I must have killed at least a half-dozen Germans coming over the bluff, but I was not thinking of killing, only of survival. The firing of the GIs around me was just as frenzied as they repulsed other assailants ascending the bluff.

Suffering a slaughter, the Germans were soon forced to halt their attempt to climb the bluff, but they continued to target our position with heavy small arms fire. Although it remained impossible for me to engage the enemy soldiers immediately beneath the ledge with my machine gun, I finally managed to depress the barrel low enough to bring at least a portion of the attacking force under fire.

Making the best use I could of the still dim predawn light, I began firing off short bursts at any movement below. As I swept the machine gun back and forth, the darkness was lit with streaking tracer rounds from my machine gun.

Taking aim at the source of this tracer fire, the enemy return fire against my machine gun was withering in its intensity. Only by crouching way down and sighting under the barrel did I survive the hailstorm of incoming rounds.

But I did not let up on my fire, running through about two and a half ammo belts—600 rounds—over the course of the ensuing half-hour. And the GIs around me and our mortar crews in the rear were just as busy pouring fire upon the Germans.

Throughout this fierce struggle, grenades flew in both directions. I tossed nearly all of my dozen grenades down on unseen targets below. At least three or four enemy potato mashers were tossed up toward my position. One exploded on the ledge not far from me, but, amazingly, failed to cause any injury.

About half an hour after the Germans had ceased trying to ascend the bluff, there was a pause in the firing. Shouted orders in German echoed up from beneath the cliff. Fearing they were organizing another attack, I grabbed my last hand grenade, yanked the pin, and dropped it over the edge of the bluff.

Just as a German soldier was crying out for a medic, the grenade exploded. Only silence ensued.

By about 7am, roughly a quarter of an hour before dawn, the enemy seemed to have given up on driving us from the bluff after a battle that had lasted for more than an hour. While noise from the fighting off to the right over at Post Number Two still resounded, our Post Number One appeared secure for the moment.

Taking advantage of the lull in combat at our position, a number of the riflemen and all the other members of my squad except Jesse were ordered away from our position on various details. Most of my squad headed back to our jeep a half mile in the rear to retrieve ammo boxes for both our gun and the gun at Post Number Two. Some of the riflemen were dispatched to Post Number Two or began helping the medic carry the dead from their foxholes to a location in the rear.

Meanwhile, Jesse remained squatted a foot from my left shoulder, the post he had held throughout the struggle to defend Post Number One. Just after sunrise and perhaps 15 minutes after the end of the fighting in our sector, he leaned toward my ear.

"I ain't gonna let nothin' happen to you, Andy," he whispered. "I wanna see where they are."

Before I realized what he intended, Jesse leaned on my shoulder for support as he stood, raising his head just over the edge of the bluff in an effort to peer down.

A second later, a loud noise like the clap of a hand resounded. Jesse's head jerked sharply. His blood splattered on the arm of my field jacket as his body slumped face down beside me.

One of the medics rushed over. "Hey, little man, let me help you," he offered. When the medic pulled Jesse's body up, I could see a bullet had struck him squarely in the forehead. As blood gushed from Jesse's mouth, nose, ears, and even his eyes, his throat gasped for air that would not come. It was terrible to look upon.

"He's gone," the medic said. In an instant, the life of a man who was a husband and father as well as my closest friend in the Army had been snatched away by a bullet.

A quarter of an hour later, a medic pulled Jesse's body away. Other than a couple of riflemen and the medics, the only other soldier now active at our position was my buddy Sergeant Carpenter, who had been running back and forth between Posts One and Two to direct men where needed. He had also assisted the medics in helping the wounded to the rear and grimly dragging away the dead.

Shortly after Jesse's body had been taken back, I watched as Carpenter pulled another dead GI from a foxhole about 15 yards from me. After lugging the corpse away, he came over to me in a low crouch.

"Andy, we need you on the gun at Number Two where the fighting is. Almost everyone in the machine-gun squad over there is dead," Carpenter whispered, gesturing toward our other machine-gun post off to the right.

"Are you gonna leave this position vacant? The Krauts are coming up over the cliff," I protested. With German troops still present below the bluff, it seemed dangerous to leave the machine gun at Post Number One unmanned.

Carpenter expressed surprise upon learning the enemy had attempted to scale the bluff but did not change his orders.

"The hell with 'em. Let's go! You gotta be over at gun Number Two. There's too many Germans over there!" Sergeant Carpenter snapped. Hoping to inspire me, he added that a good gunner was needed there "to give the Germans hell."

Despite my concern about turning over the defense of Post Number One to the two remaining riflemen, I gave up trying to dissuade Carpenter and followed him on my hands and knees toward Post Number Two 40 yards to our right.

A moment later, I came across a sad sight. To the right of the narrow path, the lifeless bodies of Jesse and a half-dozen or more other dead GIs lay neatly side by side, almost as if they were sleeping.

As we crawled past them, I could see that three of the soldiers were from our section's first machine-gun squad at Post Two. All of these men had been shot in the forehead, reflecting the fact that the gunner's head was most exposed to enemy fire. One after another, three previous machine gunners had given their lives trying to defend that position from the enemy.

Defending Post Number Two: early morning, November 19

When Carpenter and I reached Post Two a couple of minutes later, a desperate struggle was playing out in the early morning light with an intensity of small arms fire greater than anything I had ever heard.

Ten yards to the right of the unmanned machine gun, five riflemen in a network of foxholes were firing frantically to hold back German troops advancing up the gently sloping footpath that led down to the bottom of the hill. Although the trail was narrow, its partial concealment by dense brush gave the enemy a far easier route of attack than the sheer cliff face they confronted back at Post One.

The machine-gun emplacement here was out in the open, protected only by a small mound of earth. Next to the gun, six more bodies lay side by side, including more men lost from our first squad. My sense of foreboding mounted, but I had a job to do.

As I hurriedly squatted down low behind the gun, Sergeant Carpenter issued a final warning. "You just keep an eye on 'em. If you have to, swing your gun back over there," indicating that I should swivel the barrel to the left if the Germans captured our now lightly defended Post One and began attacking Post Two from that flank as well. Carpenter then slipped down into a foxhole a half-dozen yards to my right.

Immediately, I started firing on the enemy coming up the trail, using tracers to guide my aim as I targeted all movement from that direction. The riflemen and I received support from our two mortar squads in the rear, who were lobbing a round onto the enemy's route of advance every five minutes or so. It seemed unthinkable the Germans attacking Post Two would persist in the face of such firepower.

Yet despite losing 20 or 30 men, at least a dozen more Germans were moving up the trail, with the closest about 20 yards to the right of my gun. Matching our own fusillade, they returned fire with submachine guns and rifles. Periodically, grenade detonations resounded above the more constant din of small arms fire.

Crouching ever lower to ensure my helmet stayed well-hidden below the back of the machine gun, I rapidly burned through belt after belt of ammo. As our riflemen continued to get hit, a few new GIs arrived to replace them, but I wondered how long we could hold out. Then things got worse.

Perhaps a half-hour after my arrival at Post Two, the ground around me suddenly erupted in a series of small explosions.

Taken completely by surprise, it took me a moment before I realized what had happened. Exploiting our focus on the frontal assault against our lower positions on the hill, the Germans had sent another force to circle around behind us and wipe out our two gun crews higher up.

Having gained control of the high ground, the dozen or more enemy troops up there were now shooting down at us. Because of the angle, I could not elevate the barrel of the machine gun high enough to fire back at them, and even if I had been able to shoot up at them, my vantage point below made it nearly impossible to see the Germans who were firing down at me.

Miraculously, the bullets whizzing past my head and kicking up the earth around me seemed poorly aimed. After a minute, the fire from above slackened and then remained intermittent, permitting me to refocus my attention on the more urgent threats in front of me. Combat is utterly terrifying, but I knew I had to try to master my fear and do what I was trained to do.

By this time, enemy troops were now also assaulting our left flank from the direction of our old position at Post One, with their strongest push coming 20 yards to the left of my gun. Luckily, a GI 30 yards away was furiously resisting the enemy's advance on this flank. Positioned out at the end of a barren rocky outcropping that stuck out above the German route of attack, he was blazing away with his rifle. As shell casings poured out, the soldier slammed one magazine after another into his weapon.

Seeking to support him, I let loose short bursts of six or eight rounds toward the enemy force coming along the path on my left. However, just as on my right flank, the German route of advance on my left was largely hidden from my view by dense undergrowth.

"Keep the machine gun going," shouted the GI on the outcropping, observing the deadly results of my fire from his superior vantage point. "That's the way. You're mowing 'em down!" he encouraged, as I kept shooting in short bursts.

After a few moments, the soldier hollered at me to increase my fire. I responded with a steady stream of fire for 30 seconds until the gun barrel was steaming hot.

Realizing the barrel could warp if I did not let up, I reduced my rate of fire. In between short bursts, I noticed the rifleman on the knoll was no longer shooting.

All of a sudden, he came hobbling toward me, half-crawling, half-trying to run to the aid station behind my gun. As he made his way past my gun on his hands and knees, I could see a gray-whitish matter oozing from a long red open wound across the right side of his head just above his ear. About two yards from me, he collapsed to the ground, where he passed out.

A medic hustled over and did the best he could to bandage the wound, which was obviously the work of a German sharpshooter. The medic then pulled the soldier a short distance away where a few other seriously wounded men lay.

Just after this GI had been dragged away and perhaps five minutes after the Germans had begun firing down at us from higher up on the hill, there was a sharp clap of rifle fire. It was followed by a peculiar noise like nothing I had ever heard, closely resembling the sound of a canoe paddle slapping the surface of the water.

Swinging my head rightward toward the noise, I could barely comprehend the surreally gruesome sight before my eyes. A few feet away, Sergeant Carpenter was weaving back and forth on his feet like a battered boxer still trying to fight, but his entire face had been blown off. Everything inside his head was gushing out of the gaping hole where his face had been in a sickening torrent of blood and tissue.

In a moment, he sank down into a kneeling position with what remained of his helmeted head resting against his rifle. Finally, his body toppled forward face down on to the stony ground. Seeing a man die like that was one of the most horrible sights I ever witnessed.

Apparently, Carpenter had decided to come out of his firing position in the foxhole in an effort to determine the location of the enemy shooter who had just targeted the rifleman on the outcropping. Standing up, he had instantly been struck in the head by a bullet, probably one fired from our left flank.

His death again drove home to me the terrible cost of war. He had been the best sergeant under whom I had served. More importantly, he had been a close friend.

Only minutes after Carpenter's death, an infantry sergeant in a foxhole further off to my right suffered the same fate when he stood up. As I watched, his whole head seemed to explode when the bullet struck him. A medic arrived a moment later to take him to the rear, but his brains were spilling from his head.

The infantry sergeant's corpse was dragged over next to that of Sergeant Carpenter, the fallen riflemen, and the dead from the machine-gun squad, adding to the neat row of bodies beside me. *Why were they being lined up there?* I thought to myself. It was a ghoulish sight.

With almost all my fellow GIs on Hill 232 dead or dying, I wondered again why God had spared me so far and whether I would survive the morning.

A fight to the end: morning, November 19

Among the small number of riflemen who remained to defend our position, only a couple were still unwounded, leaving me feeling very alone. Still caught between the German troops coming up the trail on our right, others attacking from the left, and those on the high ground above us, our situation at Post Two was at a crisis.

Just when it looked like we were about to be overwhelmed, what seemed to be a single artillery shell—but could have been a salvo of several shells arriving simultaneously—blasted the enemy force 30 yards above us with indescribable force. The enormous, deafening explosion radiated heat and a concussive shockwave strong enough to knock me over if I had not already been crouched behind the gun.

As I looked up in stupefied fascination, the slope above me literally erupted, lifting a fiery jumble of trees, bodies, and the hillside itself upward into the morning sky. A moment later, dirt was raining down upon me.

Everyone and everything in that part of the hill was instantly obliterated in what was the largest explosion I witnessed in the entire war. Sometime later, I heard that an American artillery observer operating from a concealed post atop the hill had realized our whole position was about to be overrun. Seeing no other way to hold the hill than to request a fire mission on his own location, he radioed back the coordinates to a battery of our heavy guns. In calling down the artillery strike that annihilated the German force atop the hill, the artillery observer won the battle and undoubtedly saved my life.

Afterward, it was as if some kind of magic spell had been cast over the battle space. The end of the enemy fire from above was matched by a halt in all shooting as the Germans ceased their assault on our position at Post Two, perhaps concluding they now had no chance to recapture Hill 232 following the elimination of their troops on the high ground. The heavy losses the Germans had sustained in the effort may also have made their attack simply too costly to continue.

About half an hour after the explosion, one of our new lieutenants appeared near Post Two from somewhere in the rear. I did not know him well, but the officer was a friendly, gregarious fellow who everyone liked.

Without speaking to me, the lieutenant stepped out onto the small rocky outcropping 30 yards to the left of my gun position, the same location where the rifleman had earlier been hit. Watching the lieutenant, I thought he was out of his mind to stand up in full view of the enemy, but he had obviously concluded the shooting was over.

Cupping his hands around his mouth, he shouted in English, "Anybody want to surrender? Come right this way!"

Just as the last word left his mouth, a German machine gunner answered with a burst of fire that caught the lieutenant in the gut, causing him to double over.

With his hands gripping his abdomen, the lieutenant began to struggle back to the aid station on his own. Before he got very far, a couple of medics came forward to assist him. As he passed near me, I could see his guts spilling out between his fingers. The officer ultimately survived but paid a high price for his recklessness.

Everything again fell quiet, but I remained alert for any movement up the trails on either of our flanks, keeping watch under the gun barrel from my crouched position. A few of our riflemen remained off to my right, but I did not speak with them.

When another quarter of an hour passed without more Germans appearing, I began to believe the enemy might truly have given up their effort to seize our position and retreated down the hill.

Just at that moment as I started to relax my vigilance, a German soldier sprung up only feet away from me. Rising to his full height in one swift motion, he cocked his arm back to lob a potato masher at me as I swung the machine gun toward him.

While his arm was still coming forward, I squeezed off a quick burst. As if in slow motion, tracer rounds marked out the trail of bullets stitching down the left side of his body, the force of which knocked the German backward and out of sight.

My fire having caused an errant throw, his grenade sailed over my head in a high arc. Landing half a dozen yards behind me, it detonated with a loud bang, spraying shrapnel in every direction.

With what felt like a blow from a steel fist, one of the shards slammed into the back of my right shoulder. Striking the same spot where a piece of shrapnel had hit me during the fighting at the bunker a month and a half earlier, the sharp pain was intense, but lasted only briefly. Mainly, I just felt a little stunned by what had happened.

As the momentary rush of adrenaline faded, I refocused my attention and the gun on the dirt mound behind which the wounded German had disappeared, even though it seemed likely he was already dead. Despite his desperate assault, it was becoming clear we had beaten back the enemy's effort to retake Hill 232. They had paid a terrible price in lives in the attempt, but we had also suffered heavily.

Thinking back to my mom's parting assurance of the Lord's protection, I recalled her words from Psalms 91:7: "A thousand shall fall at thy side, and ten thousand at thy right hand; but it shall not come nigh thee."

By God's grace, I had survived.

CHAPTER 14

A Break from War:
November 19–December 22, 1944

After the battle: morning, November 19

An odd quiet followed the grenade attack, a silence magnified by its sharp contrast with the battle that had raged during the previous hours. While the fighting was almost certainly over, I remained crouched low behind my gun, hyper-vigilant for any movement, whether from my last assailant or any other direction.

After perhaps 20 minutes, a scuffling noise came from behind the earthen mound 10 feet in front of my machine gun. As I tensed for action, a small white handkerchief attached to the end of a stick rose into view above the mound, waving back and forth.

"May I surrender? Please, may I surrender?" a voice loudly pleaded in German-accented English.

"Yes, you may," I replied. Though happy to accept his surrender, I suspected it might be a trick. Withdrawing my .45 pistol, I leveled it at the flag, ready for anything.

A moment later, a young face appeared under a German helmet. Grimacing in obvious agony, the soldier pulled his shoulders up over the mound. Finally, with a tremendous effort, he managed to drag all of his thin, short body onto the ground in front of my machine gun. Examining his dirty, blood-soaked uniform, I could see his left side was riddled with a series of wounds extending down from his torso to his thigh, which confirmed he was the same guy who had tossed the grenade at me.

Seeing the German no longer posed a threat, I holstered my pistol. Bending down to the ground, I wrapped my left arm around him, while trying to avoid aggravating the injury to my right shoulder. With a heave, I pulled the soldier up over the smaller mound just in front of my machine gun, laying him down beside me.

The German was bleeding badly and needed urgent medical care, but I knew our medics working at the small aid station in the hill's cave already had their hands full dealing with our wounded. Since my right shoulder also required medical attention, I decided to help the enemy soldier walk back to our larger aid station at the edge of woods, located near the spot where we had first fired on the hill the previous day.

After permitting the German to rest for a few minutes, I again extended my left arm around his shoulder to help him stand. With my arm tightly around his waist and his arm around my back, we set out for the aid station, though he had no idea where I was taking him. Neither of us spoke as we hobbled along together down the hill in the fall's cool morning air, retracing the path I had ascended the previous afternoon.

Perhaps 20 minutes later, we reached the bottom of the hill, at which point we passed within 10 yards of one of H Company's mortar squads. Situated in a large ditch, their firing position was surrounded by stacks of ammo boxes.

"Who's left up there, Andy?" one of the mortar crew called out to me.

"There's only four guys that I saw still up there. And the ground is full of dead men, Germans and Americans," I explained, describing a scene beyond words.

"You mean everybody was killed?" he asked.

"Almost everybody," I sadly acknowledged.

The sergeant in charge of the mortar squad walked over to me and the German.

"You're a lucky man," he said. The sergeant informed me an officer had just reported over their field telephone that only five men were left unwounded on Hill 232, confirming the heavy losses I had witnessed over the course of the fighting.

As the German and I continued our slow trek across the field toward the aid station, I noticed his eyes repeatedly glancing over at the pistol holstered on my right hip, something he had been doing since we had first started down the hill. Clearly, he was terrified I was delivering him to some dark fate.

"You shoot me? You kill me?" he finally blurted out.

"No, no, I'm not going to shoot you. I'm a Christian. I don't murder people," I adamantly objected.

"I Christian too!" he proclaimed with a wide grin, no doubt greatly relieved to know he was not being led off for execution.

With that connection made, I asked his name.

"Erich. I 17. I drafted," he declared. "How old you?"

"I'm 21," I replied.

"My officers say, 'We surrender, you kill,'" Erich told me.

"That's not right. We don't do that. Americans do not shoot unarmed prisoners," I explained, hoping to reassure him. I then attempted to describe my own German heritage in a mix of poor German and English. "*Mein Grossvater* was a medic in the German Army before World War I."

Erich nodded that he understood, though I do not think he really did. However, his English was good enough that we went on chatting about all kinds of things.

When we were about halfway across the large open field that lay between Hill 232 and the aid station at the edge of the woods, Erich halted. Reaching into his left shirt pocket, he retrieved a little gold cross attached to a short chain. After proudly displaying it to me, he placed the cross and chain in my hands.

"Giff-giff. Giff-giff. Giff-giff," he exclaimed.

Not wanting to deprive him of this cross that he obviously treasured, I tried to refuse his gift. But Erich insisted, so I put the cross in my jacket pocket, offering my thanks for this symbol of our common faith and new friendship.

As we resumed our trek to the aid station, I was feeling a real sense of comradeship and Christian love toward my recent enemy. Erich exhibited an unusual warmth and humanity I had not expected from a German soldier.

Despite being on opposite sides of the war and the four-year age difference between us, it was easy for me to put myself in his boots. Erich struck me as a sincere Christian and young "Boy Scout" much like me, a fellow soldier fighting for his country.

It was impossible for me not to reflect on the irony of the situation. We had been enemies trying to kill each other an hour earlier and now we were arm-in-arm like old buddies. The absurd, brutal tragedy of war was never clearer.

From the aid station to a field hospital: November 19–22

Roughly 45 minutes after setting out from Post Two, Erich and I arrived at the main aid station located under the trees at the edge of the forest. About 10 wounded men were lying on the ground and another three or four stood nearby with their arms in slings. Only four or five medics wearing white arm bands with red crosses were in sight, but they were supported by a larger number of medical orderlies.

A couple of medics immediately approached me.

"Take care of this guy first. He's really hurt," I informed them.

Working with the medical personnel, I helped lay Erich down onto a stretcher. They immediately removed his tunic and shirt and cut open his pants leg in order to dress his wounds. I watched for another quarter of an hour as they treated Erich, giving him the same care they would have provided a wounded GI.

My own wound to my right shoulder felt more annoying than serious, but I asked one of the medics to take a look at it once they had finished with Erich. Leading me to a large tent, the medic directed me to remove my field jacket and shirt so another medic with the rank of sergeant could examine me. I did not have to wait long.

After determining that a piece of grenade shrapnel was lodged in my shoulder, the sergeant carefully twisted my arm and then pushed on my shoulder with both his hands in an effort to loosen it. Finally, he informed me I would have to be evacuated back to a field hospital to have the shrapnel surgically removed.

"I don't think I need to go to the hospital." I protested.

"You got a piece of shrapnel in there and it's gonna get infected, so you need to go back to the hospital," he insisted. "We're going to send you and the German you brought in back there in an ambulance in just about a half-hour."

While I realized removing the shrapnel was necessary, the medic's decision to evacuate me to a field hospital several miles in the rear frustrated me. I was anxious to get back to the machine gun at Post Two, knowing there was almost no one else left to defend that part of Hill 232. The order also ruined my plan to inspect the site of the enormous explosion at the end of the battle. Additionally, I thought returning to the hill might help me deal with the painful loss of Jesse Beaver, Sergeant Carpenter, and other buddies earlier that morning, deaths I had not begun to come to terms with.

Like many soldiers, I never had any personal expectation of receiving a medal for bravery, fighting, or otherwise doing my duty. However, it seemed to me that if any GIs were ever deserving of commendation, it was those men who had given their lives in that morning's bitter struggle to hold on to Hill 232. They were true heroes.

It was already apparent the Germans had suffered heavier casualties, but I later heard they had lost some 250 men from the two companies they sent to retake the hill. This included a number of enemy troops who had been captured, of whom at least a dozen or more were now under guard as prisoners at the aid station.

By repulsing the *Wehrmacht*'s counterattack at Hill 232, we had retained control of the superior artillery observation point in the area, isolating the remaining German troops in Hamich. With the main line of enemy resistance broken at Hamich, the southern part of the Stolberg Corridor was opened to further advance. Yet, despite having been in the middle of the fight, none of us had any real understanding of the military significance of our victory. We simply had to believe our lives were being risked and sacrificed to help defeat the Nazi regime and achieve a lasting peace.

As promised, an ambulance arrived about half an hour after my shoulder had been examined. Medics swiftly loaded Erich's stretcher and three others into the vehicle before the ambulatory patients boarded. Since I was not exactly enthusiastic about the order to go back to the field hospital, the medic sergeant was keeping his eye on me to make certain I complied. When my turn came to board the ambulance, he did not exactly shove me inside, but his hands firmly guided me into the vehicle.

Once I joined the half-dozen other GIs already seated in the ambulance, we sped off to the field hospital. Erich was suffering too much for me to converse with him any further, so I made small talk with the other fellows as we bounced around in back.

When the ambulance pulled up at the busy field hospital an hour and a half later, the other men quickly disembarked, but I waited behind with Erich. A couple of minutes later, medical personnel arrived. They unloaded his stretcher first.

"We're going to put him in the German unit," one of them informed me, referring to the secure area of the hospital reserved for treating enemy patients.

Before the orderlies lifted his stretcher out, I patted Erich on his shoulder. "You'll be okay," I told him, offering a final reassurance.

"I okay. I alive," he replied, staring up at me. With tears running down his cheeks, he managed a smile as they took him away. It was the last time I ever saw Erich, but our brief association had given me the rare chance to get to know a German soldier.

In weighing whether to surrender back on Hill 232, Erich had confronted one of the worst fears a soldier faces. You never know the attitude of the enemy after a battle. If enemy troops have been wounded or just seen some of their close buddies killed during the preceding action, they may take revenge on you if you surrender. When you surrender, you give up everything. You are completely at their mercy.

Horribly wounded, this 17-year-old German boy had realized he could either lie there on that hill and die in a pool of his own blood or place his life in the hands of the enemy. Terribly afraid, Erich had chosen to surrender.

Maybe they will treat me decently and take care of me. Maybe I will receive medical care and live, he must have hoped.

Even having made it this far, Erich still faced an uncertain future in an Allied prisoner of war camp once he recovered from his wounds. I was never able to find out whether Erich survived, but I sincerely hope he did. He was a good kid, one of the countless millions of decent Germans caught up in this catastrophic war waged by an evil Nazi regime.

Erich's surrender taught me an important lesson about my Christian faith. I realized it was one thing to accept Christ as my savior, it was quite another to fully surrender myself to Him. Like a solider giving up, I had to give up control over my life: *Lord, I want to do what you want me to do, whatever you say.* That is surrender.

After Erich was taken away for treatment, I was directed to a barracks-like ward of the field hospital, which was packed with injured American troops, many of whom had been severely wounded.

"We'll get to you in maybe an hour," an Army surgeon told me.

When my turn came, I was taken into the surgeon's office where a medical orderly carefully removed my shirt so the surgeon could examine my shoulder.

"You are lucky. The wound is slight. Some of these guys lying here have had their arms totally blown off. We're just going to take a chunk of that flesh out of your shoulder," he explained.

Following his diagnosis, the surgeon immediately had me prepped for surgery, giving me anesthesia to put me under. A surgical team then excised the shrapnel along with a circle of flesh from around the wound to eliminate any infected tissue.

When I awoke, my shoulder was bandaged, but there was no immediate soreness—that would come later.

"You want this shrapnel?" the surgeon asked me, holding up the piece of grenade he had just removed from my shoulder.

"No, I don't want it," I told him. I liked war souvenirs as much as the next fellow but was not interested in holding on to a memento of my war wound.

To give my shoulder time to heal before I returned to duty, the surgeon informed me I would have to convalesce for a few weeks at an Army hospital back in France.

At the convalescent hospital: November 22–December 16

Three days later on November 22, three other lightly wounded soldiers and I departed the field hospital for the U.S. Army's 7th Convalescent Hospital. Located just outside of the French town of Étampes, the hospital was roughly 30 miles south of the center of Paris and 250 miles southeast of Hill 232.

The trip took most of the day and it rained the entire way. Fortunately, we had been assigned a top-notch Black driver and an almost new ambulance. Folding back the seats, the other GIs and I used the time to catch up on sleep.

Thanksgiving fell the day after our arrival and every soldier recuperating at the 7th Convalescent Hospital had a lot for which to be grateful. After the perpetual noise, filth, and commotion of life on the front line, the hospital seemed unbelievably quiet, clean, and orderly. Patients could use lights at night and had newspapers to read. There were cold and hot cereals for breakfast and meat and vegetables for lunch and supper. In short, we had returned to civilization.

My assigned hospital room was a pretty good size, with enough space for a dozen beds situated three or four feet apart. Since my shoulder was not hurting too much, I was often up walking around and chatting with other wounded soldiers.

Venturing outside the hospital into the town of Étampes, I searched local tobacco shops for a nice pipe for my dad, but instead ended up buying myself a tiny pipe shaped like a shoe for three dollars. Though not a smoker, I collected tobacco pipes as a sort of hobby and wanted to have some souvenir from my time in France.

While the other patients and I were taking it easy, doctors in white coats and nurses dressed in white uniforms calmly went about their work with practiced efficiency, although crises sometimes disrupted the regular routine.

In one instance, a large number of seriously wounded troops arrived at the hospital from the front, requiring all but one of the nurses on duty to help deal with the influx. The nurse who remained in our room was a striking blonde with an hourglass figure. Naturally, she caught the attention of all the patients, notably the sergeant in the bed next me. A fun sort of guy who also happened to be the ranking soldier on our floor, the red-haired sergeant was short, rather heavyset, and loud.

When the nurse requested help making up empty beds, the sergeant stepped in. "Okay, you guys, get your asses out of bed and help the lady, and that's an order. I'll go back to the nurse's quarters and help her straighten things out back there."

"Listen, bright eyes, you stay right there in your bed. When I need your help, I'll let you know," she retorted.

All of us got a huge laugh out of that exchange, but our irrepressible sergeant did not surrender so easily. On several further occasions, he tried to win her affection, but the nurse was always ready with a quick comeback for each of his flirtations.

The sergeant liked to have fun with us as well, ordering everyone around while he lounged there in his bed like a king on his throne.

"Yes, Sergeant, just as you say!" we would respond to each command, which we would then proceed to ignore.

"That's what I like to hear, soldier," he would reply to our pretended compliance.

Of course, these lighter moments were balanced by the serious business of the hospital. Just a few days after my arrival, three nurses rushed to a nearby bed. A moment later, they called a physician over to examine the patient.

"He's dead," the doctor sadly pronounced as he pulled a sheet over the soldier's head. A few minutes later, orderlies wheeled the lifeless body away.

Fortunately, most patients convalescing at the hospital recovered from their wounds and deaths were relatively rare.

Letters from home

Word of my injury on November 19 eventually reached my family back on Signal Mountain in Tennessee. A telegram dated December 4 read as follows:

> Regret to inform you—Your son Pvt. Ernest A. Andrews Jr. was slightly wounded in action on Nov. 18th, in Germany. You will be advised as report of condition received.

Although concerned by this telegram, my family was more relieved the news was not worse. With five sons in the military, my parents needed a sturdy Christian faith just as much as we did to see them through the war.

In her role as our family's "prayer warrior," my mother devoted herself to asking God's protection for my brothers and me. Knowing she was constantly praying for us comforted me with a reassuring sense of peace, just as her deep and abiding faith in God gave me tremendous encouragement and fortified my own belief.

While my mother prayed for the five of us on a daily basis, my dad was our family's letter writer. Each week, he mailed one or two-page letters to me, usually with a brief note from my mother. In every letter, my parents never failed to remind me that they loved me and awaited my return home.

For all troops, letters provided a huge boost to our morale and served as our connecting rods to home. The mail could not always get through if fighting was especially intense, but it was delivered in most situations. Its arrival every month or so was always a big event on the front line. If we were in the middle of combat, one soldier would act as postman, crawling from foxhole to foxhole to distribute the mail.

Because of the frequency of my dad's correspondence, there was almost always something for me. Sometimes, I would get as many as eight letters at once bound with a rubber band. These occasionally included a V-mail (Victory Mail), a single page folded into a square with an address on one side. More than once, I heard other guys grumble, "Lucky Andy got another letter."

These letters from my dad or my sister Peggy maintained my spirits and kept me updated on folks back home, but also sometimes carried sad news about my friends who had been killed in combat. Even though death is an inevitable part of war, it did not make it any easier to bear the pain of their loss, especially for the families.

If letters from home sometimes delivered bad news, that was far better than having no news. A few men in H Company heard nothing from home and never received a single care package. They reminded me how fortunate I was to have parents who loved me enough to write me regularly.

Watching me read a letter, one fellow remarked, "It's from your dad, huh? I ain't got no dad." Looking over, I could see the tears rolling down his face.

In another instance, I received a bundle of mail containing several letters. Putting them in chronological order, I started reading.

"Letters from your dad again, Andy?" a nearby GI inquired.

"Yeah," I replied.

"You're a lucky soldier. My daddy dudn't give a damn if I come home."

That remark really got to me, cutting deeply into my heart. After he left, I cried openly. The absence of a loving father was simply unimaginable to me.

A "Dear John" letter was especially hard for a soldier to bear. On learning that his girlfriend had gotten involved with some guy back home and was breaking up, most men just tore the letter up, tossed it aside, and cussed a little. While a lot of GIs suppressed their feelings about these breakups, others were simply fatalistic. How could a soldier at the front hope to revive a relationship when he had not seen the girl in many long months and was thousands of miles away?

In addition to receiving letters, we were also issued copies of the U.S. Army newspaper *Stars and Stripes*. As I read the paper, my main interest was trying to glean information about the fronts where my brothers and friends were serving.

Two of my older brothers—Don, a paratrooper, and Bennett, a jeep driver—never wrote me, but I did maintain a limited correspondence with my other two brothers. Though my oldest brother Karl and I had never been especially close growing up due to the 12-year age gap, he wrote me several letters describing how he helped to outfit thousands of troops going off to war as an Army quartermaster in Colorado.

My younger brother Bill had volunteered for the U.S. Navy in 1943. Writing me a few times from his ship in the Pacific, he compared our circumstances.

"I'm sure you would like to be in my position with a clean bed, clean white sheets, clean clothes, and a nice hot meal, safe aboard this big ship," he gibed.

After slogging across Europe through a series of foxholes amid heat, dust, rain, mud, snow, and cold, it seemed to me Bill raised a valid point. I drew little satisfaction from the fact that we did not have to spend our time endlessly repainting a ship, which Bill noted was a constant feature of life in the Navy.

Though my mom seldom sent me letters, the sand tarts she mailed me every so often were as much an expression of her love as any words she could have written. Baked from a simple recipe of flour, sugar, and real butter, they were the best cookies you ever put in your mouth—and home-baked food tasted even better at the front.

Like everyone else in my squad who received a cake or cookies from home, I would rip open the big package of cookies and pass it around to others.

"C'mon, guys, let's eat. We may be dead by suppertime, so let's eat it all now."

Beyond just our families, we knew everyone in our local communities back home was behind us. As part of the effort to support the boys fighting overseas, the ladies and girls at my Presbyterian Church assembled miniature survival kits for all the GIs from Signal Mountain. In a neat trick, they somehow crammed 30-odd useful items into a small, waterproof, tin film canister: a couple of Band-Aids, one needle and a yard of thread, five matches and a sandpaper striker glued inside the lid, one single-edge razorblade, two fishhooks, 10 feet of weighted fishing line, two fishing lures, four large paperclips, five aspirin tablets, five safety pins, one small can opener, five nails, two round-headed thumbtacks, one foot of thin wire, and a stick of chewing gum.

Of all the mail from my dad, it was his closing words in a letter I received shortly after the fighting on Hill 232 that most touched my heart.

"Son, try not to hate ... Your lovin' Dad"

Sadly, hatred and even loathing of the other side became all too common among soldiers amid the war's constant violence and brutality, where we were killing the enemy and the enemy was killing us. My dad's letter reinforced my determination not to entertain such animosity, though, in truth, hatred toward others, even our wartime enemy, was alien to my nature. While my father's German heritage might have given me a different perspective than most GIs, my Christian faith was a far more significant force shaping my feelings toward the Germans. The Bible's admonition to love your enemies served as a bulwark against poisonous and dehumanizing animosity.

Thinking back on the hate tactics taught during our training in England, I had come to believe even more firmly that the U.S. Army's effort to inspire loathing toward the Germans was both unneeded and immoral. A soldier can fight and, if necessary, kill the enemy without such hostility in his heart. My conviction that these hate tactics were wrong was strengthened by my conversation with Erich, a guy who was much like me. He and most other German prisoners were not supporters of the Nazis. In fact, many of them expressed disgust with the behavior of the Nazi regime.

Though firmly believing in the righteousness and necessity of our struggle against Nazi Germany, my faith in the justice of our cause did not alter my conviction about the barbaric nature of war itself, with its terrible violence that wrought such catastrophic suffering and death. The experience of killing other men, especially at pointblank range, weighed heavily on my soul.

My heart was pained by the knowledge I had ripped a man my own age away from his family and his community, deprived him of the chance to fulfill his life's dreams, and denied the world his irreplaceable talents. Even if those enemy soldiers I had killed had been trying to kill me, I prayed God would bless and comfort their parents and loved ones, just as He would my own family if I were to die in this war.

Of course, the recent deaths of my buddies in combat grieved me far more profoundly. While I had seen many GIs killed in the previous six months of fighting, witnessing the deaths of my friends Jesse Beaver and Sergeant Carpenter right before my eyes had been particularly gut-wrenching. I would remember them often.

With my shoulder nearly healed by mid-December, I knew my release from the convalescent hospital was imminent. Though a sense of duty and a bond of camaraderie made me want to get back to my buddies at the front, it was difficult not to feel dread at the prospect of returning to combat after the terrible things I had experienced.

Like any soldier, I naturally wondered about my own fate in this war.

Would some random bullet or piece of shrapnel ever have my name on it?

The warning issued during our basic training also always lurked in the back of my mind: "A machine gunner's life expectancy in actual combat is seven minutes." The bodies of the dead machine gunners laid side by side on Hill 232 had driven home to me again the peril for the gunner, who was always a priority target for the enemy.

But there was no point in dwelling on these dark thoughts, so I sought to block them from my consciousness. As ever, my refuge was my Christian faith. In God, I found the strength to overcome my fears, trusting that His will would be done.

The Battle of the Bulge begins: December 16–20

As I had experienced firsthand during the fighting in the Hürtgen Forest and on Hill 232, the offensive toward the Roer River by the First Army's VII Corps in Operation *Queen* had run into ferocious German resistance, resulting in the toughest combat our outfit had yet encountered in the war. Only later did I learn the course of events for the 1st Infantry Division following my medical evacuation from the front on November 19.

After overcoming the *Wehrmacht*'s defensive line at Hamich and Hill 232, the Big Red One continued its attack northeastward against bitter enemy opposition. By early December, the division had battled its way through the Hürtgen to a position roughly three miles from the Roer, where it ended its part in Operation *Queen*.

Already, by November 27, most elements of our 16th Infantry Regiment had largely concluded offensive operations and H Company was pulled off the front line for a week of reorganization and training. On December 4, the rest of the 1st Infantry Division began handing over its front-line positions to other American units.

By mid-December, other elements of VII Corps succeeded in pushing the final three miles up to the Roer but did not advance beyond it toward the Rhine. Incredibly, during the three months since we had first fought our way into the Schill Line fortifications near Eilendorf back in mid-September, the front line had only moved about a dozen miles further east into Germany. Particularly in the Hürtgen Forest, the 1st Infantry Division and other divisions had paid a tremendous cost in casualties for every inch of ground won. There was little solace in knowing the Germans had also paid a very heavy price in resisting our advance into the Roer Valley.

On December 9, as winter snows began to fall, all elements of the Big Red One, except for the 16th Infantry Regiment, proceeded to a rest area 10 miles southwest of Aachen near Henri-Chapelle, Belgium. Meanwhile, on December 5, the 16th Infantry had been slotted back into the front line in the Roetgen sector, where H Company took up a defensive position at Monschau, roughly 16 miles south of Aachen.

Finally, between December 11 and December 13, the 16th Infantry Regiment was relieved of its front-line positions and transferred about 20 miles west into rest camps around Verviers and Herve, Belgium, located about 16 miles southwest of Aachen. As part of this movement, H Company was relieved of its position at Monschau on the morning of December 13 and traveled to La Minerie, Belgium, 19 miles west-northwest of Monschau. Upon their arrival, troops received word they would have at least three weeks to rest, reorganize, obtain reinforcements, re-equip, and train.

Hitler wrecked these plans.

On the morning of December 16, 200,000 German troops supported by 1,000 tanks launched a massive counteroffensive in winter fog, completely surprising the American units holding a previously quiet sector of the Ardennes Forest in Belgium. Spearheaded by the enemy's Fifth and Sixth Panzer Armies, the attack extended along a 50-mile front between Monschau in the north to Echternach in the south, with its main effort slamming into the U.S. First Army's VIII Corps and V Corps.

In the Ardennes Counteroffensive, more commonly known as the Battle of the Bulge, the *Wehrmacht* aimed to seize the Belgian port of Antwerp over a hundred miles away, isolating the largely British forces to the north from the American forces in the south. If the desperate gamble succeeded, Hitler hoped to compel the western Allies to negotiate a separate peace, splitting them from the Soviet Union.

The alarming reports of a major German breakthrough reached us back at the 7th Convalescent Hospital in Étampes on the evening of December 16. For the next couple of days, we anxiously listened to the radio as announcers issued news bulletins describing German tanks crashing through the woods and penetrating American lines.

Although I was surprised the *Wehrmacht* had been able to keep so many men and so much equipment in reserve during the recent heavy fighting, the German assault into Belgium did not come as a total shock. If the scale and timing of their offensive was unanticipated, an attack by the enemy is something that has to be expected in war.

Return to the front: December 20–22

On December 20, one of the doctors on the hospital's staff walked into our room and gave several of us our discharge papers, informing us we were needed back at the front. I had orders to board a train that would travel to Belgium the following day.

About an hour before my departure on December 21, the beautiful nurse who the sergeant had been chasing came to my bed with a glass of water and a laxative.

"You are going to need this, soldier. Most soldiers need a good cleaning out," she explained. She added it would also help ensure my "regularity" once I switched back to eating normal Army rations. I swallowed the laxative without a second thought.

Around noon, about 20 of us boarded three trucks for the short drive to the railway station. Upon our arrival, we headed straight for the waiting train. An MP directed eight of our group into a 40-foot-by-8-foot boxcar, which was already packed with about 20 newly arrived replacements from England.

Each replacement had an oversized duffel bag alongside him containing all his earthly possessions. As always, these fellows were well-supplied with a couple of boxes of rations, extra clothing, a raincoat, gloves, and a spare pair of boots, which was a real luxury. In contrast, we veterans had only the uniforms we were wearing, the jackets on our backs, the old boots on our feet, and the helmets on our heads. We would have to wait until we reached our outfits to obtain gloves and other cold weather gear.

Despite being the last to board, the eight of us coming from the hospital felt our status as combat veterans gave us seniority. Pushing and shoving our way inside, we claimed seats on the wooden slats of the boxcar's floor. While uncomfortable, sitting was far more preferable to standing for hours in the overcrowded space.

About half an hour after our arrival, a shrill train whistle signaled the start of our journey toward the front. With coal ash from the locomotive seeping into our boxcar through the air vents, a thick layer of soot soon coated our clothes and hair. We could even taste the coal ash in our mouths. All of us were also very cold.

As the train chugged along eastward, it made frequent stops, halting for several minutes before resuming its progress. Before long, the combination of the train's jerking starts and jarring braking to screechy stops accelerated the work of the laxative supplied by the nurse. Unfortunately, heeding nature's call in the boxcar presented a serious problem, especially with the hollering of my bowels growing ever more urgent.

Determined to take care of business at the next stop, I made my way through the obstacle course of sleeping bodies and edged to the boxcar's huge, heavy door, sliding it open just far enough for me to get out. When the train made its next stop somewhere in the middle of the French countryside on that freezing, pitch-black night, I leapt down from the boxcar into soft snow and sought a good spot to relieve myself.

As I squatted 15 feet away, the halted train presented a just-visible dark silhouette against a moonless sky. Thanks to the thoughtful and farsighted nurse at the hospital, I even had tissues stuffed in the pockets of my battle jacket. All seemed well.

Ten minutes passed quickly. Sooner than I anticipated, a metallic clink reached my ears. The railcars were taking up the slack in the couplings as the train started to move slowly down the track. Facing abandonment in a strange country, panic struck.

Haste took on new meaning. Rising to my feet, I clumsily lumbered through the snow toward the train, which was steadily gathering momentum. With my pants half on and my battle jacket half off, I hobbled alongside my boxcar, my fingers fumbling in the darkness for the rungs of a ladder to haul myself aboard.

As the train's speed gradually exceeded my own pace, I fell behind my original car. Now the danger was that I would fall behind the train itself. Desperation drove my legs to run faster.

Finally, at the end of a three- or four-minute chase, I managed to pull myself up onto a ladder on the side of the train, but now had to put myself back together. Clinging tightly to an ice-cold metal ladder with my gloveless hand in a freezing wind, I performed a series of acrobatic maneuvers in order to button my pants, buckle on my belt, and slip on my jacket. But I had to wait until the next stop to try to find my boxcar.

After I had endured the biting icy wind for 10 minutes, the train at last halted. Heaving open the sliding doors, I bent my head inside to make shouted inquiries. Bewildered voices responded they did not know which outfit they were with, much less the location of my car.

Upon sliding the fourth door open, one fellow recognized my voice and shoved aside a few GIs to make space for me on the floor of the boxcar. When he asked where I had been, I replied matter-of-factly.

"Hanging off the side of this train. If we had gone through a tunnel, I'd have been hanging on it." Everyone laughed and I knew I was back in good company.

As the train continued its long, slow stop-and-start journey through the night and into the next morning, some of the guys around me slept deeply the whole time, snoring loudly. For me, sleep on the uncomfortable wooden floor came only fitfully.

Like many of the other soldiers heading back to the front, my mind turned to sober, quiet reflection, very reminiscent of that long night back on the troopship before D-Day. With the Germans on the offensive and combat imminent, each veteran and replacement had to overcome his fears and steel himself for battle.

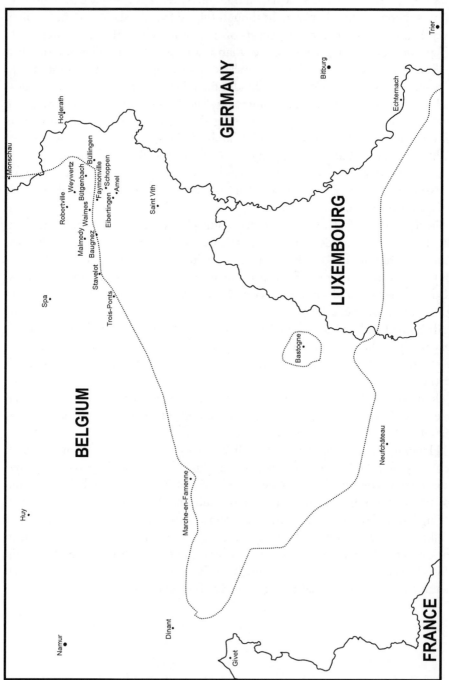

Map 4: The Battle Of the Bulge

CHAPTER 15

The Battle of the Bulge:
December 22, 1944–January 15, 1945

Into the Bulge: December 22

The *Wehrmacht's* surprise counteroffensive on December 16 cut short the Big Red One's just begun and long-awaited rest period in Belgium. Temporarily reassigned from the U.S. First Army's VII Corps to its V Corps, the 1st Infantry Division received urgent orders to rush a short distance to the south, where the massive German thrust westward into Belgium was opening a "bulge" in the front.

On reaching the front, the 1st Infantry Division would take up a defensive position on the northern shoulder of the Bulge at the western flank of V Corps. The mission of V Corps was to prevent a widening of the German breach in the Allied lines and protect the well-stocked U.S. Army supply depots north of the Bulge.

Over the night of December 16–17, the 1st Infantry Division's 26th Infantry Regiment sped 15 miles south from its rest area to the Belgian town of Bütgenbach to block a German advance northward. At the same time, its 18th Infantry Regiment deployed to take up a front-line position in the center of the 1st Infantry Division's sector. Meanwhile, our 16th Infantry Regiment prepared to shift south from its rest area around Herve and Verviers down to the vicinity of Waimes, located some 16 miles southeast of Verviers and a little over four miles west of Bütgenbach.

As part of this movement by the 16th Infantry toward Waimes, a convoy carrying H Company set out from its bivouac area at La Minerie five miles north of Verviers on the night of December 17. Over the following day, elements of the 16th Infantry assembled in the area around Robertville, 19 miles southeast of La Minerie. From Robertville, the 2nd Battalion of the 16th Infantry was to proceed about three miles further south to Waimes, where it would occupy a defensive position on the western flank of the 16th Infantry's sector on the northern shoulder of the Bulge. The 16th Infantry's 3rd Battalion would hold the position a little to the east of it, while the 16th Infantry's 1st Battalion would remain up near Robertville as regimental reserve.

Late on the afternoon of December 19, H Company moved out for the short trip down to Waimes, which it reached about a half-hour later. Just before H Company's arrival, 2nd Battalion infantry patrols scouting the area around Waimes ran into the first enemy opposition. It was soon determined that a large German force was concentrated in the town of Faymonville, located just a mile and a half east-southeast of Waimes.

As 2nd Battalion troops took up defensive positions and began laying mines, H Company's machine-gun and mortar crews established their emplacements and laid wire communications to the rear. During the ensuing night, H Company's mortar crews engaged the Germans, who retaliated with mortar and artillery fire on our positions.

From December 19 to 21, enemy mortars and artillery kept the 16th Infantry under sustained fire, while German troops probed the regiment's defenses. Though the enemy's intentions in this sector of its northern flank remained unclear, the repeated assaults against the 26th Infantry's position a few miles east around Bütgenbach suggested a similar large-scale attack was a real danger in the 16th Infantry's sector.

Naturally, those of us making the rail journey from Paris had no knowledge of these military movements in reaction to the German counteroffensive. While rumors were rampant, we knew little except that the enemy was on the attack.

Indeed, when our train lurched to a halt early on the very cold morning of December 22, we were not even aware our long stop-and-start trip was at an end. Only when our boxcar's sliding doors were yanked open, and a sergeant ordered us to exit onto the railway station's small wooden platform, did we realize we had reached our destination. We were now roughly 225 miles from Étampes, though our circuitous rail journey to this spot in the Belgian countryside had been much longer.

Immediately, several sergeants began calling out our names and issuing our unit assignments. My orders stated I would be rejoining H Company, which came as a huge relief since returning soldiers were not always reassigned to their original outfit.

Taking charge of a group of replacements and others who were fresh from the hospital, a hulking sergeant announced we were only five miles from the front line and directed us to board three of the 15 or so waiting Army trucks. Painted with the words "Red Ball Express" on their doors, these were the familiar two-and-a-half-ton U.S. Army cargo trucks commonly known as "Jimmies."

A large Black soldier sat behind the wheel of my assigned truck. His engine running, he was clearly eager to get on the road and deliver us to our units at the front. However, the laxatives were continuing to work their magic. As the other men were loading up, I was anxiously looking around for a good place to relieve myself.

"What the hell you waitin' for soldier, get in the damn truck!" the sergeant barked at me.

"I've got urgent business to attend to, so you gotta wait a few minutes," I said.

"Business?" he questioned. "My business is to get you to the front as fast as I can, so get in right now!" Under several kinds of pressure and not knowing how else to communicate my situation to the sergeant, I knew I had to lay it on the line.

"I gotta take a shit," I announced.

"Why didn't you say so? Let me know when you're ready to set sail," he told me. As it happened, I had spoken for many of the GIs who had been cooped up on the train and needed to relieve themselves before proceeding.

Less than half an hour after our arrival at the train depot, about three dozen of us, including the sergeant, set off for our units aboard three trucks, tailed by a couple of Army squad cars. Our route took us through devastated Belgian villages filled with wrecked tanks, trucks, and jeeps, all evidence of the recent heavy fighting in the area. However, our convoy did not encounter the enemy before we reached the first outfit, where three or four soldiers disembarked.

Five minutes after we got back on the road, a tremendously loud bang resounded from just in front of our truck. Instantly, those of us with combat experience recognized we were under fire. Scrambling out of the trucks, everyone took cover in the drainage ditches beside the road.

Peering out from the ditches, we could see that an enemy shell had struck the engine compartment of the lead truck in our column. Although the explosion had completely destroyed most of the front end of the vehicle, everyone in the targeted truck had miraculously escaped the attack unharmed.

We were almost certain our convoy had been ambushed by a German tank hidden in the nearby woods. However, it remained a mystery why the tank had not fired a couple more rounds to take out our other two trucks and then opened up on us with its machine gun. Whatever the reason, it was clear we had been very lucky.

After hunkering down for about a quarter of an hour in anticipation of further enemy fire, the sergeant in charge decided we had to seize the initiative. While those of us without weapons waited in the drainage ditch, he led about two dozen riflemen from our convoy into the woods to hunt for the enemy.

As we looked on, the riflemen soon located a camouflaged German tank about 40 yards from the road. A moment later, the tank's commander hoisted the white flag, surrendering without any resistance. When the young enemy crewmen climbed out of the tank with their hands in the air, they looked happy to be out of the war, which probably explained why they had not put up much of a fight. Directed into one of the squad cars in our convoy, the prisoners were driven off to the rear for processing.

Loading back aboard the two surviving trucks, we resumed the journey to our assigned units. Even though not all of us had participated in the crew's surrender, everyone was excited about the capture of a German tank. We had gotten back into combat even before reaching the front line.

Defending the northern flank: December 22/23

A little later that morning, I was dropped off at H Company headquarters, which was located in a bomb-damaged house just outside the town of Waimes. In the distance, artillery shelling could be heard as American and German crews traded fire.

Fifteen minutes after reporting to First Sergeant Huber, I caught a lift in a jeep to the rear area, where I reunited with my second machine-gun squad as they were eating breakfast. My old buddies Wayne Newsome, Lincoln Welser, Hector Gonzalez, and Chief were all there, but the other two men were strangers to me, recent replacements to our squad.

Before I could join them for some hot chow, we received urgent orders to move out. Immediately, all of us got busy preparing to head up to the front. As I was collecting the tripod and my pistol, a sergeant issued instructions to our squad.

"Andrews, there's your machine gun, and you're in charge. The front-line position is already established."

Within minutes, both squads in our section of the platoon and a detachment of infantry from G Company were on our way up to the newly established front line about 500 yards away. Five football fields may not seem like a long way, but it was slow going with all our gear, especially with snow that was up to a couple of feet deep in places.

More importantly, we also faced the threat of enemy mortar and artillery fire. If we had taken the main trail that led up to the front, we would likely have come under sustained shelling, since the Germans had zeroed in their guns on that path. Thankfully, this danger was recognized and we took an alternate route. As a result, the enemy artillery fire was sporadic and did not hinder our progress, although there were still enough incoming shells to remind us we were in a combat zone.

Upon reaching the front line, we found a series of abandoned German dugouts. Selecting a large gun emplacement, sheltered by a group of fir trees and on slightly elevated ground, our machine-gun squad had a commanding view of the surrounding terrain. With our section's other gun squad posted just 30 yards away, the position would also allow us to have interlocking crossfire if the enemy tried to advance through the open field to our front. Our two machine gun squads had further support from a half-dozen riflemen scattered around our emplacements.

Our lieutenant explained we would be helping to defend the northern flank of the German breakthrough to prevent "the Bulge from spreading sideways," making it clear we might have to remain stationed at this location for some time. Later, our engineers would plant mines in front of our lines for added protection, but, for now, we would have to rely on our machine guns and small arms to resist any enemy attack.

After watching a couple of guys in my squad struggle to clear away snow in order to make a space for our machine gun at the front of our dugout, I suggested they use a small fir branch as a broom. Once enough snow had been swept away to mount the machine gun, we jammed two sticks into the snow on either side of the weapon to mark the limit at which it would be safe to swing the barrel without endangering the other machine-gun squad and the riflemen dug in on either side of us.

While one member of our squad kept watch behind the gun, I worked with the rest to continue to improve our emplacement. We had carried out a similar project back near Zweifall a month and a half earlier before our attack into the Hürtgen, but here we had a big head start thanks to the existing shoulder-deep trench and the log walls left behind by the Germans.

Our biggest enhancement to the dugout was a roof made of thick, fresh-cut branches roped tightly together. After covering the branches with a canvas tarpaulin to keep snow out, we piled earth over the top in an effort to camouflage our small bunker until the next snowfall fully concealed it. In the freezing winter weather, the "roofing" would also help to keep us warm as well as provide limited protection from shrapnel, though not from a direct hit by a mortar or artillery round.

Realizing that not many soldiers knew how to lash logs together to create a roof, build a small fire that would generate minimal smoke, or sharpen knives and bayonets, I was once again grateful for my years in the Boy Scouts that had developed these types of skills. With the arrival of freezing temperatures, other simple tricks like inserting newspaper into our helmet liners and wrapping newspaper around our feet for added warmth in our boots also proved invaluable. Beyond these practical skills and problem-solving techniques, Scouting had also taught me how to work with and trust others, something that was just as vital in combat.

As we labored to improve our gun emplacement, our lieutenant informed us of the recent "Malmédy massacre" in which "German SOBs"—members of the notorious SS—had ruthlessly machine-gunned a large group of captured American soldiers in cold blood. While the details were not known to us at this time, the massacre had occurred just five days earlier on December 17 at Baugnez, a crossroads near Malmédy that was only a couple of miles west of our new position south of Waimes. Word of the atrocity would make us fight even harder to prevent our position from being overrun. We had to avoid falling prisoner to such murderers at all costs.

My buddies in the squad also caught me up on what had happened in our outfit during my month-long absence. Naturally, they gave me a hard time about having it easy during my hospital stay near Paris. With my long respite from combat, the others had no difficulty determining who would take the next shift behind the machine gun once we finished the improvements on our dugout.

"You've been resting, boy. You get your ass up on the gun," they directed.

Despite still feeling a bit weak physically, I willingly slid behind the gun for my first turn on duty, glad to get back into action. It soon seemed like I had never left.

Carefully surveying the snowy ground ahead of us, I tried to make sure its features were clear in my mind in case it later became a battlefield. Perhaps a hundred yards beyond the clearing in front of us lay German-held woods filled with tall evergreens, giant pines, and a forest floor covered with tiny young tree growth.

As the darkness descended early that winter afternoon, it began to snow and grow colder. Fortunately, antifreeze (ethylene glycol) had been added to the machine gun's water jacket and water chest to ensure the weapon's coolant would remain liquid in these freezing temperatures.

When my first turn on gun duty came to an end, I grabbed some chow. Though we would have to eat lots of cold rations up on the front line, our stationary position permitted us to get a hot meal in the evening. While half the squad remained to defend our position, the other half would trek back a hundred yards to the rear. On reaching our jeep "Little Joe," they would gobble down hot chow brought forward from H Company's kitchen further in the rear. Over the next few weeks, we often ate these meals with guys from our section's other gun squad and some of the half-dozen riflemen posted near our gun emplacement, giving us all a brief escape from the front.

After claiming a few hours of sleep, my second shift on the gun began in the middle of the night as snow was falling. By the following morning, the new shroud of snow had made our bunker almost completely invisible to any enemy observer.

In the dim light of daybreak before the fog had cleared, I heard the sound of a patrol approaching from the direction of the German lines. Because I had hunted squirrels in this kind of fog when I was growing up back on Signal Mountain, my ears were attuned to tracking movement crunching through the snow. Probably believing they were protected by the fog, the enemy patrol was making its way towards our position without much concern about making noise.

Taking careful aim in that direction, I fired off a dozen rounds. I was pretty sure some of the bullets found their mark, but there was no return fire, only dead silence. The Germans would now keep quiet as they probed our lines.

Later that same day, December 23, the weather cleared, allowing Allied aircraft to go after the *Wehrmacht* for the first time since the start of their counteroffensive a week earlier. Though the battered *Luftwaffe* also managed to get a few aircraft into the sky, the sight of our planes conducting missions over the enemy lines was reassuring.

Enemy infiltrators: December 23/24

As German mortar and artillery fire continued to target our lines, our officers and NCOs alerted us to prepare for an enemy attack on December 23 and 24. While the anticipated assaults failed to take place, our squad was ready for anything.

Beyond the threat of a conventional attack, we had also been warned that specially trained German troops had infiltrated behind our lines dressed in American uniforms and speaking American-accented English. By cutting communication links, altering road signs, and carrying out other acts of sabotage, these infiltrators sought to create confusion and disrupt our efforts to resist the *Wehrmacht*'s offensive.

On an afternoon a couple of days after my return to the front, I was crouched behind the gun when a trio of soldiers passed through the snow about 10 yards from our bunker. Two fellows I knew from H Company were holding on to a prisoner who had his hands bound behind him. These three were trailed by a half-dozen more GIs who were obviously interested in what was happening.

Although the prisoner wore an American uniform, the group following the trio informed us this man was, in fact, an English-speaking German soldier who had been caught just behind our front line and was about to face a firing squad. The laws of war dictated that enemy infiltrators captured in such circumstances would be shot as spies, but I had never imagined I would witness a summary execution.

As I looked on, the party halted about 30 yards away. An officer I did not recognize requested three volunteers from the assembled GIs to serve as a firing squad. Once that was done, the prisoner was led in front of a large tree and blindfolded.

My view of the execution was blocked by the soldiers who stood clustered together to observe the proceeding, but I heard the command to fire and the shooting. A moment later, I saw the German sprawled on the ground beneath the tree.

It was hard not to have mixed feelings about the execution of this enemy infiltrator. Certainly, the German was guilty of his crime, but it was difficult for me to accept the killing of a prisoner away from the battlefield. Reflecting on the episode, I was glad not to have been chosen for the firing squad and certainly hoped I would never be ordered to sneak behind enemy lines in a German uniform. For those who were captured, execution as a spy seemed an inglorious way to die for one's country.

Keeping watch: December 25

On my third night back on the front line, I started my four-hour turn on gun duty at 2am. Night shifts seemed to drag on forever, but at least our bunker had been rendered as comfortable as circumstances permitted in the icy cold.

In the clearing before me, everything remained utterly quiet, as if frozen still. Suspicious of the silence and repeatedly warned to remain vigilant, I strained my eyes in search of any movement in the darkness.

About half an hour into my watch, the sky's thick cloud cover began to break, allowing moonlight to momentarily flood the winter landscape.

All of a sudden, there was movement out in front of me. My heart leapt into my throat. Automatically, my right hand gripped the trigger as my left hand went to the ammo belt, ready to feed it into the machine gun the instant the enemy appeared.

That is when I saw her. A small doe deer emerged from a thicket of trees 20 yards to my right, followed by another, and then another. As they playfully pranced across the clearing, night birds darting through the air chirped out musical accompaniment. Snow on the branches of the nearby trees added to the pastoral scene.

If this isn't a perfect postcard, I don't know what is. At that moment, the war seemed as far away as at any time since our landing in Normandy six and a half months earlier.

As quickly as the deer had appeared, they scampered back out of sight into the woods. With clouds returning to blot out the moonlight, the birds ceased their chirping and the night reclaimed its silent, pitch-black veil.

Perhaps 20 or 30 minutes later, the clouds again parted, once more bathing the field in moonlight. Nothing appeared amiss, yet there was some almost indefinable alteration in the landscape.

No deer were present. No night birds fluttered. Nothing was moving.

It was clear to me something out there was very definitely different than before.

Oddly, although all of the foliage was covered with snow, it seemed to me the tree growth had become thicker than the last time the moonlight had shone on the clearing. The landscape was now dotted with what appeared to be six or eight small new trees, all roughly the height and shape of a five-foot Christmas tree.

But perhaps I had simply failed to note these smaller trees during the previous moonlit interlude. My mind began trying to convince me they must have been there all along, even as my gut was signaling alarm.

Then it happened. After scrutinizing these trees for a quarter of an hour as the moonlight sporadically broke through the clouds, the closest "Christmas tree" 30 yards away shifted sideways about a foot.

It was so hard to accept what I had just witnessed that I thought the moonlight must be playing tricks. Yet even as I blinked to make sure my eyes were not deceiving me, I knew I had not imagined that tree moving.

Picking up the field telephone that connected us to our section's other gun squad and our company's mortar crews in the rear, I spoke in a low voice.

"Enemy out front approaching disguised behind Christmas trees. Look carefully and be prepared to shoot. I'm gonna count to 10 and start firing and you do too."

As soon as I hung up the phone, another "Christmas tree" off to the left moved a foot closer toward us.

Sure of myself now, I squeezed off a short burst from my machine gun. A second later, our section's other machine gunner 30 yards away also opened fire. Brilliantly marked out by the tracer rounds, our murderous crossfire ripped across the clearing and into the forest beyond. The other members of my squad not yet awake roused themselves to take up firing positions alongside me as the nearby riflemen also added the weight of their fire. A few seconds after that, our mortar crews went into action, sending rounds swishing down toward the enemy.

With all hell breaking loose around them, it was obvious to the Germans their attempted sneak attack had utterly failed. Casting aside the small trees they had used for concealment, a ghostly force of two dozen or so white-clad enemy troops appeared. Returning our fire, they surged toward our line in a wild, Japanese-style "banzai" charge like those recounted in newsreels from the Pacific.

As always, the tracer rounds that helped me adjust my aim also exposed our position. But while enemy bullets began striking all around our bunker, the attacking Germans out in the open had it far worse. None made it closer than 20 yards before getting mowed down by our machine guns, rifles, and exploding mortar shells. But the fighting was not over.

Within moments, a second wave of two dozen more white-garbed enemy troops emerged into the clearing from the edge of the forest a hundred yards away. Supporting the attack, a number of vehicles, including three self-propelled guns, also came crashing out of the woods. Known in German as *Sturmgeschütz*, these fearsome armored monsters had their main guns mounted in a fixed position on a tank chassis, rather than inside a turret.

Responding to our request for a fire mission to repel this larger attack, our artillery crews immediately opened up. There was a whoosh of air around me as the shells zoomed overhead with a noise like a passing freight train.

The furious artillery barrage shattered the German force before it had advanced 10 yards out of the forest. As the self-propelled guns and other vehicles were hit, they exploded in flames, hurling burning bodies into the air. In the forest behind them, some of our shells detonated in the upper branches of the trees. As the tree trunks split in two like they were matchsticks, the burning treetops snapped off and whirled down to the ground in a fiery conflagration. Before long, many of the trees still standing caught fire, acting like giant torches to illuminate the battlefield.

The brief but sharp clash ended in a lopsided rout of the Germans. Surprisingly, our own position had not suffered any enemy mortar or artillery fire during the attack, making the engagement feel more like a massacre than a battle.

While we were relieved to have survived the firefight with no losses, the now familiar aftermath of battle was grisly. The air was filled with the acrid smell of cordite mixed with smoke from burning trees, oil, and bodies, creating a nauseating stench that irritated the throats and eyes of everyone in our squad. All of us were left gagging as we tried to avoid vomiting.

A few hours later, the day dawned bright and clear, but the brilliance of the winter sky above stood in stark relief against the desolation below. A thick pall of smoke hung over a bleak panorama of mud, death, and devastation that only hours earlier had been a picturesque snow-covered landscape.

Some of the fires ignited by the earlier shelling continued to burn. Even green fir trees had been set ablaze, transforming much of the once beautiful forest across from us into a wasteland of charred trunks. Meanwhile, the once lovely green foliage covered with snow was now scorched and splattered with blood. Interspersed among the smoldering hulks of the destroyed vehicles, the torn bodies of several dozen enemy dead lay strewn across the mud where they had been cut down.

An hour after daybreak, German medics emerged from the forest wearing white arm bands marked with a red cross. As they moved among the bodies in search of any wounded among the dead, no one fired on them from our lines. We were always careful not to shoot their medics, just as they tried to avoid shooting ours.

At about the same time, the sound of music became audible, though it was so faint I momentarily wondered whether my ears were deceiving me. When I realized the sound was emanating from the field telephone, I lifted the receiver to my ear and heard a familiar Christmas carol coming over the line.

> Silent night, Holy night, all is calm, all is bright, round yon virgin mother and child, Holy infant so tender and mild, sleep in Heavenly peace, sleep in Heavenly peace …

As the song played, my thoughts drifted away from the carnage of the battlefield before me. When the music ended, our commander came on the line.

"Merry Christmas, guys. Merry Christmas."

It was Christmas morning, but we had not really been aware of it until this moment. Reflecting on the peaceful, comforting, powerfully moving message of the carol while staring out at the terrible ruination of battle, I shook my head with tears in my eyes. There could have been no more poignant contrast.

God, there has got to be a way we can have peace so that this kind of thing does not happen, I prayed. Even in the midst of war, Christmas inspired hope.

To celebrate the day, we took turns heading back to the rear for a hot Christmas dinner of roasted turkey, dressing, cranberry sauce, and other rare treats of the season. As we ate our holiday meal under a sunny sky that warmed the winter day, everyone seemed to catch a bit of the Christmas spirit.

Stalemate in the Bulge: December 26–30

While our repulse of the small German attack early on Christmas Day marked a victory for us, the *Wehrmacht* had already given up on any major effort to crack the 1st Infantry Division's lines a couple of days earlier. As part of V Corps on the northern shoulder of the Bulge, the Big Red One had helped prevent the Sixth Panzer Army from widening the breach and reaching the valuable American supply dumps further west.

The enemy's failure to break through V Corps also meant the German offensive was funneled into a narrower salient and a more limited road network. Enemy traffic along these routes was kept under heavy fire by American artillery, which played a crucial role in breaking up enemy assaults against our lines.

The fighting also turned against the enemy in other sectors of the battlefield. On December 24, the *Wehrmacht*'s drive to reach the Meuse River had been blocked near Dinant, some 54 miles west of our position near Waimes. Then, on December 26,

American forces broke the roughly week-long German siege of Bastogne, located a little less than three dozen miles south-southwest of Waimes.

The *Wehrmacht* had been checked, but their forces inside the Bulge were not defeated. In the final days of December, enemy troops were moving westward along the roads just beyond our position as the Germans brought infantry forward to replace the armored forces that had spearheaded the offensive. These soldiers dug into their positions, aggressively patrolled, and continued to conduct small-scale attacks.

Unaware of this larger military picture, our machine-gun squad remained hunkered down in our front-line defensive position, vigilant for further enemy assaults. Over the night of December 27/28, we were alerted to prepare for a possible large-scale attack based on the movement of enemy forces near our lines, but none took place.

During the final days of December, the Germans took advantage of the clear weather to target our front-line positions and rear area with artillery shells and rockets from their "Screaming Meemies." Though some fell in our vicinity, we were not hit. Meanwhile, our aircraft, artillery, and mortars struck back hard against German troop and vehicle movement, hammering concentrations of enemy forces day and night.

No large engagements occurred in our sector of the line after December 25, but skirmishes occasionally erupted near our position when our infantry's patrols ran into German troops. These patrols were always risky, but vital for capturing prisoners in order to collect intelligence on the enemy's plans.

In one instance, I witnessed three GIs ushering a half-dozen SS troops to the rear for processing as prisoners of war. Abruptly, one of the American soldiers yelled "Halt!" stopping the six Germans in their tracks. Gesturing with his pistol, this GI made one of the prisoners hold up both his hands.

While the other two Americans kept their weapons trained on the prisoners, the GI unstrapped a concealed MP 40 burp gun from the suspicious SS man's back. In the nick of time, this observant soldier had spied the unusual bulge in the backside of this prisoner's uniform, no doubt preventing the German from later yanking out his hidden submachine gun to shoot unsuspecting American troops further back.

After the confiscation of the hidden weapon, the other prisoners were all thoroughly searched before the party resumed its march to the rear.

Battling the cold: December 30–January 15

Following a little nicer weather on December 29, winter storms at the end of the year brought heavy snowfall, temperatures that stayed below freezing, and a vicious icy wind. The bitter cold and the deep drifts of snow were unlike anything that most of us had ever experienced back home. But just like the men from the northern states, I pretty much took the weather in stride after my years spent hiking, fishing, hunting, and camping during the cold winters back on Signal Mountain. Of course, all of us appreciated any gear that would help keep us warm.

About this time, H Company's quartermaster issued us dark green wool trench coats. Although we were almost unable to move in the stiff coats and regarded them as a bit of a joke, they did a decent job of keeping us warm in the extreme cold and were just fine when we were not on the march.

However, on the whole, the Army failed to issue us adequate cold-weather clothing and equipment to protect us from that winter's arctic temperatures. In the absence of this gear, hundreds of GIs suffered severe frostbite, sometimes so bad they never returned to duty.

While the standard Army boots I had received just before D-Day held up pretty well during the ensuing months of heavy use, they were ill-suited for winter conditions. In November when it first turned cold, we got word that warm, waterproof "shoepack" boots were on the way, but they never reached us. Except for the trench coat, the only item of clothing I received that winter was a new pair of socks.

However, rumors circulated that shoepack boots had been shipped to Europe, but that rear-echelon clerks in the Army's supply depots had sold them on the black market, a criminal racket which had become highly developed by that time. We certainly hoped this story was false. Though nobody in our machine-gun squad ever got trench foot, the lack of winter-weather boots led to countless cases of the ailment among front-line troops.

Amid the freezing, snowy weather, we were always looking for ways to get warm. On one occasion during a heavy snowfall, several of us headed back a short distance to the rear for a hot meal. With the falling snow obscuring German observation, the other guys concluded it would be safe to build a fire, something normally too risky at the front since the source of any smoke could be targeted.

When they decided to build the fire under a fir tree, I told them it was a bad spot, pointing out that the overhanging branches were heavily laden with snow. From experience, I knew what would happen and stayed back, but the others ignored my warning, convincing themselves it was too cold for a small fire to melt anything. Before long, the fire's heat got to work on the snow in the tree above.

The collapse came with the force of a minor avalanche, knocking the C-rations from the hands of the men and leaving them all coated in snow. So much for trying to share another lesson from my Scouting days, I thought, as everyone broke into laughter.

Other than going back a short distance to the rear for our meals, we had little time away from our bunker during the first couple of weeks of the Battle of the Bulge. Recognizing that we needed a break after two weeks of front-line duty, the brass granted our machine-gun platoon a three-day rest period. After men from another unit relieved us of our position, we marched back through deep snow to the rest area, which had been established in a forest clearing several miles in the rear.

On reaching the rest area, each of us was issued a helmet full of hot, clean water from a huge barrel to use as we saw fit, whether for brushing teeth, shaving, washing up, or laundering clothes. While it was impossible to do much with such a small amount of water, we all made the best of it.

Shaving and washing my wavy black hair with a small bar of harsh Army-issue oxygen soap was as good as it got for a GI. At a more basic level, the rest area offered us a refuge from combat, a place where we could stand up without fear of getting shot or stretch out to grab a nap.

That afternoon, about four hours after our arrival, we received hot chow, which included a meat stew, green beans, warm cornbread, and coffee. While we were in the middle of eating this meal from our mess kits, a jeep sped into the rest area. An officer stood up and raised a megaphone to make an announcement.

"Get your gear ready. The Germans have broken through. We gotta go back to the front immediately."

Surprised and shaken by this news, we immediately gathered our equipment. With bits of shaving cream still on my face, I climbed aboard one of the trucks headed up to the front line a few minutes later. Alongside the road, tanks had slid into ditches and flipped on their sides, making clear the treacherous nature of vehicular movement on the snow-shrouded, ice-slicked roads. But whatever hazard this posed to our trucks, we were just thankful not to have to trudge back through the snow on foot.

Ironically, when we reached our position, no significant enemy action took place in our sector of the line, which only added to our disappointment at having lost our promised three-day rest period. Those brief hours at the rest area proved to be our only real break from front-line duty at the bunker, though I did later have an opportunity to head back a short distance to the rear for a quick shower under a hundred-gallon canvas tank with holes cut in the bottom.

While the icy roads made travel risky for almost all types of vehicles, there was one that could operate reliably in these conditions. This was the Army's M29 Weasel, an amazing tracked vehicle about the size of a jeep. However, to my knowledge, the 2nd Battalion had only one lone Weasel. But even if a couple more Weasels had been available, they could not have begun to meet the food, ammunition, and other supply demands of our battalion's four companies.

Despite the perilous roads, the quartermaster still somehow managed to deliver our essential requirements. Likewise, our jeep, "Little Joe," continued its regular trips to the spot a hundred yards in the rear of our bunker where we ate our meals, though the chow it brought up often arrived cold. In at least one instance, mugs of steaming hot coffee were sent up to our position, but, by the time these reached us, the cream on top had frozen solid and the coffee under the cream was already cold.

Whatever our daily struggles with the extreme winter weather, the presence of German troops a few dozen yards in front of our bunker and the ongoing exchange of artillery fire kept our minds focused. If anything, our mood became even more tense now that a thick frozen fog and falling snow provided the enemy's infantry with excellent cover to sneak up on us. Cloaked under the white sheets they wore over their uniforms, the German soldiers were already difficult enough to spot.

In these conditions, your eyes could play tricks on you. On at least two occasions, I fired at dark shadows in a thick fog, thinking it might be the enemy. With everyone on edge, there was also a real risk of getting hit by friendly fire.

While our V Corps maintained its defensive posture on the Bulge's northern shoulder during the first part of January, other elements of the U.S. First Army launched the first phase of a major counterattack against German forces inside the Bulge on January 3. Though snow and fog hampered Allied air support for these ground operations, V Corps shelled enemy positions and patrolled in strength in an attempt to fool the Germans into believing we were joining in a general attack.

As part of this effort, our battalion's riflemen regularly conducted patrols, struggling through the deep snow that made any movement overland exceptionally difficult. But the winter weather also helped conceal these patrols, which aided them in taking German outposts by surprise and bringing back a haul of prisoners.

Of course, the Germans also took advantage of these conditions to carry out similar raids against our lines. Our squad learned that three GIs from our 2nd Battalion had apparently been captured in one such incident during the night of January 5/6, which heightened our caution. The high level of tension only began to subside when the Germans stationed across from us departed their position a few days later.

On January 12, our preparations to join the offensive finally got underway, though, in the initial phase, other American units would pass through our sector of the front before we commenced our own operation. However, it really only became apparent to us that something big was in the works when engineers arrived to clear a path through the minefields that had been planted in front of our lines. In shouting "Fire in the hole!" as a warning before the detonation of a half-dozen of these mines, they might as well have been announcing that our attack was imminent.

Our squad spent that day cleaning our weapons and putting the rest of our equipment in order. Packing our jeep's trailer, we carefully stacked ammo belts and crates of grenades next to boxes of rations. Another section of the trailer was stocked with extra 5-gallon water chests and spare rubber condensing hoses for our machine gun. When it was finally all done, we threw a heavy tarp over the trailer, which "Little Joe" would haul behind us when the attack began. We were ready to move out.

Early on the morning of January 13, American artillery, tank, and mortar units opened a hurricane of fire against German lines, which was quickly met with an intense retaliatory bombardment of our front line and rear areas. Though the enemy artillery fire snarled traffic and caused casualties, elements of other American divisions were still able to carry out their planned assault against the German positions. Attacking from the 16th Infantry Regiment's lines close to our location, these troops received close air support from P-51 fighter planes, which managed to fly in spite of the weather.

That evening, our machine-gun platoon officially handed over its front-line position to another American unit. The 16th Infantry Regiment was scheduled to commence its part of the 1st Infantry Division's attack the following day, January 14. Ordered to prepare for a fast-moving advance across German-held territory, we were anxious for the offensive to jump off. However, word came down that the assault would be postponed for a full day due to intensified enemy movement ahead of us.

Warned that the Germans might carry out a preemptive spoiling attack against our force, we maintained a close watch on the area ahead of us over the next day, but none of us really considered an enemy assault as likely. In fact, there was a rumor the Germans were about to surrender after the failure of their offensive at the battle of Bulge. In short, nobody really knew what to expect.

That night, it turned miserably cold as a heavy new snow fell, but our officers ordered us to get ready to attack the next morning. Despite the horrible weather and the possibility of strong German opposition, everyone felt we had been on the defensive long enough.

We wanted to attack. We wanted to finish off the enemy. We wanted to win the war.

CHAPTER 16

Winter War:
January 15–February 6, 1945

On the attack: January 15–16

Launching its assault on the morning of January 15, the Big Red One joined in the general counteroffensive against German forces in the Bulge. Seeking to trap enemy troops holding the western part of the Bulge, American forces on the eastern flanks would cooperate in a giant pincer movement. Advancing from the northern flank, the U.S. First Army, with our 1st Infantry Division in its V Corps, would drive south to link up with the U.S. Third Army pushing north from the southern flank.

As part of the 1st Infantry Division's offensive, the 16th Infantry Regiment commenced its attack before dawn on January 15. While the 1st Battalion fought its way toward the town Faymonville roughly a mile and a half east-southeast of Waimes, the 3rd Battalion pressed forward to seize the ground northeast of Faymonville.

Once Faymonville was seized, our 2nd Battalion was to push beyond it to seize the town of Schoppen, located a mile and a half east-southeast of Faymonville and three miles east-southeast of Waimes. If our battalion was not able to take Schoppen, its orders were to capture the high ground to the west of the town.

Struggling to advance through the deep snow, troops from the 16th Infantry's 1st and 3rd Battalions drove forward despite meeting stiff resistance from German mortar and small arms fire. When night fell on January 15, Faymonville was still being cleared of enemy opposition in house-to-house combat.

Early the next morning, H Company and the rest of the 2nd Battalion began our part of the attack at the start of a bitterly cold, windy day under clear skies. Attached to F Company, our second machine-gun platoon moved out toward the front line at Faymonville at 4:15am, a little over four hours before sunrise. On reaching the town, we took cover in the basement of a bombed-out home, where I grabbed a little more sleep out of the cold.

Once Faymonville had been cleared around dawn, the 2nd Battalion began its push toward Schoppen with our machine-gun platoon advancing close on the heels of F Company. Many of the riflemen had donned white sheets obtained from Belgian civilians to camouflage their olive-drab American uniforms, but I chose not to wear one. A sheet draped over a soldier with a tripod on his shoulders was simply impractical, not to mention the enshrouded tripod carrier would resemble a moving igloo, presenting the enemy with a large and inviting target.

While our group did not immediately encounter any German resistance as we advanced across the hilly Belgian countryside, the accumulated snow posed a real enough obstacle. A foot or two deep in most places, the snow was much deeper alongside the roads and where the wind had piled it into banks. Trudging through this depth of snow was as physically demanding as anything we had experienced, with the extra weight of the tripod on my shoulders magnifying the labor of each step.

Even with short rest breaks every half-hour, all of us soon grew exhausted. Furthering our misery, the snow that found its way down inside our boots rapidly melted, leaving icy water to slosh around our feet, while a piercing wind intensified the sub-freezing cold. Inevitably, there was plenty of griping about our attempt to carry out an attack in these awful conditions. Indeed, the front-line bunker where we had been cooped up for the preceding three and a half weeks started to seem downright inviting.

Whatever our fatigue, we had to remain alert for ambushes from German troops, who typically remained hidden behind large snowbanks. When the enemy did make an appearance, it was not always immediately clear whether we faced a few riflemen, a machine-gun nest, or a larger force. Luckily, our riflemen could usually flush out the opposition without much difficulty, either killing them or forcing them to retreat or surrender. If we met a stronger force, close air support was available from our P-51s.

Though our squad deployed for action more than once that morning, the advance initially proceeded without us needing to engage the enemy with our machine gun. While these deployments of our gun permitted me to put down the heavy steel tripod for a moment, we soon had to resume our slog. Each time I hoisted the tripod back onto my shoulders, it came with a load of snow, some of which got under my clothing to melt against my skin and leave me even wetter and colder than before.

"K Company": January 16

Late that morning, we heard a commotion up ahead. A German officer waving a white flag on the end of a rifle barrel emerged from the woods in front of us, leading out a small party of enemy soldiers with their hands raised. Swiftly rounded up, the surrendering troops were marched to the rear under guard as we entered the woods.

On reaching a field on the far side of the woods, we discovered a scene of slaughter. The bodies of roughly 30 dead German soldiers and 20 dead horses were all jumbled together and frozen solid. Especially macabre was the fact that a number of the horses were still hitched to two wagons filled with hay. Though it was unclear how long ago their deaths had occurred, it was apparent this detachment of enemy troops and animals had been caught out in the open by artillery fire or an airstrike.

Entering the field, we began exploring the carnage up close. Just as our investigation was wrapping up, a couple of Allied planes appeared in the sky overhead and dived steeply toward our location, no doubt mistaking us for Germans. Expecting them to come in strafing at any second, I lunged headlong into a hole for cover.

When I crash-landed in the hole, my head struck a large rock. Although my helmet protected my head from injury, my glasses were knocked from my face. After a moment of fumbling around blindly, I managed to locate them. One lens had been cracked and the frame was slightly bent, but they were still functional.

Only once my glasses were back on did I realize I was staring directly into the face of a dead German soldier whose still open eyes were hidden behind the lenses of his frosted spectacles. In front of his head, his right hand was unnaturally twisted forward into a tight crook. Except for the top of his torso, the rest of his corpse was buried under the snow. It was a truly ghastly sight.

Luckily, by this point, the two Allied aircraft had flown off without attacking us after the pilots had apparently spotted our guys waving frantically to signal we were Americans. Just before climbing out of the hole I shared with the frozen German, I noticed a red and black swastika patch that had partially torn away from the soldier's uniform, so I pulled it loose and stuck it in my pocket as a souvenir. When I later related the story to one of the other fellows in my squad, he jokingly admonished me.

"You were laying in a ditch with a dead German soldier, why didn't you get his watch?" His question was callous, but it epitomized how the daily brutality of war was dehumanizing us.

Departing the frozen enemy dead near the woods, our platoon and F Company set off down a snow-blown road. The sound of intense firing a mile or so ahead gave me an ominous feeling combat was imminent.

Before we had gotten a few dozen yards down the road, a strong voice hollered at us from somewhere nearby.

"Hold your fire, K Company's coming through!"

Sharply defined in the crisp winter air, a group of perhaps four dozen men clad in white capes came tramping over a knoll about 50 yards away. Passing across our intended route of advance from left to right, the troops began trotting at a brisk pace, their weapons held at the ready.

A second later, someone shouted out a warning.

"K Company? Hell! We don't have a K Company in this sector! Tear 'em up, men! They're Krauts!"

Realizing their ruse had failed, several of the Germans opened up on us with their MP 40 burp guns. As bullets began whizzing through air, my squad and I instantly shed our machine-gun components and took refuge in a long drainage ditch that ran alongside the road.

At almost the same time, an American P-51 Mustang swooped down and began strafing some enemy target beyond our field of vision. As the plane raced overhead, we were close enough to see the smile on the pilot's face. The close air support against the enemy's rear was great, but we had Germans right in front of us to fight.

Seconds after entering the ditch, my squad and I had the machine gun ready for me to fire. Adding our weapon's heavy firepower to that of our accompanying riflemen, I raked the field in front of us.

Immediately, the Germans scrambled for cover in the snow. Though possessing only burp guns and rifles, they fiercely returned fire as they pulled back over the knoll. Targeting the retreating enemy troops amid the blowing snow was difficult, but I fired in the direction of three or four large snowbanks, aiming the gun wherever I thought I saw movement. While it was impossible for me to judge how many of the Germans were hit, I was sure some of the rounds found their mark.

After about 10 minutes of skirmishing, "K Company" disappeared and the fighting petered out. But I remained crouched in the ditch behind our machine gun for a few minutes longer, waiting to see whether more Germans would appear.

Just as we were preparing to climb out of the ditch and resume our advance, this big German soldier in a field gray overcoat came lumbering toward us along the wind-swept road that ran straight past our position. Mumbling loudly to himself, the man took large strides in a sort of drunken stumble.

There had been no artillery or mortar fire during the engagement, but the man's wild-eyed, incoherent babbling suggested a severe case of shell shock, what was officially referred to as "Combat Stress Reaction." I had witnessed incidents of combat fatigue, like that of the sergeant who shot himself in the foot, but, despite all of the heavy artillery barrages our company endured, this German was perhaps the only soldier I observed who seemed to be suffering from a true case of shell shock.

Of course, the German could have just been acting crazy in order to reach our lines and get out of the war. Maybe this man who seemed so nuts was actually smarter than the rest of us. Whatever the explanation, he was unarmed and clearly presented no threat, so no one fired on him as he plodded past us to be taken prisoner further back.

Following the firefight, we renewed our slow, wearying trek toward Schoppen. Late that afternoon, the GIs at the head of our advance came under heavy fire from a German blocking force positioned all around the road. Their first shots wounded three or four of our guys and sent the rest of us darting for cover.

Forced to pull back in the face of strong enemy opposition, our machine-gun squad helped provide covering fire as the battalion retreated to a location about a mile from Schoppen, where we halted for the evening to regroup. During our retreat, we tried to bring along all of our wounded, who otherwise risked freezing to death in about half an hour. That night, three of our guys returned to the site of the firefight, where they retrieved a wounded GI who had somehow managed to avoid succumbing to the cold. They also brought back the bodies of a couple of our dead. Later, we discovered the corpses of three more of our soldiers frozen solid.

With the ground turned hard as stone by the extreme cold, digging out foxholes that night was impossible. Instead, each of us had to scoop out snow with our shovels until we had a shallow hole in which to sleep. By locating our snow holes next to the base of large trees, we obtained some additional protection from shrapnel in the event we came under German shellfire.

After clearing out a snow hole and consuming a supper of very cold rations, I headed back to the rear to see my old friend First Sergeant Huber about replacing my damaged glasses. Having already replaced my glasses on two previous occasions during the fighting near Eilendorf, I was determined to try to obtain two pairs of glasses this time so I would have a backup on hand in the future.

"Listen, I'm up there really in the thick of the battle. I need to have a spare pair of glasses. When you send in the requisition to have this pair replaced, why don't you order an extra pair? I can't leave the front line this many times," I stressed.

Huber could not make any promises but agreed to submit the necessary paperwork for two pairs of glasses. For now, I would have to manage with a broken lens, though it was not a situation I wanted to put up with for long.

As we prepared to sleep that night, a new use for our trench coats was devised. By spreading them over the ice at the bottom of our snow holes, we had a sort of blanket or rug on which to rest.

An accidental hero: January 17–19

When we awakened the following morning of January 17, most of us discovered our trench coats were frozen solid to the bottom of our holes. Those who could not eventually work their trench coats free had no alternative but to rely on their light battle jackets to stay warm until they were issued a new trench coat, a process that normally took a few days. However, any lengthy exposure to the subfreezing temperatures without the warmth of a trench coat was not only an inconvenience, it was dangerous.

Following the hard fighting over the previous two days, the 16th Infantry Regiment paused its advance on January 17. Because of F Company's high casualties, H Company was reassigned to support G Company in the 2nd Battalion's next operations.

Facing strong resistance from the German forces in our sector of the front line, H Company pulled back a short distance on January 17 to improve its position. Amid an exchange of fire between tanks, artillery, and mortars that lasted throughout the rest of the day, our squad stayed hunkered down in our gun emplacement, which we had established inside a thickly wooded area. If anybody needed to move, they had to hustle as shells intermittently exploded around us.

On January 18, the 16th Infantry's 1st Battalion resumed its advance southward, while the 3rd Battalion was temporarily in reserve. For now, our 2nd Battalion stayed in its existing position, where we remained under fire from German tanks and artillery.

While I was on gun duty late that afternoon, an enemy patrol of a dozen or so soldiers approached our position. Camouflaged in white sheets that made them nearly invisible against the snow-shrouded landscape, the Germans evaded our notice until they had come within 40 yards. However, they also completely failed to detect our presence in the woods and advanced directly toward our gun emplacement.

When my squad and the neighboring riflemen spotted them and opened fire, two or three of the Germans were hit while the rest scattered like quail, taking cover in the deep snow beside the road. Despite being outgunned by our machine gun, the surviving enemy troops refused to give up, prolonging the firefight.

At last, after perhaps an hour, one of the Germans finally raised a white flag, but this turned out to signal only his own surrender, rather than that of the entire force. The other enemy soldiers slowly gave up one by one, further dragging out the skirmish.

After all our prisoners had been sent to the rear under a two-man guard, we began cleaning our weapons in preparation for a move to a new position. While this work was underway, our lieutenant directed me to retrieve as much ammo as I could carry from our jeep, "Little Joe," which was parked about a quarter of a mile behind us.

Leaving our gun emplacement, I soon came to the road the lieutenant had advised me to follow to reach our jeep. However, once there, I could already see the jeep parked in some woods on the far side of a football-field-sized piece of open ground. This gave me two options. The easiest way for me to reach the jeep would be to follow the road that ran around the edge of the field, trekking along the vehicle tracks through the snow. However, the more direct route across the field would cut a mile or more from the trip and save time, but it involved crossing deep untrammeled snow.

Deciding that taking the shortcut would allow me to get back to our gun position before dark, I set off across the field. Making use of a walking stick to help keep my balance, I high stepped my way through snow that was a foot or more deep.

On reaching the far side of the field, I noticed a three-foot-high signboard posted on a stake at the edge of the woods near our jeep. The sign was facing the other direction, so I circled around to the front to read it.

"*ACHTUNG MINEN!*" was printed in big black capital letters.

Stunned, a chill shot through my veins as it hit me I had just crossed through a German minefield, utterly oblivious of the danger!

Saying a quick prayer of thanks to God for protecting me, I went over to "Little Joe" and slung six ammo belts over my shoulder. In the fast-fading daylight, I was now faced with a more difficult choice. Hoping to get back to my outfit before dark, I had to decide whether to take the long route following the road or the more direct route back across the minefield. Saying a prayer, I elected to retrace my tracks across the minefield.

Taking meticulous care to ensure each of my steps slid into my original boot-tracks through the snow, I moved very slowly, always making sure to retain my balance under the burden of all the ammo. Aware of the potentially lethal consequence of even a minor misstep, my second passage through the minefield seemed to stretch into an eternity. Despite the subfreezing temperature, I was sweating hard.

Thirty long minutes later, I stepped out of the minefield onto the road. I had made it safely across. In another 10 minutes, I would be back with my buddies.

By the time I reached our squad's gun emplacement in the woods at twilight, my stress was only just beginning to dissipate.

"Halt! What's the password?" shouted a voice ahead of me.

Never imagining a sentry would challenge me on my return, I was dumbfounded. Standing there in my foxhole was an armed GI from another H Company platoon, which must have shifted into our squad's old position during the hour or so I had been gone. Not only did I not know this guy, but everyone serving on sentry duty had grown a lot more suspicious of any unfamiliar GI after the recent instances of English-speaking Germans in American uniforms infiltrating our lines.

"What's the password or I'll blow your damn head off!" the soldier demanded. His rifle was pointed right at my face, its muzzle appearing as big as a cannon.

Scared out of my wits, I was unable to remember the current password, even if I had been given it. The only passwords I could recall now were the completely useless ones for the previous day and the day before that. My mind raced to think of something to tell the sentry before he squeezed that trigger.

"I'm Andy Andrews from Signal Mountain, Tennessee, and I just got back from getting extra ammo for our gun squad. Hold your fire. I'm in your company, but I can't remember the password. Please hold your fire!" I pleaded, hoping my honesty would sound convincing. A tense pause ensued as we stared at each other.

"Okay, but you sure as hell better learn that the password is 'Red Fox' or somebody is gonna blow your ass off. You can come on by but I got my rifle pointed right at you," he warned.

It had been the most dangerous moment I had ever faced with one of our own men. Indeed, I was more terrified at that moment than I had been at any point crossing the minefield. I believe I remained alive because God held that man's trigger finger.

When I managed to locate my own squad a hundred yards away, our lieutenant was focused on the enemy threat to our front. But after I told my buddies what had happened, someone passed the story along to him.

"Soldier, you're mighty brave to walk back through that minefield," the lieutenant declared.

"Well, on that first pass I didn't know it was a minefield. If I had known I would be playing Russian roulette with mines taking the shortcut, I would certainly have chosen the long route on the road," I explained.

Nonetheless, because of my act of unintended bravery, the lieutenant put me up for a Bronze Star, which I was later awarded. In light of all my other experiences during the war, it seemed a great irony this was the incident for which I earned that decoration, but war is funny that way.

Our squad's new position included a network of abandoned German dugouts, one of which was claimed by my buddy Lincoln Welser and me. Excavated three feet deep into the rock-hard frozen earth, the dugout was spacious and well-built, with pine branches laid across its low earthen walls to create a roof. To help retain the warmth inside the dugout, Lincoln and I cut a few more pine branches to thicken the roof.

That night, our shelter was warm enough that Welser and I were able to take off our boots and stretch out our aching feet before going to sleep, marking the only time that winter when I left my boots off overnight. As a matter of fact, the dugout was so comfortable we both overslept.

Risking life and limb: January 19

Welser and I awakened just before dawn the next morning. Five minutes later, a sergeant yelled down into our dugout that our platoon was about to move out in an attack. Despite a blinding snowstorm and the bitter cold, we were supporting a rifle company in its assault on the German position at the edge of the nearby woods.

With everyone else already up and getting ready for the attack, Welser and I hurriedly gulped down a breakfast of cold rations, laced up our boots, put on our coats, and collected our gear. In the mad rush to join our outfit, I was unable to find the glove for my left hand and had to leave it behind.

Our assault on the morning of January 19 was part of the resumption of full-scale offensive operations by the 16th Infantry Regiment. The mission of advancing south-southeast to seize Schoppen was now assigned to the 3rd Battalion. Operating in support of the 3rd Battalion's attack, our 2nd Battalion would drive south toward the Amblève (Amel) River running southwest from Schoppen. Meanwhile, the 1st Battalion would push south toward Eibertingen a couple of miles south-southwest of Schoppen.

As a freezing wind whipped snow into our faces and reduced visibility to only about a dozen feet, we struggled forward through the knee-deep snow toward the enemy line about a hundred yards away. Unable to observe our advance until we were almost right on top of them, many of the surprised Germans quickly retreated into the neighboring woods. But other enemy troops stubbornly resisted, shooting at us from close range from their hidden positions in the snow.

Because of the deep snow, our squad was unable to deploy the machine gun and instead had to rely on our carbines. Despite German opposition and the miserable weather conditions, we won control of the enemy position within an hour of launching our assault, suffering only light losses during the engagement.

Captured Germans expressed profound astonishment at our relentless attacking in every kind of weather, whether drenching downpours or blinding snowstorms.

"We could not rest. We could not sleep. We were always getting up and trying to get out of the way of the advancing Americans," they regularly complained. Nothing stunned the enemy more than our offensive operations in the middle of that terrible winter. "Nobody with any brains attacks in all kinds of weather, but you do," one half-frozen German soldier bitterly grumbled before being led back to the rear.

If we were pleased to hear that our dogged determination to advance kept the enemy off balance, there was plenty of griping on our side about conducting offensive operations in such miserable winter conditions. Battling the *Wehrmacht* was hard enough in good weather. The German infantryman was a resourceful, tenacious, and resilient foe who could never be underestimated in any circumstance. Indeed, they had started their big counteroffensive on December 16 under the cover of winter weather.

Shortly after the capture of the German position at the edge of the woods, our section of the platoon set out along a path through the trees toward our next objective. Though the snow in the woods was not as deep as on open ground and the blizzard had slackened by this time, our advance soon left us all tired and chilled to the bone.

In the sub-freezing temperatures, my ungloved left hand clenching one of the metal legs of the tripod was suffering badly from exposure. Already, it had begun to lose any sensation and I could barely move my fingers. Aware of the danger of frostbite, I asked around to see if anyone had a spare glove. When no one did, I checked with the officer in command of our detachment.

"Lieutenant, you don't have an extra glove?" I inquired.

After a string of obscenities, he lectured me. "That serves you right, Andrews. You oughta take better care of government equipment. Besides, we're heading into a big battle and we need you up here. Your hand will improve with a little action."

Lacking a glove or anything else with which to wrap my freezing hand, I was left with the vague hope of coming across a dead enemy soldier wearing gloves.

An hour or two after our section began its trek through the woods, American artillery opened up, targeting the sector ahead of us. When we reached the edge of a clearing in a valley later that afternoon, the barrage's devastating impact was evident.

Situated among several still-smoking shell craters, a burning German tank 20 yards to our left had taken a direct hit that blew off its treads and wrenched its turret sideways, so that it now tilted skyward. The lifeless body of the tank's commander dangled from the turret, while three other dead crewmen lay nearby on the snow.

With such battlefield carnage having become numbingly commonplace, we gave little thought to the enemy dead once we determined no one posed a threat to us.

Word was passed that we would rest for an hour in a three-story stone house located about 50 yards away from the tank. Cold and exhausted by our hours-long slog through the woods, all of us were ready for a break.

But only moments after we passed the destroyed tank, a second German tank suddenly burst out of the forest behind us. We had walked right by without spotting it. Usually, once a tank started moving, the metallic squeal of its treads gave us enough warning to take cover, but we had heard nothing before this one appeared.

Re-energized by fear and hoping the tank's crew had not observed us, we hustled through the snow toward the house along a narrow ravine. On reaching the house, we circled around back and found a door that led down to the basement.

Just as those in the lead began making their way down to the basement, there was a shrill whistle of an incoming tank shell followed by a terrific explosion above us. Nearly annihilating the house's third floor, the blast sent an avalanche of brick, wood, and glass crashing down around those of us at the rear of the home.

Somehow, all of us managed to dodge the falling wreckage and make it safely down to the small, dimly lit basement. But as we huddled together, I had more hope than confidence that the basement would really protect us from what came next.

A moment later, we heard the loud whistle of another incoming round. Slamming into the second story with an earsplitting crash, the shell's detonation rocked the house as violently as if it had been struck by an earthquake. In the basement, we crouched down with our arms thrust over our helmets in an effort to shield ourselves as chunks of concrete, stonework, and other debris rained down on us. Amid the thick cloud of dust, we found it difficult to see or breathe.

"If that tank shoots another round, we're all done for!" someone called out, stating aloud what all of us feared. Feeling helpless as we waited for the tank to complete its systematic demolition of the house, I was praying hard.

Dear God, if you see fit, please distract the German tank crew so that they will not fire another shell into our basement wall.

Miraculously, the anticipated third round did not come. Observing the home's destruction, the panzer's crew must have assumed they had already wiped us out.

The pause gave us the time to retaliate. Using a walkie-talkie, a fire mission was radioed back to our artillery batteries. The speed of their response was astounding.

Within a minute or so, we heard the reassuring sound of artillery rounds plastering the area from which the tank had been firing.

After waiting a quarter of an hour, we left the basement, making our way out of the rubble that had once been a house. Everything in the vicinity had been pulverized into a moonscape of scorched stumps and smoking craters.

The second tank sat burning about 20 yards away from the one that been knocked out earlier. As with the first tank, its dead commander also hung out of the turret of this tank, but this man's lower torso was on fire. The other dead crewmen lay scattered around the vehicle. Observing the scene, I thanked God for protecting us down in that basement. We had been very fortunate to escape with our lives.

A couple of hours later, as it grew dark, we reached our objective, where a mopping-up operation was underway. Even if the Germans had been forced to retreat from an area, stubborn holdouts always remained behind. These had to be cleared out of the local villages and towns, a process which often sparked costly firefights.

Assigned to a detachment that was checking homes at the edge of a village, I was under the command of a lieutenant who I barely knew. Intending to search one of these houses for Germans, he stepped onto the porch and kicked in the door. As it swung in, he was almost sliced in half by the fire of a machine gun hidden inside.

For the enemy, this was suicidal. Immediately, one of our guys with a Tommy gun sprayed the interior of the house as another lobbed in a grenade. In 10 seconds, the three Germans inside had been wiped out, but the action had cost the life of the lieutenant.

Frostbitten: January 19–27

As a result of my ungloved left hand's extended exposure to the extreme cold over January 19, it had frozen as hard as stone, lost all feeling, and begun to turn purple by the end of the day. Aware that many GIs had to have their frostbitten fingers and toes amputated, I had a real fear of losing my hand, but did not want to overreact. Hoping it might improve by morning, I decided to wait to seek medical attention.

That night, we were quartered in a damaged home, out of the extreme cold. But when I awoke the next morning, my hand had still not regained any sensation and looked worse, having turned deep blue and black. Even some of our officers expressed concern about its condition. Though I moved out with my squad that morning as usual, I intended to look for an aid station where I could get my hand treated.

Following the previous day's advance toward the Amblève River, our 2nd Battalion continued to push southward on January 20. As our squad proceeded through the woods amid falling snow, everyone was continuing to complain about fighting in the icy cold, but my focus was on my left hand. Though wrapped around the metal foot of the tripod, it was frozen solid in a folded hook. Growing ever more fearful of losing my hand to frostbite, I knew medical attention could not be put off any longer.

When we came to a sign that read "AID STATION ONE HALF MILE" with an arrow pointing to the right, I saw my chance. But just as I was peeling off to head that way, the lieutenant at the head of our column turned back in my direction.

"Hey, Andrews, where the hell are you going?" he demanded.

I had been considering how to inform the lieutenant that my hand required urgent medical care, but knew his reaction was not likely to be sympathetic, based on his caustic response to my request to borrow a glove the previous day.

"I gotta go back to the aid station to try to get some help for my frozen hand. I can't work my fingers around the tripod. I can't move my fingers. I can't shoot the gun. If I fart around out here in this freezing weather, I'm liable to lose all my fingers."

"If you want to be a chicken, go ahead," the lieutenant smirked, apparently convinced I was faking a case of frostbite to get out of combat and the freezing cold.

"I do. I want to be a chicken … I want to get my hand thawed out," I retorted.

"Okay, you're chicken, just remember that. You remember that when the Nazis come to your house on Signal Mountain and jerk out your mother and sister and rape 'em. You'll remember that you were a chicken!" he jeered.

"Okay, I sure will remember that," I replied. Though I was indifferent to the lieutenant's gibes and knew my hand required immediate medical attention, I still hated to go back to the rear. I did not want to leave my buddies behind and realized it was going to be hard to return to combat after time away from the front.

At the aid station, I was placed in a ward with other GIs, many of whom also needed treatment for frostbite. Before long, an Army doctor came to examine me.

"You could lose your hand," he grimly pronounced. Its complete lack of sensation, hardness, and purple discoloration indicated a severe case of frostbite. While I started praying, the doctor directed me to board an ambulance that was preparing to travel to another medical facility which could provide more extensive treatment.

When we left the aid station, I had thought the ambulance was headed for a larger aid station, but it instead took us to an Army hospital. Comprised of several buildings, the hospital was treating a large number of soldiers suffering from frostbite as well as a few more seriously wounded troops just brought in from the front line.

A medic led me from the ambulance to the second floor of a three-story brick building about 50 yards long. Guiding me down the middle of a long room with a dozen or so beds on either side, the medic pointed out an empty one and showed me where to stow my gear, adding that a physician would visit me shortly.

The doctor who examined my hand did not sugarcoat his prognosis. Warning me that it might be necessary to amputate my hand if gangrene developed, he explained the hospital would administer a therapeutic treatment in an effort to save it.

Despite the number of patients in the hospital, the medical care I received over the ensuing week was absolutely first-rate. The basic treatment for those of us suffering from frostbite involved gradually re-warming the affected limb and keeping it raised to prevent fluid from collecting. Three times a day, two pretty nurses took turns gently massaging my hand to stimulate circulation. At night, a doctor came by to work my fingers back and forth in order to try to restore their flexibility. I also received a couple of shots of the new drug penicillin to ward off infection.

Thankfully, my hand seemed to get a little better each day, but not every soldier was so fortunate. Just as during my previous hospital stays, I observed several nurses gather around a GI's bed and pull the sheets up over his head after he died.

As they rolled away his body down the middle of the room and out the door, I prayed for the soldier's mom and dad, who would soon receive the dreaded telegram.

Following a week of intensive therapy, I awoke one morning with my hand in throbbing pain as a doctor vigorously bent my fingers back and forth. Apparently, the doctor believed that if he was able to manipulate my fingers to this extent, my hand had recovered. Confirmation of his evaluation was not long in coming.

"Congratulations, soldier, you're ready for the front," he told me later that night.

If I had been awake to see the doctor coming that morning, I just might have displayed a bit more discomfort during his examination in order to extend the treatment on my hand a little longer. But despite my hand's lingering stiffness at that time, the nerve damage had not been severe and it did eventually recover fully with no loss of either dexterity or sensation. Having at first faced the possibility of amputation, I was profoundly grateful and knew God really had been watching over me.

The week of treatment at the hospital had saved my hand, but my apprehension about returning to action weighed more heavily on me this time than when I had been headed back to the front in early August and late December after my earlier hospital stays. As the horror and brutality of combat replayed in my mind, I darkly wondered how many of my buddies might have been wounded or killed while I had been at the hospital. Oddly, I was also preoccupied with more mundane questions about where I had left my pistol and grenade belt and how I would go about finding them.

At the same time, I still felt compelled to get back to my outfit as soon as possible. Forcing my mind to stop dwelling on my experiences in combat, I started focusing on rejoining my buddies. As for the lieutenant who had given me a hard time for seeking treatment for my hand, I was not concerned about him at all. I figured he would just be glad to have me back on the gun.

Mail from anyone outside my family was rare, but I did receive a letter at this time that greatly boosted my spirits. Bill Fenn, a man who worked with my Boy Scout troop on Signal Mountain, offered words of encouragement. Reminding me of my friends and church back home, his remarks made a real impact on my psychological state, putting me in the right frame of mind to return to the front.

Meanwhile, back home, my family received the following brief telegram dated February 9, 1945:

> Regret to inform you your son Private Ernest A. Andrews, Jr. was slightly injured in action 20 January in Belgium. Further report states he returned to duty 22 December from previously reported wound.

Whatever our many complaints about the Army's failings, the War Department did a really good job of keeping families informed about their loved ones off at war.

Back with H Company in Faymonville: January 27–February 5

On the morning of January 27, I left the hospital aboard an ambulance headed for Faymonville, the town that had been the initial objective of the 16th Infantry Regiment's attack back on January 15. Badly damaged in the fighting, Faymonville now served as a temporary rest area for H Company.

Following six weeks of continuous front-line duty in the wake of the German offensive on December 16, H Company and the rest of the 2nd Battalion had finally been pulled out of combat the day before I arrived in Faymonville. As a result of our outfit's assignment to a rest area, I did not face the immediate return to combat I had expected back at the hospital.

Shortly after my departure from H Company for medical treatment on January 20, our 16th Infantry Regiment had largely paused offensive operations in order to consolidate its control over territory already won. When the regiment resumed its attack on January 23, it had shifted its axis of advance from south to east, so it was now aimed toward Germany. Pushing forward a couple of miles against what was now diminished enemy resistance, it succeeded in taking a few more towns before ending offensive operations. For the next week, elements of the 16th Infantry would have time to rest and recuperate in the vicinity of Waimes and Faymonville.

When I reached Faymonville on January 27, my old buddies in the machine-gun squad kidded me good-naturedly about being "blessed" with a hospital visit that had gotten me out of the last few days of fighting in the freezing cold. Agreeing that the recovery of my frostbitten hand had indeed been a blessing, I also assured them I had received top-notch care from two lovely nurses.

In truth, I was also very fortunate to be back with my old machine-gun squad in H Company. The fact I had received reassignment to my original outfit following each of my three hospital stays was nothing short of amazing. A GI never knew where he would end up on returning to duty and many never saw their old units again.

Though very lucky in this respect, I was frustrated to learn I would remain at the rank of Private First Class after having been promised a promotion before I had gone back for medical treatment on my hand. This was not the first time an officer had reneged on a pledge to promote me. Both in Normandy the previous summer and in Germany earlier that fall, one lieutenant after another had similarly assured me, "Andrews, you're going to be a sergeant." While promotion directly from private to sergeant without serving in the intermediate rank of corporal might have been unusual in normal circumstances, a constant supply of proven veterans was needed to replace the many sergeants who were getting killed and wounded in the war.

But these promises of promotion had been made before my hospital stay in England to treat the infection in my face and my hospital stay in France to recover from the removal of grenade shrapnel in my shoulder. Each time when I returned to duty, some other guy had been made sergeant. It was not that I harbored some burning ambition to be a sergeant, but I did feel a real sense of disappointment after various lieutenants had raised and then dashed my expectations. Nonetheless, even if my rank never changed, I continued to take on a leadership role as one of our squad's veterans.

While the sergeant in charge of our squad bore primary responsibility for instructing our replacements, I often filled this role when he was not available. No one ever ordered me to work with the new men. I simply took on this task out of necessity. Rather than considering it a burden, training our replacements was a duty I enjoyed. Naturally, the other veterans in our squad were also willing to help.

Almost all the replacements lacked combat experience but were eager to learn from anyone who had been in battle. The knowledge that they were acquiring the skills that could ensure their survival and enable them to do their part in the squad made them enthusiastic students. This training lacked any type of formal structure but was instead conducted on an ad hoc basis as time permitted and the situation dictated.

Beyond teaching our replacements about their particular responsibilities in the squad, we also instructed them on the operation of the machine gun, its tactical placement in combat, where they should dig their foxholes, and the performance of sentry duty. Sometimes, we even had to include more fundamental infantry skills like how to use a hand grenade. Incredibly, several of these GIs had never tossed a grenade during their basic training and had no idea what it could do. As one of the soldier's most devastating weapons, every man in our squad needed to be able to handle a grenade as well as a pistol, a carbine, and the machine gun.

At one point, I received a question that truly caught me off guard.

"Do we wear our pistols all the time?" the replacement inquired.

Restraining my amusement, I realized he held a certain naïve conception about the nature of soldiering in wartime. Even though our outfit would not be in combat all the time, we had to be ready to fight at any time. If it was tough to get the replacements to accept they would soon be fighting and killing the enemy, it was even more difficult for these men to accept that the Germans also wanted to kill them.

In our instruction of the replacements, the other squad veterans and I tried to treat the new men extremely well. Even if we did not immediately develop close relationships with our new replacements, it was vital for us to build a strong sense of camaraderie inside the squad. Because we had to rely on and support each other in combat, we needed each replacement's commitment and willingness to be in the fight.

While it was easy to predict whether a soldier was going to be a good fighter from his attitude, we tried to express confidence in all our replacements in order to encourage them. Despite knowing they faced a higher danger of becoming a casualty due to their inexperience, I never saw a single replacement fail to fulfill his assigned combat duties out of cowardice.

One of the replacements we received around this time was a tall, outgoing Indiana farmer named Cecil Painter, a guy who had a deep fondness for horses and made friends easily. Somehow, he always managed to remain neat and clean-shaven, which was not an easy feat for a soldier on the front line. More importantly, Painter also turned out to be one of the most steady members of our squad.

Though much of our week in Faymonville was devoted to training our new squad members and maintaining our equipment, there was still plenty of time for R&R. While the local Belgian civilians we encountered were always very hospitable to us, relatively few remained in the town. Fortunately, we could visit the American Red Cross Clubmobile, a sort of mobile food truck. Staffed by a couple of friendly American girls, the Clubmobile offered coffee and donuts, which were the best thing anywhere around. To add to the home-like atmosphere, the Clubmobile played popular American tunes, although the speakers were turned up to a volume that made the music almost too loud to enjoy. For recreation in the evenings, movies were shown inside one of Faymonville's large buildings that remained intact. Afterward, everyone tried to get as much sleep as possible, taking full advantage of our relatively comfortable accommodations in the basements of the town's ruined homes.

Until my return to H Company on January 27, I had been wearing the same pair of glasses that had been damaged 11 days earlier when I had made a hard landing in the ditch with the frozen German soldier. When I went to pick up my new glasses from First Sergeant Huber, he presented me with two pairs. Thanks to his efforts, the Army had listened for once and did something that made sense. Now, I would at last have a spare backup pair of glasses in case something happened to the first pair.

While our 16th Infantry Regiment was resting in the area around Waimes, other elements of our 1st Infantry Division were continuing to advance eastward toward the German border. By the beginning of February, the division reached a sector of the Siegfried Line near Hollerath, roughly 13 miles east of Waimes. On February 5, the Big Red One was relieved by another unit in preparation for a new mission.

In the Battle of the Bulge, the final German counteroffensive had been repulsed. With the Western Allies now closing in from the West and the Soviet Red Army closing in from the East, anyone but the most obstinate Nazi recognized that Germany was beaten. Facing defeat in World War I, Germany had requested an armistice. Under Hitler's Nazi regime, the Germans would continue to fight and die until the bitter end.

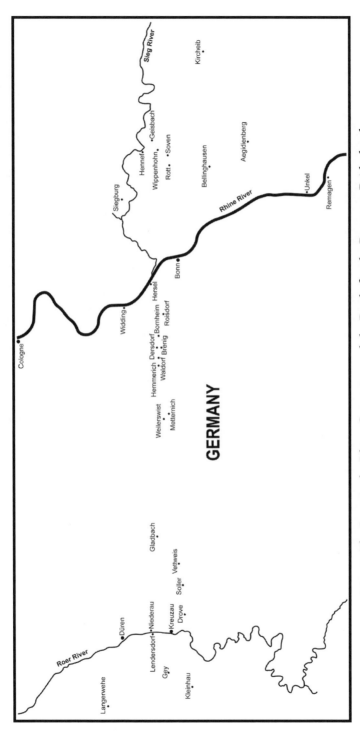

Map 5: The Roer to the Rhine Campaign and the Battle for the Remagen Bridgehead

CHAPTER 17

The Roer to the Rhine: February 6–March 18, 1945

At the Roer River: February 6–25

On the morning of February 6, our rest at Faymonville came to an end. Loading up on trucks, H Company motored two dozen miles north-northeast to an assembly point near Kleinhau, not far from the Roer River. This move left us just a half-dozen miles south-southeast of Hill 232 and, even more tellingly, only 10 miles east-southeast of our old bunker position on the Verlautenheide ridge near Eilendorf, a spot we had reached four and a half months ago. When we had crossed the German border back in mid-September, the war had seemed to be nearing its end. Instead, we had endured our hardest fighting so far in the battles for Aachen, the Hürtgen, Hill 232, and the Bulge.

Our push into the heart of Germany now confronted two major natural obstacles, the Roer River and the far greater barrier of the Rhine, some 25 miles further east. It was no secret our 1st Infantry Division would soon be attacking across the Roer, but the operation's timing remained uncertain. For now, H Company's assignment was simply to take over existing positions along the river from another outfit.

With all the approaches to the forward positions near Kleinhau under direct German observation from across the Roer, we waited until after dark on the evening of February 6 to relieve the other unit, occupying the relatively comfortable bunkers they had constructed. Though we experienced only intermittent German artillery fire, the exposure of our position to the enemy's forward observers meant the kitchen personnel had to be careful when bringing up our chow during daylight hours.

While things were mostly quiet in this sector of the front, H Company's mortar crews did engage a force of enemy tanks and several dozen troops on the far side of the river just before midnight on February 8. Out of concern the Germans might be preparing a night assault across the river, we were all placed on alert.

On February 9, our company shifted two miles further north-northeast from Kleinhau to the town of Gey, which was likewise just a couple of miles from the Roer River. Taking up quarters in German-constructed concrete bunkers, we were now even better protected from the enemy's sporadic artillery salvos. Though the dozen or so built-in bunkbeds in each bunker lacked mattresses, the bunkers still provided us with a good night's sleep as well as a safe place for a nap when we were free from other duties.

Our crossing of the Roer did not come as quickly as had been anticipated due to a steady rise in the river's waters and, more importantly, the speed of its current. This increased flow resulted from the heavy spring rains and from Germany's opening of the sluice gates on the Roer's dams. Nonetheless, our outfit continued its preparations for the crossing. Beyond briefing us on our upcoming mission, our officers and NCOs stressed the importance of cleaning and oiling our weapons in the expectation the combat would be intense once we reached the enemy-held far bank.

Many of us were also assigned to aid the engineers in clearing the area's poorly marked German minefields. Spaced about three feet apart from the man on either side of us, we cautiously advanced in a line to search for mines dispersed among the mud and weeds, planting a small flag in the ground to identify the location of any mines we discovered. Later, our engineers detonated them with a shout of "Fire in the hole."

After two weeks spent waiting for an opportunity to get across the swollen Roer, the 8th Infantry Division carried out a heroic assault crossing of the still raging river from February 23 to 24. With a foothold on the far bank at a point a little south of Duren and only a couple of miles away from our own position at Gey, Army engineers hurriedly built a pontoon bridge across the river later on February 24, despite coming under fierce German fire. Meanwhile, our own 1st Infantry Division, now operating as part of the U.S. First Army's III Corps for the campaign to the Rhine, received orders to cross the Roer on February 25, with our 2nd Battalion of the 16th Infantry Regiment in the lead.

On the night of February 24/25, the *Luftwaffe* mounted a series of air raids. Apparently hunting for specific ground targets, the enemy aircraft roared through the sky directly overhead, sounding like a group of four or five giant bulldozers with their engines at full throttle. When two of the planes strafed a target near us, the stony ground deflected many of the bullets, causing them to ricochet wildly in all directions. But while these air raids harassed us, they did not halt our plans to cross the river.

Early on the morning of February 25, our two machine-gun platoons from H Company linked up with E and F Companies and marched three miles east-northeast to the town of Lendersdorf on the western bank of the Roer. As our 2nd Battalion set out across the river over the new pontoon bridge about 8:30am, all of us were expecting to come under intense fire from German artillery, mortars, and machine guns at any moment. If the bridge was hit, it seemed almost certain we would plunge to our deaths in the Roer's fast-moving current that swirled beneath our boots.

Fortunately, the smokescreen laid down by our artillery and mortars obscured the view of the enemy. There was no machine-gun fire and the few artillery shells the Germans fired failed to hit the bridge. Relieved to reach the relative safety of the town of Niederau on the eastern bank, our 2nd Battalion passed through the 8th Infantry Division and headed south, moving parallel to the river.

On the enemy's flank: February 25

Arriving at the wooded edge of a flat, football-field-sized piece of open ground just south of Niederau, we halted behind a line of trees to assemble for our attack. With the Roer somewhere off to our right, our position was about half a mile north of the German-held town of Kreuzau. Rather than attempting a direct frontal assault on Kreuzau from across the Roer as the enemy was anticipating, our 2nd Battalion would strike southward against the northern right flank of the force garrisoning the town.

While awaiting the start of our attack on Kreuzau, we were under strict orders to avoid doing anything that might alert the *Wehrmacht* to our arrival on their right flank. At present, no enemy troops were visible, but no one was to fire on any Germans who might appear, unless it was absolutely necessary for self-defense.

Selecting a spot behind some bushes under a tree for our machine-gun emplacement, I spent the next hour digging out a foxhole deep enough for me to crouch down in. The rest of my squad dug in nearby.

A few minutes after finishing this task, I decided to explore the area to get a better sense of our overall position. But just as I was climbing out of my foxhole, two German generals came walking out into the open right where I had supposed the enemy to be located. Easily identifiable by the gold-braided epaulets and red-striped trousers on their tailored uniforms, the officers remained completely oblivious to our presence as they proceeded in my general direction, casually strolling along a road that passed behind a clump of trees about 50 yards to the right of our gun emplacement.

Immediately ducking back into my foxhole behind our well-hidden machine gun, I watched the officers and pondered my options. A short burst from our gun could take them out, though the trees in my line of fire would make it a difficult shot. On the other hand, these officers might be able to offer us valuable intelligence.

"Why don't we sneak over there and capture those Germans?" I whispered to a nearby buddy, only half-joking about the scheme.

But the orders to hold our fire and make every effort to keep our force concealed had been clear. Indeed, the appearance of these officers provided confirmation of both our proximity to the German lines as well as the enemy's apparent ignorance to our arrival in the area, validating the extreme caution of our commanders.

A few minutes later, the sound of approaching aircraft became audible.

"Fw 190s!" a spotter warned from an antiaircraft battery 20 yards to my left.

Coming from the rear, a pair of German Focke-Wulf 190 fighter planes loudly zoomed right overhead. Passing less than two dozen yards above me, I could have shot at them with my pistol, though they were moving so fast I had no time to react.

Since the pilots almost certainly must have observed our force and radioed our location, there no longer seemed to be any point in holding our fire, but our antiaircraft crews made no attempt to target the planes. With mounting frustration, I tracked the aircraft with the barrel of my machine gun as they flew off but did not shoot.

Swooping upward about a quarter of a mile away, the two fighters executed a tight 180-degree loop and came racing back toward us over the open field. With my gun trained on the planes, I was perfectly placed to blow them out of the sky. Certainly, the loud and distinctive firing of an American machine gun would have irrefutably announced our presence, but, by now, the Germans must already know we were here.

Lord, are you sending these planes for me to shoot down? I asked in a silent prayer. I had about 10 seconds to decide what to do.

As the fighters passed within three dozen yards of my machine gun's muzzle, I felt an almost overpowering impulse to fire off half a belt of .30-caliber rounds at the aircraft. It was all I could do not to pull the trigger. At this range, I felt sure I could knock at least one of the fighters out of the sky.

Even if it would mean a merciless chewing out by our captain, it was not likely they would court-martial me for shooting down one or two German fighter planes. There could not have been too many machine gunners who achieved such a feat.

While my weapon remained silent, the order not to fire was the hardest command I ever obeyed. Letting those two aircraft escape unscathed was something I would always regret. Later, those same planes may well have been responsible for the deaths of other Americans because of our pointless forbearance.

From Kreuzau to the Neffel: February 25–March 5

Our two-hour wait north of Kreuzau ended about noon, with our artillery opening up to pound the German lines and lay down a smokescreen to conceal our 2nd Battalion's attack. Supported by a platoon of Sherman tanks on our left, our two machine-gun platoons began advancing southward with E and F Companies.

When we entered the open field in front of our position, German infantry began steadily popping away at us with their rifles. But though receiving some support from their artillery and a few *Luftwaffe* aircraft, the enemy troops failed to halt our push toward Kreuzau. As intended, the *Wehrmacht* force defending the town had remained focused on the threat of a direct assault across the Roer by the 16th Infantry Regiment's 1st Battalion on the far bank, leaving their northern right flank poorly defended.

Our advance did not slow until we encountered a German machine-gun nest in a factory complex at Kreuzau's northern edge. Bringing our machine gun up, we targeted the factory with heavy fire, which soon ended enemy resistance.

After pressing a short distance further south toward the town, my squad and I were forced to take cover in a network of abandoned German foxholes. A moment later, as I was adjusting the grenades in my belt, someone yelled "Incoming grenade!"

Luckily, my head was below the surface of the foxhole, so the explosion of the enemy grenade did not injure me. However, the force of the blast knocked the right arm of my glasses off my ear. While I was still trying to secure my glasses back in place, the order came for us to renew our attack. Jumping out of the foxholes, we hustled forward toward a railroad bridge that spanned a small creek.

As I leapt onto the wooden floorboards between the railroad tracks to dash across, a German fighter plane began strafing the bridge. With bullets glancing off the bridge's steel support structure and striking uncomfortably close to me, I dropped and flattened myself against the floorboards to present less of a target.

When I did, my head came down hard, causing my poorly secured glasses to bounce from my face and drop between a gap in the boards down into the creek below. Immediately, I reached into my jacket pocket and yanked out my back-up pair of glasses. Stuck in the middle of combat, I was mighty glad to have them.

Making our way deeper into Kreuzau, we discovered our earlier shelling had set many of its houses and buildings ablaze. The German defense inside the town was mostly limited to scattered pockets of troops and sniper fire. Where our riflemen ran into enemy strongpoints in the town, they would point out these positions for us to target. Our section's two machine guns sprayed these strongpoints with heavy fire until the resisting troops were killed or hoisted a white flag.

When enemy opposition became more substantial in the southern part of the town, tanks were brought up to deliver heavier firepower. By sunset, the surviving Germans had been forced to retreat a mile southeast from Kreuzau toward the town of Drove, which was also subsequently seized by our troops later that evening.

For me, the day's fighting had confirmed the value of having a spare pair of glasses. If those glasses had not been on hand, I would instantly have been rendered useless in the middle of combat. That night, I asked First Sergeant Huber to requisition me a new back-up pair.

The following morning of February 26, German troops supported by self-propelled guns counterattacked toward Drove, but were repulsed by our infantry and artillery with heavy losses to their force. While the enemy continued to lob artillery rounds on Drove and Kreuzau, we pushed into the woods just beyond Drove.

When darkness fell, our machine-gun platoons, operating in support of the 2nd Battalion's rifle companies, had advanced to within a half-mile of Soller, a couple of miles east of Drove. After taking control of Soller the next morning, we remained in a holding position for the next 24 hours or so while the Big Red One's 18th and 26th Infantry Regiments passed through our position and pushed further eastward.

On the afternoon of February 28, the 2nd Battalion proceeded a couple of miles eastward from Soller to Vettweiss, a town already taken by other elements of the 16th

Infantry Regiment the previous day. Later that same night, we marched a couple of miles further northeast to the town of Gladbach. Won in hard fighting earlier that day, Gladbach was located on the west bank of the Neffel River.

Following an early breakfast on the morning of March 1, our battalion prepared for an attack to seize a foothold on the east bank of the Neffel, which was actually more of a creek. To help overcome the German force holding the creek's far bank, our assault would be bolstered by American tanks.

After raking the far shoreline with machine-gun fire to force the enemy back, we began wading across the shallow creek, with our machine-gun platoons advancing in support of the rifle companies. The jeep-type weapons carriers interspersed among our infantry force splashed up head-high cold water on everyone near them, bringing laughs as just about all of us got soaked. But the fun did not last long.

A moment later, a storm of enemy artillery, tank, machine-gun, and rifle fire began clobbering us, forcing everyone to crouch close to the water as we continued toward the Neffel's far bank. Over the next couple of hours, we pressed forward several hundred yards beyond the riverbank in hard fighting, knocking back the inevitable German counterattack.

During this attack, our machine gun was employed in a more mobile way to speed our ability to fire and move. Instead of fully setting up the gun in a supporting position and then disassembling it when enemy resistance ended, we carried the gun on its tripod, placing it on the ground to fire a few quick bursts before moving forward again. While this allowed us to get the machine gun into action immediately, lugging the assembled weapon on its tripod was extremely awkward.

Amazingly, it was the enemy who again lost heavily in troops and armor, while we suffered only light casualties and the loss of a few tanks. Though the Germans were continuing to oppose our advance, it was now very evident the enemy's overall fighting spirit had noticeably diminished since the Battle of the Bulge a month earlier. Less willing to put up protracted resistance than in the past, more and more of the surrendering soldiers informed us they were glad to be done with the war. These disproportionate combat losses, as well as the greater readiness of the German troops to surrender, clearly signaled the declining quality and morale of the *Wehrmacht*.

By noon on March 1, our engineers had bridged the Neffel and the Big Red One's 26th Infantry Regiment was advancing through our lines in a leapfrogging of attacking forces. For the next couple of days, the 18th and 26th Regiments continued the 1st Infantry Division's part of the campaign eastward toward the Rhine.

Meanwhile, our 16th Infantry Regiment pulled back to Gladbach, where we received a short reprieve from combat operations. Following several days of almost nonstop advances mixed with bouts of intense combat, we all enjoyed the chance to rest, grab hot showers, and eat hot chow.

Into Bonn: March 5–10

When our 2nd Battalion rejoined the 16th Infantry Regiment's offensive toward the Rhine on the morning of March 5, our assigned objective was the town of Metternich, located about 11 miles east-southeast of Gladbach and a couple of miles southeast of the then-existing front line at the town of Weilerswist.

Metternich was captured by noon in a quick operation. Located on higher ground, the town gave us our first look at the Rhine, which was still some seven miles away. With all the recent rain, the river appeared swollen as it flowed swiftly northward. Unfortunately, our enjoyment of this spectacular vantage point was somewhat spoiled by German artillery, which pounded our new position in the town.

After dark on March 6, we proceeded a couple of miles northeast to the town of Hemmerich. Taken earlier in the day by other 2nd Battalion troops, Hemmerich was part of a string of small towns stretching eastward toward the Rhine.

Before dawn on March 7, our 2nd Battalion's new assault jumped off, following a heavy barrage laid down by our mortar platoon. With our machine-gun platoons in support, the rifle companies made a rapid thrust a couple of miles eastward to take the towns of Waldorf, Ullekoven, Dersdorf, Brenig, and Bornheim, which were located so closely together it was difficult to tell where one town ended and the next one started. As our attack progressed, we came across German women and elderly men still milking their cows and collecting eggs, studiously ignoring the fighting around them.

Our advance to Bornheim left us only a couple of miles short of the Rhine and less than a half-dozen miles west-northwest of the center of Bonn, a large city which was the 1st Infantry Division's next objective. In the operation to take Bonn, the 16th Infantry Regiment planned to enter the city through a highly unconventional maneuver set to begin in the predawn hours of the following day, March 8.

Relying on stealth and surprise rather than the usual artillery preparation, the 16th Infantry Regiment's 1st and 3rd Battalions would form up in long vehicle columns and attempt to drive into the northern and central parts of Bonn before the Germans realized what was happening. During their advance into the city, our 2nd Battalion was assigned the task of defending the regiment's northwestern left flank and cleaning out pockets of enemy forces bypassed by the 1st and 3rd Battalions. Meanwhile, the 18th Infantry Regiment would seize the southern part of Bonn.

Never privy to any of these larger operational details, we knew only that our mission was to "mop up" any remaining German forces northwest of Bonn. With our second machine-gun platoon continuing to operate in support of the 2nd Battalion's rifle companies, this two-day mopping-up mission that began on March 7 turned out to involve some of the toughest combat we had experienced since taking Kreuzau.

"They've got antiaircraft guns on us," a member of our machine-gun squad hollered over to our section's other squad in an action at the outset of this fighting. This warning marked the start of our first encounter with well-trained enemy *flak* crews armed with 20-millimeter guns. Long stationed in the region as part of Germany's air defense against Allied bombers, these troops had now been thrown into battle as infantry.

Their fearsome *flak* guns gave us a real jolt. Spewing out lead faster than anything we had, they forced us to go to ground and shoot back as best we could. Thankfully, during this particular firefight, the enemy possessed only four of these weapons, so our force outnumbered them. Following a short but intense engagement, they finally raised the white flag. Afterward, the surrendering German soldiers showed off their *flak* guns with some pride before handing them over.

In another one of these mopping-up actions, I was posted behind our squad's machine gun when I heard the whistle of some type of incoming round. As I crouched tightly to brace for an explosion, it detonated just behind me, flinging a cloud of white-hot metal shrapnel in every direction.

A blow that felt like a sledgehammer walloped my right shoulder, striking the three-month old scar left by the Army surgeon's removal of German grenade shrapnel from that shoulder after the battle on Hill 232. A few weeks before that wound, I had been hit in this same unlucky spot on my right shoulder by a piece of shrapnel from a German rifle-grenade during the fighting at our bunker position near Eilendorf. This time, the shrapnel that struck my shoulder turned out to be the rounded bottom piece of an American pineapple-shaped grenade. In what must have been a case of friendly fire, a poorly aimed rifle-grenade had failed to reach its intended enemy target.

Although the grenade shrapnel failed to penetrate the fabric of my field jacket, my re-injured shoulder began throbbing with intense pain. By the time I was able to pull aside my uniform to take a look, a large purple welt had already risen. Hoping to obtain some salve, I headed over to our medic. When he saw the welt, he urged me to get treated back at the aid station, but the wound did not appear that serious to me and I declined his advice. I wanted to remain with my squad where the action was.

A second brush with serious injury occurred during this same round of combat northwest of Bonn. A moment after I had taken a German position under fire with the machine gun, the enemy began returning fire, spraying our position with bullets. One of these incoming rounds ricocheted off a tree branch and struck the right side of my glasses, bending the frame and cracking the lens on that side. While very fortunate to have escaped injury, I was stuck wearing my badly damaged "spare" pair of glasses until I could obtain a replacement.

Beyond having to deal with enemy military resistance, our operations were also hampered by the soaring number of German civilians who crowded the roads in an effort to escape the fighting. Lacking shelter, food, and medical care, these frightened and vulnerable refugees presented a pitiful parade of war's victims.

There were exhausted young mothers coaxing along little children so weary they could barely take another step, frail elderly couples who could hardly walk, and ill and injured people being pulled in small wagons or pushed in wheelbarrows. Hardened as we were by combat, the plight of these German refugees was as heart-wrenching as anything we witnessed in the war. It was impossible not to feel compassion for them.

While we were busy mopping up bypassed pockets of enemy troops northwest of Bonn, the 16th Infantry Regiment's operation to seize the northern and central parts of the city by stealth had largely succeeded. Apparently thinking the advancing columns of the regiment's 1st and 3rd Battalions were retreating *Wehrmacht* forces, confused German defenders stationed along the routes into the city had failed to put up any resistance. But once the bypassed enemy troops realized their blunder, they tried to block the roads to cut off the American troops now inside the city.

Departing our position near Roisdorf on the regiment's northwestern flank, our 2nd Battalion moved swiftly to reopen the roads into Bonn during the night of March 8/9. Though we ran into stiff opposition at some points, other German troops posted along the route allowed us to take them prisoner without firing a shot. Spilling out of our trucks, we simply rounded up all the surrendering enemy forces in the vicinity of where we had halted.

There were some tense moments as we pushed down the road. In one instance, an enemy tank erupted from its concealment in thick brush beneath a clump of small trees. It could have wreaked real havoc upon us, but not knowing which way to go or what to do, the tank's crew simply waved a white flag and gave up.

On the morning of March 9, H Company and the 2nd Battalion's three rifle companies united with the rest of the 16th Infantry Regiment inside Bonn. Now tasked with clearing all remaining enemy soldiers from the city, we were cautioned to stay alert for stubborn Nazi diehards who were not yet ready to surrender. Fortunately, not many of these were encountered.

The surrendering German troops included a few men not in uniform, but they were processed in the same way as the other soldiers, once they informed us who they were. Deserters also emerged from cellars, where they had sometimes spent weeks hiding out. Others gave up with their girlfriends who had served alongside them as female soldiers. A number of these men begged us to permit their female "friends" to be accepted as prisoners of war so they could remain together, but we had orders to treat the women as civilians and turned them loose.

All resistance in Bonn officially ended by the afternoon of March 9. While the enemy force defending Bonn had managed to destroy the city's bridge across the Rhine on the night of March 8, the Germans had failed to blow up all of the bridges across the river. Late on the afternoon of March 7, the U.S. 9th Armored Division in our III Corps had seized an intact bridge across the Rhine at Remagen, a dozen miles south of Bonn.

Wild celebration broke out on word of this brilliant feat of arms. Everyone began cheering, with some guys firing their rifles into the air and breaking out booze. The Rhine posed the last great natural obstacle to our advance into the heart of Germany. If the Remagen bridgehead could be expanded, we could use it to launch the final offensive operations that would bring an end to the war.

At the Rhine: March 10–18

On March 10, the 16th Infantry Regiment turned Bonn over to another outfit and took up a temporary defensive position back around Bornheim, with its companies spread out along the western bank of the Rhine. While most of H Company occupied the town of Widdig, our second machine-gun platoon and part of the mortar platoon were attached to F Company and assigned to the Rhine town of Hersel, located a couple of miles south of Widdig and about three miles northwest of the center of Bonn.

Following our advance of two dozen miles over the previous two weeks, a jubilant mood held sway among us. Our expectation of a quick end to the war back in September had been dashed by the grinding battles at Aachen, the Hürtgen, and the Bulge, but now victory was truly within sight. But while all of us were eager to get back into the fight and finish the war, it would be another few days before we could cross the Rhine.

With only light duties at Hersel, a half-dozen of us from my platoon decided to explore the area on our second day in the town. Wandering down close to the Rhine, we came upon an old stone-walled church that had been damaged in the recent fighting. Inside, we found that most of the sanctuary's roof had been blown off and the majority of its windows had been shattered, scattering shards of stained glass across the floor.

Despite the destruction, the church's quaint splendor was still evident. The sanctuary's beautiful wooden pews matched the huge wooden beams that supported what remained of the roof. Soon, my eyes fell upon the church's pipe organ. Located in one corner, it had been protected by a small portion of the ceiling that remained intact.

"I'll just try it out," I announced to the others.

After dusting off plaster and other debris from the organ and the bench in front of it, I took a seat. Running my fingers across the keys, I played a few notes from "The Old Rugged Cross," one of the hymns in my limited repertoire.

"Hey, that sounds good," remarked one of the guys, all of whom now gathered around the organ.

Agreeing with his verdict, I pushed down the lever to increase the organ's volume. The hymn boomed out majestically through the ruined church. It felt terrific to be playing music again for the first time since I had left my assignment as the chaplain's assistant just before D-Day.

A couple of minutes into the song, a distant thump of artillery fire resounded from the far side of the Rhine. It was followed by the distinctive high-pitched whine of an incoming artillery round, which rose above the deep notes of the organ.

An instant later, a shell exploded about 30 yards from the church, shaking the building, the organ, and all of us. Apparently, the German audience across the river did not appreciate my performance. Luckily for us, the round had not fallen that close, perhaps because the wind made it difficult for enemy observers to determine the source of the music at that range.

"Let's cut out the organ, Andy," someone shouted. The concert was over.

Hustling out of the church, we took refuge in the basement of a neighboring German home about 50 yards away. Although the four ensuing artillery rounds that followed the first shell never placed us in any real danger, it was the last time we ventured so close to the Rhine during our remaining three days in Hersel.

Up until our crossing of the Roer, we had encountered few German civilians. After we crossed the Roer, almost every pause in our campaign placed us in the midst of a German village or town. Most of the time, a natural fear and hostility toward foreign troops limited the local population's contact with us. But whenever we opened up our ration boxes to eat, a half-dozen or more starving German kids would promptly appear from out of nowhere, imploring us with their eyes as they held out rusty cans.

Despite our own hunger, few of us had the heart to eat in front of starving children and not share what we had. Breaking my ration's cheese bar into five portions and my crackers into three portions, I would try to distribute the pieces fairly among the kids around me so as to make sure each one received something. They would gulp down anything they received as fast as they could get it in their mouths.

On one occasion, I watched a German mother and her three kids approach the crew of a Sherman tank to plead for food as the men were eating their chow. The tankers passed the family all the rations they had, including some unopened K-ration boxes. Before the family departed, one member of the crew even leapt down from atop the tank to give one of the little girls a hug. Such small acts of kindness to others in need helped us to begin to regain the sense of humanity the war had stripped away.

On the night of March 14, a detachment from another division arrived to relieve us of our position at Hersel. Proceeding four miles to the west, we reunited with the other elements of H Company at Waldorf, one of the towns captured a week earlier during our rapid advance to the Rhine.

Over the next four days, we drilled and cleaned our equipment, but also had time to take showers and watch a movie, offering us another brief taste of civilian life. On March 16, several officers and men in our company were awarded military commendations. During the ceremony, I received a Bronze Star for my accidental crossing of the German minefield back in January.

To make-up for our recent casualties, a few new troops trickled into H Company, but replacements were now extremely hard to come by. While our machine-gun squad had grown used to operating without its full complement, losses from combat over the previous days and nights had reduced us to four guys, so we were glad to get anyone we could. As was the case with our other recent replacements, the GIs who arrived almost always lacked adequate training and were entirely unprepared for combat. They would have to learn fast in the tough fighting that awaited us.

Reassigned to the U.S. First Army's VII Corps, our 1st Infantry Division was preparing to move south to the Remagen area, where a fierce battle to expand our Rhine bridgehead was raging. Though excited at the prospect of crossing the famous river, we held no illusions about the bitter combat that lay ahead before Germany would finally accept defeat. We would have to keep fighting, each of us hoping and praying we would be among the living when the war's last battle was over.

CHAPTER 18

Breakout from Remagen:
March 18–April 6, 1945

The battle for the Remagen bridgehead: March 18–26

A couple of hours after midnight on March 18, H Company motored out of Waldorf in a convoy of vehicles with me riding aboard our squad's jeep "Little Joe." Following a long, slow trip that lasted until dawn, we arrived at a newly constructed pontoon bridge that spanned the Rhine River at a point roughly 16 miles south-southeast of Waldorf and just a mile or two north-northwest of the recently captured bridge at Remagen. Setting out across the pontoon bridge on foot, we joined a long column of troops and vehicles headed for the town of Unkel on the river's eastern bank.

Pondering some way to mark our crossing of the Rhine, my thoughts turned to my glasses that had been badly damaged during the fighting near Bonn 10 days earlier. Tired of putting up with the bent frame and cracked right lens, I decided the river would be a fitting spot to get rid of them. Since this was the back-up pair I had been wearing since the other pair had been lost near Kreuzau three weeks earlier, discarding these glasses would require me to be placed on temporary kitchen duty while I awaited the arrival of the new pair that had already been requisitioned for me.

My glasses had remained a constant source of aggravation for me throughout my time as a soldier. Beyond trying to keep the lenses free of rain, frost, mud, and blood, there had been at least five instances when the frame had been bent or a lens had been cracked or scratched. Without my glasses, I was useless as a soldier. If I was running the War Department, any GI with glasses would be banned from serving in combat. While such a change was not going to happen, my disposal of the damaged pair in the Rhine at least ensured I would be wearing new glasses the next time I went into combat.

When we reached the town of Unkel early that morning, I hunted down First Sergeant Huber, wondering how I would explain the loss of my glasses in the Rhine. But when I reported their loss, Huber simply assigned me to kitchen duty without asking any questions.

That evening after supper, H Company shifted a half-dozen miles northeast from Unkel to Aegidienberg, a town just cleared of German troops. We remained there in a secondary defensive position for the next couple of days, which allowed time for my new glasses to reach me just ahead of our company's next move.

By the evening of March 20, H Company had advanced a further three and a half miles north-northwest from Aegidienberg to Bellinghausen, which was still under enemy artillery fire after its capture by other elements of the 16th Infantry Regiment earlier that day. While our 2nd Battalion had been held in regimental reserve since crossing the Rhine, the other two battalions of the 16th Infantry Regiment were already in action with the rest of the 1st Infantry Division as it attacked northwards to expand the Remagen bridgehead.

On March 21, our 2nd Battalion joined the battle, carrying out an operation to seize Rott and Söven, neighboring towns located three miles north of Bellinghausen. In the attack on Rott, our machine-gun platoon supported E Company. While the riflemen checked each house for German troops, our machine-gun squad was posted nearby in the street or on the sidewalk, moving forward half a block at a time once the homes around us had been searched. Though this placement of our gun enabled us to provide immediate fire support for the infantry, it also left us vulnerable to enemy fire.

It soon became clear the Germans had dug tunnels between the houses and were shifting from one location to another to dodge our infantry. As a result, we rarely saw enemy soldiers out in the open and had no chance to engage them with our machine gun. Eventually, our guys located the tunnels and chased the evasive Germans for several blocks, until they were eventually forced out into the open and surrendered.

By the time darkness fell on March 21, we had overcome enemy resistance in Rott, which now lay in ruins. While taking few casualties ourselves in the operation, the inexperienced German troops suffered far worse. We also took a large number of prisoners who appeared to be scared and shocked as they were led to the rear.

With continued close support from our artillery and aircraft, we pushed a couple of miles further northeast of Rott and Söven the next day. After advancing through the town of Wippenhohn, we reached the outskirts of the city of Hennef spread along the banks of the Sieg River, a 100-mile-long tributary of the Rhine running east to west. At this point, our drive further northeast was blocked by the Germans, who hammered us with a heavy barrage of artillery fire.

On March 23, our 16th Infantry Regiment began concentrating along a ridgeline as we made preparations to cross Hanf Creek, a narrow, shallow stream flowing northward into the Sieg River. Though the creek was fordable on foot, our vehicles needed a bridge, which took time to build. Once across, our objective would be the seizure of the high ground beyond.

The larger aim of the operation was to eliminate all German resistance south of the Sieg and to secure the Remagen bridgehead before a planned offensive leap eastward. Meanwhile, the *Wehrmacht* was rushing armored reinforcements into the same area for a counteroffensive designed to wipe out our foothold on the eastern bank of the Rhine. Unaware of the enemy's plans, our forces were headed for a collision.

To soften us up for their attack, the Germans plastered our front line on the ridge west of the creek, making especially heavy use of rockets. Increasing the rate of fire that afternoon and evening, the enemy mounted one of the heaviest barrages we experienced in the entire war. Maintaining our positions while trying to remain hidden from enemy observation, we all wondered when the bombardment would end.

Shortly after midnight on March 24, the 2nd Battalion began pushing northeast in the direction of Geisbach, a town located a couple of miles northeast of Rott and Söven on the eastern bank of Hanf Creek. E and F Companies, supported by our second machine-gun platoon, quickly ran into heavy German opposition, including self-propelled guns. In the meantime, G Company, supported by the first machine-gun platoon, succeeded in advancing to the edge of Geisbach, only to be counterattacked by a strong force of enemy infantry and armor posted inside the town. In hard fighting, G Company and the first machine-gun platoon were forced to pull back a short distance to the southwest, causing the rest of our 2nd Battalion to likewise give up some ground.

"Let's don't retreat too far. Let's just retreat a little bit," an officer cautioned us, as our second machine-gun platoon was pulling back toward Söven with E and F Companies in order to support G Company and other elements of H Company.

By mid-morning, the German counterattack was blunted and then driven back to its starting point. In furious combat that lasted through the afternoon, our artillery and P-47 Thunderbolt fighter-bombers hammered the enemy, helping us beat back repeated counterattacks. When evening fell, our 2nd Battalion had achieved its assigned objectives, but G Company paid a particularly high price for the capture of Geisbach.

Our battalion renewed its attack early on March 25, seeking to consolidate control over a stretch of the south bank of the Sieg River. Backed by strong support from our company's mortar platoon, highly accurate fire from our artillery, and airstrikes, the 2nd Battalion succeeded in its mission, despite numerous salvos of enemy rockets and stiff resistance from German self-propelled guns and tanks.

The 1st Infantry Division's offensive across Hanf Creek on March 24 and 25 had spoiled the enemy's plan of attack, but the ensuing battle had been as hard-fought as any we had experienced since the combat in the Hürtgen Forest and on Hill 232 back in November. By taking the high ground east of Hanf Creek and forcing the Germans to retreat north of the Sieg, we had helped to secure the Remagen bridgehead for the U.S. First Army. While the enemy's losses in the fighting were far heavier, our own had also been high. Indeed, our medics wondered aloud how we could have sustained so many casualties.

By now, we had received word that George Patton's U.S. Third Army to the south and General Bernard Montgomery's British forces in the north were also crossing the Rhine. Meanwhile, the Red Army was grinding its way into the heart of the Nazi *Reich* in the east. Clearly, Germany's military situation was growing worse by the day.

The battle for the Remagen bridgehead was only a prelude to a more ambitious operation. Just to the south of the 1st Infantry Division's position, the U.S. 3rd Armored Division had already begun an operation to break out of the bridgehead.

Serving as the spearhead of a new offensive by the U.S. First Army's VII Corps, the 3rd Armored Division would advance east-northeast with our 1st Infantry Division on its left and the 104th Infantry Division on its right. In seizing additional territory south of the Sieg River, the U.S. First Army would act as the southern arm of a giant pincer movement, while the U.S. Ninth Army, swinging east-southeast, would form the northern pincer. If the linkup succeeded, the two Armies would encircle an enormous part of the *Wehrmacht* in the Ruhr Valley, the major industrial region of Germany.

As part of the Big Red One's operations on the left flank of VII Corps, our 16th Infantry Regiment's new mission would be to push east through the narrow corridor forced open by the armor and then clear enemy forces from the ground north of it. Shifting further east a day or two later, the regiment would continue the process of securing the northern left flank of VII Corps of the U.S. First Army. While those of us up on the front line knew nothing of these larger operational plans, it was soon apparent we had received a new mission.

A close call: March 26/27

Just after midnight on March 26, elements of another American division arrived to relieve our 2nd Battalion of its hard-won positions in the Remagen bridgehead. After spending the rest of that night and the following day back in Söven, we departed the town that same evening in a column of trucks and jeeps.

On reaching the newly captured town of Kircheib, eight miles east-southeast of Söven, a couple of hours later, H Company took up a defensive position behind the 3rd Armored Division. By this point, the division had largely battled its way into the open after punching a hole through the perimeter of German infantry and tank forces surrounding the Remagen bridgehead.

That night, as we were trying to figure out where to sleep, a well-liked lieutenant called together a group of about 16 of us, including a number of riflemen from one the 2nd Battalion's infantry companies. Always a firebrand for adventure, the lieutenant spoke to us with an animated look on his face.

"I'll tell you what. Let's take this next town. Let's just go into this town tonight," he exclaimed, issuing something between an invitation and a command. Neglecting to mention that he lacked orders from above for this scheme, the lieutenant had impulsively decided to seize a nearby German town on his own initiative.

Although preferring to get some rest and move out in daylight when we could see what was going on around us, the lieutenant's enthusiasm for capturing a town got us fired up. With nearby German defenses already shattered by the 3rd Armored Division's earlier advance through this sector of the front line, he made us confident that it would be easy for us to take control of the next town in the darkness and hold it until the main body of American troops arrived later that day.

About midnight, we collected our gear and set off down the road in high spirits. Even the start of another spring rain failed to dampen our mood, since it offered us cover if we ran into the enemy. Strung out two men abreast so as not to present an inviting target, I was halfway back from the rifleman at the head of our column and could see little more than the pavement under my boots and the guy just ahead of me.

Despite the rain and the heavy tripod slung over my shoulders, the three-mile trek to our objective did not take long. At the town's outskirts, it began to thunder and lightning. In the downpour, the GI leading our column made a wrong turn and took us onto the town's main street, rather than the intended backstreet route into the town.

As we proceeded along the main street in the storm, it was just possible for us to make out the two-story buildings lining either side of the road. Within a block or two, we began passing the shadowy silhouettes of tanks, about 10 of which were parked along both sides of the street. No doubt part of the 3rd Armored Division, the presence of American tanks was reassuring, but it was also somewhat disappointing since it meant we would not be able to claim credit for capturing the town.

Just at that instant, a long streak of lightning flashed in the sky. Momentarily illuminating the street, it revealed a spine-chilling, heart-stopping, and mind-boggling sight. On the tanks closest to us, large Nazi swastikas were plainly visible.

"These are German tanks, guys," I whispered in astonishment. We had stumbled right into the middle of an enemy panzer unit.

"*Halt!*" a German-accented voice shouted from about 30 yards ahead of us. The enemy sentry then issued a demand in German for what seemed to be a password.

For a few seconds, there was a nerve-racking pause as he waited for a response.

A moment later, the sentry fired a shot that echoed loudly off the surrounding buildings. With that, all hell broke loose in the stormy darkness.

Within seconds, a full-scale firefight was underway as several of the GIs at the head of our column began returning the sentry's fire, while the rest of us continued advancing along the street toward the gunfire.

Alerted by the shooting, German panzer crews began spilling out of their quarters in a two-story building ahead of us. Amid the darkness and confusion, they slipped past our column to reach their tanks behind us, ending any opportunity we had of destroying the tanks while they were unmanned.

Rising above the din of gunfire, the ominous rumble of the tank engines cranking to life warned us we were about to be massively outgunned.

Spotting an open hatch atop one of the tanks 10 feet away from me, I lobbed a grenade toward it, but it bounced off the turret and exploded on the far side of the tank. A softer touch might have improved my aim, but I was not going to risk underthrowing a grenade and having it bounce back toward me.

Recognizing we stood no chance against tanks, the firing rapidly subsided as all 16 of us set off in a mad flight through the rain in search of a building in which to hide. By the time the panzers began to roll down the street a moment later, the guys ahead of me had already dashed 50 yards down the sidewalk.

On finding an open set of double doors at the entrance of an old building, the others hustled inside. Lagging a few steps behind under the weight of my cumbersome tripod, I feared the Germans might see me if I followed them up the staircase that led to the doors, thus divulging the location of our refuge. So instead of ascending the stairs, I dumped the tripod on the sidewalk out front and concealed myself in the dark alcove just to the right of the staircase.

Despite having found cover in the shadows, it was hard to control my fear as I stood there breathless. Aware the enemy troops might have observed us heading for the building or notice my tripod six feet away on the sidewalk, I pressed myself deeper into the alcove. Yanking out my .45 pistol in case the Germans tried to charge up the building's staircase, I felt ready to deal with anything other than tanks.

Our situation was far from hopeless, but the tension of the moment overcame one of the GIs hiding just inside the entrance to the building a few feet above me.

"Let's give up!" the panicked soldier blurted out in a loud, high-pitched whine.

An instant later, I heard the unmistakable sound of a fist smashing into a face, followed by silence. There was no way that one man's loss of nerve could be permitted to expose our location to any German troops who might be in earshot.

By now, the enemy tanks were rolling down the street toward the building where we were hiding. Long bursts of machine-gun fire rose above the metallic clanking of tank treads. Uncertain where we were, the Germans had apparently decided to blindly spray both sides of the street in order to suppress any potential threat.

A flash of lightning exposed the first of the 10 panzers less than a block away, motoring toward my location from the right. As the column of tanks made its way up the street in the rain, the commander in the turret hatch of the lead tank was raking my side of the street with machine-gun fire.

Boxed into the corner between the staircase and building's concrete wall, there was little chance I could avoid being chewed up by machine-gun rounds when the tank passed in front of my position in the alcove. But I felt sure that if I attempted to dash up the stairs, the tank commander would spot me and probably order the building be destroyed, so I was stuck where I was with no good alternative.

As the commander continued blazing away, the lead panzer rumbled inexorably toward me, moving right down the middle of the street, which was barely wide enough to accommodate the vehicle. Feeling doomed and utterly helpless, all I could do was flatten my body deeper into the dark corner and do some hard praying.

An instant before the first tank reached a point opposite the staircase, the fire from the machine gun abruptly ceased.

Moving from my right to left, the monster rolled by me with a thunderous clatter. As it passed just 10 feet from my concealed position in the alcove, the tank's treads came within two feet of the bottom of the stairs, barely missing my tripod out on the sidewalk. It would have been easy for me to shoot the unsuspecting commander in the turret hatch with my .45 pistol, but that would have been suicidal.

A second later, the tank commander resumed firing, as if he had been reloading his machine gun at the precise instant the vehicle had been passing my location. As the column's remaining nine panzers clanked past me without incident, I knew my reprieve from what had seemed certain death was nothing short of a miracle.

But I was not yet out of the woods. Unless I retrieved my tripod from the sidewalk, the German infantrymen trailing closely behind the tanks would surely see it, which might lead them to suspect our party was concealed in the building.

As soon as the last of the enemy panzers moved down the street, I could already hear voices quietly conversing as the German soldiers approached my location, coming up behind the last tank.

Calculating I had just enough time to make the grab before they arrived, I darted toward my tripod six feet away. Instead, my hasty move nearly caused me to run headlong into a half-dozen enemy troops.

Reacting instinctively, I sprang backward into my dark niche before anyone caught sight of me. At almost the same moment that I regained my cover in the alcove, one of the German soldiers stumbled over the tripod, causing the other troops who had gone a few steps further down the street to return.

As the rain was letting up, the enemy soldiers gathered only feet away from me, circling around the tripod. From their excited whispers, it was evident they were trying to figure out how it got there and debating what to do.

Terrible scenarios began to race through my mind, causing me to break out in a sweat, despite the coolness of the night.

Would they start searching the area? What if they figure out where our guys are hiding and decide to storm the building? What if they toss hand grenades through the door? How should I react?

It would have been simple for me to start shooting or toss one of my grenades at the Germans. Yet, even if I managed to kill all of them, the noise would certainly alert others nearby to our location. On the other hand, if I did nothing and they decided to assault the building, my concealed position would at least give me the chance to ambush them when they tried to ascend the staircase.

Finally, after several long, anxious moments, the Germans ran off to catch up to the tank column without conducting a search of the building. For a second time, a sense of relief flooded over me. Believing I was at last in the clear, I decided to make another attempt to retrieve my tripod.

But as I stepped forward, one of the German soldiers reappeared on my left. Moving backwards along the street from the direction that the other enemy troops had just run off, the man was turning his head from side to side while holding out his rifle. He appeared to be trying to fend off some threat in front of him, though nothing was visible to me. With each step backward, he was moving closer and closer to me, forcing me to withdraw back into the dark corner beside the staircase where I had hidden.

As I looked on in disbelief, the soldier steadily retreated directly toward the alcove, until he stood only an inch or two away from me and the muzzle of my pistol pointed at his back. My sharp awareness of his breathing and his pungent odor suggested he must likewise be able to hear and smell me, but the German seemed to remain utterly oblivious as he continued to remain focused on the unseen menace ahead of him. Still, I feared he would sense my presence at any second.

Once again, tension gripped me as I considered my options. I could try to thrust my arm around his neck and take him prisoner, but it might be less risky if I shot him in the back with my pistol.

It then struck me that it might not even be necessary for me to squeeze the trigger. In his already terrorized state, just uttering, "Hi there, Fritz!" would probably cause the German to die from shock.

No matter which alternative I chose, the soldier's failure to return to his outfit would no doubt cause his buddies to come looking for him, though a gunshot would certainly bring them a lot faster. With the risks of any action outweighing the benefits, I did not see any choice but to wait, hoping he would leave.

An excruciatingly long minute later, the German at last bolted off into the darkness to catch up with the rest of his unit, apparently having overcome his fear of whatever was out there. After three close calls, I wondered whether my long night was finally over as I offered a silent prayer of thanks for my survival thus far.

When another quarter of an hour had passed without any further movement in the street, I quickly snatched up my tripod and hurried up the staircase. Passing the GI guarding the building's entrance, I made my way down a darkened flight of stairs to a large basement, where I joined the rest of the guys.

Following my arrival, the street outside remained quiet. However, to be certain the entire German force had pulled out of the town, we decided to stay concealed for another couple of hours, waiting until daybreak to exit the building.

At dawn, sunlight began to filter through the basement's windows, illuminating what turned out to be our truly ghoulish surroundings. While we had thought it odd one wall of the basement was made of glass, its function only now became clear.

Behind a six-foot-high pane of glass, a dozen human corpses floated in a sort of giant aquarium filled with gallons and gallons of formaldehyde or some other type of embalming fluid. Eerily lifelike, the eyes of the dead seemed to stare back at us as we gaped in horror.

The realization that we were in the cadaver storage area of what appeared to be a medical school helped spur us on our way.

"Guys, let's get out of here!" someone shouted.

Needing no additional encouragement, we swiftly exited the basement and clamored up the steps to the building's main entrance, where our sentry was posted.

Just as we reached the entrance, a roughly 50-year-old German civilian was coming up the staircase that led into the building. Evidently heading for his office inside, he was dressed in a business suit and carried a briefcase.

Before the German had time to react to our appearance, the sergeant in our group seized the guy by his collar and literally yanked him the rest of the way up the stairs to the landing. Eye to eye with the sergeant, the man was now staring into the face of the roughest looking and largest soldier in our group.

Speaking in halting German, our sergeant demanded, *"Wo sind die deutschen Soldaten?"* ("Where are the German soldiers?")

"Amerikaner! Amerikaner!" the German cried out as his shock turned to fear.

"Ja, Amerikaner. Wo sind die deutschen Soldaten?" the sergeant calmly repeated.

By now, the man was deathly pallid and choked with terror, as close to having a heart attack as anyone I had ever seen. Somehow, he managed to convey through gestures and words that the tank unit had pulled out of the town.

This confirmed the town was now in our hands, but our lack of good intelligence had deprived us from achieving a far greater success. If we had known in advance a German panzer unit was holding the town, we might have been able to sneak in and disable the first and last of the tanks parked along both sides of the main street. Tightly jammed front to rear, the remaining tanks would have been blocked in between them.

With a machine gun or two in the street, it would have been a simple task to have prevented the escape of the tank crews quartered in the neighboring building. At that point, an announcement could have been issued in German.

"You are surrounded with machine guns. We're going to kill every last one of you, if you don't surrender right now. Send your commander out here."

While that opportunity had been lost, we had to be grateful our party had evaded both casualties and capture. The night could have turned out very badly.

Departing the town a bit later that morning, the 16 of us formed two columns along either side of the road. Coming around a sharp bend, we found ourselves facing directly into the barrel of a panzer just 30 yards in front of us.

Instantly, all of us lunged for cover.

Amazingly, nothing happened. After a few moments, a couple of our guys moved forward to check it out.

"Hell, there ain't nuthin' in that tank. Let's go!" one of them exclaimed.

It appeared the crew must have been forced to abandon the tank as the Germans were withdrawing from the town the previous night. Since there was no obvious damage, we concluded the vehicle had probably experienced mechanical problems. Had the tank been manned when we came around the corner, it could have easily wiped us all out with a burst from its machine gun. Another prayer of thanks was in order.

Our unsanctioned advance the previous night had given us a real face-to-face close encounter with the enemy. While it had been an adventure, it had been a terrifying one. It had also provided a cautionary lesson to our gung-ho lieutenant, who acknowledged the risk we had taken.

"Boy, that was close, wasn't it?" he declared with a grin as we moved on. The war might be nearing its end, but the chance of being killed before it was over was as real as ever.

Closing the Ruhr Pocket: March 27–April 6

Later that same morning of March 27, our group linked up with the rest of the 2nd Battalion, which was beginning its part of the 1st Infantry Division's new mission to mop up German resistance on the northern flank of VII Corps behind the hard-charging 3rd Armored Division. Backed by dominating air power and meeting only limited and sporadic opposition from German small arms, mortars, and artillery fire, we pushed through a string of small towns to Kuchhausen, roughly five and a half miles east-northeast of Kircheib.

After halting for the night at Kuchhausen, our mopping-up operation continued the next day. On entering a small German village along our route of advance, my squad and I overheard loud female voices. Heading toward the commotion, we came upon a group of three women, one of whom was viciously berating a small, emaciated man, who was wearing a dingy, over-sized shirt and pants lined with a series of broad, vertical blue and light gray stripes. From his wretched appearance and uniform, it was obvious he had suffered under the Nazis as some type of prison camp inmate, possibly as a slave laborer.

As the irate *Frau* continued ranting at the man, a soldier in our squad translated the German for the rest of us. In response to the poor fellow's request for a set of clothes to replace his prison garb, the woman was dispensing a harsh rebuke, cruelly assailing the man like he was some type of inferior beast rather than a human being.

Feeling sympathy for the man's plight, I tried to intervene with the woman in an effort to help him obtain something else to wear. But rather than considering my appeal, the woman instead turned her venomous tirade on me.

In a lightning quick movement, my buddy Wayne Newsome reached around in front of me and whipped his open hand across the woman's face.

"Oh!" she gasped indignantly.

"Don't let her talk to you that way, Andy!" Newsome chided. A GI who lacked much warmth toward the Germans, he was not going to put up with such disrespect toward a buddy.

My astonishment that Newsome would strike a woman was matched by my amazement at the force of the blow. In my whole life, I had never seen anyone slapped that hard, but his intervention achieved its intended effect. Though still glaring bitterly at us, the *Frau* had shut up, while her two friends looked shocked.

Shortly after the three women retreated into a nearby home, one of them returned with a shirt and pants for the man, who stepped out of sight to change into them. The new clothes immediately seemed to restore a little dignity to him.

This man's dehumanization was a central aim for the Nazi regime in dealing with its enemies. The disdain these German women displayed toward this destitute victim of Nazi barbarity showed how deeply they had been infected with the belief of their superior status as the Master Race. In losing their ability to feel compassion for a fellow human being, it was apparent they themselves had become dehumanized.

Our next fighting took place on the night of March 29/30 as we battled to seize control of Wilgersdorf and then Rudersdorf, neighboring towns located a little over two dozen miles east-northeast of Kuchhausen. Over the course of March 30, the 1st Infantry Division went on to take control of the commanding heights above Siegen, a city located in the basin of the Sieg River about six miles west-northwest of Wilgersdorf and Rudersdorf. Since pushing out of the Remagen bridgehead on March 27, our drive east-northeast had claimed more than two dozen German towns. In a mood of dogged determination rather than exuberance, all the GIs around me simply wanted to "get on with it."

At the vanguard of our advance, the 3rd Armored Division was meanwhile already nearing the town of Paderborn about 65 miles north-northeast of Siegen, closing in on the location where the U.S. First Army was to link up with the U.S. Ninth Army coming down from the north. Reacting to this impending danger of encirclement that would isolate them from the rest of Germany, enemy forces west of Paderborn appeared to be assembling for a breakout to the east. In response to this threatened German counterattack in the rear of our armored spearhead, the Big Red One was ordered to race northeast to support the 3rd Armored Division.

On the morning of March 31, our 16th Infantry Regiment boarded trucks and jeeps for the journey up to Büren, about 14 miles southwest of Paderborn. The roundabout route that we traveled from the Siegen area to Büren made it more like a 100-mile trip rather than the 50 miles indicated on a map, ranking it as our longest movement since we had trucked from Normandy to Paris back in August of the previous year.

But Büren turned out to be just a pit stop. The day after the 16th Infantry Regiment's arrival there, our 2nd Battalion was rushed a further half-dozen miles north to the town of Geseke in order to deal with the urgent threat of a German breakout to the east in that sector. Though our rapid drive northward to join the operation around Geseke limited the Easter celebrations on April 1, our chaplain still managed to hold worship services with small groups of us to mark the holy day.

By the end of April 1, we had seized Geseke, putting us in position to help block enemy efforts to escape eastward from the Ruhr Pocket. The ensuing combat was relatively light, but included some difficult night engagements, as German troops tried to slip past our lines in the dark. While no doubt some got through, we succeeded in capturing substantial numbers of enemy prisoners and equipment.

Following the fighting on April 1 to 2, H Company remained in a defensive posture as our 2nd Battalion consolidated its control over the area around Geseke. Some limited skirmishing persisted, but most of the German soldiers trying to pass through our lines were now moving individually or in small groups, often outfitted in civilian clothes rather than their uniforms. In an effort to hunt down enemy troops who might be hiding among the area's civilian population, our squad joined in searches of local homes and farms. We rarely found any concealed German soldiers, but that did not mean the farmers had nothing to hide.

During a check of one isolated farm, the German-speaking member in our four-man detachment asked the older German gentleman who answered the door if any soldiers had taken refuge in his home and whether he possessed any extra stocks of food.

After the man responded that no German soldiers were sheltering with his family, he added in English, "We don't have any food. We don't have any wine. We're hungry."

This was the usual response, but it did not stop us from carrying out a thorough search of the property. After completing an inspection of the house, we descended to the cellar with the four members of family in tow.

Once there, our eyes immediately fell upon barrels, shovels, and hoes stacked against a door, placed there as if to suggest the door was never opened.

"Where does that door go?" the German-speaking GI in our party inquired. Immediately, the two other members of my squad began sliding away the barrels and tools.

"*Nein, nein! Nein, nein!*" the elderly woman in the family loudly objected.

Ignoring her strenuous protest, our two guys finished clearing away the obstacles and jerked the door open, revealing a large room literally crammed full of food. None of us had seen anything like it.

Eight to ten hams, three sides of beef, and numerous wheels of cheese hung from the rafters. A dozen wicker baskets stuffed with corncobs were neatly stacked on the floor, while an equal number of crates filled with apples were piled against the opposite wall. Sweet potatoes and beets were heaped knee-high in two separate mounds. Several free-standing shelves built into one wall held perhaps a hundred neatly arranged bottles of wine. Stored down in the cool cellar, it would all keep for months.

The old German gentleman who had told us there was no food looked a little sheepish. Although there were strict orders against stealing from civilians, we felt justified in liberating a small ham, a wheel of cheese, a number of sweet potatoes, several cobs of corn, and a few bottles of wine as punishment for lying to us.

However, shortly after our departure, all of us began to feel we had been wrong to simply swipe the items from the family. Returning to the farm, we offered to trade cigarettes and candy in exchange for what we had taken from the cellar.

"*Ja, Ja! Ja, Ja!*" the now extremely friendly German gentleman agreed, nodding his head repeatedly to assure us he sincerely wanted us to retain the food and wine we had removed from the cellar. When we left the farm this time, the man had a big smile on his face, obviously very pleased with the bargain.

On a couple of other occasions, German women gave us small hams, potatoes, and fresh eggs as a gesture of goodwill. But however we obtained the items, we did not always keep these goods for ourselves. In one instance, we seized most of a stash of hoarded food and distributed it to a group of starving refugees.

More than once during our searches of local homes, elderly German gentlemen proudly showed us their hunting rifles, which were often quite impressive. While these weapons could have been seized as contraband, we chose not to confiscate them.

Our assignment in the Geseke area lasted only a few days but allowed us to play a very small part in a major Allied victory. The successful linkup of the U.S. First and Ninth Armies had trapped hundreds of thousands of German troops inside the Ruhr Pocket, delivering a catastrophic blow to the *Wehrmacht*. Relieved of our position by another American division on April 6, the Big Red One prepared for another new mission further east. The war was clearly nearing its end, but Germany had not yet surrendered.

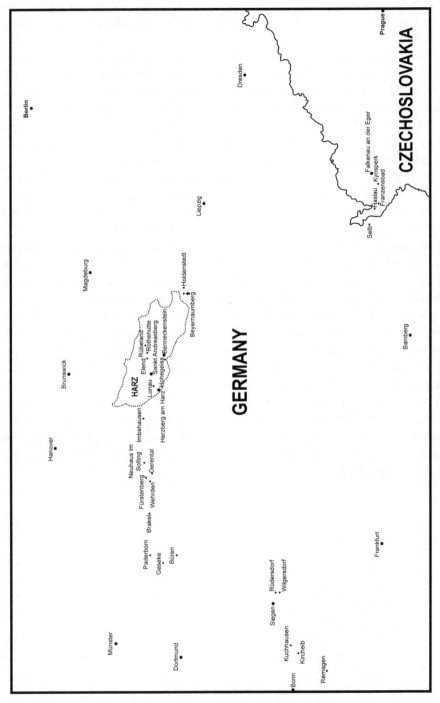

Map 6: The Campaign Across Germany

CHAPTER 19

The Harz to Czechoslovakia: April 6–May 8, 1945

Across the Weser: April 6–8

In the new operation, our 1st Infantry Division was again supporting the 3rd Armored Division, which was already thrusting further east into Germany. Seeking to head off any attempt to rescue the *Wehrmacht* units encircled in the Ruhr, our target was the group of German forces assembling in the Harz Mountains, the western edge of which lay some 75 miles east of Geseke. But before VII Corps could deal with this threat in the Harz, it first had to reach and cross the Weser River.

Setting out from Geseke on the morning of April 6, H Company motored 30 miles eastward to the town of Brakel, where we assembled with the rest of the 16th Infantry Regiment that afternoon. The following evening, our outfit departed Brakel and advanced nine miles further east to Wehrden, located on the Weser. Upon our arrival in the town, we moved into position to cross the Weser the next day, as German artillery and small arms targeted us from the far side of the river.

On April 8, other elements of the Big Red One launched the first phase of our division's attack across the Weser, with the initial crossing taking place a few miles south of our company's location. When the 16th Infantry Regiment's turn came that afternoon, our two machine-gun platoons boarded boats with E and G Companies. As we began our first real assault from boats since D-Day, it was hard not to feel a little anxious about what awaited us on the other side of the river.

Concealed by a smokescreen and backed by our artillery and mortars targeting German positions on the far bank, our crossing was successful. After we landed, enemy troops resisted with 20-millimeter guns and small arms but failed to prevent our capture of the high ground near the town of Fürstenberg, a mile north of Wehrden.

Most of our immediate haul of prisoners were teenage SS troops, but this soon changed. Over the ensuing days, we began capturing soldiers from various German replacement units, a mix that was unsurprising since the area stretching between Paderborn and the Harz Mountains served as the *Wehrmacht's* central training ground.

By now, we had a fairly clear picture of the German Army. Most regular *Wehrmacht* units were made up of draftees who had been called up for several years of military service. German troops were well-trained, tough, and highly capable, but their close adherence to standard tactical doctrine made them more predictable in their conduct of military operations. In contrast, American GIs were usually less experienced as soldiers, but usually demonstrated more flexibility and ingenuity in action, doing whatever was necessary to accomplish the mission. In general, troops on both sides sought to fight honorably. Of course, it is difficult to kill people in an "honorable" way.

Over the months of combat since D-Day, regular German troops had always fought hard, but surrendered when the jig was up. As they were pushed back into their homeland, the Germans had fought harder, which had made combat from Aachen to the Bulge such a tough slog. But after our crossing of the Rhine three weeks earlier, the rate of enemy surrenders had mounted as more and more Germans came to believe the war was lost. Usually, they surrendered in small groups of fewer than 10 men, though sometimes these surrenders included as many as 50 to 100 men.

Certainly, the composition and quality of the German forces facing us had also diminished over time. While most enemy soldiers in the field after the Battle of the Bulge were still of typical military age, we also increasingly captured older reservists in their forties as well as quite a few younger Germans in their mid-teens. As for the foreign citizens who had been conscripted into the *Wehrmacht*, their lack of commitment to Germany and low morale made them even more ready to give up quickly.

Particularly when it came to the surrender of older German troops, it was apparent from their faces that many of them were happy to be out of the war. Having performed their duty as soldiers, they were normally talkative and even friendly once the fighting was over. If we had ever had enough time to speak at length with these prisoners, I would really have enjoyed the chance to talk with them about hunting, fishing, and their lives before the war.

Though we engaged a range of *Wehrmacht* units in combat, we had run across relatively few members of the dreaded *Waffen* (Armed) SS up until the Bulge. As the military wing of Hitler's SS, they were organized into elite combat divisions. Throughout our training, we had heard they were a rough bunch of Nazis, made up of an altogether different breed of German soldier. Tough, extra-hardened, and generally better trained and equipped, SS troops battled us far more fiercely, stayed in the fight longer, and were seldom taken prisoner.

Deeply indoctrinated with the ideology that proclaimed the Germans to be the "Master Race," these hardcore Nazi troops were bound to find it difficult to accept defeat at the hands of the inferior American "mongrel race." Of course, SS troops were still sometimes forced to surrender. I heard that some SS who tried to give up were shot on sight by our guys, but never witnessed such an incident. In my experience, captured SS men were roughly handled and more closely watched, but were treated correctly.

Most SS troops we encountered at the Weser and elsewhere were quite young and looked to their older officers for direction. Taught to resist our orders, these soldiers at first exhibited an arrogant, hostile, and defiant demeanor that contrasted sharply with other German prisoners. When told to do something, they would often respond, *"Ich verstehe nicht"* ("I don't understand").

However, this uncooperative attitude abruptly changed when their officers were faced with the business end of an American .45 pistol, the barrel of which looks like a cannon when the muzzle is jammed right in your face. Afterward, these officers and the men under their command became very compliant, perhaps harkening back to their earlier training when obedience was absolute.

Overall, our treatment of German prisoners was generally pretty fair as far as I could judge. Naturally, before transferring them to the prisoner facilities in the rear, we stripped these soldiers of any military hardware, such as pistols and knives, as well as watches and compasses, liberating these items as war souvenirs.

Spotting a knife with deer-foot handle sticking out of one captured German's belt, I asked the soldier to surrender it to me and he readily complied. In contrast, enemy officers sometimes proved less receptive to such requests, as was the case when I directed an officer to hand over his fine pair of field artillery binoculars.

"Ich verstehe nicht," the officer replied, pretending not to understand.

"I want those field glasses," I insisted, pointing at them with my .45 pistol.

"Ja! Ja! Ja!" he readily agreed with the situation clarified.

Now facing defeat, German troops, including some of these same soldiers, had once marched across Europe as conquerors. Wearing belt buckles inscribed with the phrase, *"Gott Mitt Uns"* ("God With Us"), most German soldiers probably did believe God was on their side. Fed a steady diet of Nazi propaganda, the majority of Germans were convinced their cause was right as their nation battled to crush Soviet communism and overturn what they viewed as the injustice of the Treaty of Versailles that had ended World War I.

In truth, Germany had fought a brutal war of conquest that produced tremendous suffering and death under the direction of a truly evil criminal regime. In our fight to liberate Europe from this Nazi tyranny, we firmly believed God and justice were on our side.

Into the Harz Mountains: April 8–13

After gaining a foothold on the eastern bank of the Weser on April 8, the Big Red One moved to consolidate its position the following day. Operating with the other elements of the 16th Infantry's 2nd Battalion, H Company pushed toward Derental, a couple of miles southeast of Wehrden. Our advance ran into limited opposition in more populated areas and only a series of lightly defended or undefended roadblocks outside of the towns. In one spot, a dozen huge trees growing beside the road had been felled across it. As foot soldiers, we simply circled around the trees, though our tanks had to take a longer route to bypass the obstacle.

On April 10, the 1st Infantry Division continued its drive toward the Harz Mountains, operating on the left flank of VII Corps. With the 16th Infantry's 1st and 2nd Battalions acting in a mop-up role as the divisional reserve, we advanced to Neuhaus Im Solling, a half-dozen miles north-northeast of Derental. The following day, H Company leapt almost two dozen miles further east to Imbshausen.

As we neared the Harz, the Germans made greater use of roadblocks, small arms and tanks to resist our advance. When they blew up bridges at several small rivers, our engineers rapidly spanned these with pontoon bridges, a marvel of fast work that allowed us to press onward. But during our mop-up operations, it was increasingly uncertain where, when, how, or in what numbers we might encounter enemy soldiers, who stayed well-hidden and held their fire until the last minute.

On April 12, the 16th Infantry Regiment moved up to take a leading position in the 1st Division's advance on the following day, ending our brief assignment as the divisional reserve. Our resumption of front-line operations coincided with the intensification and improved organization of the German opposition.

The new push brought us into the thickly forested hills near Herzberg am Harz, situated roughly 15 miles east-southeast of Imbshausen. This marked our entry into the Harz Mountains, where the *Wehrmacht* was making a last-ditch effort to concentrate and reorganize the troops and armor of two German armies into a cohesive fighting force. Though the details of the enemy's desperate plan were unknown to us at the time, it was clear from the outset we were likely to face stiff resistance.

Reminding me a lot of my home back on Signal Mountain, the Harz Mountains had long served as a picturesque vacation spot, with jutting peaks and steep hills that towered above low valleys. However, like the Hürtgen Forest, this extremely rough, broken, and densely wooded landscape was far less inviting as a venue for offensive military operations. While German forces were too disorganized to exploit the Harz's naturally defensible terrain to its full potential, the region provided the available enemy troops with plenty of spots to stage ambushes as well as a limited road network that could be easily obstructed at countless chokepoints.

Pressing forward along forested mountain tracks, our battalion soon became dispersed into small units. As our machine-gun squad made its way along one of these backroads, we were expecting to come under enemy fire at any moment. Instead, we stumbled upon a small, isolated shack that was home to a German family.

Unlike most German civilians who appeared wary of American troops, this family warmly welcomed our squad, offering us fresh water, hard biscuits, and homemade jelly. Despite their generosity, it was obvious they had very little to eat, so we handed over a few of our K-ration boxes, a gift they gratefully accepted.

Wandering down to a stream beside the home, we saw good-sized trout.

"Do you ever catch and eat these fish?" inquired one of our guys in German.

"We're not supposed to catch these fish," a member of the family told us. Apparently, the trout were protected by some type of local ordinance, but we all agreed we should catch a few to help feed the family.

"Okay, we'll help you," the German-speaking member of our squad explained.

The detonation of three hand grenades in the deepest pool of the stream kicked up a fountain of water and an instant bounty of fish. Before the pool had even settled, the family's two young boys waded out into the cold water to scoop up a dozen or so trout floating on the water's surface. A couple of minutes later, the family was cooking up the fish inside their shack.

As our squad departed, the whole family waved goodbye, saying *"Danke! Danke!"* Helping them out made us all feel a bit more human.

Advancing through the Harz: April 13–16

On April 13, the capture of Herzberg am Harz was assigned to the 16th Infantry Regiment's 1st Battalion, while our 2nd Battalion was ordered to seize the small town of Lonau. Only three miles north of Herzberg am Harz, Lonau was much deeper inside the Harz. As on the previous day, we remained on alert for a German ambush, but on this day the surprise came far away from the battlefield.

While eating a lunch of C-rations, we received the stunning news that President Franklin Delano Roosevelt had died on April 12. Deeply saddened, all of us at first fell silent as we came to terms with the president's death.

Voting in my first presidential election the previous year, I had cast my absentee ballot for Roosevelt. He had been president since I was nine, serving three four-year terms before his election to a fourth term in November 1944. During both the Great Depression and the war, I thought FDR had displayed strong leadership. In particular, I valued his close collaboration with Britain's Prime Minister Churchill in developing an effective strategy to win the global struggle against the Axis powers of Germany, Italy, and Japan.

Most of the time, the political situation back home seemed remote to us at the front, but Roosevelt's death marked one of the rare occasions that I discussed politics with the others in my outfit. There was general agreement FDR had been a great president as well as a strong commander-in-chief who had been concerned about the welfare of the common foot soldier. We also talked about how his leadership would be missed by the generals commanding the Allied forces.

But the majority of our conversation centered on Harry Truman who, as vice-president, had succeeded to the presidency upon Roosevelt's death. While none of us anticipated any major changes to Allied military strategy, we wondered about who Truman was and how he would handle the war going forward.

Late on the afternoon of April 13, the various elements of our 2nd Battalion reached Lonau and began clearing it of enemy troops. Once the town was secured, we assumed a defensive posture for the night, though patrols and bazooka teams were directed to scout ahead for enemy positions and armor. Meanwhile, the 1st Battalion had advanced from Herzberg am Harz to take the town of Sieber, three miles east of Lonau.

The following day, our objective was the high ground north of the larger town of Sankt Andreasberg (now part of Braunlage), located about seven miles east of Lonau. Compared with our previous campaigns, our advance through the Harz was proving less difficult, though it was not without its challenges. Trudging through the rugged terrain in small detachments, we frequently became lost. The mountains also prevented any rapid support from other troops and armor in the area. If we did run into the enemy, we would initially be on our own.

With the Germans exploiting every possible means to slow our progress, we never knew what awaited us around the next bend as we made our way along the steep, narrow roads that wound through the mountains. In at least one instance, the enemy had laid a minefield to block our advance, but their demolition of small bridges was a more frequent problem. Even more common were roadblocks constructed of logs, which we came upon two or three times a day. Created by felling countless tall trees with explosives, axes, and saws, these obstructions ranged from just a few trees to many dozens of trees, with the timber often downed for hundreds of yards along the route of our advance. It was a shame the beautiful forest lining the roads had been spoiled in this way, but that was war.

On several occasions, the Germans attempted to ambush us near these roadblocks, firing at us with machine guns and mortars from camouflaged positions in the surrounding forest. At other times, they allowed our troops to move past their location and then began lobbing mortar rounds at us from the rear. This tactic often caused casualties and delayed our progress, forcing part of our battalion to backtrack in order to clear out the enemy pocket. Because the brass sought to maintain a solid line of advance, these relatively small-scale engagements temporarily halted all progress.

Fortunately, these pockets of German troops rarely put up resistance for more than a few hours, just long enough for the men to feel they had fulfilled their sense of duty. Recognizing they would ultimately have to give up, most thought better of killing more GIs in such circumstances. As usual, when these soldiers did raise the white flag, they mostly appeared delighted to be out of the war.

Beyond enemy opposition, we also endured almost incessant cold spring rains that thoroughly saturated the ground. The resulting slick and muddy dirt lanes were quickly transformed into quagmires by foot and vehicle traffic, further hampering our advance. Soaked to the bone, we plodded on, hoping for a break in the weather. Whenever the precipitation did let up, our body heat would gradually evaporate the moisture, though the rain seldom stopped long enough for us to fully dry out.

Late on the afternoon of April 14, our 2nd Battalion and the 1st Battalion arrived at a location within a few hundred yards of Sankt Andreasberg, which the guys in my squad had dubbed "Saint Andrewsberg" in honor of my last name. From our superb vantage point above the town, we could look down on its streets and observe the enemy's movements. Pummeled by our artillery, most of the German troops garrisoning Sankt Andreasberg were already evacuating, making us feel like we had won control of the town before we had even reached its streets.

Supporting the 2nd Battalion's infantry, our machine-gun platoons entered Sankt Andreasberg that evening as it was getting dark. Enemy resistance was fairly light, but sniper fire slowed us down a bit as we advanced along the town's streets past burning buildings. At the price of a number of casualties, we succeeded in clearing most of the German rearguard from the town by around midnight. Later, many additional enemy soldiers surrendered, emerging out of the surrounding woods in large groups.

After securing Sankt Andreasberg, my squad and I spent a cold night in foxholes we had dug just inside the town, hoping that the next day would be clearer and maybe a bit warmer. On the following morning of April 15, we left our foxholes and huddled behind rubble. As we were scanning the surrounding area for any remaining enemy troops, the mess sergeant delivered a hot breakfast up to our position, a rare treat that was greatly appreciated.

Just at that moment, three strikingly attractive German girls between 18 and 20 years old appeared on the deserted street from out of nowhere. The scene was as bizarre as anything I had witnessed in the war. Decked out in fancy, carefully coiffed hairdos and bright, clean, neatly pressed dresses, these *Fräuleins* promenaded arm-in-arm down a street littered with chunks of brick and concrete from buildings bombarded into charred ruins. Every so often, they stopped to gaze into the blown-out shop windows, chatting away merrily as if out for a normal day of shopping.

Our company mess sergeant, who spoke a little German, greeted the young ladies, who responded in a friendly manner. Going over to the *Fräuleins*, he inquired about their fashionable dresses. Obviously proud of their stylish attire, the girls explained the dresses were gifts from their boyfriends in the *Wehrmacht* who had been stationed on occupation duty in Paris before the city's liberation.

With a radiance that stood in stark contrast to the desolation all around us, the girls were no doubt hoping to catch the eye of the American soldiers now occupying their town. Certainly, they made a far more favorable impression on us than we grubby footsloggers must have made on them.

Since crossing the Rhine about a month earlier, we had occasionally taken improvised showers or bathed in ice cold creeks and streams when we were out of combat, but none of our washing had been very recent. Our hygiene was good enough to avoid lice, but I am sure we developed a unique "American scent," the counterpart of the particular odor of German troops I had noticed on my first morning in Normandy. But if the ripe smell of our unwashed bodies became offensive during the long interludes between bathing, it did not seem to be much of a deterrent to the German females we encountered. Indeed, by this point in the war, there was an increasing amount of friendly fraternization between American GIs and the local *Fräuleins*.

When one fellow in our outfit discovered an almost new two-seater bicycle that had been left on the porch of a bombed-out house, he claimed the tandem bike as loot, tossing it into the trailer behind our jeep "Little Joe" for future use. Sometime later during a halt in our advance at a small German village, the soldier spotted a couple of teenage girls. Removing the bike from the trailer, he rode it over to them. The GI spoke German pretty well and invited one of the girls to hop on the other seat for a short ride. Figuring a bicycle built for two might as well as carry a third person, he urged the other *Fräulein* to sit sideways on the bar in front of him.

All went pretty well until the soldier turned his head to glance back at those of us who were watching. Not looking where he was going, he collided with a dog that was following along and crashed to the pavement with his two young female passengers. This marked the first occasion we employed our first-aid kits to patch up cuts and scrapes from a bike accident. To compensate the girls for their injuries, the soldier gave them the tandem bicycle.

But not all interaction between the men in our outfit and the local *Fräuleins* was so innocent. Whenever our machine-gun platoon spent the night in an abandoned home, one or more of the guys almost always brought back a local German girl who was ready to exchange her intimate favors for cigarettes, candy bars, or money. While such liaisons were frequent, only a minority of the men actually engaged in such activity. Far more rare were instances of American soldiers forcing German women to have sex, no doubt in part because of the harsh punishment meted out to GIs convicted of rape.

Later on the morning of April 15, H Company was ordered to form up in Sankt Andreasberg as if we were assembling for an inspection. This came as a surprise to us, since we had been expecting to receive orders to depart the town.

As our captain called us to attention, a beautiful German blonde stood at his side.

"This young lady has been raped. We'll walk up and down the lines to see if she can identify the man who did this," he announced.

The tension was palpable as she began scrutinizing the face of each soldier in our company in search of the guilty man. Rape was utterly abhorrent to me, but I was terrified at what might happen if she mistakenly fingered me as the rapist.

What if she points to me? What if she misidentifies me as the culprit? "There he is, that's the one," I imagined her telling the captain as my mind played out dark scenarios.

When the two of them passed in front of me, the girl looked me in the eye for a long second before moving on.

After her review of our company concluded, the captain expressed his pleasure that she had not identified anyone in our outfit as the guilty party. Needless to say, all of us were even more relieved than he was.

The end in the Harz: April 15–27

As soon as the 1st Battalion took over our positions in Sankt Andreasberg, we set out from the town, only to discover a long stretch of the road running eastward was blocked by freshly downed trees. Once the route was cleared to allow the passage of vehicular traffic, our 2nd Battalion began to make its way southeast.

Yet again, our advance was hindered by periodic ambushes from pockets of dug-in enemy forces. Ranging in size from a squad to a platoon, these German troops deployed machine guns, mortars, self-propelled guns, and other weapons, giving them substantial firepower. Despite Germany's dire military situation, the soldiers facing us certainly appeared to have no lack of ammunition.

By the night of April 15, our battalion had made good progress in its drive southeastward toward Hohegeiss, located some seven miles southeast of Sankt Andreasberg. With Hohegeiss and the larger neighboring town of Benneckenstein already in the hands of the 16th Infantry's 3rd Battalion, our 2nd Battalion used the next couple of days to secure the sector to the north of these towns, a process which sparked a few sharp, but brief firefights.

Early on the morning of April 18, our battalion launched a new attack through the Harz to clear the three or four miles of road leading north to the town of Elend. Supported by Shermans and tank destroyers, we advanced toward Elend in a steady light rain and dense fog, meeting varying degrees of resistance from the enemy forces posted along our route. Where the Germans did engage us, they got the worst of the fighting. Any survivors were usually ready to surrender.

On reaching Elend, which had already been captured by the Big Red One's 26th Infantry Regiment, our 2nd Battalion turned east toward the town of Rothehütte, with E, F, and G Companies advancing the three miles along parallel routes. Confronted by a German King Tiger tank along one of the routes, as well as three more Tiger tanks in Rothehütte, we had to obtain artillery support before we could move forward. After all the tanks had been eliminated or forced to retreat, we took control of Rothehütte on the night of April 18.

On April 19, we pressed eastward with E and G Companies another three and a half miles to the town of Rübeland, which had already been seized the previous day by the 1st Battalion. Following our steady advance through the Harz Mountains, word began filtering down that more than 300,000 German troops trapped in the Ruhr Pocket to the west had surrendered, further raising our hopes for Germany's imminent defeat.

By this point, German resistance in the Harz was completely disorganized and collapsing, but it still required another couple of days for us to clear the enemy's infantry out of the surrounding woods. Most of the German soldiers emerged from the forest unarmed and ready to give up. Once these men had been taken prisoner, my squad and I entered the woods to search foxholes for holdouts. Waving my pistol at these men, I simply directed them toward the rear. Nearly all the surrendering troops were extremely compliant. It was almost as if they were glad to have orders to follow, even if these came from the enemy.

During our five days in Rübeland, our 2nd Battalion captured hundreds of enemy prisoners. The fact that these came from several different corps within the *Wehrmacht* confirmed earlier intelligence that the enemy had been engaged in a desperate effort to assemble a major force in the Harz Mountains before our arrival. If the tens of thousands of German troops gathered here had been more effectively organized to defend the region, the seizure of the Harz would have been a far more challenging and costly operation.

On April 24, our 16th Infantry Regiment was relieved of its positions in the Harz and received new orders to occupy the towns around a place called Holdenstedt. To carry out its part of this operation, H Company boarded trucks early that morning for a more than 50-mile trip down to the town of Beyernaumberg, located roughly 30 miles southeast of Rübeland and a couple of miles west of Holdenstedt.

As our convoy was nearing its objective, the arrival of warmer spring weather brought a new sight. In the meadows alongside the road, sunbathing *Fräuleins* in swimsuits lay seductively on big blankets, practically inviting GIs to fraternize. When we reached Beyernaumberg late that morning, some of our guys slipped away to chat with the girls we had passed just outside of town. After flirting in a mix of English and German, many of these men visited the homes of these girls.

How does a guy know that a home isn't booby-trapped? Such cavorting with German girls still seemed risky to me, even if the war was so close to ending.

While some of our guys spent time with local *Fräuleins* in Beyernaumberg, we all took advantage of the break for some badly needed bathing and clothes washing. On our second day in the town, we learned from Armed Forces Radio that advancing American and Soviet forces had come together at Torgau on the Elbe River, just 70 miles east of our current position in Beyernaumberg. As the Allies won control over more and more of Germany, it was clear the Nazi regime could not hold on much longer.

Into Czechoslovakia: April 27–May 5

With the war "melting down" to its end, we were surprised to receive orders two days later for a new mission. By the afternoon of April 27, H Company was back aboard trucks travelling south.

After a tiring 150-mile, nine-hour journey, our company finally reached the Bavarian town of Selb, Germany, where we were welcomed by enemy soldiers sniping at us from the darkness. Located 95 miles south of Beyernaumberg, Selb had been designated as the 2nd Battalion's assembly area. As our battalion and the rest of the 16th Infantry Regiment collected around Selb, the 18th and 26th Regiments of the 1st Division were also gathering nearby. This positioned the Big Red One just across the border from the Sudetenland, a German-speaking region of Czechoslovakia annexed by Nazi Germany in the fall of 1938, less than a year before the start of the war.

On April 28, our second machine-gun platoon moved out from Selb in support of E Company. Pressing forward a half-dozen miles to the east, we crossed the old German-Czech border and entered the town of Haslau (today's Hazlov, Czech Republic) in the Sudetenland. Following the recent pattern, German troops fiercely contested our advance in some spots, but, elsewhere, others happily gave up. At one location, we came upon small groups of Germans sitting in the woods who had decided that the war was lost and were simply waiting for us to "capture" them.

While the *Wehrmacht*'s desperate need for troops had led to the conscription of many older Germans and foreigners less motivated to fight, the U.S. Army had also been experiencing a manpower shortage in its front-line units since at least the Battle of the Bulge. One measure taken to address these losses involved the transfer of Black American soldiers to formerly all-white combat outfits as replacements. Previously, Black troops had served in separate quartermaster and engineering units, so the integration of combat units marked a dramatic shift in what had been a segregated army. Even if it was intended as an expedient to augment our combat manpower, it made sense to me that Black Americans would now participate fully in the war in which our country was engaged.

As a result of this new policy, Black soldiers had begun transferring into H Company and our 2nd Battalion's infantry companies as replacements sometime around March, just before we crossed the Rhine. From among the 10 or so Black GIs received by H Company, a fellow named Jerry McClain had been assigned to our machine-gun squad, where he was treated like any other replacement. As with many other replacements who had passed through our squad, I had not immediately had much of an opportunity to get to know him.

That started to change when I found myself sharing a foxhole with McClain after we came under intense German artillery fire during the first day of our push into Czechoslovakia. In the middle of the furious bombardment, there was nothing for us to do but crouch down low in our hole and hope it would end soon. The shelling only lasted a few minutes, but it gave me my first chance to begin to bond with McClain. While we never became as close as my long-time buddies in the squad, Jerry did soon become a friend, the first Black friend I ever made.

On April 29, we moved deeper into a nearby forested area and came across a huge abandoned German roadblock located at the base of an intersection shaped like the letter "T." Constructed mainly of tall fir trees that had been felled across the road, the roadblock was reinforced with enormous boulders that had been bulldozed into place. With its command over all traffic coming from the left and the right, the roadblock provided our squad with the perfect gun position from which to prevent any enemy movement along the route.

Just after dawn the next day, two runners arrived to inform us that several of the brass were coming forward to inspect this unusually large roadblock.

A short time later, a group of about four officers and ten enlisted men came strolling down the road in our direction, laughing as they cracked jokes. All of the sudden, I noticed one of the officers had two white-handled pistols on his belt.

"Well, I'll be damned, that's General Patton," I exclaimed. All of the other guys joined me to get a look at the famous general, the commander of the U.S. Third Army.

Unfortunately, the officers never came close enough to our gun emplacement for us to meet Patton. After about half an hour, the officers departed, leaving behind the enlisted men in their party to eat breakfast with us. These GIs confirmed that General Patton had indeed been with the group. They also recounted his celebrated remark: "I am going to Berlin to shoot that paper-hanging SOB Hitler," a boast we all found amusing.

Views regarding the top brass were rarely discussed at the front, but Patton's boldness and love for being in thick of battle had earned our respect. Widely known as "Old Blood and Guts," the joke was that it was his guts and our blood. But knowing the fear he inspired in the enemy, our admiration for him ran deep.

General Omar Bradley presented an interesting contrast to Patton. In command of the 12th Army Group comprised of the U.S First and Third Armies, Bradley was also popular among the GIs, but for different reasons. Known as "the soldier's general," he truly cared about the lives and conditions of the men fighting on the front line.

Following the advances of April 28 to 29, our operations remained primarily defensive for the next few days. For now, our infantry companies actively patrolled the front line, while American artillery shelled enemy-held villages and towns nearby. Each day, hundreds of Germans continued to surrender, including more old soldiers and young kids. It was always fascinating to watch them lay down their arms and suddenly become quite friendly.

While halted at a location just behind the front line, my squad and I happened to be standing next to a large group of recently captured Germans. Six of these prisoners had been separated out and moved to a spot very close to us. Five of the six appeared to be afraid of us, but the other one was belligerent and full of malice, despite being small in stature. Out of the blue, this particular prisoner started haranguing me in German, delivering a furious tirade that I could not understand a word of.

Suddenly, the prisoner broke away from the other five and charged toward me, covering the short distance in a few strides. On reaching me, he viciously lashed out with his fingernails, clawing at my arms and chest through my field jacket.

More irritated than shaken by the attack, I realized something was strange about this enemy soldier with the boyish face. Dropping my tripod on the ground behind me, I clutched my assailant's uniform to shove him back.

To my astonishment, I was stunned to feel what seemed to be breasts under the soldier's tunic. Stepping back, I swung my pistol to knock the German's helmet off. The shoulder-length brunette hair that spilled out onto the prisoner's shoulders confirmed my suspicion. This "man" was actually a *Fräulein* in her early 20s.

"Fellas, I believe I've got a girl soldier here!" I proclaimed to a half-dozen of my buddies within earshot. As I pushed her away, she swung her arm back to slap me. Seeing what was coming, I managed to dodge the blow.

But my bemusement at the situation was short-lived. Like some kind of wild beast, the woman continued her savage assault, all the while fiercely cussing me out in German. Despite my efforts to hold her off, she soon managed to tear through my field jacket with her long, tiger-like claws.

As my buddy Wayne Newsome had demonstrated a month earlier when he had slapped the German *Frau* who had been berating the former slave laborer, he was not one to tolerate bad behavior from a German, especially when it was directed toward an American soldier. Circling around in front of me, Wayne slapped the girl's face with so much force that he nearly broke her neck. But in contrast to the submissive reaction of the other woman after her slapping, my female assailant quickly resumed her physical and verbal battering of me with renewed ferocity.

"Don't let her treat you like that, Andy!" Newsome shouted. "Kill her, Andy! Kill her! She's a Nazi! Shoot her right now! Don't let her claw you like that!" he exhorted.

"Kill her, Andy! Kill the bitch!" the other guys chimed in, goading me on.

It would have been easy to kill an enemy prisoner in this situation but taking the life of an unarmed woman or man was not an action my conscience would allow. Beyond considering such an act to be immoral, I also knew that shooting a prisoner would discourage other nearby enemy troops from surrendering. Even now, two Germans were giving up peacefully right behind her.

Still, I had put up with this girl's thrashing long enough. Quick as a flash, I slammed her temple just above her right eye with a hard blow from my .45 pistol held flat in my hand, causing her to collapse to the ground unconscious.

Noticing a small stick pin on her uniform, I bent down and removed it as a souvenir of my struggle with her. The lettering on the face of the pin read, "*Reichstreubund*" (*Reich* Loyalty Federation). Apparently, she was finding it difficult to accept the defeat of the Nazi regime.

The whole incident had not lasted more than four or five minutes but proved to be the most demanding hand-to-hand combat I experienced in the entire war.

Perhaps because my attacker had been a woman, it was also one of my most emotional moments.

It turned out that the other five prisoners with whom my assailant had been standing were also female soldiers. Coming forward, they helped their still groggy comrade to her feet before all of them were taken back further to the rear.

Though female German soldiers were not a common sight, a group of women prisoners of war was not particularly surprising by this point in the war. A few had been captured as early as Bonn, but we were now increasingly running into women who were fighting alongside their boyfriends and husbands. The challenge was trying to figure out how these women should be handled once they were taken prisoner.

Meanwhile, events elsewhere promised Germany's defeat in a matter of days. Some 150 miles to the north of us, the Red Army was completing its conquest of Berlin. Most of the GIs around me felt it should have been American troops who took the Nazi capital, despite recognizing how costly this prize would have been in terms of American blood. Whatever our feelings about the Soviet capture of Berlin, we all celebrated when the radio announced Adolf Hitler's suicide there on April 30.

A final push: May 5–8

Placed under the command of the U.S. First Army's V Corps on April 30, the Big Red One and the rest of V Corps were very shortly reassigned to General Patton's U.S. Third Army for a final offensive. Confronted with continued German resistance, the brass decided the *Wehrmacht* forces holding out in Czechoslovakia needed one last little push to force their surrender.

At the end of our weeklong halt in a holding position near Haslau, the 16th Infantry Regiment received orders on the afternoon of May 5 to reposition southeast about four miles to the town of Franzensbad (also known as Frant Lazne, today's Františkovy Lázně, Czech Republic) in preparation for the new offensive.

While we were in the last stages of packing up our jeep "Little Joe" for this move, the Germans unexpectedly began lobbing artillery rounds into the area. Leaping aboard the jeep and trailer, our squad took off across an open field with enemy shells exploding all around us.

As our jeep was bouncing across the field, a man came dashing toward us as fast as I had ever seen anyone run. Thinking he might be a German, we prepared to shoot him, but someone shouted that he appeared to be wearing a Red Army soldier's uniform. When the man caught up to our still moving vehicle, he stretched out his arm and one of our guys hauled him aboard.

Once the enemy artillery fire was behind us, we tried to learn more about our guest. The man spoke very little English but managed to convey that he was a Soviet soldier named Alex who had escaped from German captivity. Feeling a natural camaraderie with this Russian, we "adopted" Alex into our squad and he tagged along with us for the next couple of weeks.

The following damp, misty morning of May 6, our 16th Infantry Regiment joined other units launching the final attack, with all three of the regiment's battalions advancing abreast toward Falkenau an der Eger (today's Sokolov, Czech Republic), located roughly 14 miles east-northeast of Franzensbad.

As our machine-gun platoons and mortar platoon pressed forward in support of the 2nd Battalion's rifle companies, we remained alert for surprise attacks from our left and right flanks. Particularly at road junctions and village strongpoints, our advance ran into stubborn opposition from enemy troops firing small arms and machine guns. These forces included men of various ages from several German-occupied countries, who were augmented by small detachments of fanatical SS troops.

By the end of the day, our battalion had advanced several miles and taken numerous prisoners but was still some nine miles short of our objective of Falkenau. The ground already gained had cost us a number of casualties, a price that was increasingly difficult to justify as the war neared its end. Nonetheless, until the German forces capitulated, the pressure would be maintained.

Early on the morning of May 7, our attack thus resumed. But just a couple of hours later, orders came down the line to cease all offensive operations and hold fast at our current position. While these orders foretold an imminent end to the fighting, the German force that we faced refused to surrender and continued shooting at us. Yet even as we exchanged fire, some of the enemy troops were crossing our lines to give up.

Dug in around the machine gun, everyone in our squad kept to his foxhole, staying as low to the ground as possible whenever the need to move arose. With the chow jeep located about a hundred yards to the rear, all of us had to be especially careful not to expose ourselves to German snipers when it was our turn to head back for a meal. Knowing the war would soon end, none of us wanted to be one of the last men to die.

During one of my turns on gun duty, my buddy Chief came over to my foxhole and nudged me to gain my attention.

"Andy, do you see that German in that field over there?" he asked, pointing in the direction of a bull in the green pasture in front of us. My eyes scanned the field, but the only thing I observed was the bull peacefully grazing about 50 yards away.

"No, I don't see a German," I replied skeptically.

"I want you to look carefully. He's right over there in that field," Chief urged.

"I don't see anything but a bull," I said, wondering if he was imagining things.

"Did you ever see a bull with six legs?" he chided.

"Oh yeah!" I exclaimed, finally noticing an extra set of legs protruding under the bull's body. Since this enemy soldier was using the bull for cover in an effort to sneak up on our position, I was grateful for Chief's sharp eye.

"Watch this!" he announced. Taking careful aim with his carbine, Chief squeezed the trigger. The shot punched right through the bull, killing the concealed German, who fell dead on the far side. Meanwhile, the bull remained frozen like a statue, despite receiving a mortal wound.

Observing the shooting from his home 50 yards away, the bull's owner could not bear to let the animal go to waste. Within half an hour, the man arrived on the scene leading a horse harnessed to a big sled, apparently unconcerned for his own safety. Shoving the bull's carcass onto the sled, the man headed off to the slaughterhouse, leaving the body of the dead German soldier where he had fallen.

Mercifully, this was the last enemy soldier I saw killed in the war. Having fought across countless battlefields, all of us had witnessed more than enough death and destruction. Now, we anxiously awaited the promise of peace.

CHAPTER 20

Peace:
May 8–October 19, 1945

Taking the German surrender: May 8–June 8

When Nazi Germany's unconditional surrender became effective at 11:01pm Central European Time on Tuesday, May 8, we were holding our still active front-line position in Czechoslovakia. It took a little time for word to filter down to us that the war was at last over.

Beyond exulting in our survival and an end to the fighting and killing, we also experienced a tremendous psychological release at being free from the constant danger of someone shooting at us. Yet, the war's ragged ending matched our mood and we somehow just did not feel like celebrating. Whatever excitement we felt at the Allied triumph was tempered by a numbing emotional and physical fatigue as well as a deeper sense of loss for all our buddies who had given their lives to achieve this victory.

Over the course of the war, probably something like 30 different guys had served in our seven-man machine-gun squad, with more than half of those being killed or wounded. These losses rapidly multiply as one progresses from the level of squad to section, platoon, company, battalion, regiment, division, and larger unit formations. In the European Theater, our 1st Infantry Division alone suffered 15,374 casualties, including 3,307 battle deaths, but such tragic statistics do not even begin to measure the real human cost of the war.

Later, on May 9, orders came down for H Company and other elements of the 2nd Battalion to assemble at a location close to the town of Kynsperk on the Ohre River (also known in German as Königsberg an der Eger, today's Kynšperk nad Ohří, Czech Republic), about eight miles east of Franzensbad. Upon our arrival, a huge open field was swiftly converted into a temporary internment camp for enemy prisoners of war.

At first, the boundaries of the enclosure were delineated only by twine. If a German prisoner crossed the twine, he would be shot by one of our machine guns positioned at each corner, with each gun carefully situated so that our fire would not hit a fellow gunner. Recognizing the inadequacy of such poorly secured boundaries, Army engineers erected a barbed-wire fence around the site by the end of the day.

Soon, thousands of German soldiers began pouring out of the woods to hand over their weapons and surrender. If it was astonishing that the *Wehrmacht* still had so many men in the field, the large number of troops surrendering to us was partly due to the fact that all of the remaining German soldiers in the area were trying to reach American lines to give up. They greatly feared what would happen to them if they were captured by the Red Army, which now occupied territory very near our location.

Some of the Germans arrived aboard trucks, but most came on foot. Emerging from the surrounding forest, they gave themselves up individually or in small groups. In a few instances, entire units surrendered, bringing along a number of horses. Some of the German soldiers hauled wounded comrades in small wagons like those a child might possess. In contrast, their wounded officers were normally carried on improvised sleds, formed by a piece of canvas or blanket spread between two long branches.

Watching it all unfold from my machine-gun post near the compound's entry gate, I became engrossed in the progress of the mass surrender. We had been fighting these men just yesterday, but I found it impossible not to feel sympathy for our prisoners.

While most of the men's faces wore a blank expression that matched their vacant stare, some bore a more revealing mixture of exhaustion, fear, sadness, humiliation, and relief. Furtive glances toward the nearby American troops displayed their complete uncertainty about their future in the wake of Germany's defeat. At our mercy, they appeared to be thinking, *What's next for us?*

Unsurprisingly, a dozen or so uniformed female German soldiers arrived among the thousands of surrendering male troops. Just after the internment camp had been established, I overheard one of these women speaking with a GI posted at the entrance. In broken English, she explained that the man beside her was her husband and begged for permission to join him inside the camp.

Of course, it was impossible for females to remain inside the compound with the male prisoners, so the guard directed her to head up a dirt road with the other women. My heart went out to the German couple as they embraced in tears before separating, no doubt wondering if they would ever see each other again.

As the woman walked away in despair, a soldier from my machine-gun platoon approached her. I was out of earshot of their conversation, but it was clear to me from his gestures that he was offering her shelter. After a moment, she nodded her head in agreement and they headed off to the house where our platoon was billeted. As it turned out, a couple of other guys in my outfit had found local "girlfriends," so this woman would not be the only female in the house.

While attempting to sleep that night, I heard the young wife repeatedly fighting off the soldier who had offered her shelter. Over and over, he was trying to force himself on her against her will, threatening *"Ich schieße Sie"* ("I will shoot you") if she refused.

Listening to him bully this poor woman from my nearby spot on the floor, I knew I should intervene. Despite lacking any authority over this GI, I should get up and tell him to stop, pulling out my pistol if necessary. To my deep and lasting regret, I was so dog-tired that I simply failed to rouse the energy to stand up to this soldier. Thankfully, the woman eventually managed to escape him and flee the house.

The next morning, I angrily confronted the soldier about his brutish behavior.

"You're a lowdown, white-trash coward! You're not strong enough to get it on your own!" I shouted, hoping to shame him in front of the other men in the room.

Feeling guilty about what he had done, the GI turned away without responding. Later, I reported the incident, but, to my knowledge, nothing ever came of it.

As a Christian, this soldier's treatment of the woman made me ask myself, *How can God bless us with a clear victory with this kind of brutality going on?*

We had believed God was on our side as we fought to liberate Europe from Nazi tyranny, but I wondered what liberation meant if some of the men in our army were already abusing our position of power. Sadly, some American soldiers seemed to believe that, having conquered the Germans, whatever they had was ours to take.

By this time, we had started to get to know our new Russian comrade. While Alex did not exactly win our affection, he did turn out to be an interesting character with some different habits. For example, our latrine consisted of a long, raised board with a series of holes cut through it. When a GI needed to take care of business, he seated himself on the board above a hole, but Alex would instead step up onto the board and crouch down catcher-style over a hole. When we pointed this out, Alex laughed along with us, but I am not sure that he really understood what was funny.

Shortly after Alex joined us, we discovered he possessed an unusually bitter hatred toward the Germans, a sentiment I suspect was common among Red Army troops at that time. A couple of days after the war ended, Alex came up to a bunch of us as we were gathered around a table eating lunch. Holding up a large photograph of a teenaged German wearing a Hitler Youth uniform, he angrily jabbed his finger at the boy's picture. With one of our guys translating, Alex excitedly explained to us that this German teenager lived in a nearby house.

Later that day, I saw Alex hauling off this same teenager as the boy's mother stood on the porch weeping. Knowing Alex's hatred of the Germans, I deeply regret my failure to intercede and return the teenager to his mother. I never learned the boy's fate, but it seems very likely that Alex killed him. Not long afterward, Alex departed our outfit, presumably having been repatriated to the Red Army.

Our overall feelings toward our wartime Russian ally were mixed. Certainly, the Red Army had played a paramount role in Nazi Germany's defeat, but this did not mean we felt any great warmth toward the Soviet Union. Indeed, we distrusted the Russians, though none of us expected a war between the United States and the Soviet Union. Whatever our thoughts, we did not spend much time discussing such matters.

Our squad's main responsibilities were guard duty at the machine-gun post and patrolling the perimeter of the internment compound on foot, which was an easy job since none of our German prisoners were seeking to escape. We also carried out wider patrols of the sector around Kynsperk, during which we observed the Russians conducting similar patrols. Otherwise, our days were mostly filled with exercises to keep us in shape, close order drill, weapons maintenance, and kitchen duty. Fortunately, we had access to showers and were soon issued new uniforms, so our situation was certainly better than it had been in combat.

But conditions for the thousands of German prisoners crowded into the open-air camp soon became miserable, despite the U.S. Army's efforts to meet their basic needs. Beyond trucking in food as well as canvas tarps and wooden stakes to build shelters, the Army also supplied soccer balls and other recreational equipment.

Meanwhile, the Germans themselves worked to improve their living conditions: constructing simple shelters, digging latrines, and generally organizing the camp. After clearing a large piece of ground, they regularly played a rough version of soccer that turned the game into a full-contact sport. They also occupied themselves with card playing, exercising, and singing in harmony—and boy could those guys sing! Whatever their feelings about Germany's defeat, the men appeared to accept their internment as a temporary condition and put the war behind them.

The camp gave me my best chance yet to claim a Luger pistol, the prized war souvenir I had sought to acquire since D-Day. While on duty at our machine-gun post, I had spied the weapon that I wanted in the holster of a German lieutenant, but it was subsequently announced that *Wehrmacht* officers would be permitted to retain their side arms to help them keep order among the prisoners. This policy only further stoked my desire, but I was never able to find a GI willing to sell me a Luger. However, I did manage to trade the cigarettes I had collected from my rations for a smaller-bore German pistol, which was an especially great deal for me since I did not smoke.

By this time, we had learned of the Nazi concentration camps where millions of Jews and other innocent victims had been brutalized and murdered. Just before the end of the war, other elements of the 1st Infantry Division had helped liberate Zwodau and Falkenau an der Eger (today's Svatava and Sokolov, Czech Republic), two subcamps of the Flossenbürg camp located in Bavaria.

While Flossenbürg was more than two dozen miles south of Kynsperk, Zwodau and Falkenau an der Eger were only a few miles northeast of us. Hoping to visit one of these nearby subcamps, I put in a request to our captain through First Sergeant Huber. A day or two later, my request was denied. Our company was apparently too busy to be without all of its gunners, even for a short time.

Within a few days of the war's end, Army intelligence began taking two dozen prisoners at a time for brief interrogations in order to determine whether the men could be released. Observing the speed of this process, I wondered whether such cursory conversations could truly be effective in weeding out members of the Nazi Party or the SS from among the regular soldiers, but the Army's focus was on getting the processing done.

By the end of May, the Army began releasing some of the interned German troops, permitting them to return home to their families. Other prisoners were transferred to more permanent detention facilities inside Germany for additional interrogation and investigation. But while the German soldiers were starting to go home, the Army had other plans for our outfit.

Occupation duty in Bamberg: June 8–October 1

On June 8, the 16th Infantry Regiment concluded its postwar mission in Czechoslovakia. Motoring 75 miles west-southwest from Kynsperk, we arrived in the city of Bamberg in the Bavarian region of Germany for a long-term assignment on occupation duty. Beyond overseeing the local population, our initial responsibilities also included guarding several thousand German prisoners of war held in the city.

Despite Bamberg's many bombed-out buildings and bridges, the city's residents appeared to be making the best of their circumstances. Already, the streets had been largely cleared of rubble and many local businesses were reopening. Citizens were out strolling the streets with their children and dogs, giving the city a feeling of normalcy.

Billeted in a large boarding house taken over by the U.S. Army, we had access to showers, flushing toilets, and much better chow than what had been available during our months in combat. Ordered to make sure the American presence in the city "looked right" at all times, we observed strict dress codes. However, the Army's rules against fraternization with German civilians were now essentially lifted. After a few weeks, a "speaking and greeting" relationship developed with the locals, giving most of us our first real chance to get to know the German people in a more personal way.

As our own feelings toward the Germans softened, any hostility that citizens of a defeated nation might be expected to feel toward a foreign occupier also rapidly faded. While it is fair to say the Germans could do little about the occupation and so perhaps had to act halfway civil, Bamberg's residents came to treat us with genuine cordiality and there was never even a hint of tension in my encounters with them. My impression was that the Germans just wanted to forget about the war and move on with their lives.

Naturally, we wanted to put the war behind us as well. The Army announced the establishment of the ASR (Advanced Service Ratings) Points System to determine the order by which troops would ship back to the States for discharge from the armed forces. Points were awarded to a soldier based on his number of months in service, his number of months overseas, his number of decorations, the number of campaigns in which he had fought, and the number of children under 18 he had back home.

Before long, many of the long-serving veterans in our ranks began departing for the States, their spots being filled by a steady stream of new replacements. Despite close to two years in the service and nearly a year in combat, I was still 11 points short of the 85 points necessary to return home in June 1945. With the cessation of the accumulation of points as of May 12, 1945, it was unclear how long I would remain in the Army.

For those of us who remained on occupation duty, our hopes of returning home crowded out any fears we might have of transferring to the Pacific Theater for the invasion of Japan. But if it was simply impossible for us to imagine that we would again be called upon to fight on the other side of the world, the rumor mill churned out a steady stream of gossip about our impending reassignment to the Pacific.

With all the 1st Infantry Division's incoming replacements, the Army might well conclude it needed to retain an experienced cadre of veterans. A leavening of battle-tested troops would be essential if the Big Red One was going to participate in the invasion of Japan, a campaign that was certain to be savage. German troops had generally surrendered when the jig was up, but we were told Japanese soldiers were fanatical, fighting until they killed you or you killed them.

After surviving months of combat in Europe, none of us had any desire to risk our lives anew, but we would not have a choice if orders came for our redeployment to the Pacific. I thought the odds of this happening were about 50/50, but that was just a guess. In the meantime, we continued to conduct close order drill, carry out weapons maintenance, and watch training films at night. There was also an ongoing program of physical exercise to keep us in shape, including long marches around Bamberg.

Since our military duties were limited, plenty of time remained for us to relax and wander around the city. I occasionally spent time with my fellow squad members Wayne Newsome, Lincoln Welser, Hector Gonzalez, and Chief, but my main circle of buddies was now First Sergeant Huber, Private Painter, and a fellow named Bob Lane, who stood out because he was at least six feet tall. During our outings to Bamberg's shops and small stores, local kids always tagged along, trying to engage us in conversation. Though the language barrier made real communication difficult, there was always plenty of laughter to fill the gaps.

While rarely eating out in the city's restaurants, we did regularly patronize one newly opened ice-cream shop. With its quaint round tables, wire-backed chairs, and pictures of large ice cream cones and hefty mugs of chocolate sodas, the establishment's ambience and aroma reminded me of an old-fashioned drugstore soda fountain back home. As we enjoyed its ice cream, ice cream sodas, and chocolate milkshakes, the elderly gentleman who worked behind the counter would often chat and laugh with us. His friendliness was pretty typical of what we encountered in Bamberg's shops, though this warmth was not always immediately evident.

When our group visited a local photographer's studio, the proprietor's ability to speak English at first appeared to be rather limited. However, his language skills seemed to show sudden improvement as soon as we asked to have our studio portraits made. Once he learned that we also wanted enlargements, his English became even better. The proprietor ultimately turned into a friend after I told him about my German ancestry.

In addition to having my portrait made, I also had quite a few of my own photographs developed in his studio. Having recently acquired a camera, I roamed around Bamberg snapping pictures of the bomb damage to the city's buildings and bridges as well as taking shots of some of my buddies.

In the evening, my free time was mostly spent watching movies, writing letters, and reading, but a number of guys in our outfit dated local German girls. At the time, I was unaware of any GIs from our unit being involved in more serious romantic relationships with the city's *Fräuleins*, but I later learned my buddy Lincoln Welser became very attached to a German girl who worked in the U.S. Army PX in Bamberg.

Occupation duty in the city was far from unpleasant, but the purpose of our presence seemed increasingly unclear. Within a couple of months of our arrival, most of the German prisoners of war in our custody had been released, leaving only 500 or 600 men under guard. And Bamberg's residents certainly posed no threat.

"Why are we here?" we began to ask. But with no real say in the matter, all of us sought to make the best of the situation while we awaited new orders.

Paris and Yeovil

One thing I wanted to do was to see more of Europe, especially Paris. Having passed just south of Paris in late August 1944 and spent a month recovering from shoulder surgery in a military hospital at nearby Étampes from late November to late December, I looked forward to visiting the city itself. In late July, a number of us received three-day passes to travel to Paris. Paired with another GI from H Company, the two of us made the 400-mile train trip from Bamberg.

Paris lived up to its dazzling reputation, with beautifully lit streets, blooming flowers overflowing their huge pots, elaborately dressed shop windows, and music playing from loudspeakers outside its stores. Most amazing to me were the open-air urinals located along the street with only "courtesy walls" to provide some limited privacy. While men entered and exited these outdoor toilets, their ladies pretended to be interested in window shopping. The Parisians made it all seem very natural.

After dropping off our bags in our assigned room at a hotel reserved for American soldiers, we headed back outside to see more of the city. Reaching a corner half a block from our hotel, we began studying our map to figure out where to go.

While we were standing there, a couple of attractive young women approached us from the direction of a small hotel nearby.

"*Zig-zig?*" they sweetly inquired, issuing an invitation for sex in the contemporary slang without first even offering so much as a "*Bonjour.*" Pointing to their hotel, they repeated the words "*Zig-zig?*" just to be certain we got their meaning. No doubt they saw us as easy marks who could pay in highly prized dollars.

"Yeah, yeah, yeah! C'mon, Andy!" my fellow GI exclaimed, enthusiastically embracing their proposition.

"No, no. Not for me," I declared, shaking my head. But when I waved the girls away and started to head off, the guy grabbed my shoulder and pulled me aside.

"Man, this is our chance!" he pleaded in an effort to persuade me.

"It's a chance to get syphilis," I retorted.

"I don't think so," he protested, though the look of concern on his face made me skeptical that he really believed what he was saying.

"You don't know," I cautioned, trying again to get him to consider the risk. "I'm not interested. Go ahead. I'll wait for you," I told him, since we had to stay together.

"Wait a minute, Andy! Wait a minute! We are missing a fantastic opportunity. Here is our opportunity to have sex!" he implored.

"You've got a hotel full of whores and you can go if you want to," I said bluntly.

"Sex in Paris!" he kept repeating in the vain hope of changing my mind. Finally, after a couple of minutes, he gave up and sent the girls away, making it clear to them that I was the one who was turning down their offer.

But this fellow still would not let the issue rest. "I can't believe this. We have missed our opportunity," he kept saying over and over. Later that day, as we were sitting in a coffee shop, he vented his frustration at me.

"You know, Andrews, you're a real horse's ass."

"I know it, but I am a free horse's ass. I have my conscience. I've made my decision on that subject and I'm not changing," I explained. As we drank a good cup of hot chocolate, I shared my Christian faith, the source of my convictions regarding pre-marital sex. He seemed to respect my position and let the matter drop.

With that behind us, we spent the remainder of that day and the ensuing day sightseeing. Between wandering around Paris on foot and taking a bus tour, we managed to visit the Eiffel Tour, the Cathedral of Notre Dame, and the Louvre Museum. Less than a year after the city's liberation from the Germans, the Parisians themselves appeared to go about their business like the war had never happened.

On August 6, about a week after my return to Bamberg from Paris, we learned that the United States had dropped an atomic bomb on the Japanese city of Hiroshima. At first, none of us had any idea what an atomic bomb was or the true significance of the event. We only knew that the bomb was an incredibly powerful weapon that had caused enormous devastation. Three days later, word came that a second bomb had been dropped on Nagasaki.

On August 15, we received the thrilling news of Japan's surrender. We would not be sent to the Pacific to invade Japan! World War II was over!

Even as we found out more about the horrific consequences of the atomic bombs, none of us questioned the use of a weapon that had helped to bring an early end to the war. At the end of our occupation duty in Germany, we would be headed home.

Later in August, I was awarded a seven-day pass based on my length of service with the 1st Infantry Division. With this much leave time, I decided to return to England to visit the West family. Luckily, I was able to hitch a free ride aboard a U.S. Mail plane flying out of a U.S. Army Air Force base in Germany.

Landing in London, I caught a lift to a U.S. Army base near Yeovil. The following day, I began a grand and fun-filled reunion with the West family. With Captain West and one of his fellow British officers at home for the weekend, the three of us exchanged war stories of battles, close calls, wounds, and the like. While most of my leave was spent catching up with the West family, I also paid a visit to my old friend Bert Chapman and his wife, which included lots of talk about fly fishing and beekeeping that made me miss home.

When I returned to Bamberg from England, all the remaining H Company veterans were increasingly impatient to receive their military orders to return home. As of September 2, 1945, the Army modified its points system that determined when soldiers were eligible to ship back to the States for demobilization, cutting the critical score for enlisted men from 85 to 80 points. Not long afterward, the required score was further lowered to 75 points.

With 74 points, I was now just one point short and expected that a further reduction was imminent. My spirits were further boosted by a fantastic piece of news that I received in a letter from my dad. My four brothers had all survived the war! Karl, Don, Bennett, Bill, and I would soon be going home to our family.

Traveling back to the States: October 1–October 12

On October 1, 1945, the Army reduced the critical point score to 70 points and issued my long-awaited orders to ship out. The other departing veterans and I were one excited bunch of soldiers as we set off from Bamberg's railway station toward France and home. With plenty of sandwiches to eat, we joked that our only concern now was that our train might derail at some forlorn spot in the middle of nowhere.

At the end of a roughly 650-mile rail journey, we disembarked at the U.S. Army's Camp Calas near the French port city of Marseilles, a staging area for troops shipping back to the United States. Established on a large piece of open ground, the camp was filled with hundreds of good-sized tents, each furnished with four cots.

After stowing our gear in our tents, we made use of the camp's bathhouse, checked out the PX, and enjoyed some really decent chow in the "dining hall" tent. Once these basic needs were met, there was not a lot else for us to do. While the Army had provided the camp with recreational facilities like Club Lamas, heavy rains made our two-day stay primarily an adventure in muck.

On the morning of October 4, a convoy of trucks delivered us to the harbor of Marseilles, where the USS *Mount Vernon* was docked. Tramping up to the top of our troopship's gangplank in mud-caked boots, we stepped onto the shiny deck of the former luxury ocean liner. Met by U.S. Navy sailors in spotless white uniforms, we were escorted down to our quarters. The sailors did not comment on our grimy appearance, but I am sure they were not particularly impressed.

Accommodations for the 6,000 GIs aboard the *Mount Vernon* were infinitely superior to those we had experienced on the *Île de France* on our way over to Scotland more than a year and a half earlier. The meals were good and the desserts were even better. Equally important, everything on the ship was clean and no toilets were overflowing. Of course, the absence of any German U-boats was an added bonus.

Our primary entertainment was supplied by daily talent shows, which were held out on deck in the sunshine. While many GIs with some type of skill performed for us, a particularly gifted harmonica player turned out to be the real star. Teaming up with a guitarist, he regaled us with a rendition of "The Fox and Hound" that had everyone howling with laughter and wildly applauding. Our repeated calls for an encore brought the duo back out on stage over and over.

On October 12, after an eight-day, roughly 4,500-mile voyage from Marseilles to New York City, an announcement was broadcast over the ship's loudspeakers.

"Attention all soldiers! This is the captain speaking. Our observers on the top deck have reported to me that the landmass of America is in sight."

With those magical words, I began weeping like a little boy. Around me, hundreds of tough, battle-hardened men were crying and hugging complete strangers as if they had been lifelong friends. More men swarmed up on deck from their quarters down below and the jubilant celebration grew even louder and more boisterous. Clapping and hollering, everyone flocked to the rails trying to catch sight of "the land of the free." I honestly do not know how the *Mount Vernon* did not capsize.

Our emotional outburst was a pent-up, cathartic release from all we had witnessed and endured during the war. The announcement that home was so close seemed to mark the true end of slogging forward and living in foxholes; the end of fighting in mud, dust, freezing rain, and snow; the end of killing and seeing our buddies die; and the end of that constant haunting fear that sooner or later amid battle's noise and clamor, a bullet or shard of white-hot shrapnel would find its way to you.

We had survived! Praise God!

An hour after alerting us that America was in sight, the captain made a second announcement to the thousands of us cramming the rails.

"Get on deck if you can. We are going to see the Statue of Liberty." Somehow, even more men now squeezed toward the rails of the *Mount Vernon* for a look.

As our ship eased into the harbor, we thrilled at the sight of thousands of people crowding the pier four stories below us. Waving American flags of every size, they presented a fluttering mass of red, white, and blue. Up and down the docks, bands were playing, people were shouting greetings, and women were blowing us kisses. Everywhere there were signs like "Welcome Home Yanks" and "Good Job Boys."

Tears of joy did not stop. Answering my mother's prayers, God in His grace had spared me from death on the battlefield countless times. Delivering me safely home, I believed God had refreshed my soul and given my life a higher purpose.

This is America. This is my country for which I have been fighting. God has been so good to me. If He has brought me back to this free country, I am going to use every opportunity I can to tell young people about His grace and protective care, what freedom really means, what they need to learn and be and do in order to keep the Star-Spangled Banner flying high over the land of the free and the home of the brave.

My patriotic reverie was interrupted by a band just below us playing "Boogie Woogie Bugle Boy." It went on to perform other popular hits like "Jersey Bounce, Cow Cow Boogie," and "Chattanooga Choo Choo."

After an hour of these festivities, the ship's loudspeakers announced we would begin our disembarkation. Upon our eventual arrival at the bottom of the gangplank, we were ushered over to a young man and young lady in blue and white uniforms who worked for the Bell Telephone Company. They informed us Bell would allow each soldier to make one free phone call, a gracious offer that was much appreciated since most of us were not carrying any change.

Claiming a spot in one of the several snaking queues, I awaited my turn to place a call from one of about four dozen phone booths. Despite lines up to three or four blocks long, I did not mind the wait. Just the simple act of standing on American soil again was profoundly satisfying. The anticipation of talking with my family made the moment that much more exhilarating.

When my turn finally came, I was so excited I was shaking. As soon as I picked up the phone, an operator's friendly voice came on the line.

"Welcome home, soldier, where are you calling?"

"Signal Mountain, Tennessee, ma'am, to the residence of E. A. Andrews."

After a few short rings my mother answered. It was fantastic to hear her voice.

"Is this Mrs. Andrews?" I asked.

"Yes," she responded somewhat hesitantly.

"Mom, this is your son Ernest calling from New York City. We've just arrived and I'll be home in a few days."

The line went silent as my mother began to cry.

"Thank you God, hurry home!" she at last whispered through her tears.

Overcome with emotion, she could not say much else, so I asked her to phone my dad at his print shop, since I could only make one call. Before hanging up, I told my mom I loved her and would see her soon.

Discharge from the Army: October 12–19

Departing New York by train from Grand Central Station, we traveled 35 miles to Camp Kilmer in Piscataway, New Jersey, for a short period of debriefing and review of our records. Each of us also received a new uniform for the unit to which we would be temporarily attached for our discharge from the U.S. Army. I was assigned to Company C, 27th Armored Infantry Battalion.

Once our processing was completed, we headed to the mess hall for a special dinner. To welcome us back, we were treated to an American feast of steak, mashed potatoes and gravy, biscuits, apple pie, and ice cream. Some of the other GIs left the table without finishing the meal, but I cleaned my plate. After all those months in the field subsisting on cold Army rations, I was not about to let one bite of such fine food go to waste.

The next day, I joined other demobilizing troops for the roughly 700-mile rail journey from Camp Kilmer to Camp Atterbury in Edinburgh, Indiana. As our train rolled down the tracks, I gazed out the window at the passing American farms, towns, and rivers, reflecting on how amazing it was to be back in the States.

At Camp Atterbury, we began the last phase of our separation from the U.S. Army. The most interesting part of my final two days of processing turned out to be a brief interview conducted by an Army clerk. Seated at a desk behind a typewriter, this young kid had been tasked with preparing a short record of my Army experience.

"Tell me about what you've been doing," he inquired in a casual tone, as if he was asking what I had been up to the previous weekend. "What did you do?"

"What do you mean, what did I do?" I responded, confused by his question.

"What did you do?" he repeated without offering any further clarification.

"Well, I killed a lot of people … I was a machine gunner. I've been on the front for 11 months and was wounded several times. What else do you want to know?" I queried, still unsure what he wanted from me.

The clerk typed up what I had said, though it was obvious this kid could not conceive of killing anybody or the larger brutality, terror, and tragedy of war.

"Well, give me some information. Did you go to high school?" he asked.

"Yes, I went to high school," I confirmed. He typed in the information.

"What did you study in high school?"

"English, algebra, general science, biology, sociology, history, manual training, and music," I explained.

"I'm not even going to try to type that in," he declared. Perhaps there was not enough space in that section of the form.

"You were a machine gunner?" he continued, returning to my earlier response.

"Yes, that's right."

"What did you do?" he probed, repeating the earlier question.

"Well, I just had a whole lot of fun."

"No, no, seriously. Did you load the machine gun?"

"Yes, I loaded the machine gun."

He dutifully typed that onto the page.

"Did you clean the machine gun?"

"Yes."

"Did you fire the machine gun?"

"Yes."

"Did you aim your weapon at the enemy?"

"Yes."

"Did you ever shoot at the enemy?"

"Yes."

"How many of the enemy did you see?"

"A lot."

Through such perfunctory questioning, the clerk eventually obtained the necessary information for his report on my military service. It stated, "Heavy machine gunner: Loaded, aimed, fired, and maintained care of gun for fire power in breaking through enemy positions. Also set sights and estimated ranges."

That interview was only one element of our demobilization processing. In addition to receiving a couple of new immunizations to prevent who-knows-what disease, I had a final medical evaluation.

As the Army physician reviewed my paperwork, he confirmed I had been wounded in the left cheek in Normandy, had developed a frostbitten left hand during the Bulge, and been hit twice in my right shoulder, first by a piece of grenade shrapnel at Hill 232 and later by another shrapnel fragment near Bonn. The even earlier shrapnel wound to my right shoulder that had occurred during the fighting at the bunker near Eilendorf was not included in his paperwork, probably because it did not require significant medical attention. It was therefore not a part of our ensuing discussion.

"What hit you in your right shoulder the second time?" the doctor inquired, referring to the wound I had received during combat near Bonn.

"I was hit by the butt end of a grenade," I explained, without going into detail.

"You've got four wounds. So why don't you have another Purple Heart if you got hit a fourth time?"

"I don't know. I just didn't report it," I replied.

"Soldier, if you got injured, you get credit," he declared.

Going into more detail about my injuries, I explained that the Army had not even initially counted the bullet wound to the left corner of my mouth as a war wound, though it had caused the severe infection in the left side of my face that necessitated my medical evacuation to England at the end of July 1944. The Army only officially credited it as a wound a month later. Since that bullet wound had not at first been deemed a war wound, I questioned whether the Army would count the second injury to my right shoulder, a wound that had not even required me to visit to an aid station.

"Well, I do. You're getting a Purple Heart for it, do you understand that?" he declared, as he completed the paperwork to give me a belated fourth Purple Heart.

"Yes sir, whatever you say," I assented. As a result, my Purple Heart for my first wound ended up with three oak leaf clusters for my three subsequent wounds.

Our separation processing also included an inspection of our war souvenirs to determine whether any of the items were contraband. As I had anticipated, the officer confiscated my German pistol, which he placed in a box with firearms removed from other soldiers' collections. It was hard for me not to feel a little dubious about the ultimate fate of the best souvenirs in that box, but I did not protest. Indeed, I was very pleased that I was permitted to retain all of my other two dozen or so war souvenirs: the three beautiful German daggers, the knife with a deer-foot handle, the Nazi flag and diadem liberated from the women's sewing committee, the small Nazi *Reichstreubund* badge taken from the female soldier who had attacked me, three German military compasses, artillery field glasses, a small flag from a German command car, and several German medals.

With my final demobilization processing completed, I received my official honorable discharge from the U.S. Army, which included a resume of my military service. Since the start of my basic training on July 7, 1943, I had been on continental service inside the United States for six months and 17 days. Departing the United States on January 17, 1944, and returning on October 12, 1945, I had been on foreign service for one year, eight months, and 26 days, participating in the Normandy, Rhineland, Ardennes, and Central Europe campaigns.

During the 11 months that stretched between D-Day, on June 6, 1944, and the end of the war in Czechoslovakia on May 8, 1945, I was in combat as a machine gunner for about nine months. For the remainder of those 11 months, I spent approximately six weeks in the hospital on three separate occasions and about 10 days on kitchen duty at different points while waiting for replacement pairs of glasses to reach me.

On my arrival at Camp Atterbury, I possessed about $300 in cash that I had saved from my monthly salary over the previous two years. This salary had varied from $50 while I had been on active duty in the States, to $65 once I arrived in England, to $75 when I was in combat, and back to $65 once the fighting ended. However, I had requested that a portion of my pay be sent directly to my parents to help them meet the mortgage for the new home they were building on Signal Mountain. On top of that, the U.S. Government had matched the first $25 per month I had sent back to my family with another $25. My four brothers had done the same thing with their military pay, so the money my parents received from us each month had been a substantial sum.

As a final parting gift, the Army issued me a shirt, pants, jacket, and cap. I also received $100 in mustering-out pay as well as another $19 to cover the cost of my travel expenses from Camp Atterbury to Chattanooga, Tennessee. When added to my other cash, I left the Army with over $400 in my pocket, a tidy sum worth roughly $5,000 in contemporary dollars.

Homeward bound: October 19

Boarding a chartered bus on the morning of October 19, I took a seat among 50 or so other happy new civilians bound for homes in Kentucky, Tennessee, Georgia, and Florida. It was roughly a 450-mile trip to Chattanooga, so I sat back to enjoy the ride.

Two dozen miles out of Camp Atterbury, our bus pulled over to the side of the road and the driver opened the door. An unsavory character stepped aboard to announce he could provide us with faster transportation home via his unmarked taxi. Of course, this taxi driver charged a special fare for this service, a fee from which the bus driver no doubt received a kickback. Two guys from our bus departed with the taxi driver, but I thought it was despicable to make a quick buck off war veterans trying to get home as fast as possible.

Once we were back on the road, the mood on the bus turned reflective. Staring out the window, I started thinking about my homecoming, wondering what to expect when I saw my family for the first time in almost two years.

That afternoon, as we were traveling the last hundred miles between Knoxville and Chattanooga, the bus driver announced to the roughly 30 of us still on board that we were stopping for an early supper. It was an unanticipated, but much appreciated, pit-stop where we could stretch our legs, grab something to eat, and use the restroom.

When our bus pulled into a nondescript roadside diner, we were not expecting much, but at least the picture of a hamburger on the door looked appealing. Entering the establishment, most of us claimed bar stools at the counter. Others took seats in chairs with uneven legs at one of the diner's wobbly tables.

As our food was cooking, I just happened to glance toward the screen door at the back of the diner. Waiting alone outside was Jerry McClain, the same Black soldier with whom I had shared a foxhole back in Czechoslovakia. Although there had not been enough time for us to become really close friends, he was a war buddy whom I liked.

While I had failed to notice the sign about segregated service posted in front of the establishment, Jerry had not missed it. Like nearly all restaurants in the South, this diner prohibited its Black patrons from eating their meals inside the restaurant, requiring them instead to obtain their food out the back door. But instead of using the conventional "WHITES ONLY" wording on the sign, this diner's sign read

"NO *NEGROES*"—but with an explicitly racist word for Negroes. The use of this slur seemed intentionally designed to convey open racial hostility toward Black folks, though a "WHITES ONLY" sign would have been painful enough to any Black person.

A pang of conscience came over me. McClain was an American soldier who had fought for his country and for freedom. Now, his country, in this restaurant, would not grant him the simple freedom to sit with his fellow veterans to enjoy a hamburger.

Gaining the attention of three or four other members of our group nearby, I quietly expressed my concern.

"Guys, there's something wrong here. There is a guy at the back door who was in a foxhole with me who can't come in here and order."

The injustice and absurdity of the situation hit home as we heatedly discussed the matter up and down the bar stools and around the tables.

A hulking buddy sitting beside me rallied to Jerry's defense.

"Well, I tell you what let's do neighbors, let's tell the owner to let that Black soldier in here or we'll tear this place all apart!"

"Hey, hey, let's not cause any trouble," I cautioned, anxious that things were getting out of hand. Another fellow in our group reminded everyone that this was the South and the owner had a right to set the rules on his property the way that he wished.

As some of us were working to calm the situation, the owner of the diner pulled out a .45 pistol from behind the counter.

"I own this place and I can do whatever the hell I want to. And, if anybody don't like it, I'll shoot 'em!" he exclaimed. Despite his menacing language, I did not really believe he was threatening us so much as defiantly proclaiming his right to post whatever sign he wanted about who could eat in his diner, however offensive that policy might be.

If the owner had actually shot and killed a soldier returning home, it would have been a big deal, but a jury of his Southern peers would likely have found him guiltless. The owner's armed response to our demand for equal treatment for a Black soldier was extreme, but most people in this part of the country strongly supported segregation and would judge his defense of it acceptable. The law was on his side.

After a long moment of tension in which everyone in the diner fell silent, the owner put his pistol away. Feeling powerless to do anything, I took my hamburger and drink to Jerry at the back door. He said he understood the situation, explaining he had grown accustomed to such treatment before the war. Things had not changed.

Thinking back on this incident over the ensuing years, I deeply regretted Jerry's treatment, asking myself how I would have felt if the restaurant had posted a "BLACKS ONLY" sign and I had been the one standing humiliated at the back door. While I had grown up with segregation, our fight for freedom against the Nazis made me question that way of life.

An hour later, as our bus was traveling down the final stretch of rural highway toward Chattanooga, a fellow sitting near me spoke up.

"Hey, driver, at the next little road to the right, I want you to stop. That's my road," he announced.

Grabbing his Army backpack out of the overhead storage rack, the guy made his way up to the door at the front. As the bus began braking to a stop at the dirt road, he could not contain his excitement and turned to speak to us.

"Y'all see that light up there? That's my house at the end of the road. I ain't got no daddy, but my mama's waiting on me!"

As he stepped off the bus and trotted off down the narrow, dusty road, all of us applauded the man's safe return home to his mother. When our bus got back on the highway, the eyes of every hardened veteran aboard were wet.

The Postwar Years:
October 19, 1945–April 22, 2016

Back on Signal Mountain: October 19, 1945–Spring, 1946

Early that evening, we pulled into the main bus terminal in downtown Chattanooga. While the friends and family members of some of the men had gathered to welcome home their loved ones, no one was waiting for me since I had not been able to notify my parents of my arrival ahead of time.

After retrieving my backpack, I thanked the bus driver and began walking the dozen blocks to my dad's shop. Some of the city's businesses were already starting to close up for the day, but not Andrews Printing Company.

When I came through the door, Dad was going full force, feeding papers into the printing press with that practiced easy motion. Hearing the rattle of the glass from the closing door, he looked up from his work. As soon as he realized it was me, his face lit up with a big smile. Shutting off the press, he bounded toward me across the floor.

"God brought him home! God brought him home!" he cried, throwing his arms around me in a tight bear hug. As we embraced, it surprised me how much bigger I was than him. But though he appeared leaner and shorter than I recalled, he was my same old dad. After nearly two years, both of us found it hard to believe I was home. My four brothers would soon be returning as well, but I was the first one to make it back.

Using the phone in his shop, I rang our house up on Signal Mountain.

"Hey, Mom, it's Ernest. I'm at Dad's shop and will be catching the next bus to the Mountain."

"Oh, thank you Lord! Thank you Lord!" she exclaimed.

After chatting with Dad for a few minutes, I left the shop and headed to the nearby bus stop to wait for one heading up to Signal Mountain. As I thought back to the fellow on our bus who had been so thrilled to return to his mother, the idea of not having a father tugged at my heart. How much that soldier had missed by not having a dad like mine who loved him and was waiting for him to come home.

To this day, I deeply regret my failure to ever adequately thank my dad for all his marvelous words of support in the letters he had written me throughout the war.

They meant everything to me, conveying my family's continuing love and prayers for me and keeping me connected to my community and my church.

On the bus ride up to Signal Mountain, it was a real thrill to see the familiar sights along the winding route. Half an hour later, I exited the bus and briskly walked the last few blocks to our family's home on Fairmont Avenue just as the last light of day was fading from the sky.

Mom was waiting for me at the top of the steps with tears in her eyes. Overcome with emotion, neither of us could say much, but there was no need for words. We simply embraced each other and quietly thanked God for this blessing of being together again. Later that evening, I had another happy reunion with my younger sister Peggy.

A day or so after my arrival, my mother remembered there was a package for me from Europe stored in a closet. On checking inside, I instantly recognized the tablecloth in which I had mailed the double-barreled .30-30 hunting rifle that had been given to me by the German man who did not want it destroyed. Having forgotten about the rifle, I had never really imagined this fine souvenir would make it all the way home. Seeing it again, I felt profoundly grateful to the U.S. Army's postal service.

If I was surprised the package had made it back, it was even harder for me to accept that I was really home after two years away. I had sorely missed my friends, the members of my church, and all the other hometown folks. Over the ensuing weeks, I wandered all over Signal Mountain just to look at the houses that had been a part of my life when I was growing up, images that had often filled my dreams at the front.

As I settled into home, it was a challenge to adjust to the quietness and slow pace of civilian life. After experiencing rough conditions on the front line and witnessing the far worse plight of Europe's starving, homeless refugees, the war had taught me to be deeply grateful to God for the simple blessings of hot water, soap, a dry towel, clean clothes, good hot food, and a roof over my head at night.

The next few weeks were a blur of more happy reunions as my brothers returned home. Bennett arrived about a month after me. He had spent the war as his company's bugler as well as the driver for his company commander. Chauffeuring his commander and other officers turned out to be only part of his job as a driver. For much of the war, he was jeeping around Europe to hunt up wine cellars for the brass to liberate, though he had also found time to fish the trout streams of Bavaria.

A month after Bennett's arrival, Don came home after completing his service as an Army paratrooper. In comparing experiences, we discovered that Don's outfit had fought near mine during the Battle of the Bulge. He had suffered wounds in his leg and in his arm that were pretty severe, though not life-threatening. Since none of our other three brothers had seen combat, the two of us gave them a hard time.

My younger brother Bill was discharged from the Navy just after Don's return. A guy who found humor everywhere, Bill's time aboard a warship in the South Pacific gave him lots of material. In one story, he recounted how every time he and a buddy had tried to sit down or lean against the wall to have a snack, some sailor with a can of paint would approach them. "Pardon us, Mac, but we gotta paint where you're sitting."

My oldest brother Karl had been the first of us to enter military service and was the last to leave it. While serving as an Army quartermaster at Camp Carson near Colorado Springs, he met a girl who he went on to marry. Karl and his new wife decided to live in Colorado following the war, but he traveled back to Signal Mountain after his discharge to join our family for several days of celebration of our safe return.

While my brothers were returning home, my mother was voted Tennessee Mother of the Year for 1945 and was invited to attend the national meeting of State Mothers of the Year in Washington, D.C. The national title was ultimately won by a lady from another state, but my mom was elected runner-up, which was still a great honor.

Moving on from the war: Spring, 1946

Over the days and weeks that followed a family dinner celebrating our return, my brothers and I sometimes discussed our travels during the war, but rarely spoke about actual combat. Interestingly, my parents never once asked my brothers or me about the war. Perhaps they were trying to respect our privacy or simply just did not wish to know any of the horrible things we had witnessed or experienced.

For my brothers and me, it was not so much that talking about the war made us uncomfortable, but rather that we were busy swapping ideas about our future plans. Whatever challenges came with the return of peace, we were blessed to be able to move on with our lives. With tens of millions killed in the war, countless other families around the world were far less fortunate, including a number on Signal Mountain.

Very late in the war, I had received a letter passing along news of the death of my best friend from home. Apparently, an aircraft had malfunctioned during takeoff and crashed on top of him. Two other friends of mine from Signal Mountain had also been killed in the war, likewise depriving their families of sons and brothers.

The profound grief of each family was beyond measure, a microcosm of the anguish felt by so many. Looking back, I cannot understand why I never visited the parents of my friends who had been killed to offer my condolences. I certainly owed the families that much, however little consolation I might have provided.

My sister told me the War Department's notification telegrams had been personally delivered to each family's door by men driving specially marked Western Union cars. When these vehicles came around, a somber mood would descend on the community and neighbors would gather at the home to support the family. If the family had lost a son, they would cry with them. If the telegram brought news that a son had been wounded, the neighbors would offer encouragement for his recovery.

During the war, my family had received several telegrams notifying them that one of their sons had been wounded. While none carried the news that every family dreaded, I never gave consideration to the terrible heartbreak my parents must have suffered with each telegram's arrival. But despite bearing the daily burden of concern for their sons, my parents' abiding faith in God had remained constant.

On the day that I left home back in late November 1943, Mom had sent me off to war with Psalms 91:7 ringing in my ears and in my heart. "A thousand shall fall at thy side, and ten thousand at thy right hand; but it shall not come nigh thee."

Many times during combat, my own faith in my survival had been tested, but the certainty of my mother's unswerving faith and unceasing prayers reassured me the Lord would protect me, guide me, care for me, forgive me, and help me to be a strong soldier of Christ while I was serving as a soldier for my country. And, through God's grace, my four brothers and I ultimately returned safely home.

Yet, consumed with my future plans, I neglected to fully express my gratitude to my mother for her prayers, just as I never adequately thanked my father for his letters. It was terribly thoughtless of me to take the blessing of my parents' love and concern so for granted. They would have appreciated knowing how much their faith, prayers, and letters helped to sustain me and keep me on balance amid the war's unrelenting fighting and killing and the cries of the dying.

As a young boy, I had heard that local veterans of World War I did not want to share their stories from combat, perhaps seeking to put the conflict out of their minds and spare others from the brutal and ghastly reality of war. While many former American GIs coming back from World War II shared the reticence of the World War I veterans, I personally felt compelled to talk about what the war was really like and how God had watched over me through the conflict. It was my conviction that if those of us who had fought did not share our stories with our fellow Americans, they would not appreciate the true value and cost of freedom.

In the spring of 1946, I began giving talks about my war experience. Speaking to audiences interested in a firsthand account, I quickly discovered that I enjoyed telling my story. With my outgoing personality, it is fair to say it would have been unnatural and unhealthy for me to have kept my vivid recollections of combat bottled up inside. Talking through my experience helped give me some type of psychological and emotional closure on the war so that I could move on with my life.

Giving college a try: Spring–Fall 1946

When I had entered the Army back in 1943, it had been my intention to become a minister in the Presbyterian Church after the war. My wartime encounters with

German children had helped further refine my career plans, leading me toward service in some type of church ministry working with young people or as a church youth director.

Whatever my career in ministry, I would first need to earn a college degree. My past academic struggles made it clear that college would be a real challenge for me, but the recently passed GI Bill at least ensured I would have the means to pay for it.

During the spring of 1946, I received encouragement to attend King College that coming fall. With my combat experiences still so recent, I was very concerned I was not yet in a psychological state to begin classes. I found it hard to sit still and read for more than a few minutes. However, in the end, I decided to give college a go.

In August 1946, about a month after turning 23, I made the 225-mile trip from Signal Mountain to King College, located in the town of Bristol in northeastern Tennessee. After starting my courses in the Bible, history, science, biology, and civics, the Bible class unsurprisingly emerged as my favorite. I had no trouble memorizing a full chapter for class each week and several times was called on to recite the chapter before the class. When the professor told the class I sounded like I was preaching, everyone laughed, but I took it as a compliment. Unfortunately, my other classes somehow just did not click with me and I quickly started falling behind in my studies.

Meanwhile, my new roommate and I soon became involved in campus activities. Possessing reasonably good singing voices, we began participating in campus skits, where we performed country songs. We also joined the King College Glee Club.

Beyond my school-related activities, I also regularly attended Sunday morning worship services at the Central Presbyterian Church, located just across the state line on the Virginia side of the town of Bristol. Doctor Ben Lacey Rose, the Church's pastor, delivered powerful sermons from the pulpit, which seemed to augment his already towering six-foot-three-inch height. A reserve military chaplain, he sometimes preached in his Army uniform, which gave me a sense of connection. With our shared experience as combat veterans of the war in Europe, we soon developed a close bond of friendship.

Seeking to work with young people, I volunteered to help out with the church's youth group on Sunday evenings. Because the youth group's meetings were held in the homes of members of the congregation, Dr. Rose had asked Hellon Coffey, the young church secretary, to be present at each gathering in order to keep an eye on things.

An attractive five-foot-three-inch brunette, Hellon always dressed in perfectly coordinated color combinations, as if she had just stepped out of a bandbox. Her looks were matched by a winning personality that made all the kids love her. While I still barely knew her, Hellon had definitely caught my eye and soon won my total attention.

Though busy with my classes, Glee Club, Debate Club, and church-related activities, I also still made time to tell my war story at prayer meetings and other venues in Bristol. Whereas I had shared my story only a few times before college, these talks now became much more frequent. Perhaps in part because I regularly spoke about my war experience, I did not suffer much from nightmares. However, my time in combat did affect me. As I had feared, my limited ability to sit still and concentrate hindered my academic success. I did try to focus on my schoolwork, but it was a real struggle.

With my difficulties in studying and my heavy involvement in extracurricular activities, I ended up flunking nearly all of my courses that fall, except for Bible class. While I had been aware most of my classes were not going well, actually failing them came as a real surprise. Even if it simply had been too soon after the war for me to have started college, I could have worked harder and should have done better.

Finding love and a calling: Spring 1947–October 1949

Following my return to King College in January 1947, I joined a group of my friends in a long line of students waiting to sign up for spring classes. When I reached the window to register, I was told I would not be permitted to enroll that spring as a result of my poor grades in the fall. It was a humiliating moment.

Before departing Bristol for Signal Mountain, I headed down to Central Church to say goodbye to Dr. Rose. As I was discussing my plans to return home and my hopes to continue working with church youth, we were joined by Hellon Coffey. She and I still barely knew each other, so I had no idea what to expect when she opened her mouth.

"Reverend Rose, this guy knows a lot about Scouting," she announced.

"You do?" he inquired, turning to me.

"Well, I used to be a Scoutmaster," I acknowledged. Shortly after my return from the war, I had served as the Scoutmaster for a local troop on Signal Mountain for a few months before enrolling at King College. Surprisingly, my long participation in the Boy Scouts had never come up in any of my previous talks with the pastor.

"You're hired as temporary youth director," Dr. Rose declared.

I was stunned. Apparently, he had been weighing the job offer over the course of our conversation, but my work with the Scouts clinched it for him.

Gladly accepting the six-month paid position on Central Church's staff that he had more or less just created for me, I immediately began working as the youth director and helping to organize a new Boy Scout troop at the church. It was an amazing opportunity that gave me practical experience toward a career in youth ministry.

By the summer of 1947, the Sunday night youth groups and the Scout troop were both enjoying tremendous growth in numbers and activities. This was matched by the increasing time Hellon and I were spending together eating out, going to the movies, and hiking. After several months, Dr. Rose approached me with another idea.

"You'd be a dead ringer as a Director of Christian Education (DCE), if you'd go to ATS." Created to educate lay workers outside of the ordained ministry, the Presbyterian Assembly's Training School (ATS) was located in Richmond, Virginia, about 275 miles east of Bristol.

"If you would go up there for two years, I'll start a 'whispering campaign' here in our church and, hopefully, we'll hire you as our DCE," he proposed. It was another opportunity I could not refuse.

While I was attending ATS, a local YMCA facility provided my housing free of charge. In exchange, I served as a boys Hi-Y (High School YMCA) advisor to three local clubs in the city. The need to concentrate my time and attention on my studies and my work with the clubs limited my ability to give war talks or do much of anything else, but this focus helped me to do much better in my classes.

By the fall of 1948, my relationship with Hellon was growing more serious and we arranged for her to visit Signal Mountain to meet my parents over my Christmas break from ATS. One night, I took her to "the Brow" to see the view of Chattanooga and the Tennessee Valley, a stunning sight in the moonlight. It was the perfect moment to ask Hellon to marry me, but I chickened out. However, not long afterward, I finally got up the courage to propose. To my great joy, she immediately accepted.

Four months later in May 1949, I graduated from ATS with a degree in Christian Education. As Dr. Rose had planned, I straightaway went to work at Central Presbyterian Church in Bristol as their new Director of Christian Education.

But this was only the first of my dreams to be fulfilled that year. The second came on October 7, 1949, with my marriage to Hellon.

Building a career and a family: 1949–1960

Over the ensuing four wonderful years in Bristol, I worked hard as DCE to enhance all aspects of the Church's Christian education program, especially for the congregation's youth. As DCE, I also supervised the Boy Scout troop that met at our church, occasionally serving as its Scoutmaster. Meanwhile, Hellon continued to work as the church secretary for a couple of more years but resigned a few months before the birth of our first child, a beautiful little girl named Sarah Louise.

During these years, I regularly showed off my collection of war souvenirs to the boys in the Scout troop. After pulling out the items a few times, I decided just to leave them out on permanent display. Setting up a little "museum" in the basement of our home, I exhibited the three beautiful daggers inscribed with Hitler's signature and my prized knife with the deer foot handle that I had liberated from a German soldier.

About six months later, the most valuable items in the collection were stolen, including the three daggers and a few German medals. It is my belief one of the Scouts carried out the theft, an act that left me more sad than angry.

In 1953, I received an offer to join the Presbyterian Church's Division of Men's Work in Richmond, Virginia. After all that Dr. Rose had done for me, I had never even entertained the thought of leaving Central Church until this moment, but the new offer was another great opportunity I felt I had to accept.

Not long after our move to Richmond, Hellon and I celebrated the birth of our son Al in 1954. Meanwhile, my position as program director and, later, Executive Director for Presbyterian Men, proved to be exciting and rewarding, even exceeding my expectations. My meetings with leaders from the National Council of Churches also brought me in touch with officials from the World Council of Churches.

Through these connections, I received the chance to serve for a year and a half on the staff of the World Council of Churches in Geneva, Switzerland. Shortly after our family's arrival there in 1958, I was invited to visit American military bases in neighboring West Germany to speak to the local chapters of Men of the Chapel, a Christian fellowship organization for American servicemen. Naturally, I was thrilled to accept the offer.

Traveling around West Germany, I was surprised and impressed at the nation's rapid physical and economic recovery from the war. With the Cold War between the West and the Soviet Union now in full swing, the Germans who I encountered appeared to have put World War II in the past and to have embraced their country's membership in the NATO military alliance with other Western democracies.

The final speech of my tour took place before a large audience of American servicemen at a convention of all the chapters of Men of the Chapel in the town of Berchtesgaden. Located in the southeastern corner of Bavaria, the area around Berchtesgaden had once been a scenic retreat and headquarters for Hitler and the Nazis, but now served as a recreation spot for American forces stationed in West Germany.

During my 25-minute talk, I mixed the theme of Christian responsibility with several humorous stories from my experiences in the Army. In particular, I joked about the military brass. With three generals seated beside me on the platform, the crowd of soldiers had a good laugh. When I finished, the men cheered before being dismissed.

After the audience departed, the general in charge pulled me aside.

"Private Andrews, this is the best speech that we've had. And you are now promoted to Brigadier General Andrews," he proclaimed with a smile.

"Yes, sir!" I replied with a crisp salute. After all the fun I had had at the expense of the brass, I was relieved to have earned such a favorable review from the officer.

"I want you to tell me where you'd like to go. I am going to place my driver and my command car at your beck and call," the general graciously offered.

"I want to go to the Dachau Concentration Camp, which some of our guys helped liberate," I responded without a moment's hesitation. During the war, my request to visit a Nazi concentration subcamp in Czechoslovakia had been denied.

With Dachau located just a hundred miles east-northeast of Berchtesgaden, I was not going to miss out on this unique opportunity to see the notorious concentration camp there.

"Andrews, I can't understand you. I'm giving you the chance to go anywhere in Europe that you want to go and you want to go to Dachau?" he questioned.

"Yes, sir, I do because I want to be able to say that I witnessed Dachau, even if it's been years since the war," I affirmed. With that settled, his driver and I set off.

As the general's staff car passed through the streets of various German towns on the way to Dachau, the residents would stop and stare. When the car stopped at intersections, American soldiers passing by would come to attention and salute. Flourishing a casual salute in response, I found it easy to embrace my new rank.

On my arrival at Dachau, I was met by a German guide who led me on an individual tour of the concentration camp. Having served as the model for subsequent Nazi concentration camps, Dachau had been preserved as it had existed at the end of the war, a memorial to the millions of Jews and other victims who had been persecuted and murdered in the larger system of camps created by the Nazi regime.

Just inside one of Dachau's main buildings, a lifelike statue of a small man was garbed in a frayed over-sized jacket lined with broad gray and light blue horizontal pinstripes, part of an inmate's shabby uniform. Underfed and overworked, prisoners had been crowded into long, shack-like barracks, where they slept on crude wooden "shelves" with so little space between each pallet that it was almost impossible for anyone even to rest on their side. Trying to survive another day, the inmates were confronted by disease, filth, and stench, abominable conditions designed to inflict the total degradation of human beings. Yet far worse was to come in the camp.

Pointing out a particular location on Dachau's barbed wire fence, the guide described the gruesome fate of three inmates who had attempted to escape by climbing over here. Machine gunned by the guards, their bodies were left hanging on the fence where they had been murdered, a brutal warning to the other prisoners.

Leading me on to the camp's whipping post, my guide explained that the guards had punished prisoners at this spot, viciously flogging their backs for even minor infractions. When inmates received a death sentence, they were either hanged or marched to the camp's execution wall to be shot in the back of the neck. Those shot were left to bleed out into the blood ditch dug along the wall.

Finally, we visited the camp's infamous "shower," which was actually a gas chamber. Records indicate the gas chamber at Dachau was never used, but this method of mass murder was regularly employed at the Nazi death camps. Once an unsuspecting group of innocent men, women, and children had been herded into these sealed chambers, poison gas would be released into the room from the ceiling. When the gassing was finished, the dead were removed to a neighboring room, where their corpses were cremated in brick ovens. A wire screen under the ovens collected their teeth so that any gold fillings could be extracted. It was utterly incomprehensible that any government could have conceived such a wicked thing, but it was all too real.

Speaking as a former *Wehrmacht* soldier, my German guide shared his grief at what had happened at Dachau. It was difficult to believe that the Germany which had created some of the world's most beautiful music had also spawned this monstrosity. The horror of the place simply staggered one's conscience. Though I was only able to visit the camp a decade and a half after the war's end, nothing better epitomized the inhumanity of the Nazi regime or the moral justice of our fight against it.

The decades after 1960

Returning to Richmond from Switzerland in 1960, our family moved into the second story of an antebellum mansion. Word was that the Presbyterian Church's Board of Christian Education had purchased the 200 acres around the home in anticipation of eventually transferring its main offices out to the property.

Over the next few years, our children Sarah and Al took full advantage of the place, with both becoming particularly proficient at fly fishing. In my younger days back on Signal Mountain, fishing and hunting had both been a big part of my life. After my return from the war, I continued to fish whenever I could, but had no heart for killing anything with a gun. I never hunted again.

At the end of 1964, I started a new job with the Mountain Retreat Association (MRA) in Montreat, a small mountain town in western North Carolina about 20 miles east of the city of Asheville. Over the next 15 years, I served as the MRA's Conference Director, assisting conference participants in any way that I could.

In 1969, I was persuaded to run for mayor of Montreat and managed to win the job. In the end, I served two terms and sat on the town council for 20 years. During this period, other leadership positions in the region also came my way, including President of the Asheville Area Tourism Association and President of the Black Mountain Rotary Club. Even after the MRA was reorganized and my job as Conference Director was eliminated in 1980, I never lacked for work and hobbies to keep me busy.

In 1990, Hellon retired from her position as Director of Student Activities at Montreat College and, several years later, from her job as manager of the College Bookstore. Tragically, in 1999, Hellon was diagnosed with Alzheimer's at about the same time that we moved from Montreat to a retirement center in the neighboring town of Black Mountain. After her hospitalization early in 2002, Hellon's condition worsened.

On June 4, 2008, my dear wife and closest friend passed away. Two weeks later, a memorial service was held in Montreat's Anderson Auditorium in remembrance of a beautiful person. For days on end, my mailbox was stuffed with cards and letters, and phone calls came from relatives and friends all around the country, a measure of how Hellon had been a blessing to so many.

A celebrated return to Europe

Over the passing decades, my main connection to the war came through my ongoing talks about my own experience. Once I began my career in 1949, these speaking engagements became less frequent. However, when I left my position as the MRA's Conference Director in 1980 and had more time, I started speaking more often. But while continuing to give these talks about the war, I had never had the opportunity to return to Normandy or any of the other battlefields where we had fought during the 1st Infantry Division's campaign through Europe.

Early in 1994, a newsletter for 1st Infantry Division veterans announced a mid-May trip to Europe just ahead of the fiftieth anniversary of D-Day. The tour was scheduled to revisit not only the Normandy beaches, but also the division's entire route of advance across France, Belgium, and Germany. I immediately telephoned my then 40-year-old son Al, who agreed to join his 70-year-old dad on a fascinating trip.

Every stop on the First Division Tour was remarkable, including a profoundly moving visit to the Normandy American Cemetery. Walking among the sea of white crosses and Stars of David, we grieved and prayed for our fallen buddies who had made the ultimate sacrifice. We later visited a German military cemetery, where crosses of black granite marked the graves. Kneeling before one, I prayed that God would also extend his mercy to the German families who had lost these fathers, sons, and brothers.

Many store windows in Normandy displayed large signs reading "WELCOME LIBERATORS." While we all greatly appreciated the warm welcome, the term liberator seemed strange to me. I had not really recalled myself in that way, but that is exactly what we had been to the French living under Nazi occupation in 1944.

In celebration of our return, three Norman communities prepared receptions for us. The first one at Vierville-sur-Mer was held in the local schoolhouse, the largest room in the town. All the desks had been pushed back against the walls to make space for three long tables in the center of the room, which must have been groaning under the lavish spread. There were gourmet cookies, pastries, chocolates, cheeses, crackers, breads, and bottles of wine as well as the locally fermented apple cider.

Adorned in the colorful sash of his office, the mayor warmly greeted us, proudly explaining through our interpreter that local residents had saved their money for the past three months to purchase the food, while the beverages had been donated by a local store. After the mayor's short speech, other town officials presented us with small pins to commemorate the invasion and their liberation. It was an amazing welcome.

The next day, a torrential rain was beating down as we drove into Bayeux for our second reception, also held in a local schoolhouse. As we entered the building, an elderly former French soldier in his World-War-II-era uniform stood rigidly at attention at the right of the door as an honor guard, holding out a French flag with one arm and an American flag with the other. For the next two hours, we enjoyed another round of generous hospitality from our hosts in a happy babble of French and English.

When we exited the building, that lone French sentry remained stoically at attention holding out the two flags. Despite getting drenched in the continuing downpour, the elderly man had never moved from his post. Circling around in front of him, I presented him with my sharpest salute. For me, the simple tribute he paid us was one of the most moving experiences of our entire trip.

The following morning, a Sunday, we entered the town of Caen to the loud chiming of church bells. Looking out on deserted streets, we naturally assumed that most of its residents were attending church services. When our bus reached the main courthouse, our tour guide entered the building to check whether we were at the right place for the reception. Ten minutes later, he returned with tears in his eyes.

"In all my tours, I've never seen anything like this. The reason you don't see anybody is because everybody's in the courthouse. For three stories, there are little kids, teenagers, middle-aged people, and folks on canes and crutches lining both sides of the steps, all of them holding American flags. There are so many that they couldn't all get in the big reception room upstairs, but they wanted to greet you."

Ascending those steps single file through the phalanx of townspeople was a welcome none of us could ever forget. Waving little American flags, the citizens of Caen hailed us with warm words of thanks, kisses, and hugs, reminiscent of the jubilant throngs we had met in the newly liberated French towns and villages 50 years earlier.

At the top of the stairs, double doors opened into a large room with three long tables placed end on end, covered with beautiful purple tablecloths. Wine and cider bottles and trays of cookies stood on the two end tables, while the center one was adorned with small French and American flags. Behind this table stood five immaculately attired political leaders and senior clergy from the town.

After a gracious greeting from the mayor, the other local dignitaries gave speeches commending our heroic efforts in the Allied liberation of France. With the formal welcoming ceremony concluded, the town's citizens who had been observing the proceedings came forward to join the festivities. It was another wonderful event.

When our First Division Tour arrived in Liège, Belgium, we received an equally warm reception from town officials decked out in their full regalia. Afterward, Belgians came up to us individually to express their gratitude. Just as in France, the fervent joy and exuberance of the locals made the occasion seem as though the war was just over and victory just won. Seeing their faces, we former soldiers were convinced more than ever that all the blood sacrificed, all the bitter fighting, all the tragedy and suffering, and all the intense effort put into defeating the Nazis had been worth it.

After further receptions in Belgium, we traveled to the Aachen area, where we were reminded of the terrible battles that had taken place there. Our visit to Germany provided an emotional conclusion to an unforgettable trip.

At Normandy's Cemetery

Ten years later in May 2004, Dr. Bill Forstchen, a history professor at Montreat College, invited me to return to Normandy with three Eagle Scouts, two dads, the *Boys' Life* photographer, and himself. An article covering our trip has been published in *Boys' Life* magazine's June 2004 issue, the sixtieth anniversary of the Normandy invasion. Since *Boys' Life* presents a full account, I will offer only my own highlights here.

Our arrival at Omaha Beach was a deeply poignant experience for me, despite being my second visit to the site since the war. As waves softly nudged the shoreline, we treaded along the smooth sand in contemplation. The quiet solemnity of the place presented a sharp contrast to my memories of that long ago landing in 1944.

With the Scouts close by, I pointed towards England and described our training there, the loading of the invasion armada in the port, the long hours down in the bowels of that troopship carrying us across the Channel, our first sight of the French coast under a white cloud of smoke, the ocean teeming with landing craft and ships of all types and sizes, and the noise of the mighty battleship USS *Texas* blasting away at inland targets. All this and more passed through my mind as I reminisced with them.

Following our stroll along the shore, we drove to the Normandy American Cemetery just above Omaha Beach. Just as I remembered from my previous trip, the sight of 172.5 acres of white crosses and Stars of David aligned in perfect order was astonishing, breathtaking, mind-boggling, quieting, and sobering. Nobody spoke.

Moving ever so slowly, we tried to comprehend what we were seeing. It is too easy to be captivated by the austere beauty of the place without feeling the weight of sacrifice of so many young lives, so that the true meaning of the loss is not fully appreciated. The cemetery holds the graves of 9,385 American military dead killed in the invasion and the ensuing combat, including many of the roughly 2,500 Americans killed on D-Day. Among the graves are 307 unknown burials inscribed with this simple epitaph: "Here rests in honored glory a comrade in arms, known but to God."

The cemetery is a profound testament to so much heroic sacrifice as well as a stark reminder of war's terrible waste. With my heart in my throat, it was difficult to say anything. It was awesome and humbling. Looking to the right, there was the ocean, a sight that brought back other memories I was unable to communicate.

The silence was broken by our photographer's request to the Scouts that they fan out and locate the cross of a soldier from my home state of Tennessee. One was selected and I was asked to kneel at this cross with the Scouts kneeling around me. After sharing a few of my own D-Day stories, I began talking about the GIs who had given their lives.

"When you look out at a field full of white crosses, you see only a cemetery. If you could imagine the lifeless body of that young American soldier laid out on the ground at the foot of each cross, then you would get idea of the true cost paid."

"What were their thoughts as they fought? Were they afraid? Did they expect to be killed?" I asked, urging the Scouts to consider the men who had fought on that day.

"These boys were about your age, mostly 18 or 19. No soldier who I knew really wanted to give his life for his country, though all the guys I knew were ready to stand in harm's way for their country. War is very ugly, very trying, and very stressful for all soldiers. If it was destined to be that their life would be sacrificed in this conflict, then okay. But, like everyone else, they believed that death would come to someone else, not to them."

"The soldiers who ended up under these crosses did not die a comfortable death. They died violently. They did not die easily. They died by direct fire from rifles and machine guns, from grenade and artillery shrapnel, from landmines that blew up in their face, or in some other violent situation."

"Many of these boys received a direct hit from an artillery or mortar round that literally ripped them apart. If his dog tags could not be found, there was often not enough left of the soldier to identify him. Those are the horrible things of war, but that is the reality of war."

"The heroism of those who died shows how raw courage overcomes fear and this cemetery testifies to their willingness to lay down their lives. But without our remembrance, their sacrifice is meaningless."

"America was robbed of their contribution by their ultimate sacrifice. Like you three Scouts, each of these young men had hopes and dreams of finishing school, pursuing a career, falling in love, getting married, and raising a family. But war ended their lives, placing on our shoulders the responsibility of preserving and advancing freedom for people everywhere. By the very way we live and work, we must also seek to preserve the freedom for which these men fought and died."

"When I look out on this cemetery, I think about how God spared me from laying under one of those crosses and about my responsibility before God and those men. Since the end of the war, my heart has daily been driven by the question: What can I do with my life that might achieve something that some of these dear guys wanted, but were never given the chance to accomplish? Our job is to ask: What can we possibly do that might fulfill some of the dreams these boys had?"

"So, when you see a military cemetery, remember that the soldiers there sacrificed their lives so that you could be free," I concluded.

While the First Division Tour on the fiftieth anniversary had given me the chance to bond with other veterans and meet with those we had liberated, my trip with these Eagle Scouts gave me the opportunity to try to share what we had experienced with the next generation.

Final trips

My third postwar trip back to the war's battlegrounds came just two years later in 2006. Conceived, encouraged, planned, and executed by my friend Maury Hurt, it was labeled "Trip of a Lifetime." Taking me as his guest, we would visit Omaha Beach, Saint-Lô, Aachen, the Hürtgen Forest, Hill 232, the Battle of the Bulge, and a number of military museums. Beginning in London and ending in Frankfurt, Germany, the tour would run from May 15 through May 25.

Maury had enlisted five other friends for the trip, a group that included my son Al and Bill Forstchen. As our tour guide, he selected Lieutenant Colonel Andrew Duff, a retired British Army officer now working as a professional battlefield guide. Duff's research into the history of my outfit's campaign in Europe was a highlight of the whole experience.

After a couple of days touring war-related sites in England, we crossed the English Channel to France and traveled to Colleville-sur-Mer, where Duff led us to the spot where we had entered the village in 1944. With the rest of our party trailing behind, Bill Forstchen and I approached an intersection with a narrow street.

When I came around the corner, a sudden wave of anxiety made me freeze in my tracks. Bill turned back to me. "You coming, Andy?" he asked.

"Yeah, I got to," I whispered, trying to overcome my instinctual reaction.

"What's the matter?" he queried, observing the horror on my face. So vividly real, so hauntingly visceral was my wartime memory of the place, that it seemed to me that the window in the barn loft at the far end of the street still held an enemy sniper searching for targets. It was not the last time I would experience such a flashback.

Following visits to other key sites along the route of our campaign through France and Belgium, our next stops were in Germany. At the frontier, a German border control agent asked me, "Where is your passport?"

"When I was here before, I was a soldier and didn't need a passport," I protested.

"You need one now!" he responded, obviously not amused at my bit of humor.

Before touring the Hürtgen Forest battlefield, our group stopped at Hill 232. My return to this place for the first time since the war felt almost like a pilgrimage.

Rain was pouring down when our van arrived, but I was determined to visit the hill and led the way up the mud-slicked dirt road to the top. By the time we reached it, gale force winds were blowing. As sleet turned to hail, big chunks of ice began pelting us. Taking shelter behind a dirt mound, everyone got out of the wind so I could tell them what had happened at this place more than six decades earlier.

As I began speaking, it felt like I was not so much remembering as actually reliving my worst experience of the war. The others later told me my voice became that of a 21-year-old, almost as if I was in a trance. Duff told me that in all his years as a soldier, combat veteran, and guide, he had never witnessed such a transformation.

Despite being on the site of the battle, my attempt to explain the brutal fighting proved difficult because much of the terrain atop the hill had been leveled off. We heard later that this was part of the German government's effort to eliminate sites that contained wartime bunkers, fearing these might be used as gathering spots for groups of neo-Nazi teenagers. While understandable, the physical alterations to the site came as a disappointment. Nonetheless, our visit to Hill 232 was an intensely emotional experience for me, marking a highpoint on a trip filled with many special moments.

Not surprisingly, the reaction of contemporary Germans to the war is very different. Passing through a town near Hill 232, the staff of a restaurant welcomed us warmly, but the locals did not seem particularly interested in our tour of World War II battlefields. Most Germans today have no personal memory of the war and wish to move beyond those dark days in their country's history.

Shortly after my return home to North Carolina from that fantastic trip in the summer of 2006, I was invited to participate in the HonorAir program. Created to honor America's veterans for their sacrifices, HonorAir (now Honor Flight) is a non-profit organization that flies veterans to Washington, D.C., to visit the capital's war memorials.

After our flight landed in D.C., we boarded buses and drove to the National Mall, where we disembarked at the large new World War II Memorial just completed in April 2004. Located between the Lincoln Memorial and the Washington Monument, the World War II Memorial has 56 granite pillars arrayed in a semicircle around a pool. The triumphal arch on the northern side represents the Atlantic Theater, while the one on the southern side represents the Pacific Theater.

The most impressive thing for me was the Freedom Wall on the western side. Each of the 4,048 golden stars on the wall represents 100 Americans who died during World War II. Pondering this host of stars standing for the more than 400,000 Americans who gave their lives, I wept, unable to take it in. There was simply too much death for my mind to comprehend.

Sharing my war experience

Though the war often occupied my thoughts in the decades after 1945, I lost touch with Wayne Newsome, Lincoln Welser, and all my other old buddies from H Company. At the end of the war, Hector Gonzalez had urged me to come visit his home after we got back, but, unfortunately, that reunion never happened. Now, like so many of our generation, I think all of these men have passed away. Soon, no veterans will be alive to offer a first-hand account of World War II.

While combat veterans deal with their experiences in different ways, few like to discuss the war or describe its brutal reality. But if I had not been able to tell my own war story, I would probably have thrown a fit or gone crazy. Bringing my war experience into the open has helped me to work through those traumatic events, allowing me to come to terms with my time as a soldier and find a certain psychological peace as a human being. Indeed, I believe it is because of my frequent war talks that I largely avoided reliving the war in my dreams and waking up in a cold sweat.

Every time I give a talk, people tell me they wish their father or grandfather would share their war experiences. While sympathizing with a family member's desire to hear these stories, I certainly understand the reticence of these veterans. Despite all the talks I have given, sharing my war story is often still very emotional for me. It remains particularly hard for me to discuss killing another man at pointblank range in combat, though such a terrible thing is impossible to ever forget.

Many former soldiers simply do not believe an audience will be able to grasp the terror of combat and the horrors they have witnessed on the battlefield. Other veterans may simply believe they were not heroes and have no stories worth relating. Whatever concerns a veteran might have, it is my experience that audiences have a hunger for these firsthand accounts from World War II.

As that time grows ever more distant, the need for the war's few remaining veterans to share their stories grows ever more urgent. It is my hope that telling my story in this memoir will encourage combat veterans who have remained silent to preserve their own accounts before they are lost. If we are unwilling to recount our personal war stories, those who were not there will never know what it was really like. By helping to bring to light the terrible suffering and horrors that inevitably accompany all wars, I also believe we veterans can perhaps help prevent history's repetition.

We remember wars not to celebrate them, but to understand them. War is tragic, brutal, and gruesome, but holds an intense fascination for me as I try to comprehend my own combat experience. The war is part of my life and my service in the U.S. Army is a source of deep pride that helped to shape me into the person that I am.

In discussing World War II, I always stress that when I am speaking about Germans, I am talking about our fellow human beings. The Nazi regime was our enemy, but a lot of the Germans were good people. About every three months, I have lunch with my friend Bill Lubbeck, a former German soldier who served on the Russian front for four years during World War II. After the war, Bill immigrated to America with his family and now lives in Asheville. A wonderful man, he has given me new insights into the German experience in the war.

Whatever the contrasting experiences among soldiers from various countries, all combat veterans share a larger experience in common. Any attempt to communicate the stark reality of battle to those who have not been under fire is very challenging.

Indeed, whether I am recounting my war story to younger kids, college students, or adults of various ages, people from the audience often approach me afterward to express their amazement at what they have heard.

"There's just no way that I can imagine that. You make it seem just like we were there and I just can't believe it." If recounting my story has made combat more vivid for them, I am glad because people should have an idea of what war is really like.

After I finished speaking to a group of students and their parents, most stood up to clap and shout, but one dad in the audience had a different perspective on my talk.

"It just looks like to me that you would fill your life with beautiful thoughts, instead of all this stuff about the war," he told me.

"Well, sir, I appreciate your feeling, but I've got news for you. You don't blow your fellow man's brains out at pointblank range and forget about it. So I have to talk about it. I hope you'll understand," I replied.

On the 63rd anniversary of D-Day in 2007, I had the chance to share my war story on a live radio talk show. In reply to a question about my strongest memories from the war, I replied that my sharpest recollections are the awe-inspiring array of troops and equipment stockpiled in England in 1944 before the invasion as well as the terrible carnage and wreckage left behind at the end of a battle. While these are perhaps the two sides of combat, it is the latter that reflects war's true nature.

I went on to tell the show's host that it was God's magnificent grace that most stands out for me. Throughout the war, God remained with me and protected me. Too many times, I should have been killed. God brought me through battles that claimed the lives of so many good men, good men on both sides. I believe that God had something special for me to do with my life, particularly working with young people.

I further explained that I drew a close parallel between my Christian faith and the freedom for which we were fighting in World War II. While Jesus Christ sacrificed his life on the cross to free each of us from the power of sin, our soldiers sacrificed their lives on the battlefield to free the world from the Nazi's earthly tyranny.

The public response to the radio show was tremendous. By the end of the first hour, we could see a group of people beginning to congregate outside the big glass window in front of the studio. As they listened for the last two hours of the program, many had tears rolling down their checks.

When the program concluded, several people came up to hug me or shake my hand in appreciation. Although they were thanking me, I knew they were really expressing their gratitude to all the veterans who served in that war as well as to those Americans who had given their lives in the fighting.

Last reflections

If talking to the public was often an emotional experience for me, some of the most poignant questions came from my own family. In high school, my son Al wrote a paper based on an interview with me. In it, he addressed the question: How did you feel when you killed your first enemy soldier?

My response was that there was no time to think, it was kill or be killed. But when the battle ended, I prayed for the mother and father of the men who had fallen in front of my machine gun. I asked that God console them, just as he would have comforted my own parents if I had been killed in battle. As a Christian who was taught to love my fellow man, there has always been a deep sadness in my heart that it is the soldier's fate to kill so many boys fighting on the other side.

Was World War II the "good" war?

War is never good or glorious, but sometimes it is necessary to prevent or overcome an even worse evil. You have to weigh the calamity of war against the evil of allowing Hitler and the Nazis to continue with their ruthless wars of conquest, their harsh oppression of occupied nations, and their mass murder of millions of Jews and other equally innocent human beings out of racial and ideological hatred. It was and remains my deep conviction that our war against the Nazis was just. Helping rid Europe and the world of Hitler's tyranny was both my patriotic and moral duty.

To this day, I get excited talking about freedom. Our fight against the Nazis taught me the true value and cost of freedom in a way that nothing else could have. Whenever I see the Star-Spangled Banner flying, I feel that same passion for freedom that I felt when we landed at Normandy and returned home to welcoming crowds in New York City. I believe many Americans have forgotten that the freedom to lead their lives as they see fit was purchased through the priceless sacrifice of countless lives.

As citizens of a democratic republic, it is vital for Americans to learn about the government and remain vigilant about what it is doing. Through our participation in it, we ensure the government serves the public good and never abuses its power. A free people likewise bears the responsibility for protecting its liberty from foreign threats as well as to advance the broader cause of human freedom in the world.

At the same time, you have to wonder if humanity can ever escape the endless cycle of wars, permanently beating its swords into plowshares. Why does one nation have to pit its young people against another nation's young people in wars?

When sharing my recollections of the war, I often push young people to seek ways to prevent new wars and ensure peace in the future. Hoping to inspire them to be ambassadors, I tell them that, if I had my life to live over again, I would be a linguist and learn every language I could. When you speak another person's language, you can get along better. You can communicate and negotiate. One of the reasons we have problems in this world is that people cannot understand each other.

To achieve lasting peace in the world, it is my belief Americans should work to advance individual freedom and democratic government everywhere, while recognizing that other peoples must be free to pursue their own paths. The key to reducing conflict in the world is ultimately greater mutual understanding and respect among free peoples. Such an effort will not be easy, but it is infinitely better than war.

In sharing my war story, no audience has been more attentive than my own grandkids. It means so much to me that they want to hear and understand my experience as a soldier. Yet, I hope and pray with all my heart that children in future generations will only know war from history books.

My son Al was deeply moved by our visit to the Hürtgen Forest battlefield in May 2006, where the soil still holds the remains of unknown soldiers from both sides. Afterward, he penned the following poem.

A Word to the Hürtgen Forest

Those who sleep here are not unknown to you.
Hearing their last cries,
Sensing their final breath,
Offer them now, comfort and peace.

Blanket of forest needles and soft green moss,
Keep these fallen ones warm.
Let your gentle winds whisper songs in their native tongues.

Night owls and morning doves
Keep your constant vigil.
Light of sun and moon
Strain through the dense canopy,
Sparkle on dark graves.

Towering fir sentinels, stand alert!
Guard this place.
Let no more harm come.

Sorrow-soaked burned-out ground,
Defy these deaths.
Burst forth with hot green saplings,
Grow them into life again.

Al Andrews
May 2006

Final Note from the Author

Over the course of my work on this memoir, I have come to realize the correct dates for two of my stories differ significantly from the timeframe I have previously indicated in telling these stories elsewhere.

On several occasions, I have stated I was aboard a ship bound for the Pacific when the atomic bomb was dropped on Hiroshima on August 6, 1945, but I was mistaken about my location at this time. As my official U.S. Army records state, and this memoir accurately recounts, I was still on occupation duty in Bamberg, Germany, in August 1945 and did not ship out of France for New York until October 4, 1945.

In at least one instance, I have also provided an account of my visit to the Dachau Concentration Camp that mistakenly states my trip to that camp took place sometime in 1945. To be clear, I did not visit that camp or any other German concentration camp either during the war or in the months immediately after the war.

My tour of the Dachau Concentration Camp did not occur until I returned to Germany in about 1959. The description of what I witnessed during my visit to Dachau at that time is accurately recorded in this memoir. Although my tour of the camp occurred a decade and a half after the end of the war, the passage of time does not diminish the feeling of revulsion experienced by a visitor to that terrible place.

Acknowledgements

Many people have played a role in helping to bring about this memoir. Andy especially wished to thank the several dozen people who urged him to put his account of World War II in writing after attending one of his talks. While there are too many names to identify individually, it was their encouragement through the years that gave him the inner strength to pursue this book.

Andy and I both wanted to express our particular gratitude to my brother Maury Hurt, who first introduced us and generously supported our project from the start. Whether it was scanning Andy's photographs, passing along a chapter to Andy, or editing the manuscript, Maury always stood ready to help.

We also greatly appreciated the assistance of Jordan Edelstein, whose grandfather, Anthony J. Prahl, served as an officer with H Company during the war. An expert on H Company's history, Jordan provided us with the *History of Company "H," 16th Infantry Regiment* and *Organization History of Company H, 16th Infantry: The Invasion of the Continent* as well as other related U.S. Army materials that were extremely useful.

Our gratitude likewise extends to the producers of the video documentary: *The High Price of Victory*, directed by Louis Asbury (L.A. Image Works, 2011), who gave us a copy of Andy's full interview for the series. While Andy and I had reviewed his war experiences multiple times in the process of writing the book, it is wonderful to have his story and the accounts of other World War II veterans preserved on film.

We additionally wished to express our appreciation to a number of people who freely gave of their time to review and comment upon the draft manuscript of the memoir, including William Hurt, Mary Eleanor Hurt, Amanda Medley, Amy Trainer, and Fred Trainer. A special thanks must also be extended to Dawn Vander Galien, who kindly assisted Andy just before his passing by reading several chapters of the manuscript aloud to him and recording his editorial comments.

Finally, I would like to convey my personal gratitude to Andy's children, Al Andrews and Sarah Murray. Following Andy's passing in 2016, they allowed me time to complete the writing of their father's memoir and collaborated with me to ensure its publication.

David Hurt